Christian Reid

After Many Days

A Novel

Christian Reid

After Many Days
A Novel

ISBN/EAN: 9783337026721

Printed in Europe, USA, Canada, Australia, Japan

Cover: Foto ©Thomas Meinert / pixelio.de

More available books at **www.hansebooks.com**

AFTER MANY DAYS:

A NOVEL.

BY

CHRISTIAN REID,

AUTHOR OF

"A QUESTION OF HONOR," "MORTON HOUSE," "VALERIE AYLMER," ETC.

NEW YORK:

D. APPLETON AND COMPANY,

549 AND 551 BROADWAY.

1877.

CONTENTS.

PART I.

PART II.

AFTER MANY DAYS.

PART I.

CHAPTER I.

WILD-FLOWERS.

A WOODLAND glen into which the soft April sunshine streamed, through which a bright brook babbled, where graceful trees leaned over the water, and flowers of many kinds covered the ground like a carpet: on a flat stone at the foot of one of these trees a girl of sixteen sat dabbling a leafy branch in the current of the brook, and varying this amusement occasionally by leaning over to look at the water, which gave back a reflection of her face and of the white blossoms of a hawthorn which arched overhead.

Near by, a boy, probably two years her senior, also sat, engaged in weaving, with remarkably dexterous fingers, a wreath of wild-flowers, which he had evidently gathered in the course of a long ramble.

"I don't think there's anything in the woods prettier than this crimson honeysuckle, Amy," he said. "See what a vivid color it has!"

"It is very pretty," said Amy, glancing up. "But I care more for the sweetness than the color. Give me a spray, Hugh."

"Wait a minute," said Hugh, "and you shall have the wreath. I am making it for you. I'll put a long, trailing spray behind. There, now! I call that picturesque!"

He extended the wreath at arm's-length, looked at it admiringly, then rose and laid it on his companion's head—a head covered with unruly masses of chestnut hair, in rich, curling waves.

"It's very becoming to you!" he said, stepping backward for a better view, and nearly tumbling over an outspread root into the water. "What a lovely Queen of May you'd make, Amy!"

Amy leaned over and looked at herself in the clear brook.

"'For I'm to be Queen o' the May, mother, I'm to be Queen o' the May,'" she hummed, under her breath. "It's likely, isn't it?" she added, with a laugh that had a slight ring of bitterness. "Fancy anybody in Edgerton thinking of Amy Reynolds as Queen of May—except you, Hugh!"

"I'm not the only person who thinks you the prettiest girl in Edgerton," said Hugh. "I sometimes wish I was! Oh, yes, I do!"—as Amy looked at him, arching her brows in a challenging fashion she had. "It's no pleasure to me to hear men say, 'There goes pretty Amy Reynolds.' I always feel like knocking them down—and I'm not large enough for that," he ended, ruefully.

"I shouldn't advise you to try it," said Amy, and again her laugh rang out, this time full of unalloyed gayety. "You are not large, Hugh, and the consequences might be unpleasant. Besides"—with an almost Gallic shrug—"what does it matter? Am I injured by being called

'Pretty Amy Reynolds?' It's not respectful—but then it is meant to be complimentary."

"And you like compliments?" said Hugh, with an attempt at sarcasm.

"Of course I like compliments," answered Amy. "I'd prefer them to be respectful, but a person in my position can't expect that."

"Now you are talking nonsense," said Hugh, severely. "A person in your position! As if you are not as good as anybody!"

"Am I?" the girl asked; and her lip —too young a lip by far for such an expression—curled scornfully. "That depends on what you mean. I hope I am as honest as anybody; but I'm poor and obscure, and I don't think *that* is exactly ' as good as anybody.' But we won't talk about such disagreeable things. What are you going to do?"

He had taken a book from his pocket while she was speaking, and opened it; then he produced a pencil, and answered: "I am going to see if I can draw your head. Sit still, and look at the hill over there."

This was apparently not a new proceeding, for it excited no surprise. Amy said, "I'll look at the dogwood-tree," and Hugh went to work.

He sketched rapidly, and with the ease of one who had acquired, from long practice, perfect command of the pencil. If there had been any artist by to glance over his shoulder, he would have been surprised to see how accurate was his eye, how steady his hand; and his surprise would have increased to amazement if he had known that the boy was altogether self-taught. With clear, vigorous strokes he drew the outlines of the graceful, spirited head, the long, waving lines of the beautiful neck, and still unformed but symmetrical figure. He shaded almost as rapidly as he sketched, and his pencil was busy with the flowery wreath and rippling hair, when Amy spoke, abruptly:

"Hugh, wouldn't you give anything to be rich?"

"I shouldn't care about being rich," Hugh answered, glancing from his book to his sitter and his sitter to his book, in true artist-fashion. "If I had money enough to go away and learn to be a painter—that's all I'd ask."

"That's all you care for," said Amy. "But I care for a hundred things, and for all of them I want money, money, money! There isn't anything in the world, Hugh, that money can't buy!"

"You are mistaken about that, Amy. If you were ugly, it could not buy you a pretty face."

"And what good is my pretty face, when I never have a new dress or a becoming hat from one year's end to another?" demanded Amy, aggrieved. "Do you know how I would look if I had on that lovely hat Miss Waldron wore in church this morning?"

"I've no doubt you'd look very pretty," replied Hugh, "but it couldn't be any more becoming to you than your wreath of wild-flowers."

Amy tossed the head on which this wreath reposed. Wild-flowers were, in her sight, less than nothing compared to a French hat in the latest style.

"That is absurd!" she said, trenchantly. "You are a boy, and you don't know what you are talking about. If I was rich, I would have the most beautiful dresses—prettier than anybody here wears, except Miss Waldron—and I'd drive in a pony-carriage, and papa should never give another music-lesson, and Felix should go to Leipsic, and the other boys to the *best* schools, and Mariette should be dressed like an angel, and you should go and learn to be a painter, Hugh."

"I am much obliged to your ladyship," said Hugh. "And after I had learned, would you allow me the honor of painting your portrait?"

"Yes, and I would wear violet velvet and point-lace and pearls for you to paint it in."

"I like you best as you are," said Hugh, "and I really don't think it's right, Amy, for you to think so much about such things. It only makes you miserable, since you can't have them."

"But I will have them!" cried Amy. "I am determined on that, Hugh. I *will* be rich! I am sick and tired of the grinding life we lead, of worry and debt and scraping and pinching, and wearing washed-out dresses! People who have never known the want of money may talk of it's being wrong to desire it," the girl went on, passionately, "but I *know* that there is no prison on earth like poverty, and I hate it, and I don't mean to bear it!"

Hugh looked at her with a pair of very clear, serene eyes—the only attractive feature in his boyish face. From his earliest childhood he had known the life of which she spoke; at this very moment he was held prisoner by "those twin-jailers of the daring heart, low birth and iron fortune," but it was not in his nature to rebel with such bitterness and defiance as this.

Though he was not able to make art the pursuit of his life, its exercise was still a delight to him; and when he held a pencil in his fingers, he scarcely sighed even for the instruction which at other times he would have bartered anything to win. Young as he was, he had been tossed about the world enough to know something of its dangers, and he felt a thrill of fear as he looked at the beautiful face before him, and thought of the passionate, undisciplined nature longing so madly for the pleasures and trappings of wealth.

"You should not talk so, Amy," he said, reprovingly. "You may be sure it is very wrong. How can a girl like you make money?"

"How?" replied Amy. "Why, in this way."

Then she threw her head slightly back, curved her round, white throat, and, opening her mouth, sent forth such a clear, ringing tide of melody, that a bird in the tree over her head flew up with a startled cry. Yet, if it had paused a moment longer, it might have thought that one of its own companions was pouring out those sounds of the woodland stillness.

Certainly Amy sang with as little effort as a bird, and Hugh felt that he had never before appreciated the beauty and power of her voice. It had wonderful compass as well as exquisite purity, and was flexible as a wind-instrument.

The echo-song which she had begun to sing tested this last quality admirably. As her silver notes soared in the long-drawn call, and then sank, the hill-side joined in giving back the soft, dying echo.

"Brava!" said an unexpected voice in the rear, and a pair of hands beat enthusiastically together.

Amy and Hugh turned simultaneously, surprised and a little startled.

Standing so near, that but for the singing they must have heard his approach, was a stranger, regarding them with a smile—a young man, of handsome face and elegant figure.

Seeing how much he had startled them, he was the first to speak:

"I beg pardon," he said, lifting his hat lightly. "I had no right to express my admiration, but one does not often listen to such a voice. Allow me to say that it is wonderful, and I have heard all the best singers of the day."

"Thank you," said Amy.

She did not know what else to say, and she blushed very much in saying this.

Hugh, on his part, looked at once fierce and awkward. He considered the intrusion a great impertinence, but being only a "hobbledehoy," as Amy often called him, he did not clearly see how to manifest this opinion.

"I am afraid I was foolish to let my enthusiasm find expression," the stranger went on, with his glance fixed admiringly on Amy's face, to which Hugh's wreath was indeed very becoming. "I interrupted you, when, if I had kept quiet, I might have heard another song."

"I did not mean to sing any more," answered Amy, who had recovered her self-possession by this time. "Hugh has heard me often enough. He does not care about it."

"But *I* have not heard you often," said that gentleman, "and I should be very grateful for another song. Music is the passion of my life, and I have never heard a finer voice than yours."

"Don't sing, Amy!" said Hugh, brusquely. "It is time for us to go home."

The intruder gave him an amused and carelessly supercilious glance; then he looked at Amy again, and she thought what very handsome eyes he had!

"I fear," he said, addressing her, "that you may think me a little presuming; but I am one of the most unconventional people in the world, and there is nothing I like better than to ignore the starch and buckram of society occasionally, and make an acquaintance in a natural, informal manner. As a warrant of my respectability, allow me to say that my name is Marchmont, and I am a cousin and guest of the Lathrops, with whom, if you live in Edgerton, you are probably acquainted."

"I am not acquainted with them, but I know who they are," answered Amy, always proudly literal in her statements. "They are very rich, fashionable people, while I am the daughter of Mr. Reynolds, the music-teacher. And this is Hugh Dinsmore," she added, with an instinct of courtesy.

Mr. Marchmont lifted his hat again, with the air of one who acknowledges an introduction. "I am happy to know you, Miss Reynolds," he said. "Finding Sunday afternoon dull, I sauntered out into the woods, but I did not expect to meet either Flora or Euterpe—much less the two in one. May I hope that you will, of your charity, sing another song for me?"

"Amy," said Hugh, again breaking in, "it is certainly time for us to go home."

In return for his solicitude, Amy flashed a glance of vexation at him. "It is *not* time, Hugh, and you know it!" she said, in an irritated tone.—"Did you like the song I sang before?" she asked, turning to Mr. Marchmont.

"Very much," he replied.

"Well, I will sing you something better now," she said, quietly. Then, folding her hands and looking straight up into the blue sky, to his amazement she began the "*Cujus animam*," from Rossini's "Stabat Mater." Even Hugh forgot his anger as he listened, for it might have been a seraph singing the divine melody instead of the girl who so shortly before had been talking of violet velvet and point-lace. It was impossible to connect any earthly association with the pure notes that fell on the ear like "the music of the spheres," and seemed capable of piercing to the very courts of heaven. When the last strain ceased, Amy's eyes drooped for the first time, and then she turned them on Mr. Marchmont.

He had unconsciously advanced nearer to her, and his face was absolutely aglow with excitement. "Why, it is divine!" he cried. "Good heavens! do you know that you have one of the most beautiful voices in the world?"

"I am glad that you think so," she answered; and she looked (Hugh thought) exultant. A starry light streamed into her dark-gray eyes, a vivid flush of color shone on her peach-like cheeks. "Papa has taken a great deal of pains with my voice," she went on, "and he does not like me to sing for people in general; but, since you said you were cultivated musically—which most people in Edgerton are not," she added, candidly, "I thought I would like your opinion of my singing. Do you think that I can make a fortune with my voice?"

"I am sure of it," he answered, confidently. "No one who heard you could fail to be sure. There is gold, and triumph, and delight for multitudes in that throat of yours."

She made him a pretty little courtesy —the girl was lissome and graceful as a bayadere.

"Thank you," she said.—"And now I will not detain you longer. Hugh, it is time for us to go."

"You must let me thank *you* for the great pleasure you have given me," said Mr. Marchmont, eagerly.

"If I have given you pleasure, you have given me encouragement, so you are not all in my debt," she replied. "But you may come to my *début*, if you will."

"I shall certainly be there," he said, smiling.

As she moved away, the spray of honeysuckle which had been attached to her wreath behind dropped to the ground, and he stooped for it. "I shall keep this as a souvenir of my pleasant adventure," he said, "and on the night of your first triumph I will return it in roses. Thanks again, and *au revoir*."

"This way, Amy. We have to go for the children," said Hugh, impatiently.

CHAPTER II.

"JEWELS WILL BE BETTER."

THEY walked on in silence through the woods for some minutes. Then Amy said:

"Why are you so cross, Hugh? There was no harm in singing for the gentleman."

"Yes, there was harm," answered Hugh. "You ought to know better. I am sure your father would not like it if he knew."

"Then we won't let him know," said Amy, with that expressive play of countenance which the French call a *moue*. "Though I don't really think he would care," she added. "Papa is not a dragon."

"But he is a man," said Hugh, who was greatly vexed, "and he knows that a young girl should not sing to every stranger who chooses to ask her to do so."

"I should not have sung to him if I had not wanted his opinion of my voice," said Amy; "and I am so glad he praised it. What was it he said?—'gold, triumph, the delight of multitudes,' in my throat! O Hugh! I am so happy I could dance and sing for joy!"

She clapped her hands as she spoke, and, making a movement like a ballet-dancer's *pirouette*, darted forward several paces, and then waltzed back.

"For shame—on Sunday!" said Hugh, who had heard numerous admonitions about "the Sabbath-day" in his early youth, and in whose memory the recollection of such teaching still lingered.

"Where's the harm?" asked the girl, gayly. "May I not sing as well as the birds, and dance as well as the sunbeams? *Pouf!* as old Madame Duchesne says. I am going to be rich; I am going to be admired; I am going to *live*.—Hugh, did you know I could sing so well?"

"I never had an idea of it, Amy," replied Hugh, simply.

"And, to tell you the truth," said Amy, stopping short and looking at him, with her face flushed into radiant beauty, "I had no idea of it myself until this evening. Do you know what being inspired means? I think I was inspired when I sang that '*Cujus animam.*' Wasn't it divine? I felt as if I could do anything in the world with my voice—as if I could send it straight up into heaven if I chose. I never had such a sense of power before. I did not think of anything while I sang except the delight of uttering such thrilling sounds. Papa never praises my voice, though I know he thinks it very fine; but when I saw Mr. Marchmont's face—and hasn't he splendid eyes?—then I knew that fortune and fame are here"—she touched her throat.

"And will your father consent to your

singing in public?" asked Hugh, his face growing grave.

The girl stared at him.

"Why, that is what he means me to do!" she said. "That is why he is so careful of my voice—cultivating it, but never allowing me to strain it. He would not let me sing in the church-choir, though I have been so anxious to do it; not that I cared about the choir, but I wanted to test my voice in a large building. I am satisfied now, however. I know that I can fill any theatre in the world."

"I suppose I ought to be glad," said Hugh, "but I'm not, and I can't help it. I hope you are mistaken—I hope your voice is not as good as you think. I should be glad of anything that kept you from going on the stage."

This was more than Amy could bear. Her eyes flashed with anger instead of delight, and she fairly stamped her foot.

"How dare you!—oh, how dare you hope such a cruel thing!" she cried. "I didn't think you *could* be so mean! When there is but one chance of relief from this horrible life of poverty—one chance to free others as well as to escape myself—you grudge me that! O Hugh, I didn't think you could!"

Hugh felt stricken with remorse, yet unable to retract what he had uttered.

"I wish to Heaven I was rich and older!" he said, with a sigh.

"Wishes are of no good," said Amy, with the air of one who had given them a fair trial and found them useless. "But if you were as rich as an emperor, and a hundred years old, you could not keep me from going on the stage. Gold, triumph, the delight of multitudes—oh, I wish I was going to make my *début* to-night! You should paint my portrait in the costume of the character in which I achieved my first triumph."

"Not I," said Hugh, grimly. "I should paint you, with your wreath of wild-flowers, as *my* Amy—not the public's."

"But I am not your Amy, sir," she said, laughing; and then she began singing again, trilling her birdlike notes for very birdlike joy.

The sun was nearly down when they paused a few minutes later on the crest of a hill which they had been gradually ascending. Immediately below lay a green valley, through the midst of which wound a stream—

"A sedgy brook whereby the red kine meet
And wade to drink their fill,"

and over the fallen tree which made a rustic bridge across this a party of children were trooping in single file.

"There they are!" said Amy, waving her handkerchief.

"What a beautiful scene!" said Hugh, in the tone of one thrilled suddenly. "Look, Amy—look!"

Amy looked in the direction which he indicated, but it is doubtful whether she understood what had stirred him. She, to whom one kind of harmony was so intelligible, scarcely comprehended the harmony of another kind which filled the fair landscape, sweeping westward to the golden sky.

But to Hugh it was even more divine than the "*Cujus animam*." There was a pearly mist over everything like the haze of Indian summer, only it was more delicate, and had in it all the buoyancy of spring, the indefinable sense of awakening life—of resurrection instead of death. Near at hand the softly-swelling hills and lovely meadows were covered with emerald; afar the fringe of distant forest melted into azure softness. There were clouds of snowy blossoms in the fields, and every breeze was laden with fragrance. The sun was sinking behind the mist which near the horizon veiled his glory so that it could be gazed upon fearlessly. Filmy vapors of rose and gold floated above, and high over these the new moon rode—a slender silver boat.

"And I shall not see it again for another week!" said the boy, in a tone of keen pain. "Oh, how can people live in the world and think so little of its beauty! Amy, I could paint that sky. I know—I know I could!"

"Just as I know that I could fill an opera-house with my voice," said Amy, arching her throat. "When I am *prima donna assoluta*, you shall paint as many sunsets as you like, Hugh."

"Do you think I would take your money?" asked Hugh, flushing. "We may laugh about such things, but you mustn't believe for a minute that I would really do it."

"Then you would be very ungracious," said Amy, indignantly.

The embryo quarrel was stopped here by the advent of the children, who came running and laughing up the hill, laden with flowers and blossoming boughs. There were seven of them, ranging in age from fourteen to six years. Four of these were Amy's brothers and sister; the other three were the children of Mrs. Crenshaw, a kind woman who kept a boarding-house next door to the Reynoldses, and made no claim to social position. If she had done so, Willie, Fanny, and Hetty Crenshaw would probably have been pacing decorously to Sunday-school in their best bib and tucker, instead of running wild, like young fawns, in the lovely spring woods with "those Reynolds children."

Of the last there were three boys and one girl, besides Amy; Felix, the eldest of the boys, had been named after Mendelssohn, and justified his name by the precocity of his musical genius. He had played from the time that his tiny fingers could touch the keys, and now, at fourteen, his father—a musician himself of rare power—declared that he could teach him no more. "He knows as much of the science of harmony as I do," Mr. Reynolds would say; "he will make a great musician, if I can send him to Germany." That *if*, however, was gigantic. On this April evening, the path by which Felix was to go to Germany had not opened yet.

The other two boys, Oliver and Ernest, were more ordinary; they, too, possessed in a measure the musical talent of the family, but it was largely dominated by the tastes and habits of common boyhood. And youngest of all was pretty baby Mariette, with a face like an opening rose-bud, great eyes of turquoise-blue, and a shower of glittering ringlets falling to her waist.

It may be imagined how gayly—yet, certainly, how harmlessly—this group of children laughed and talked as they took their way homeward through the gloaming, so tenderly purple, so delightfully fragrant. Amy and Hugh led the procession—and a quaint Bohemian pair they were: the future *prima donna assoluta* was habited in a muslin dress which many washings had very much faded and slightly shrunken; her straw hat was swung on her arm like a basket, while Hugh's wreath still crowned her graceful head. So pretty and so shabby was she, that she might be described in general terms as looking like a vagabond Queen of May. Her companion, though not less shabby, was decidedly less picturesque; he was simply an undersized boy, plain of face and awkward of movement, whose clothes, though clean, were much worn and also a little outgrown.

So long as they were in the country, these trifles of costume mattered little, and it was only when they approached the outskirts of the town that Amy began to wear that air of defiance which soon comes to social outlaws.

The road which they were following left the sweet wildness of the open country and led first between grass-lots and cultivated fields, then by a stone-wall of considerable length, over the top of which evergreens drooped, showing that grounds of large extent and probable beauty lay within.

"If I were rich I would not build a wall around my grounds to deprive people of the pleasure of looking at them," said Hugh.

"If you were rich you would not care how people who had no grounds felt about it," said Amy. "It is to *keep* us from looking at their lawns and gardens that they build such walls."

"Isn't this where General Waldron lives?" asked Oliver. "He's the old gentleman who has such a big white mustache. I like his looks."

"It's a pretty place—we can get a glimpse through the gate," said Felix, stopping before this portal, which was of iron. "I see a lawn and part of a fountain, and the corner of a greenhouse—"

"Felix—the rest of you, come on!" cried Amy, sharply.

All the small faces which had been pressed against the iron bars turned quickly. The reason of Amy's sharpness was at once apparent. An open carriage, drawn by two dark-bay horses, was rapidly approaching.

"It's the Waldron carriage!" said Ernest, darting away.

The rest followed hastily, and the dignity of their retreat was further marred by Hetty Crenshaw tripping over a stone, and having to be lifted, dusted, and led away weeping.

Amy walked in front with a flushed face. She would have scorned to peep through the Waldron gate herself, but she felt compromised by the conduct of her cohort; and when a head, adorned by the hat of which she had spoken admiringly, nodded more kindly than patronizingly from the carriage, she responded with a salutation stiff enough to have rebuked aspiring presumption rather than acknowledge superior condescension.

"What an extraordinary-looking cavalcade!" said another lady, putting up an eye-glass. "For mercy's sake, who are they? Oh, the Reynolds children! I hope they haven't been rifling your flower-garden."

"Hardly," Miss Waldron laughed. "All those spoils came from the woods. Did you notice how pretty Amy looked with that wreath of flowers on her head?"

"I thought she looked very peculiar, but I didn't notice exactly what was the matter. What a theatrical idea, to walk through the streets decked in such fashion —on Sunday evening, too!"

The carriage rolled in, the gates clashed together, and the Reynolds children dropped from the conversation and minds of its occupants.

"That was Miss Lathrop with Miss Waldron," said Hugh; and Amy answered, "Was it? I did not observe."

No doubt there were numbers of other people to echo Miss Lathrop's opinion with regard to Amy's appearance, before she reached home. She passed group after group of well-dressed, Sunday-mannered folk, with the defiant expression deepening somewhat on her face, but no other token of heeding their curious glances. Yet the uncharitable only said, "There go those outlandish Reynolds children!" while the kindly remarked with a sigh, "How that poor girl needs a mother!"

When that girl thus commiserated reached the house where the Reynoldses as a family lived—or, to speak more correctly, where they scrambled through existence in a hap-hazard manner—she walked into a small low-ceiled parlor, which held but one prominent article of furniture, and that a piano. At this piano a gaunt man, with hair and beard dashed with gray, a sharp nose, and a pair of pathetic eyes, sat playing a strain from one of Mozart's masses with a touch that brought out all the divine melody lurking in the harmony. He nodded and smiled when the children came in, but did not cease playing. Felix walked forward and slipped his arm round his neck. He was his father's pride and favorite, and had as many caressing ways as a girl.

"You ought to have come with us, papa," he said. "The country is so lovely now. A walk would have helped you to rest."

"I walk enough on six days," answered Mr. Reynolds; "on the seventh

I like to stay quietly with the piano. But you have brought back flowers enough, my boy."

"Yes; see, papa, how pretty and sweet!" cried the others, thronging round.

Meanwhile Amy went up to a small mirror that held the last glow of sunset light in its depth, and looked at her reflection — the color-flushed cheeks, the dark-gray eyes shining under long lashes, the rich masses of curling hair, and the wreath of wild-flowers crowning the fair picture. Then she turned to Hugh with a smile that broke up all the gravity of her face.

"The wreath is very becoming," she said, "and you have crowned me for victory. But jewels will be better than flowers."

CHAPTER III.

" 'TIS BUT A LITTLE FADED FLOWER."

AMY had been right in characterizing the Lathrops as "very rich and fashionable people"—according to the standard of riches and fashion in Edgerton. They lived in a handsome house, with appointments every way suggestive of wealth, were gay and hospitable, and therefore popular. Mr. Lathrop and his sons were "in business" on a large scale. Mrs. Lathrop and her daughters were also in business, if the duty of leading society could properly come under that head. That it is very often far more of a business than a pleasure, no one can doubt who has ever had the opportunity of observing at close quarters the life of a fashionable woman. But to some natures there is a compensation for all attendant labor and cost in the mere possession of a power; and that Mrs. Lathrop was one of these people, was patent to the dullest perception.

In all details of life she was what is generally known as "a managing woman." Her household was organized like a police force; yet her rule was never oppressive, for she knew exactly where authority ended and tyranny began. Always suave, somewhat diplomatic, with a fine presence and a pair of large, white hands capable of holding the threads of many different interests, she was eminently fitted to administer the social affairs of Edgerton and preserve society from the chaos which always attends the want of a recognized leader.

Her daughters gave promise of following the maternal footsteps. Two were in society—not at all pretty, but noted for their style, and, from their position, always sure of receiving as much attention as if they had been beauties. A younger daughter was not yet emancipated from the school-room. One of the two sons had taken unto himself a wife, with the hearty approval of his parents, since the lady—who was not an Edgertonian—was the fortunate possessor of a considerable fortune in her own right.

"If Edward will only marry as judiciously as Paul, I shall be truly grateful to Providence," said Mrs. Lathrop, devoutly. But Edward, the younger son, was rather given to flirting with portionless girls, and sometimes disturbed his mother's equanimity by declaring that he thought it his duty to bring a pretty wife into the family, since Paul had married one whose personal appearance no man could conscientiously commend.

Of Mr. Lathrop, the head of the household, there is little to be said further than that he was his wife's most loyal admirer, and, though in no sense a henpecked husband, her opinion had more weight with him than that of any one else. In business matters he was keen, shrewd, and inclined to be hard, though always just. Socially he was genial, fond of display, and lavish with the means necessary to this end. Seen in his own house, a more agreeable host—notwithstanding the drawback of a little pomposity—never wore a white waistcoat, or boasted one of those bald, glistening heads which impart such a benevolent aspect to the countenance.

Under the shelter of the Lathrop roof Mr. Brian Marchmont, nephew of Mrs. Lathrop, had been sojourning nearly a week, on that Sunday afternoon when he met Amy Reynolds in the April woods. This young gentleman was one of those who have the reputation of "brilliant abilities," and there was a vague, general expectation in the minds of all who knew him that he would one day greatly distinguish himself. Of the abilities there could be no question, and the expectation of distinction was stronger in the mind of Marchmont himself than in that of any one else. He was ambitious, and had already decided by what steps he would mount to the height he desired. They were not to be very difficult steps, for there was an element of epicureanism in the young man's character which, under certain circumstances, might mar his plan of life. He had no fear of such an event, however. If belief in one's own power is a first necessity for achieving worldly success, Marchmont was ready with that requisite. He had so far in life vaulted lightly over all obstacles, and lifted his head so high above the heads of those surrounding him, that he could scarcely be blamed for self-confidence.

At the present time the errand on which he had come to Edgerton was well known. In the city where he lived he had, during the past winter, met Miss Waldron, the only child and heiress of her father, a man of large wealth. With Marchmont, as with a great many other aspiring men, the first step which he proposed to himself on his journey to the Temple of Fame was the step of marrying a fortune.

"I have, comparatively speaking, no money, and if I waste my life in working for that, it will be too late after I have gained it to devote my higher powers to the objects I propose; so it follows that I must marry a rich woman!"

This was what he said to himself, and to the few friends who were admitted to intimacy with him. These friends, one and all, applauded his resolution. It is well known, however, that the seekers after rich women are, in point of number, altogether out of proportion to those desirable objects, so that unless a man has unusual advantages of person or manner, his chance of drawing a prize is exceedingly small. These advantages Brian Marchmont possessed. No one could deny that he was well-born, well-bred, and above the ordinary rank and file of mankind in point of appearance.

Although his aunt, Mrs. Lathrop, was in a measure attached to him, and certainly proud of the abilities which he was supposed to possess, she would have welcomed him more cordially if he had come to Edgerton for any other purpose than the one which brought him. Not that she did not consider his object a good and altogether praiseworthy one; but it had been her cherished plan that her son should marry Miss Waldron, and though she was too sensible a woman not to recognize that all overtures to this end had been unmistakably rebuffed by the young lady, she had, nevertheless, a sore feeling in seeing the prize grasped before her eyes by the hand of her own nephew.

It was true, the prize had not yet been grasped; but that Marchmont's chance of success was better than that of any other suitor of the heiress, all who knew anything about the matter were agreed.

On the Sunday evening already recorded, Mr. Marchmont made his appearance at the Lathrop tea-table just as the church-bells were pealing out over the town on the soft, flower-scented dusk.

"Why, Brian, we have been wondering what had become of you," said Mr. Lathrop, looking up. "What have you been doing with yourself all the afternoon?"

"I saw you asleep in the hammock after dinner," said Edward Lathrop;

"but when I looked into it an hour or so later, you had vanished."

"I felt an inclination to take a stroll," said Marchmont; "therefore I left the hammock and wandered off. The woods are so delightful that I rambled farther than I intended, lost my way, and hence my late appearance."

"You don't know what you missed by strolling off!" cried Florence, the second daughter. "Beatrix Waldron has been here this afternoon, and Anna has gone home with her."

"She would hardly have been likely to take me instead of Anna—would she?" asked Marchmont, quietly.

"Hardly; but I thought it would grieve you to miss *one* glimpse of your divinity."

"And so you gave me the afflicting intelligence at once. Thanks for the consideration—but I don't find my appetite impaired.—Eunice, my dear, may I ask what attracts your attention?"

Eunice, a pale little maiden of fifteen, who sat opposite him, blushed, and pointed to his button-hole.

"I was looking at that spray of crimson honeysuckle, Cousin Brian," she answered. "It is pretty. Where did you get it?"

"I found it in the woods," he replied. "Is it uncommon? Then, have it, pray." He tossed it lightly across the table, and Eunice smiled her thanks.

"I have not seen any in a long time," she said. "I would get some and plant it in the garden if I knew where to find it."

But her cousin did not volunteer to show her where it was to be found. He glanced round the table, and, seeing that every one else had ceased eating, he said:

"I beg that you will not let me detain you, Aunt Caroline. I should not have been such a late-comer if I had remembered that your hour was probably early on Sunday."

"In order to allow the servants, as well as ourselves, to go to church," said Mrs. Lathrop. "We are a little later than usual on account of having waited some time for you, and, since you are kind enough to excuse us, I think it would be better, Florence, if we put on our bonnets at once."

Florence rose, and, with a rustle of silk, the ladies left the room. Marchmont looked at Edward Lathrop, and said, gravely:

"Do you go to church *twice* a day, Ned?"

"Not unless there is some very particular inducement," answered that gentleman, "and not even then when the thermometer stands above seventy-five degrees. I simply escort my mother and the girls to the church-door. That is what we will do to-night, if you have no objection, after which we will come back and smoke a cigar in peace and coolness."

A few minutes later Mrs. Lathrop and her daughter entered the drawing-room, whither the gentlemen had adjourned. Both were dressed beautifully, and the elder lady was buttoning her gloves.

"Eunice has a headache, so I have allowed her to remain at home," she said. —"Are you coming with us, my dear?"

"Not to-night, my dear," said Mr. Lathrop.

He always said, "Not to-night," as if he might be tempted to go on some future night; but, so far, that occasion had not arrived, and Mrs. Lathrop was wise, and never asked when it would arrive.

The young men escorted the ladies to the church-door, but declined an invitation to enter the edifice, where vivid gaslight streamed on crimson-carpeted aisles and crimson-cushioned seats. Then they strolled slowly back through the semi-darkness of the streets, past gardens from which the fragrance of roses and syringa, jasmine and honeysuckle, filled the air.

"This is rather better than blinding gaslight and simmering heat," said Edward Lathrop, as they regained the house which they had left so shortly before. "Shall we sit on the piazza, and take a smoke? My father and Eunice seem to be very well entertained."

Marchmont glanced through the drawing-room window, and smiled at the scene within.

Mr. Lathrop, leaning back in a large chair, with a newspaper open on his knee, was dozing placidly, the light from the chandelier falling with brilliant effect on the bald top of his head; while, at the farther end of the apartment, Eunice was seated at the large, carved piano, playing a simple accompaniment as she sang, in a childish voice, "There is a land of pure delight."

From the force of contrast, the voice and song reminded Marchmont of the silver tones that he had heard soar aloft in " *Cujus animam* " so short a time before.

"That girl could not have been much older than Eunice," he thought, as he dropped the lace curtain and returned to his companion.

"Do you know anybody of the name of Reynolds in Edgerton, Ned?" he asked, after they were settled in their chairs with lighted cigars.

"I know Eunice's music-teacher," answered Lathrop. "Do you mean him? —a gaunt fellow, who plays the organ in the church we left a minute ago."

"I thought there was an uncommon hand on that organ this morning," said Marchmont. "And does his daughter sing there?"

"His daughter—pretty little Amy? I don't think so. But how do you chance to know anything about her?"

Marchmont laughed.

"I met her this afternoon in the woods," he said. "It was an odd kind of adventure, and I did not mention it to my aunt, because I fancy she does not approve of unconventional ways and people."

"You might stake a good deal on that without much fear of losing," said Lathrop; "and I don't think she has a very good opinion of pretty Amy either."

"Why not?"

"If you have seen the girl, you might tell why not. The *madre* is great on making people walk a chalk-line, according to their station in life, which Amy— who is an out-and-out little Bohemian, and wild as a gypsy—will on no account think of doing. They have had one or two encounters—one was on the subject of attending Sunday-school, I believe— and Amy always came off with flying colors. Hence she is regarded in the light of a most reprehensible young person, you understand. But she is amazingly pretty —and piquant as pretty."

"Yes, she is very pretty," assented Marchmont—at that moment he seemed to see again the winsome face with its wild-flower crown—"but she has something better than her face. Do you know that she sings like an angel — pshaw! what do we know about angels?—like a prima donna?"

"Not I," and it was very evident, even in the dim light, that Lathrop stared. "How the deuce did *you* find it out? You must have progressed in your acquaintance very rapidly—if you never saw her before this afternoon."

"I never saw her before this afternoon, and I came upon her most unexpectedly then. It was out in the woods —she was sitting in a glen with no other companion than an awkward boy, singing a Tyrolean echo-song which I have often heard on the stage, but never better rendered. You may be sure I was astonished, and I could not help encoring when the song ended. She was somewhat embarrassed at first, but, when I introduced myself, she was good enough to say she knew who the Lathrops were, and then she sang the ' *Cujus animam* ' from Rossini's 'Stabat Mater,' and sang it divinely! She has not only one of the finest voices I ever heard, but it has been remarkably well cultivated."

"Reynolds is an excellent musician," said Lathrop; "at least, he has that reputation. I don't know much about such things myself. And so little Amy said that 'she knew who the Lathrops were?' Upon my honor, that's the best joke I've heard in an age! I don't really think I can keep it from the *madre!*"

"It's no joke at all," said Marchmont, "and I hope you won't think of trying to make one out of it. The girl meant no impertinence. She said, quite proudly: 'They are very rich, fashionable people, and I am the daughter of Mr. Reynolds, the music-teacher.' She's an amusing little witch. By-the-by, have you any idea who was the boy with her? She mentioned his name, but I have forgotten it."

"I have not the least idea," replied Lathrop. "My acquaintance with her is of the slightest possible description, and her friends are quite unknown to me. Reynolds has several sons. It was probably one of them."

Marchmont knew better, but he said no more of Amy or her companion. Perhaps the subject dropped from his thoughts. Certainly when he spoke again it was of something very different; and so they talked and smoked until the gate at the foot of the lawn opened and closed, and voices and steps approached the house.

"There come my mother and Florence, with somebody in attendance," said Lathrop, rising.

The somebody proved to be a young man of smooth face and immaculate dress, who was thought to have evangelical leanings, and known to entertain matrimonial intentions toward the second Miss Lathrop.

This young lady had no objection to a mild flirtation after having performed her duty by going to church in the most exemplary manner; so she retired with her captive to the end of the drawing-room, while Eunice was at once dispatched by her mother to bed.

"Close the piano, Edward," she added. "It is very injurious to an instrument to stand open."

Edward sauntered obediently to the piano and closed it. Then he returned, holding in his fingers the faded spray of honeysuckle which had already changed owners twice.

"I believe this is yours, Brian," he said, extending it with a smile to his cousin. "Eunice left it by the keyboard, but I thought I would bring it to you, since you might like to preserve it."

Marchmont took the spray and tossed it carelessly into the empty fireplace.

"Faded flowers are useless things," he said. "When they have served their purpose, the only thing to do is to throw them away."

CHAPTER IV.

"ALTOGETHER AN ACCIDENT."

"I AM going to drive to Cedarwood for Anna this morning, Brian. Will you come with me?"

It was Florence Lathrop who said this, pausing in the hall the next day, after breakfast.

Her cousin, who was in the act of lighting a cigar, looked up at once.

"Certainly I will, with pleasure," he replied. "When do you mean to start?"

"In an hour or two—not before. They never breakfast early at Cedarwood. There are no business-men *there!*"

"It is too bad that there should be some here to rouse you for anything so barbarous as a nine-o'clock breakfast," said her brother. "If you are not going for an hour or two, you can call for Brian at the commission-house. He is going to walk down-town with me."

"Very well," replied the young lady, sailing languidly up-stairs.

Mr. Lathrop emerged from the breakfast-room at the moment, drew on his gloves, exchanged his benevolent air for a decided one, and said, "We are ten minutes behind time," and walked quickly out of the front-door.

The younger men followed, and the three took their way together into the

2

business portion of the town, filling the fresh air, as they walked, with the triple smoke of their cigars.

"Lathrop & Sons" were engaged in a large wholesale commission business; and as the two members of the firm, accompanied by their idle relative, entered the great, dingy warehouse, filled with bales of cotton, hogsheads of tobacco, grain, and other products, it chanced that the first person they met was an undersized boy of seventeen or eighteen, whose face had an oddly familiar look to Marchmont, though for a moment he was puzzled to think when or where he had seen it.

"Dinsmore, I shall want you in a minute," said Mr. Lathrop, in his most brisk tones. "Come to the counting-room."

Dinsmore! Marchmont said nothing, but he thought to himself that this was the awkward boy who had been Amy Reynolds's companion on the afternoon before, and who had glared at him with such amusing indignation. For that matter, his eyes had by no means an amiable expression now, as they rested an instant on the well-dressed young gentleman, before he turned and followed Mr. Lathrop.

An hour or two later, Marchmont was reading the morning papers in his cousin's counting-room when one of the clerks appeared with the intelligence that Miss Lathrop was at the door waiting for him.

He rose with alacrity. Something in the nature of his surroundings oppressed him with a sense of weight and repugnance.

"How can you muster philosophy enough to think of spending the best part of your life in such a place as this?" he could not refrain from saying to Edward Lathrop; but the latter only laughed.

"The prospect does not overwhelm me," he said, "though I grant you it would be pleasanter to live at Cedarwood on ten thousand a year. But everybody isn't a Prince Charming, or a Prince Fortunate either."

This good-natured sarcasm effectually silenced Marchmont. He knew that if there had been the faintest chance of securing Miss Waldron and Cedarwood, his cousin would have grasped that chance as eagerly as himself; but, nevertheless, he could not help feeling that the labor which was so distasteful to his fastidious, pleasure-loving nature, was, to say the least, far more honorable than the gentlemanly profession of fortune-hunting.

These uncomfortable feelings were evanescent, however. It was with a sense of relief that he emerged into the sunshine and entered the waiting carriage, where Miss Lathrop sat with a handkerchief at her nose; for there were several tons of fertilizers in the neighborhood, the odor of which was strikingly unlike that of Araby the Blest.

"What a disagreeable part of the town this is!" she said. "I always dislike to come down here; and how papa and the boys can be content to spend their days in that horrid place, I don't understand."

It occurred to Marchmont that this was rather ungracious on the part of one whose carriage and horses, silk dress and lace-covered parasol, were all the direct proceeds of the "horrid place" in question; but he only said, "It strikes me rather in that light, but I suppose I am one of the drones of the world—and you know they are not a very estimable class."

"But you don't mean to be always a drone," said she, smiling; for they had left the fertilizers behind, and she was now able to smile again.

Marchmont thought this very true. He did *not* mean to be always a drone. On the contrary, he meant to do work more important as well as more agreeable than selling cotton and tobacco on commission. He did not remember that such an idea is one of the most common and shallow devices of self-love. There are few of us who do not excuse our present shortcomings by reflecting on the great things which we mean to do in the future

—until the future has become the past, when we think what great things we might have done had circumstances only been more favorable—Fate kinder, the world more appreciative.

Neither of these two butterflies of prosperity felt inclined to complain of Fate or the world this morning, however. The carriage rolled as if on velvet, the wheels and harness glittered in the sunshine, the glory of spring was all about them, birds were singing in the delicate leafage of the trees, flowers were blooming in all directions, windows were open, light costumes were out in force. Miss Lathrop, who was bowing now and then from under her parasol to passing acquaintances, suddenly said, with the air of one whom a sudden recollection strikes:

"Andrew" (to the coachman), "drive to Mrs. Crenshaw's boarding-house.—Brian, will you excuse me if I detain you for a few minutes? Mamma asked me to call and see how a sick lady, who is boarding there, is to-day. She is a stranger in Edgerton, but belongs to quite nice people, so, of course, we are anxious to pay her every attention."

"A modern rendition of the good Samaritan," said Brian, smiling. "My time is at your disposal altogether; don't hesitate to detain me as long as you like. I could be happy on the door-step to-day, basking like a Neapolitan in the sunshine."

The carriage, as he spoke, turned into a street where the buildings, though respectable, were by no means imposing, but where there were many shade-trees and a few good residences. The largest of these was a house which opened on the street, and had a neglected flower-garden at the side. Here the carriage stopped, and Marchmont, springing out, assisted his cousin to alight. Then, having rung the door-bell and seen her admitted, he returned to the pavement and sauntered under the flickering shade of the elms by the low garden-fence.

However neglected, all gardens in which there are flowers must be pretty in April, and this garden was no exception to the rule. The syringa-bushes were covered with white, fragrant blossoms; bees were humming over the honeysuckle; there was a large bed where lilies-of-the-valley lifted their delicate white bells amid broad green leaves; and the untrimmed rose-bushes were full of blossoms.

Bordering the fence, and on a level with it, was a luxuriant *Enonymus* hedge, from the other side of which Marchmont heard the voices of two invisible and probably liliputian personages.

"The flowers *won't* stay on, Hetty," said one. "You go and ask your mother for some more string."

"Mother said I mustn't come and bother her any more," answered another small but positive voice. "*You* go and ask Mr. Trafford for some."

"Mr. Trafford's gone to walk—I saw him go," said Number One. "But I'll go and ask Clara for some."

"Be sure and make haste back," said Number Two.

Following this came the patter of small feet, a gate in the fence suddenly swung open, and a child of not more than seven years, with a glittering mane of yellow curls, sprang out on the sidewalk. Her companion's voice followed her, saying:

"Shut the gate, Mariette, or the pigs will get in."

Mariette, who was darting away without this necessary precaution, turned back, but Marchmont closed the gate, and then said, with a smile:

"Are you Alice from Wonderland? You look like her."

"No, I'm not; but I know all about her," she answered, quickly, breaking into a laugh, and gazing up at him with fearless eyes of myosotis blue. "Mr. Trafford gave me the book—she went to Wonderland, and through the looking-glass, too."

"Did she?" said Marchmont. "I never

followed her that far. But are you certain you are not she?"

"Oh, yes," she replied, with another laugh. "I am Mariette Reynolds."

"Reynolds!" repeated Marchmont. He did not say to himself, "*C'est la fatalité*," but he certainly thought that Fate, or something else, was determined to keep the pretty songstress of the woods in his mind. "Have you a sister named Amy, and does she sing?" he went on, after a moment, as they walked along side by side.

"Of course I have," answered Mariette, surprised that any one should ask such a question. "Do you know my sister Amy? Mr. Trafford says she sings like a—I've forgotten the name exactly, but some kind of a bird."

"Who the deuce is Mr. Trafford?" Marchmont felt inclined to ask, but he restrained himself, and only said: 'I am afraid that your sister Amy would not allow me to say that I know her, but I have heard her sing. Where do you live?"

"Here," said Mariette, indicating a house adjoining the garden which they were passing.

It was a small, old-fashioned dwelling, opening immediately on the street, with high, narrow windows, and a generally shabby and uncomfortable aspect. It spoke so plainly of poverty—that poverty which manages to keep bread-and-butter on its table, but has not a sixpence to spare for the adorning graces of life—that Marchmont's fastidious epicureanism felt a thrill of much the same disgust which he had experienced in the warehouse of Lathrop & Sons.

His interest in the embryo prima donna began to abate, but nevertheless he walked on by Mariette's side, thinking that he would turn as soon as he reached the door of the house and saw the little maiden within it.

But, if not fatality, what was it that brought Amy to the window of the little parlor, and framed the piquant loveliness of her face between the chintz curtains, to startle Marchmont, like a gleam of rich color in a gray landscape?

He stopped short, with an exclamation, and lifted his hat.

"Miss Reynolds!" he said. "How fortunate I am! I did not hope to meet you again so soon!"

Amy was not much surprised—a fact which was very natural, since the windows on the side of the house commanded an excellent view of Mrs. Crenshaw's garden and the street along which Marchmont had been sauntering.

She had been engaged in dusting, with a towel tied round her head, when she first saw him, and she had flushed rose-red, cast the towel into a dark corner, darted to the small mirror, given a few hurried touches to her hair—which was always ready to curl, and never prettier than when left to its own devices—and then established herself at the window, with an open music-book in her lap.

At his salutation the long lashes lifted from her mischievous gray eyes.

"O Mr. Marchmont!" she said, with a slight start. "How do you do this morning?—and where did you find Mariette?"

"Mariette found *me*," he replied, "in a very badly-bored condition, dawdling along the street yonder. I am waiting for my cousin, who has gone into the house of your neighbor to pay a visit."

"Ah!" said Amy. "I was wondering what could have brought you into this part of the town."

"My presence here is altogether an accident," he said; "but within the last two minutes it has begun to assume the appearance of a very lucky accident. I dreamed of sirens all last night, and you can tell, I am sure, who was to blame for that."

"How can *I* tell?" asked Amy, innocently. "Perhaps you went to church, and the choir—"

He interrupted her by a laugh.

"Pray don't be so severe on the sirens

as to liken them—or to suppose that *I* would liken them—to any well-intentioned band of amateur squallers. Besides, you know better—you know that sirens don't sing in village choirs, but they are to be met sometimes in wooded glens on April afternoons."

"Happy sirens!" said Amy, with a soft little sigh. "They knew their songs intuitively, and were never obliged to learn to sing by note. How I hate notes!" she added, glancing down at the page of score in her lap.

"Drudgery is always disagreeable," said Marchmont—and *he* glanced down at the score also—"but especially when connected with harmony. What have you there?"

"A song papa has just given me to learn. When he gives me a song for the first time, he always locks the piano, so that I have no opportunity to learn the notes by the keys. Then I have to sing it for him, and then he teaches me *how* to sing it."

"All of which is very essential to prepare the foundation of your future greatness," said the listener, smiling. "And have you sung the song yet for papa?"

"Not yet, but I must to-night."

"I suppose I dare not be bold enough to ask you to sing it for me now?"

"What, here?" The gray eyes opened to their widest extent, while the pretty lips laughed. "That is impossible; everybody along the street would hear—and see me!"

"But, if you were hospitable enough to allow me to come in—"

"You are not in earnest," she said. "How could you tell when your cousin finished paying her visit, if you came in to hear me sing?"

"That is very true," he replied; "at present it is unfortunately impossible for me to have that pleasure; but if I return this afternoon, will you admit me then, and let me hear your lesson before *Monsieur votre père* does so?"

Amy hesitated. The prospect was alluring—how alluring, those of older years and different rearing can scarcely understand—but an instinct of propriety warned even this "out-and-out Bohemian," as Edward Lathrop called her, against it. Seeing her hesitation, Marchmont would not have been a man if he had not instantly conceived an added desire to carry his point.

"You did me the honor to remark, yesterday afternoon, that you sang for me because I seemed to be musically cultivated," he said; "will not the same reason plead for me now? My culture is not very great, so far as any personal acquirement is concerned, but I have heard all the best singers of the day, and I can give you a few needful hints, perhaps, with regard to your method."

"Have you ever heard any one sing this?" she asked, holding the score toward him.

"Certainly I have," he answered, glancing at it (and whether the assent was strictly true or not, Mr. Marchmont's conscience alone could tell); "I heard Carlotta Patti sing it at a concert in—"

He paused abruptly, not because his memory or his invention failed, but because at that moment Miss Florence Lathrop's gray silk dress and lace-covered parasol appeared on the steps of the Crenshaw house.

"I see my cousin has come out, and I must not detain her," he said. "I will call this afternoon—at four, shall I say?—and I trust you will not refuse me admittance."

He lifted his hat, gave one last glance out of the eyes which Amy admired, and walked away. Miss Lathrop, who, like her sister, was a little near-sighted, perceived him first as he was advancing along the sidewalk by the garden-fence.

"I am afraid your patience has been quite exhausted, Brian," she said, when he approached and handed her into the carriage. "Mrs. Ripley—poor woman!—is very unwell this morning, and she kept me a long time listening to a detailed account of all that she suffers. One should be patient with that habit of invalids, I suppose. It is all the pleasure they have. —Drive to Cedarwood, now, Andrew."

CHAPTER V.

THE HEIRESS OF CEDARWOOD.

WHEN the carriage rolled into the gates through which the Reynolds children gazed so wistfully the evening before, its occupants saw two feminine figures, escorted by a masculine one, crossing the lawn toward the house.

This house was a large, handsome building, in what architectural books call the "Norman villa" style, evidently of late erection, and containing all modern improvements and conveniences. The cedars, from which its name was derived, stood in a group on the close-shorn lawn, immediately in front of the drawing-room windows—three splendid patriarchs, under the shade of which a rustic seat was placed. The grounds were of great extent, and, on this April morning, full of the brightest beauty of the spring.

"Yonder are Anna and Beatrix and General Waldron," said Miss Lathrop, elevating one of those glasses which the French call a *pince-nez*, and regarding the three figures. "No doubt the general has been showing some of his landscape-gardening. He is always having trees moved, or hedges set out, or something of the kind done. It is a great bore to be taken to see them."

"Why has General Waldron been allowed to remain unmarried so long?" asked Marchmont, looking at that gentleman, who, with his erect figure and strongly-marked face, was manifestly a *grand seigneur*, though he wore a loose linen coat and a broad palmetto hat. "I am surprised that no kind lady has taken compassion on his widowed condition."

Miss Lathrop laughed. "It would be impossible to enumerate the number of ladies who have desired to console him," she said; "but he has so stoutly declined to be consoled, that they have at last abandoned him in despair.—Good-morning!" she added, bowing to the group of pedestrians whom they were now approaching. "I see that the charming day has drawn you all out to enjoy it."

"Yes," said the general, lifting his broad hat with the air of a cavalier; "I have just taken Miss Lathrop and my daughter to see some improvements which I have made in the grounds. Are you interested in landscape-gardening, Mr. Marchmont?"

"Very much, indeed," answered Marchmont, promptly. The carriage had by this time drawn up before the portico, which was the principal entrance to the house, and he was assisting his cousin to the ground as he spoke. When he turned, Miss Waldron shook her parasol at him.

"Take care!" she said; "if you tell papa that, he will carry you off at once to see his improvements."

"I should enjoy seeing them," Marchmont replied, readily; for at that moment he saw his way clearly to a clever *finesse*.

"Come, then," said the general, greatly pleased. "We'll walk down and look at them at once.—Miss Florence, can we not tempt you to accompany us?"

This invitation Miss Florence gracefully but decidedly declined. Not regarding General Waldron in the light of a possible father-in-law, she saw no necessity—as she afterward remarked to her sister—for tanning her complexion by walking over the grounds with him.— "And I am sorry, Brian," she added, "but it will be impossible for us to wait for you long; both Anna and myself have a positive engagement in Edgerton."

"Don't think of waiting for me at all," responded her cousin, calmly; "I should prefer to walk. As I remarked to you some time ago, on such a day as this one cannot have too much of sunshine."

More than an hour elapsed before the general and his willing victim returned; by that time the Lathrop equipage had vanished, and when Mr. Marchmont, in a somewhat heated and very tired condition, made his appearance in the drawing-room, he found Miss Waldron alone. The large, cool apartment, so darkly toned, so fragrant with flowers, so free from glare of any kind, was in itself refreshing; and it was still more refreshing to be met by a handsome woman, with amused yet sincere compassion.

"I have been really uneasy about you, Mr. Marchmont," she said, smiling. "When papa mounts his hobby, he is apt to be a little inconsiderate; and he kept you so long, I began to fear lest you might have fallen by the wayside with a sunstroke. Pray take this chair, which for comfort I can recommend, and let me give you a fan."

"How delightfully kind you are!" said Marchmont, accepting both the chair and the fan. "Pardon me if I say that I have, indeed, had a most fatiguing time. After inspecting the landscape-gardening, I was taken to see an imported Devon bull, which glared in a manner unpleasantly suggestive of tossing; then to a bottom which has been recently drained and put under cultivation on the most scientific principles; then to a new orchard, and finally to a model dairy.".

Miss Waldron laughed again.

"How unconscionable of papa!" she said. "And your cousins have gone, too! I am afraid your visit to Cedarwood this morning does not strike you in the light of a success."

"On the contrary, it strikes me very much in that light *now*," responded Marchmont. "I am glad that my cousins are gone—I meant them to go; else, perhaps, your father might not have found me so deeply interested in meadow-lands and dairies."

"For shame!" said Miss Waldron, but the color deepened on her cheek, the smile on her lip, as she spoke.

Seen thus, she was a very handsome woman, this heiress of Cedarwood. A stately, mature-looking woman for her years—she was only twenty-four on her last birthday—but with nothing hard or arrogant in manner or appearance. She was invariably self-possessed, and, perhaps, a trifle too decided in speech and bearing; but these things followed, as matters of course, from her temperament, as well as from her position in life. In figure she was tall, with a more commanding than graceful presence, though no one could accuse her of absolutely lacking the latter attribute. Her face was clear-cut as a cameo, and indicated an excellent mind, without intellectual brilliancy, and a generous, upright nature, impatient of shams, scorning deception. Under the broad, benignant brow were set a pair of dark eyes often full of satirical light; the nose was large, but not heavy, with delicate, arched nostrils; while the mouth was altogether sweet and womanly, with that dark down on the upper lip which is so common on French and Spanish feminine faces. Miss Waldron had neither French nor Spanish blood, but she was a brunette of the most pronounced type; and her color, when it came, was the rich pomegranate flush of the Southern skies.

This color was glowing in her cheeks now, and giving lustre to her eyes. She was most becomingly dressed, and, as she leaned back in a large, luxurious chair, with the rich room stretching away in the dim background behind her, Marchmont's æsthetic tastes were thoroughly gratified. This was what he liked—beauty adorned by art in the highest possible degree, and the manner of a thorough woman of the world.

There could be no doubt that Beatrix Waldron would grace worthily any position to which she might be exalted—which was a very essential point to a man at once so ambitious and so fastidious. No degree of wealth could have tempted him to marry an underbred woman, and the necessity must have been very great which could have induced him to think of marrying a plain one.

"You will remain to luncheon, of course," Miss Waldron went on, "and afterward papa will take pleasure, I am sure, in driving you into Edgerton."

"I will remain to luncheon very willingly," Marchmont replied, "but you must allow me to decline being driven into Edgerton. I was quite sincere in telling Florence that I prefer the walk—especially if I take a short cut through the fields which your father was kind enough to show me."

"It is a route which all our friends take when they come to see us on foot," said the heiress, "and, unless I am mistaken, yonder is one coming now."

Marchmont turned his head to look out of the window through which she was gazing, and, greatly to his disgust, perceived a man approaching the house, who, from the direction in which he came, had plainly crossed the fields.

"It is Mr. Archer, I think," said Miss Waldron. "Do you know him?—I suppose not," as Marchmont uttered a negative. "He is a hard-working young lawyer, who goes into society very little. Papa thinks highly of his ability, and has trusted a great deal of business to him. Probably he has come on some matter relating to it now."

"Then he will not disturb us," said Marchmont, in a tone of relief.

"Are you so comfortable?" asked Miss Waldron. "I am sorry that you must be disturbed in any event, for here comes my little page to say that luncheon is ready.—Go and find your master, Rex.—We need not wait, Mr. Marchmont; papa is in the library, no doubt."

She rose, and while Marchmont and herself crossed the drawing-room, the little page of whom she spoke—a mulatto boy dressed in livery—darted to the library. So it chanced that, when they reached the hall, they found the gentleman who had been seen from the window standing in the open door, waiting the appearance of a servant.

Miss Waldron greeted him very graciously:

"Good-morning, Mr. Archer. You are just in time for luncheon. Come with us, pray. Let me introduce Mr. Marchmont."

Mr. Archer acknowledged the introduction, and then said:

"Thank you, Miss Waldron, but I will not come in. I only want to see the general a few minutes on business, and—"

"Business always comes better after the inner man has been refreshed," said the general's voice in the rear. "Nonsense, man! come in to luncheon. I know your abstemious habits, but you must at least take a cracker and a glass of wine after such a walk."

Mr. Archer made no further demur, but followed, with his host, the trailing sweep of Miss Waldron's dress across the hall.

The room which they entered was very handsome, and the pretty lunch-table was like a picture, as it stood glittering with crystal and china.

When they sat down, Marchmont looked at the young lawyer with that sense of distrust which becomes the suitor of an heiress. He saw no material for a rival, however. A gentleman unmistakably was Mr. Archer, but evidently a man entirely unaccustomed to those easy habitudes of society which sat upon Marchmont himself like a garment. A refined, thoughtful face, with something of the keenness which is always apparent in the physiognomy of the born lawyer, and which here was chiefly expressed by the hazel eyes and attenuated nose—this was what he noted, together with a manner reserved almost to stiffness, and a coat so much worn that it fairly reached the point of shabbiness.

It was characteristic of General Waldron and his daughter that they treated the wearer of this shabby coat with a courtesy as cordial as if he had been a millionaire, under the influence of which Mr. Archer's reserve melted somewhat. There was nothing shy or awkward about him, yet he felt both as he listened to Marchmont's flow of small-talk.

Few things have a more paralyzing effect upon a man of action than to meet a man of society under circumstances like these; and Archer was conscious of a sense of inferiority, which he could not possibly have felt at any other time or in any other place.

It was a relief when General Waldron began to speak of topics with which he was familiar, leaving Miss Waldron and Marchmont to pursue their conversation aside.

"I am inclined to think that your opinion is correct with regard to the X and Y Railroad, Archer," he said. "I was talking to Mr. Trafford about it a few days ago, and he is sure that the stock will prove a paying investment before very long. I know of nobody whose opinion on such a subject has more value than his."

"Certainly he has judged very shrewdly for himself," said Archer. "No man has invested capital with greater success. I heard his wealth computed at a million the other day."

"An exaggeration, I think," said the general, filling a glass of sparkling wine. "But he is wealthy, beyond a doubt, and shrewd. There has been some talk, you know, about the unsoundness of the manufacturing company here, which has most likely brought him to Edgerton. If he sells his shares, I shall sell mine."

"It will be at a great sacrifice."

"Better that than lose the whole."

Of this conversation only one name caught Marchmont's ear with a familiar sound, and that was "Trafford." For a minute he was unable to remember where he had lately heard it, until he thought of little Mariette Reynolds, and then he suddenly became aware that Miss Waldron was talking to him.

"You are very fond of music, are you not, Mr. Marchmont? Nay, don't answer—the question was foolishly framed. Everybody professes to be 'fond of music.' I meant to say, you know a good deal of music—do you not?"

"You alarm my modesty by such a formidable question," he answered. "I know something of music—not a great deal, by any means."

"Do you sing at all?"

"Not in the least. Nature only gave me the capability of admiring the singing of others."

"It is a capability which she denies to many people. Papa, there, does not care a straw for the best music in the world, and does not know soprano from contralto, or tenor from base. But you wonder what all this leads to. Briefly, I am meditating a musical entertainment, or, at least, an entertainment which shall be in part musical; and I wish to secure a good critic-in-chief."

"To the extent of my limited ability, I shall be happy to serve in the position. What is your programme?"

"I will not bore you with it now. It is not fully matured, and immature things should never be published. If you remain in Edgerton two or three weeks longer, you will probably hear all about it."

A few minutes later they left the dining-room, and General Waldron walked with Mr. Archer to the library, while Miss Waldron and her companion paused in the hall, where, through several open doors, the golden brightness of the day was fully revealed, and multitudinous sweet odors were borne in on the soft tricksy breezes.

"It is a shame to spend such a day in the house," said the young lady, taking up a garden-hat. "Are you still exhausted by the tramp papa gave you, Mr. Marchmont, or would you like to accompany me to the fernery? I believe you have not seen it yet, and it is my show-place."

"I have entirely recovered from my fatigue," Marchmont answered, "and I shall be glad to see the fernery, or anything else that you choose to show me."

To the fernery, therefore, they took their way. It deserved to be a show-place, if only for the refreshment which it afforded them when they came into its shade and coolness from the noonday glare and heat. There were an abundance of rocks made damp by trickling water, and the green plumy grace of ferns in profusion.

"We can fancy ourselves in a mountain-glen," said Miss Waldron, after her companion had expressed his admiration. "The mountains only are lacking."

"And that is a trifle when we have the rocks and ferns," said Marchmont. "I congratulate myself afresh upon having sent Anna and Florence back to Edgerton without me! I had an instinct of something charming in store for me: and I never yet followed my instinct and was deceived."

"You are very kind," said Miss Waldron, "but I can't help suspecting that, even while making these pretty speeches, you are, perhaps, putting the fernery in the same class with papa's model dairy."

"I never justify myself when I am suspected," said Marchmont; "I always leave circumstances to do that for me. Shall we sit down? This is an improvement on a mountain-glen—and, I may add, on the model dairy—inasmuch as there are seats here for the indolent; and I am always indolent when I find myself in an agreeable place."

Miss Waldron assented.

"We can sit down," she said, "while I show you some of my prettiest varieties of ferns. Do you know much about them! Here is the maiden's-hair, with its delicate ebony stem; this is the beech-fern, this the cheilanthes, and here is the beautiful little—Mr. Marchmont, I am instructing you, and you are not listening to me at all!"

"A thousand pardons!" said Marchmont, who was looking at her instead of the ferns. "I was, indeed, not paying proper attention to what you were saying, for I was thinking—shall I tell you what I was thinking?"

"Your thoughts might not interest me much more than my ferns have interested you," she answered, lightly.

"Probably not, but still I should like to tell you—though I scarcely fancy you need to be told—what they were. I can think of but one thing when I am with you, and that is—yourself!"

"Am I a thing?" she asked, with a laugh, while a soft flush rose into her cheeks. "You are a flatterer; and since you are not at all interested in the ferns, we had better go back to the house."

"Pray don't!" said Marchmont, eagerly. "I am not a flatterer. You know—or you ought to know—that I could not flatter you if I tried. I should have told you long ago that I love you passionately, if I had not lacked the opportunity, and perhaps the courage, to do so. But I cannot be silent any longer. I love you so much that I must ask if there is any hope of winning you?" The earnestness and passion with which he spoke were not simulated, for Beatrix Waldron was a prize well worth winning, apart from the wealth which made her chief attraction; and the man who addressed her was specially fitted to appreciate this. There are many worse counterfeits of love afloat in the world than the sentiment which he felt when, with his last words, he took her hand and kissed it.

She did not draw it from his clasp, but when he lifted his head he found her dark eyes fastened on him with a steady gravity which did not augur well, he thought, for his hopes. If the lashes had drooped on the flushed cheeks, he would have felt that success was in his grasp. But that glance was not calculated to inspire such a conviction; there was too much of the woman of the world apparent in it—of the woman who had heard many other men utter such words as these. If he had suspected how quickly her heart was beating just then, he would have been reassured; but he did not suspect it, and her voice, when she spoke, did not betray the fact.

"I cannot say that you surprise me, Mr. Marchmont, for that would be foolish and untrue. But I am sorry that you have said this. We have been very good friends—now we must be something else. And I hardly know how to answer you."

"Then you do not love me?" said Marchmont, with a pang of keen disappointment. "I was mad enough to hope—"

He broke off short; but no rounded sentences could have pleaded his cause so well as that pause, and the look which accompanied it. This look went straight as an arrow to Beatrix's heart, and her lips curved into a smile, very sweet and very bright.

"I am not seventeen," she said. "You must expect a woman of my age to be a little reasonable—to consider a little before pledging herself to anything very important. But I may say to you, as the heroines of old-time novels said to their lovers, 'I am not indifferent to your merits.'"

"I am grateful for any crumb of encouragement," he replied, "but my merits are so inappreciably small, that I cannot afford to base any hope on them."

"Modesty is a great merit," said she, half laughing, "and so rare, too! I did not know before that you cultivated it. Shall I say, then, frankly, that I like you very much, but—"

"Why should you bring in that detestable word?" asked he—and now, indeed, he began to hope. "Surely you do not mean to qualify anything so moderate as liking."

"No, I do not mean to qualify the liking; I only mean that I cannot give you anything more—at present. I am doubtful of many things—my own heart among the rest. As I have already said, a woman of my age, if she has any sense at all, does not act hastily in such an important matter as this. When I give my hand, I

wish to be sure that my whole heart goes with it, and not only my heart, but my mind—in other words, I want to be sure that I can thoroughly respect as well as love the man I marry."

"And you are not sure of that with regard to me," said Marchmont, with a flush mounting to his brow.

"You must not misunderstand me," she answered, quickly. "I only mean that I know very little of you. How much of the real character do we show each other in the drawing-rooms? Marriage is called a lottery; but, for my part, I have always had a fancy to know what I was doing before taking a step which means so much. Is that desire unreasonable?"

"Very far from it," replied Marchmont; though he might have added, "It is very inconvenient!" "I am content if you give me a little hope—if you do not send me away."

"I should be sorry for you to go," she said, with a charming blush. "If you are willing to wait for a more definite answer—if you can be satisfied with a fair field and some favor—"

"I can be satisfied with anything which gives me a hope of at last winning this!" he said, again kissing the slender, delicate hand sparkling with jewels.

She drew it away now with a faint sigh. Perhaps the thought occurred to her that without the jewels it might not be esteemed so well worth the winning—at least it is certain that she had not the obtuseness with which (fortunately for themselves) many heiresses are liberally endowed. She did not exactly distrust every man who approached her, but she knew enough of the world to be aware of the mercenary side of human nature, and to feel sure that she was not indebted to her *beaux-yeux* alone for all the suitors who had thronged around her.

Philosophy and worldly knowledge, however, combined to prevent her betraying such thoughts as these. Though she drew back her hand, it was with a very winning smile that she said:

"I will not make your probation long or hard. Believe me, I have no love for coquetry, and I promise not to keep you in doubt an hour longer than I can help. But I *must* be certain of myself! I have known a great many men, and heard a great many declarations of—attachment, shall I say? But, oddly enough, they have none of them touched my heart sufficiently to make me willing to give up my freedom and trust my life to the power of a man who might make or mar all its happiness. You see"—the Spanish-like eyes gazed away from him to the sunny emerald sward of the lawn beyond—"I am not one of those gentle, trusting women to whom love is a necessity. On the contrary"—a slight laugh—"I think I am one of the women who could easily drift into a strong-minded old maid."

"Heaven forbid!" cried Marchmont, with unaffected horror. "The bare idea of such a thing is sacrilege! Do not think that I shall grow impatient over my probation," he went on. "I will wait—gladly, willingly—any length of time, if only you can finally trust your life to me, believing that I shall make, *not* mar, its happiness."

"I should be glad to believe it," she said, almost as if speaking to herself.

"Then why can you not believe it?" cried Marchmont, impetuously. "What proof can I give you? I should hesitate at none! If I could only lay bare my heart to your inspection—if you could only see—"

"Nay, that is impossible, you know," she interrupted, with another soft yet brilliant smile. "Besides, if one could always see, there would be no such thing as faith; and that is my favorite virtue. It is not because I distrust you that I hesitate: it is because I am not sure of myself. But I suppose there is an answer to all riddles after a while; and you will wait patiently—will you not?—for the answer to this. Now"—after Marchmont had again assented—"we will return to the house, for I see Mr. Archer is taking his departure, and I want to ask him to attend to some business for me."

CHAPTER VI.

UNDER AN APPLE-TREE.

ON the graveled sweep in front of the house Miss Waldron and her companion met Mr. Archer, who had parted with the general a moment before. Seeing the latter still standing on the steps of the portico, Marchmont said:

"If you are going to walk to Edgerton, Mr. Archer, and have no objection, I will accompany you as soon as I bid General Waldron good-day."

Archer responded to the effect that he had no objection, and, leaving Miss Waldron talking to him, Marchmont passed on to the general. That genial gentleman, being fond of conversation, detained him several minutes, and it was with some difficulty that he at last took leave and rejoined the others. As he approached, he heard Miss Waldron saying:

"It is a rather troublesome commission, but you are so kind about attending to such things that I have grown accustomed to imposing upon your good-nature."

"I assure you that I have never felt the imposition," Archer replied. "It gives me sincere pleasure to serve you in any way."

"Will you have a fern for a reward?" she asked, extending one with a smile. "I know you are as much of a fern-lover as myself. I have been showing my fernery to Mr. Marchmont, and trying to waken his interest for my favorites, but I failed signally."

"I think you know the reason of the failure," said Marchmont, while Archer received the fern and looked at it with the air of a connoisseur.

"This is one of your prettiest varieties, Miss Waldron," he said. "How very delicate and graceful these fronds are! You mean it for me? Thank you."

He took out his pocket-book, opened it, and placed the fern within, saying:

"A leaf like this withers sooner than a flower in the heat of the sun."

"And am I to be punished for finding you more interesting than the ferns, by not having any bestowed upon me?" asked Marchmont. "Surely you will not be so unkind! I, too, think fern-leaves beautiful—and I should like one as a souvenir," he added, with a glance that expressed a great deal.

Despite her self-possession, Beatrix's color deepened as she held out the collection.

"Take one, if you like," she said; "but I am sure you will not value it."

"I should prefer for you to give it to me," he answered. "And as for my not valuing it, I think you know better than that. I would value anything you gave me—especially anything associated with to-day."

His voice sank over the last words, so that Archer did not hear them, but he had a shrewd idea of their tenor. Having by this time put away his pocket-book, he said, somewhat stiffly:

"I am at your service, Mr. Marchmont, when you are ready to start."

"I will not detain you," said Marchmont.—"Many thanks!" as Miss Waldron gave him the fern. "I shall have the pleasure of seeing you soon again."

The gentlemen lifted their hats; the lady bowed; then they moved away over the sunshiny lawn toward a small wicket which let them into the fields, across which a path ran.

"What a charming place!" Marchmont said, as they found themselves outside the grounds. "One seems while there to breathe an air of repose and luxury. After all, there is no such beneficent genius as money, when it is united with good taste."

"It is a very powerful genius," said Archer, "but its beneficence depends altogether upon the use which is made of it."

"At least it would be difficult to find fault with the manner in which it is used in this instance," said Marchmont. "What a capital fellow the general is, despite his being a trifle prosy! And good taste is one of the least of Miss Waldron's charms."

There was something in the tone of this remark which jarred on Archer; but he was well aware that he had no right to express any feeling of the kind.

"It would be difficult to tell what charm Miss Waldron does not possess," he said. "I have known her with a partial degree of intimacy for several years, and I have never met a nobler character than hers."

"You are enthusiastic," said Marchmont, looking at him with the least possible elevation of the eyebrows.

"No; I am simply literal," was the quiet reply. "I am not talking at random. I have something more than a drawing-room acquaintance with Miss Waldron's character. At the present moment I hold a commission from her—there's nothing confidential in the matter, so I may speak of it—which shows how ready she is to think of benefiting others. There is an untaught boy in Edgerton who has a remarkable talent for painting, and a photographer employs him to color photographs, some of which fell into Miss Waldron's hands. She was much struck by the work, and she has asked me to find out all that there is to know about him, and, if he is really deserving of assistance, to send him to her. If he is deserving, I have no more doubt than I have that I am walking here that she will induce her father to give him the opportunities he needs."

"Her father must be uncommonly obliging if he suffers her to waste money on such objects. Embryo geniuses are among the most disappointing things in the world."

"The general has no one to consider but herself, therefore he does not curb her expenditure at all. I have heard a great many people talk of her 'wasting money' before this, but I fancy they would not have considered it so grievously wasted if, instead of helping the struggling, it had been spent on laces and jewels."

Marchmont's lip curled as he lifted the slight walking-cane which he carried, and beheaded two or three weeds with a single stroke. He could not exactly say, "The general should consider his future son-in-law," but he thought it. A pause of two or three minutes followed before he said, carelessly:

"What is the name of the struggling Raphael in question?"

"Dinsmore," Archer answered.

"Dinsmore!" Marchmont repeated, with an involuntary start. To himself he added, "By Jove, it is odd!"

"Do you know anything about him?" asked Archer, in some surprise.

"Nothing further than that there is a boy of that name in Mr. Lathrop's business-house."

"Probably the same. I think I have heard that he is there."

Had Marchmont forgotten his appointment with Amy Reynolds—which was not the case—this unexpected introduction of Dinsmore's name would have reminded him of it. Consequently, when they entered Edgerton, he glanced at his watch, and said:

"I believe I am just in time for an engagement which I made this morning. Do our roads part here? I am happy to have made your acquaintance, Mr. Archer. Good-afternoon."

As Archer returned the salutation and walked away, Marchmont glanced after his alert figure with a half-amused expression.

"So that is your secret, is it, my good fellow?" he said to himself. "You are certainly pretty hard hit; but it is an infernal piece of presumption for you to think of Beatrix Waldron!"

"A thorough puppy!" was Archer's equally complimentary soliloquy at the same moment, "and, unless I am greatly mistaken, mercenary to boot! How strange that such a woman should be attracted by such a man!—and she is attracted, if I am any judge of the signs of feminine fancy. Well," with a short, quick sigh, "what is it to me?

'It were all one
That I should love some bright particular star,
And think to wed it.'

I *don't* think it—I am not such a fool as that; but I should like a chance to prove what I would do for her sake, and what a pitiful soul lurks, I am sure, under that fellow's silken exterior!"

.   .   .   .   .   .

The pleasantest—in fact, the only pleasant—feature of the Reynolds domicile was a tolerably-sized garden, which, although it in part adjoined the Crenshaw garden, did not, like that, border the street. Hence it was much more retired, and, with the dwelling for its boundary in front and a high fence and tall hedges on the other sides, was an agreeable place of resort from January to December. Yet it was not much of a garden, either in an ornamental or useful sense. The vegetables which came out of it were few and poor, while the flowers that grew in it had long since assumed the entire control of their own destinies. Nevertheless, there were bloom and fragrance even here under the sweet kiss of April. Syringa and yellow jasmine, lilac and honeysuckle, these alone would redeem Sahara. A very rickety arbor was covered with the jasmine and honeysuckle, among which countless bees were humming loudly, and under which, as four o'clock drew near, sat Amy, arrayed in the best dress her limited wardrobe afforded, with lilies-of-the-valley in her hair, a score of music on her lap, and a look of expectancy in her eyes.

A clock near by struck the hour, and several minutes afterward elapsed, but still the golden quiet of the afternoon remained undisturbed. The children, on various pretexts, had been sent away, and the only sounds which broke the stillness were the chords of the piano as they rolled out under Felix's fingers. Through the open windows every note was audible; but Amy was so accustomed to this that it did not in any manner interfere with her thoughts or her power of listening. Consequently, when a peal of the doorbell came, she heard it at once, although the musician was just then in the midst of a crashing *fortissimo* passage.

Instantly she dropped her score and darted away. Clara, the half-deaf servant-of-all-work, sometimes answered the door-bell, if she chanced to hear it and was not too busy; but this, of all things, Amy least desired at present, for Clara had severe ideas of propriety, and frequently admonished the willful, motherless girl in a well-meant but not agreeable manner. If *she* went to the door, Mr. Marchmont would not be admitted—of that Amy felt sure; so she hurried away —tearing her dress in her haste on an overgrown rosebush—flitted across the latticed back piazza, walked demurely but quickly down the narrow passage, and opened the door with trembling fingers, to face—a short, heavily bearded, brightly spectacled man, who held out his hand and said:

"Goot-day, my dear! Ees your baba at home?"

"Oh!" said Amy, with a great gulp of disappointment. She felt a strong inclination to slam the door, liked a spoiled child, but she resisted it, and only answered shortly: "No, Herr Meerbach, he isn't at home; he never *is* at home this time of day."

"Ah, I haf made von mistake, den," said Herr Meerbach, smiling as he looked at her—a smile Amy felt nowise inclined to return. "I t'ought he vas done mit his lessons by now. Vell, my bretty little maiden, you shust say to heem dat I veel be glad eef he veel come to my room to-night. I haf von letter from mine friend in Leipsic."

"Oh, Herr Meerbach!" cried Amy, "is there any hope that papa will be able to send Felix?"

"Sh! sh!" said Herr Merrbach, while his bright eyes seemed to grow brighter behind the spectacles. "Ees not Felix at de piano? Do not let him know. Disappointment is hard, and your baba must say. Goot-day, my dear, and be sure you tell heem."

After the kindly little man had walked away, Amy gave one quick glance up and down the street, then drew in her curly head with a sigh and shut the door.

"It would never do to be found *watching* for him!" she said to herself.

It was in a somewhat dejected frame of mind that she returned to the garden. Picking up her score from the walk where it lay, she retreated to the farthest corner of the domain, and established herself on the low, broad bough of a spreading apple-tree—a bough easily reached without much gymnastic skill.

It was her favorite seat, and she did not care now how much she tumbled her dress.

"I was a fool to think he would remember or care to come!" she said. "Never mind; things will be different when I am a prima donna!"

Then, as a means to this desirable end, she bent her eyes and her attention on the music, and began to sing.

Considering the sounds she was emitting, it was not singular that, several minutes later, she did not hear approaching steps until her practising was interrupted by the appearance of Marchmont, who stepped round a cluster of bushes, and said, with a smile:

"I see that Fortune has marked me for its own. To find you alone, to find you here, and to find you singing, what a delightful combination of circumstances!"

"How did you get here?" asked Amy, too startled to think of any other greeting, and thrilling with a mixture of pleasure and mortification—pleasure that he had come, mortification that she should be found established, like a tomboy, in the fork of an apple-tree.

"I met my charming little friend Mariette on the street. She piloted me into the house, and your voice did the rest. Are you vexed with me for coming? If you could see yourself among those apple-blossoms, you would think the picture too lovely to be wasted; and I am at least endowed with the power to admire."

There was little doubt of that. His eyes, as he spoke, expressed this admiration so plainly, that into Amy's face the blood mounted in a roseate tide. She recovered her composure, however— helped thereto by a sense of satisfaction which was all the greater for following on partial disappointment.

"I hope my ankles are not showing very badly!" she thought. "If I had expected you in the least, you would not find me perched here in this ridiculous manner," she added, aloud.

"I don't consider it ridiculous at all," said Marchmont. "I have often sat in an apple-tree, and I know that it generally makes a capital seat. May I try it now? That bough looks very tempting."

"I cannot advise you to try it," said Amy, with a rippling laugh. "I don't think it would bear your weight. It cracked the other day when Hugh and I were sitting here."

"Oh, Hugh sits there, does he? Lucky fellow! By-the-by, I think I saw Hugh this morning—isn't his name Dinsmore?— and he did not regard me in a very friendly manner."

"Hugh is—peculiar!" said Amy. "I bear with him because he is such a good fellow, but I often tell him that he will never get on in the world."

"That must be encouraging," said Marchmont, smiling. He was not in the least interested in Hugh, but he served for a topic of conversation, and it was

pleasant to lean against a convenient tree and watch at his leisure the slanting sunlight fall on the girl opposite—on her rich chestnut hair, her exquisite complexion, her piquant features and laughing eyes. "By Jove!" he said to himself, "if she ever does go on the stage, it will be a *Veni, vidi, vici* business in more senses than one!"

"Oh, Hugh does not mind what I say," remarked Amy, answering his last remark. "We are great friends, though he is very trying—and some day when I am famous he is to paint my portrait."

"You have quite made up your mind with regard to the fame, then?"

"I have quite made up *my* mind; but"—a sigh—"unluckily there are other minds to be made up."

"Would a victory be worth anything without a struggle? But I see no necessity to wait till you are famous with regard to the portrait. Why does not Hugh paint it now? I should like a picture of you as you sit there. But I should not like him to be here to take it—at least not now."

"It is very inhospitable of me to sit here and let you stand," said Amy, debating in her mind how she should get down. "We might go into the parlor, only Felix is making such a noise there."

"Don't think of such a thing! It is absolutely sinful to spend such hours as these under a roof."

"Well, there is the arbor, if you won't be frightened by its appearance. It *looks* as if just about to fall down, but it has stood a long while."

"I should be dreadfully frightened, I am certain. I don't want to be buried, not even by an arbor. It strikes me that we are excellently placed; pray allow me to remain where I am. I never grow tired when I am well entertained."

"I don't see what there is to entertain you," said Amy, who began to find this very agreeable.

"Don't you? That is strange! However, I must not neglect business for pleasure, though happily, in this instance, business is synonymous with pleasure. Will you let me hear your song, mademoiselle?

Mademoiselle did not demur or hesitate. She lifted the sheet of music, and forthwith began to sing.

Marchmont listened and looked with an expression of amused approval.

The pretty, half-childish figure perched on the gnarled bough of the old apple-tree, her unconscious imitation of the manner of a concert-singer, and the beautiful, silvery voice—the oddity of this combination might have amused a less volatile person.

When the song ended, she received his compliments and criticisms with perfect composure.

"Of course I have a great deal yet to learn," she said; "but I know my voice will be worth hearing some day. Papa says so, and Herr Meerbach—he is teacher of music at the college, you know—and Mr. Trafford. It is astonishing how much Mr. Trafford knows about such things!"

Upon which Marchmont could no longer restrain the question which had trembled on his tongue twice before that day.

"Who is Mr. Trafford?" he asked. "Or perhaps I should say what is he? I have heard of him as a benevolent gentleman who keeps string for the benefit of small children, and as a capitalist who invests in paying stocks; now I hear of him as a musical critic. Pray, is he anything else?"

"An eavesdropper occasionally—without malicious intention," answered a voice which made both Marchmont and Amy start. The former, however, was chiefly surprised when, on turning, he encountered the gaze of a pair of acute eyes, and saw a head overlooking the high wall which shut off Mrs. Crenshaw's garden. This head was covered with iron-gray hair, and surmounted by an embroidered smoking-cap; the face was that of a man between fifty and sixty, bronzed, lined, expressing much shrewdness, yet frank and pleasant withal. A moerschaum pipe was in his mouth, which he removed as he went on:

"You must excuse me, my dear"—addressing Amy—"but your song drew me to the end of the garden, and, as I paced along the wall, I heard this gentleman's question. You can answer it as you please, for I am going back to the house now. Take care of yourself—don't fall out of that tree!"

He smiled, nodded, and disappeared. There was a minute's silence while they listened to his retreating footsteps, then Marchmont said:

"Is he a lunatic? His mode of appearance reminds one strikingly of the crazy man in 'Nicholas Nickleby.'"

"Oh, no," replied Amy; "but," she added, lowering her voice to a whisper, "he is very, very queer—what would be called eccentric. He boards at Mrs. Crenshaw's, and he is devoted to music—though you wouldn't think so from his looks, would you? The first time I ever saw him was in just that way. I was sitting here, singing, and he looked over the wall and asked if I was a thrush or a nightingale. The next night Felix was playing, and he put his head in the parlor-window, and said: 'That boy will make a great musician some day.' Then papa asked him in, and he has been coming over since."

"I don't wonder at that," said Marchmont. "How is it possible for any one to keep away who has once been admitted to your enchanted garden? If I come again very soon, will you be surprised?"

"I don't know why you should," answered Amy, blushing.

"But if I know, is not that enough? You would not have the heart to deny me, if you could imagine how dull I find everything else."

He came nearer, and leaned his arm on the bough upon which she sat.

"Speak!" he said, smiling. "May I return? Do you believe in Fate? I do; and I believe it has thrown us together for a purpose."

"I don't believe in Fate at all," replied Amy, who, young as she was, had a sufficient spice of coquetry in her to hold her own; "but you may come—if you like."

"Do you doubt my liking?"

"Yes; I doubt it. I can only sing; while you must know any number of charming ladies who—"

She stopped short, for he was laughing.

"So you think you can only sing?" he said. "Does your mirror tell you no more than that? Do you not know that your face is as uncommon as your voice?"

The unmistakable sincerity of his words seemed to impress her. She looked down with half-parted lips, a questioning surprise in her eyes.

"I did not suppose that *you* would think so," she said, simply.

Then, as she realized what her words implied, the color again rushed over her face, and saying quickly, "This is all nonsense!" she suddenly made a spring toward the ground.

In her haste and confusion she was awkward. Her foot caught, and she would have fallen heavily if Marchmont had not been so near. As it was, he had barely time to interpose and receive her in his arms.

"You see you are punished for trying to deprive me of the pleasure of assisting you down," he said, laughing, as she drew back from him, flushed and more lovely than ever. For an instant he was greatly tempted to snatch a kiss, but he felt instinctively that even this wild little Bohemian was woman enough to resent such a liberty, and he had no mind to be banished in earnest. "You might have sprained your ankle," he went on, "and a sprained ankle is no joke. Why were you in such haste? Have I made myself disagreeable? If so, it was most unintentionally. This garden is the most delight-

ful place I have known in an age, and has but one disadvantage—the probability that Mr. Trafford's head may appear over the wall at any time."

"It does not appear very often," said Amy. "He is not often at home."

"The most desirable thing would be that he should take his departure altogether. One never knows what course the eccentricities of eccentric people may follow. *A propos*, what a charming glen that was in which I first saw you! Do you go there only on Sunday?"

"Not often at any other time, because I do not like to walk so far alone, and Hugh can go with me only on Sunday, while Felix cares for nothing but the piano."

"Will you let me be your escort some time? Mr. Trafford would not be there, and I am sure we should enjoy it very much."

This proposal took Amy by surprise. Even if her social position had been different, her social experience much greater, she would have been flattered by the attention of this fine gentleman, whose appearance in Edgerton had created a flutter of interest in what newspaper writers call "fashionable circles." Being what she was, it seemed almost incredible that he should distinguish her by his admiration, and she brightened and dimpled with pleasure as she answered:

"I shall be very glad to go—if I can."

"If you can! Who will prevent your doing so?"

"Oh, nobody, I suppose.—There!" as a prolonged cry of "Miss Amy!" came from the region of the house. "Clara is calling me; I must go! Would you—would you mind if I let you out into the lane, instead of taking you through the house again? It is shorter, and Clara is *so* fussy!"

"I am in your hands; do exactly what you please with me," replied Marchmont, who for obvious reasons preferred a quiet exit.

He was therefore piloted to a small gate opening from the garden on a narrow lane.

"We keep this locked most of the time," said Amy, unfastening it, "but sometimes we find it conveniently open."

"It is very convenient," said Marchmont; "and, now that you have showed me the secret entrance, you need not be surprised if you see me often. Must I really go now? Is Clara a dragon? Good-evening, then, and do not forget that you are pledged to take a woodland ramble."

.   .   .   .   .   .

"Amy," said Mariette, an hour or two later, "see what a pretty fern I found at the foot of our apple-tree."

"Give it to me!" said Amy, quickly. When the delicate frond was placed in her hand, she knew it to be the one which she had seen in Marchmont's button-hole, and which no doubt had fallen unnoticed when he caught her as she sprang from the tree. "It is too pretty to throw away," she said to the child. Then she ran to her own room, placed it carefully between the leaves of a book, and wrote the date on the margin.

"I feel as if this is the beginning of life for me!" she said, looking at it with the pencil between her fingers.

CHAPTER VII.

HUGH RECEIVES A COMMISSION.

It is to be supposed that Mr. Archer's inquiries with regard to Hugh Dinsmore were satisfactory, for a few days later a note was brought to Miss Waldron, which contained the following lines:

"DEAR MISS WALDRON· This will be presented to you by Hugh Dinsmore, the colorist of whom you spoke when I last saw you. He bears, as far as I can learn, an unblemished character, and deserves respect and encouragement. I have the honor to be your obedient servant,

"HENRY ARCHER."

Miss Waldron, who was sitting in the library, laid down her book, and said to the servant:

"Where is the boy?"

"He said he'd wait in the hall, ma'am."

"You should have asked him into the drawing-room; but no matter now—show him in here."

A minute later Hugh entered. The change from the bright light of the hall to the subdued light of the library made him hesitate for an instant within the door; then he saw the young lady rise, and he advanced with a not ungraceful bow.

"How do you do, Mr. Dinsmore?" she said, in her pleasant, frank voice. "I am glad you have come. Pray sit down."

She indicated a chair as she spoke—a more delightful chair than Hugh had ever in his life occupied before—and as he sat down he said:

"I have come by Mr. Archer's request, Miss Waldron; he told me that you wished to see me."

"Yes," replied Miss Waldron, noticing with what an educated accent he spoke; "I requested Mr. Archer to send you—or, rather, to ask you to come. I believe you are an artist?"

"I, madam?" said Hugh. "Oh, no! I should like to be one, if I could."

She smiled cordially. "That is the right feeling," she said; "I have no doubt you *will* be one. You are very young yet. I saw a photograph which you colored the other day, and it was so well done that I thought I would ask you to touch up some for me."

"I will do it willingly," he answered.

"You are sure you have the time?"

"Yes, for I paint at night. To color a photograph is nothing; that is not artist-work at all."

"Yet artists are often colorists."

"Perhaps so—for money. But there is no satisfaction in it. Do what one will, the hard outlines, the sharp shades, remain."

"The photograph you painted, of which I speak, had less of that than any other I ever saw; the colors were so finely and softly blended."

"Who was the photograph of?" he asked. "I paint a great many."

"This was of Meta Brodnax."

"I remember. The commission came directly from Miss Brodnax, so I could afford to do my best. I cannot usually afford to do so for what Mr. Watkins pays me."

"Your best was so admirable, that I could scarcely believe this was a mere photograph taken on paper. It looked like a miniature painted on ivory."

"No!" said Hugh, shaking his head. "A photograph can never look like a miniature; the artist's hand has done everything there. And then, ivory is such a beautiful thing to paint on—or must be, I should think. I have never tried it."

"Why not? It is true that miniatures are now generally superseded by these odious photographs; but there are some people who still have sense enough to desire an enduring picture."

The boy hesitated for a moment, then he said, simply, "That may be; but I have never had the ivory on which to paint, nor the necessary instruction. And I like oil-colors best."

"Wait a moment," said Miss Waldron, and, rising quickly, she left the room.

When she returned she carried in her hand a casket which would have delighted a virtuoso. Placing it on the table by which Hugh and herself had been sitting, she unlocked it with a small key and drew forth a miniature richly set in pearls and attached to a long gold chain.

"This," she said, "is one of our most valuable family possessions. It is a miniature which was painted in Paris more than a century ago—a picture of the ancestress after whom I am named, Lady Beatrix Waldron. She was named after that unhappy princess who was the second wife of James II., and both by birth and marriage was identified with devoted Jacobites. Her husband and herself were untiring in the cause of the Pretender, and the former played an important part in the ill-fated campaign of 1745. It was owing to his wife's courage and wit that he finally escaped to France with his head on his shoulders, and there this picture was taken. Soon after, like many others who followed the white cockade of Prince Charlie, they came to America, where their descendants live at the present day. See, how lovely she is! And would you not think that the picture had been painted yesterday, from the freshness and clearness of its tints?"

Hugh answered not a word. He had received the miniature in his hand, and he now stood, with his eyes fastened on it, almost as if he had been magnetized.

"How beautiful! how beautiful!" he said at last. "I never saw anything so beautiful before!"

It certainly was exquisitely painted, and the subject was one which had given the artist's powers full scope. The lovely, high-bred face with its brilliant complexion, the fearless eyes, and rich brown hair elaborately coifed and dressed with pearls, the fair, uncovered neck, and court-dress—each was painted with a delicacy and skill that were like a revelation to Hugh.

Miss Waldron smiled kindly at his delight.

"I am glad I showed it to you," she said. "We are very proud of our ancestress, for her courage was as great as her beauty."

"She looks like a princess and a heroine in one!" said the boy. "I am sure she would have died for Prince Charlie!"

"Very likely. I have heard that to the day of her death she was an ardent Jacobite. But a thought has struck me! I think I can give you a better commission than the mere coloring of a few photographs. How should you like to copy this?"

"Miss Waldron, you cannot be in earnest?"

"I am in serious earnest. Do you think you could do it?"

There was a minute's pause before he answered—a pause during which he looked intently at the picture. Then he said, very slowly:

"I think I could."

"If you think so, you shall," said Miss Waldron. "I have a cousin who has long coveted this miniature, but of course it is impossible that I could give it to her. I have several times thought, however, that I should like to give her a copy. Now, if you can make a faithful copy, I will pay you a hundred dollars."

"Miss Waldron!" said Hugh, with a gasp. Such a wonderful prospect as that of making at one stroke a hundred dollars fairly took away his breath. "Oh, I would try my *very* best to do it!" he cried, eagerly, after a moment; "but—but you cannot mean to trust this picture to me?"

"Why should I not? See there!"—she pushed Mr. Archer's note toward him—"that is the character you bring me."

Hugh took the note and read the few lines, with a flush mounting to his face. Then he looked up, and, as he was standing just opposite the window, Miss Waldron was struck by the limpid candor of his eyes.

"Mr. Archer is very good," he said, simply, "and, as far as I am concerned, your picture would be safe. But there is the danger of accident. I hardly think I dare take it."

"There would be no danger of accident if you did not tell any one that you had it," said the young lady, whose sense of prudence was often overmastered by generous impulses. "Does any one share your room?"

"Not any one at all. I could have a better one if I *would* share it, but I cannot; I must have privacy at any cost."

"And you stay—"

"At Mrs. Sargent's. It is a very plain house, but the people are honest and kind."

"Then I see no possible reason why you should not take the picture. In fact, I insist upon it. Frankly, when I sent for you it was with the intention of offering you the means necessary to become an artist; but since I have seen you, I am sure you would rather earn money than accept it."

"I would very much rather earn it," he answered, "though I thank you for intending to offer it," he added, with a courtesy that surprised his listener. "I am glad you told me; I have always believed that people who never knew what struggle was cared little for the sufferings of those who have never known anything else; but I shall not think so again."

"Some of us are very careless," said Miss Waldron, "but we often err more from want of thought than want of heart. By-the-way, I believe you said you have no ivory. I will give you some sheets that I have. Some years ago," she went on, unheeding Hugh's remonstrance, as she crossed the floor and opened the door of a cabinet, "I took a fancy to paint miniatures. Of course I failed. But I have all the necessary appliances here, and I will hand them over to you."

Poor Hugh was so overcome by this kindness that he was fairly incoherent when he attempted to return his thanks; and when, after a little longer talk—in the course of which Miss Waldron drew forth all his hopes and aspirations—he went away, it was with a half-incredulous sense of something too good to be true.

As he was leaving the hall a carriage drew up before the door, and, crossing the portico, he found himself face to face with Miss Lathrop and Brian Marchmont.

The young lady swept by with an indifferent glance; Marchmont nodded carelessly, but Hugh did not return the salutation. He lifted his hat to Miss Lathrop, whom he knew as the daughter of his employer; but he passed Marchmont, who was a little behind, without the least notice. That gentleman smiled.

"Is it worth while to give the unmannerly young beggar a lesson?" he thought. "But, perhaps, the best lesson is the jealousy he is suffering with regard to pretty Amy. So Archer, like a fool, sent him here! But then, he would do anything to ingratiate himself with Miss Waldron. —Florence," he said, as the servant left his cousin and himself in the drawing-room, "do you know anything about that fellow Archer, whom I met here several days ago?"

"Very little," answered Miss Florence. "He does not go into society at all. When he first came to Edgerton, mamma—who knew his mother, or something of the kind—tried to show him a little attention; but he repulsed it like a bear, and since then he has been left alone. By all accounts, he must be totally unfitted for society. But why do you ask?"

"Simply because it is very evident that he lifts his eyes and his hopes to our charming lady of the manor."

Miss Florence opened her eyes.

"Is it possible?" she said. "I am certainly surprised—though I don't know why I should be," she added, philosophically. "All men want to marry an heiress, and no man believes there is any danger of his failing to please a woman."

"Until he has failed a few times," said Marchmont. "Then he learns wisdom, if not modesty. But I consider Archer's case one of flagrant presumption, and it is a pity Miss Waldron is not aware of it, that she might administer an effectual quietus."

"Do you suppose she is not aware of it?" asked his cousin. "Women usually know such things long before they let you know that they are aware of them."

"I know that the dull masculine mind hardly appreciates the quickness of the feminine intelligence," Marchmont began, with a laugh; but Miss Waldron's appearance just then cut short his speech.

She looked very handsome as she entered, dressed in black grenadine and black lace, with a crapy, rose-colored tie at her throat, a rich flush on her cheeks, a bright light in her eyes.

It was not the first time that she had seen Marchmont since his declaration in the fernery, so her manner was altogether composed as she shook hands with him, after greeting Miss Lathrop.

"I am so glad that you have both come," she said, presently. "I want to ask you about my birthday entertainment. Papa insists, as usual, on a ball—though I tell him that I am growing too old for such frivolities—but he does not object to anything else that I please being added. We had theatricals last year, you know, Florence, so I have thought of a concert—a kind of musical *fête*. What do you think of it?"

"I think that you will find it very difficult to accomplish," replied Miss Florence. "Singers will be even harder to find than actors—and harder to manage, too."

"*That* they could not possibly be," said Miss Waldron, laughing. "The managing, however, will fall on the director's shoulders—and he is equal to it."

"Mr. Reynolds, you mean?"

"Yes, Mr. Reynolds. He is permanently director of the Cecilia Society, and he tells me that any or all the members of it will assist. Since the society comprises the best musical talent in Edgerton, that settles the question of performers."

"Pray," said Marchmont, "does Mr. Reynolds's daughter belong to the Cecilia Society? *She* has one of the finest voices I ever heard—the purest, most silvery soprano."

"Little Amy?" said Miss Waldron, in a tone of surprise. "I had no idea of it."

"I have heard something of her voice," said Miss Florence; "but she certainly does not belong to the Cecilia. They are all of our class."

"I suppose she would hardly contaminate them," said Marchmont. "And really"—turning to Miss Waldron—"if you want to signalize your *fête* by bringing out a star of the first magnitude, get little Amy, as you call her, to sing for you."

"Is her voice really so good?"

"It is really most remarkable."

"And how did you find out about it, Brian?" asked Miss Florence, curiously.

"I heard her accidentally first," said Marchmont, carelessly. "Since then I have been to Mr. Reynolds's house once or twice for the pleasure of listening to her."

"And looking at her, perhaps," said Miss Waldron, smiling. "She is very pretty.—Thank you for the information, Mr. Marchmont; I will act on it at once. Perhaps it may benefit her to bring her voice into notice," she added.

"So you want another *protégée?*" said Marchmont. "Are you not satisfied with the one whom I met going out?"

"Dear me!" said Miss Florence. —"Was that shabby boy a *protégé* of yours, Beatrix? I thought, of course, he had merely come on an errand."

"I am inclined to think that shabby boy will make a remarkable man some day," said Miss Waldron. "He certainly has great talent for painting. I saw some of his work not long ago, and I asked Mr. Archer to inquire about his character, and, if it was good, to send him here."

"Mr. Archer—ah!" said Miss Florence, glancing at her cousin.

"I have given him a kind of test-commission," Miss Waldron went on. "It will show his power, enable me to help him, and serve to educate him in art—all at the same time. He is to copy the miniature of my ancestress, Lady Beatrix, which you have often admired, Florence."

"What! that picture? O Beatrix!"

"Well"—with a laugh—"why should not that picture be copied as well as another?"

"But how absurd—pray excuse me! —to imagine that he *could* copy it, or to trust anything so valuable in his hands! —Brian, have you ever seen it? No?

That is a pity, for it is the loveliest thing imaginable, and is set in pearls worth a fortune."

"My dear Florence, pray be moderate! The pearls are beautiful, but they do not by any means represent a fortune."

"And is it possible," said Marchmont, with a look of amazement, "that you have trusted such a thing to the boy whom I met?"

"I trusted it to him—yes. I am sure he is honest."

"But—pardon me!—how can you possibly be sure? There is every presumption against his honesty, and the temptation is immense. Let me urge you to reclaim the picture at once!"

"Yes—pray do!" pleaded Miss Florence. "Think how dreadful it would be if he ran away with it! Really, Beatrix, I am astonished at you!"

"Honestly," said Miss Waldron, "if I had taken time for thought, I might not have given him the picture; but I cannot reclaim it now. I feel sure of his honesty, and I could not seem to suspect him."

"It would be better to do that than to lose the picture," urged her friend.

"I have no fear of losing it.—Mr. Marchmont, can you suggest anything very effective for the programme of my *fête?* Mr. Reynolds suggests a *cantata*, but I fear that would be too long, and weary, more than entertain, an audience longing for dancing."

"I think a concert selection would be better," said Marchmont; "but your own ideas, I am sure, are good. Let us have them!"

CHAPTER VIII.

"SO LONG AS YOU ARE AMUSED."

"You don't seem glad of my good fortune, Amy," said Hugh, in rather a wounded tone.

They were in the garden together, these two young people, as the day died softly away into dusk, and in the western sky the sunset built a gorgeous temple of fretted gold and jasper, with vivid crimson melting into softest rose on the long lines of vapor.

Over their heads hung a canopy of tender green foliage, while neither thought of dew in connection with the fragrant grass on which they sat.

In response to Hugh's last speech Amy looked up, and the dreamy expression, which had of late become habitual in her eyes, faded out of them, as she said:

"Yes, I am glad, Hugh, but—I wish it had come in another way. If I were you, I would not like the idea of being patronized; and that is what Miss Waldron is doing."

"I don't think so," Hugh replied; but the color mounted to his sensitive face. "Patronage means something offensive, but Miss Waldron only intends to be kind. Of course, she desires to assist me, and makes an opportunity to do so; but why should I object to that? I would not accept charity, but it would surely be misplaced pride to refuse assistance."

Amy made a slight, petulant motion with her shoulders.

"That may be the way you look at it," she said, "but I never mean to be indebted to anybody for anything. Above all, I would not be indebted to one of those arrogant Edgerton people!"

"I doubt if people here are more arrogant than people anywhere else," said Hugh, quietly; "and Miss Waldron is not arrogant at all. She is as kind and simple—"

"I don't want to hear anything about her," interrupted Amy. "You may fall in love with her if you like, but please don't bore me with her praises."

"Fall in love with her!" repeated Hugh, with a laugh. "That is a good joke! Honor bright, Amy, don't you know that I never have been, and never shall be, in love with but one person?"

"Nonsense, Hugh! you are a boy, and don't know your own mind," replied Amy, with discouraging carelessness.

"You are mistaken about that," said Hugh, who was well used to snubbing. "I know my mind a great deal better than many men, and before long I shall be a man. Then, perhaps, you'll listen to me."

"My dear boy," said Amy, with the calmness of superior wisdom, "before you have finished learning how to paint, I shall be a queen of the lyric stage. Mr. March—"

Here she stopped short, and either a glow from the sunset sky suddenly fell over her face, or else a blush dyed it.

"Well," said Hugh, in a tone of very poorly-concealed irritation, "what has your oracle, Mr. Marchmont, told you now?"

"Nothing that would interest you," she answered, with an attempt at dignity. "You are so prejudiced against him that it is not worth while to repeat anything he has said."

"I am not prejudiced against him," said Hugh. "Why should I be? But I know that his coming here does you no good; and I doubt if your father knows how often he does come."

"Hugh, how dare you!" cried Amy, with wrathful lightning gathering in her eyes.

"I would dare a great deal, Amy, to save you from any harm," answered Hugh, gravely. "You don't know—you are so young, and have no mother—how people will talk if Mr. Marchmont continues to come here so much. Oh, you may be as angry with me as you like—I do not care how angry you are, if it makes you consider."

"What should I consider?" demanded Amy, so angry that her cheeks were ablaze with crimson. "What is Edgerton to me? I don't care a straw if people talk till their tongues drop out!"

"I think you would care if you knew," said Hugh. "And your father—I am sure he would care. He works so hard, and is so busy, that he has not time to look after you; but you are old enough to take care of yourself. Amy, dear, promise me not to let that man come here any more!"

In his eagerness he leaned forward and caught one of the girl's hands, holding it firmly in both his own. His eyes gazed at her with an almost passionate pleading; but it was a pleading which, instead of touching her heart, only made her wrath wax higher. She snatched her hand away, and looked at him with a glance which the poor fellow remembered long afterward.

"I have borne a great deal from you," she said, "but I will not bear this! You have no right to talk so to me! If you want to make mischief, you had better go and tell papa that people are talking —oh, how I hate them!" she cried, with the small hands clinched, the bright eyes flashing fire; "but it is useless to come to me. You are jealous of Mr. Marchmont—I dare you to deny it!—and that is what your warning means."

"You are mistaken," said Hugh. "I am not jealous of him in the way you mean, but I am sure he will bring trouble on you, one way or another, if you don't take care. Do you know what has brought him to Edgerton, and keeps him here? He is courting Miss Waldron for her money—some people say he is engaged to her—and yet, while he is doing this, he comes day after day and spends hours here, pretending to hear you sing!"

"It is none of your business if he does!" cried Amy, exasperated beyond all thought of forbearance. "If you have nothing more agreeable to say than this, I—I shall go into the house."

"Never mind; I will spare you the trouble by going myself. I have to leave, anyway, for I have no time to spare from my painting. I only dropped in to tell you the news about Miss Waldron's

kindness. I have spoken the honest truth, and I wish—oh! I wish very much that you would heed it. Good-evening. I don't know when I can come again."

He went away with a wistful look, which had no effect whatever upon Amy. She sent one scorching glance after the small, spare figure; then, with a shiver of passion that shook her whole frame, burst into a storm of tears.

Unconscious of the tempest he left behind, Hugh passed through the garden and into the house. He had long been in the habit of coming and going like one of the family, so no one regarded him at present except Felix, who cried from the dining-room: "Come to supper. Hugh! What are you going away for? And why don't Amy come in?"

"I don't care for supper to-night, Felix; thank you!" Hugh answered, as he let himself out of the front-door.

He spoke so truly, that he did not even think of turning his steps toward his boarding-house, but walked slowly in the opposite direction, toward the suburbs of the town. Before he reached the open country the sunset splendor had faded, and only a faint, soft glow remained to show where it had been; but the mingling of twilight and moonlight —for in the eastern heavens hung the silver, three-quarter moon—was very lovely, and might have tempted to lingering one less keenly alive to beauty.

Yet, although he felt the beauty, it is certain that Hugh was not thinking of it. In truth, he could think of nothing save the scene in Mr. Reynolds's garden and Amy's passionate resentment of his warning. He had considered deeply before he offered this warning, and, now that it had been received in such a manner, he hardly knew what else to do. He might speak to Mr. Reynolds, as Amy had angrily suggested; but would that help matters? Would his opinion be likely to have any weight with the musician?— while he felt certain that Amy would never forgive such a step.

"What can I do?" he thought. "Amy would not have been so angry if she was not beginning to care for the fellow; and he may be a scoundrel of the worst kind, for all she knows. It seems to me that if he was not, he would surely think of the harm he is doing by filling her head with all manner of foolish ideas and hopes. But, then, some people never think of anything but amusing themselves, and he may be one of that sort. What if I were to speak to him? But I hardly think there would be any good in that; and where would I find an opportunity to do so?"

It was a boy's idea, altogether foolish and impractical, but Hugh could not banish it from his mind after it had once suggested itself. Miss Waldron's words rose in his memory, "Some of us are very careless, but we often err more from want of thought than want of heart."

Was it from want of thought that Marchmont was acting? If so, a word might be enough—a word might rouse the chivalry of his nature, and make him, of his own accord, discontinue the visits that had already set the gossiping tongues at work.

Hugh absently seated himself on a stile as he made these reflections, and, with his face turned to the fading glory of the west, he did not observe that a pedestrian was crossing the field behind him—a man young, slender, well-dressed—in a word, Brian Marchmont.

This gentleman had left Cedarwood a few minutes before, pleading an engagement in Edgerton which would not allow him to accept the general's hospitable invitation to remain to dinner; and as he walked across the sweet-smelling fields in the soft gloaming, he had a comfortable sense of satisfaction with regard to his affairs, immediate and future. He had very nearly won all that he desired from Miss Waldron, and he felt thoroughly assured that securing her definite promise to be his wife was only a question of time.

Then, breaking the monotony of courtship, there was Amy—pretty, winsome Amy—to amuse his leisure hours with the piquant flavor of her Bohemianism.

"The blossoms of the garden are all very well," he said to himself, "especially such a stately rose as Beatrix; but variety is the spice of life, and now and then one likes to gather a wild-flower from the woods."

Owing to the association of ideas, he was, half unconsciously, humming one of Amy's songs as he drew near the stile—a song which Hugh knew so well that, hearing it, he turned abruptly and faced the man who was at that moment in his thoughts.

The boy's heart seemed to rise up in his throat. Here, in the most unexpected manner, was the opportunity he had been esteeming out of his reach! Should he use it? He had only a minute in which to answer this question. There was no time for reasoning or reflection; instinct alone had to settle the matter, and instinct bade him act.

He stepped down from the stile, and as Marchmont, having swung himself over, was about to pass without the least token of recognition, he gathered his courage, and said:

"If you will excuse me, Mr. Marchmont, I should like to speak to you."

Marchmont paused, and, with a great deal of *hauteur* mingled with surprise on his face, he said, curtly:

"What do you want?"

"I will tell you in an instant what I want," Hugh replied. "First, let me say that my name is Dinsmore."

"I remember you," Marchmont answered. "I never forget a face. Pray, Mr. Dinsmore, what possible business have you with me?"

There was so much *brusquerie* in the tone of this question, that Hugh felt inclined to reply, "I have no business whatever," and go his way. But the thought of Amy checked the impulse.

There was nothing he would not endure for her sake; and surely if this man knew the harm he was working, his manhood would assert itself in her behalf, and he would find some amusement for his idle hours fraught with less serious consequences. This consideration gave Hugh patience, and, lifting his clear eyes to the haughty, handsome face, he said, calmly:

"My business with you is simply this: I am a friend of Amy Reynolds, and I want to tell you that you are doing her a great injury in bestowing so much time and attention on her. Gossips are already beginning to talk about it, and a man like you must know what a misfortune it is to a young girl for her name to be on light tongues and in evil mouths."

"By Jove!" said Marchmont.

The exclamation was entirely involuntary, and addressed to himself, being an expression of irrepressible surprise at the audacity of this shabby stripling. Then he laughed, and the scornful, contemptuous cadence made every drop of blood in Hugh's veins tingle.

"My young friend," he said, coolly, "allow me to inform you that the best thing you can do is to attend to your own affairs. I have no doubt you are very jealous, but you can hardly expect to serve your cause by such absurdity as this. Pretty little Amy and I understand each other; that ought to be enough. If it is not, so much the worse—for you."

With these words he was passing carelessly on, when Hugh, quivering with indignation and fearless as a lion, placed himself in his path.

"Do you mean that you do not care what people say of Amy, so long as you are amused?" he asked. "If that is the case, I tell you to your face, Mr. Marchmont, that you are no gentleman! You know that you want to marry Miss Waldron, and yet you are trying to win Amy's heart in the most dishonorable—"

"You are an insolent young fool!" said Marchmont.

He had no cane in his hand, else Hugh might have fared badly; but, slight as he looked, he was very muscular, and taking the boy by the collar, he flung him with great force into the middle of the road. Then, without pausing to see what was the result of this stringent measure, he walked on rapidly toward the town.

Hugh lay motionless where he had been thrown—stunned into unconsciousness by the heavy fall—and he had not yet stirred when, a minute later, a horseman came cantering down the road.

The horse first perceived the odd, dark, crumpled heap lying in the moonlight, and promptly bolted. His rider, having checked him up shortly, looked round for the cause of the fright. He, too, perceived then the dark figure, and muttering, "Some drunkard lying there to be run over," dismounted, and throwing the rein over his arm, approached, and, bending down, lifted the boy's face.

"What—Dinsmore!" he said aloud, in a tone of surprise. "Why, he is badly hurt!" he added, quickly, as he found his hand wet from the blood which was trickling from a cut on the forehead.

As he spoke Hugh's consciousness returned, and, opening his eyes, he looked up, half dazed.

"I want no assistance from you, Mr. Marchmont," he said. "You are a coward."

"I am not Mr. Marchmont," said a voice that recalled his scattered senses. "I found you lying here insensible. What has happened, Hugh?"

"Oh, you are Mr. Archer," said Hugh. "I—beg your pardon. Have I been here long, I wonder? Thank you, I think I can get up."

With Archer's assistance he rose to his feet, and, though still trembling from the nervous shock, stood erect, stanching with a handkerchief the blood which flowed from the cut on his brow.

"What has happened?" Archer repeated. "How did you come to be in such a situation? Lucky for you, my horse bolted, or I should have ridden over you, for I was looking toward the lights of the town, and noticing little of the road."

There was an instant's silence before Hugh answered. Then he looked up and said, quietly: "I would rather not tell you anything about it, Mr. Archer. I am obliged to you for helping me. I think I can walk back into town now."

"You had better ride my horse," said Archer, looking at him keenly. "You have had a severe blow."

"Only from the fall," said Hugh. "There is no need for me to ride, thank you. I am used to walking, and I shall be all right in a little while."

Archer did not press the matter any further—indeed, it was never his way to press anything on people which they were unwilling to receive. But, as he mounted his horse and rode away, he felt considerably puzzled. The last person in the world whom he would have supposed Hugh likely to come in contact with was Brian Marchmont; yet Hugh had plainly mistaken him for Marchmont, and had uttered words not easily forgotten. "He meant them, too," Archer said to himself. "It is very odd! If Marchmont was the person who knocked him down and left him senseless, what could possibly have been the provocation? Surely I did not make a mistake when I recommended the boy to Miss Waldron! Every one speaks of him as quiet and inoffensive in the extreme."

.   .   .   .   .   .

Having left Hugh without even a backward glance to see whether or not he recovered from the stunning fall he had received, Mr. Marchmont walked into Edgerton, his usually well-moderated pulses beating with an excitement which, to say the least, was not pleasurable.

This was a result he had not bargained for while spending the idle hours in light flirtation with the musician's pretty daughter. To be called to account by "an insolent errand-boy," as in his thoughts he characterized Hugh, was certainly a novel and not an agreeable experience. He laughed over it, but the laugh had no ring of real mirth. With the best intentions, Hugh had done the worse thing possible for Amy; he had waked the slumbering devil in Marchmont's nature, and converted what had before been only amusement into deadly earnest.

It was, however, characteristic of the sybarite nature of the man that he shook off annoyances as a Newfoundland dog shakes off water; though putting aside the annoyance by no means implied putting aside the purpose it had wakened. His engagement in Edgerton was with two or three gay young gentlemen who chanced to be passing through the town—friends, or at least intimate acquaintances, whom he had accidentally encountered. In the course of the convivial evening which ensued, no one entertained the faintest suspicion that anything had occurred to ruffle the easy tranquillity of his spirits or cast the least weight upon his mind. In truth, Mr. Marchmont's spirits and mind were not readily affected by insignificant trifles, and in this class he included his flirtation with Amy, and Hugh's interference therewith.

Had Amy been aware of this, she might have spared herself some Juliet-like fancies, as she sat by the parlor-window, looking at the moon sailing through an iris sky, while silver lights and broad, sharp-cut shadows made up the world below.

Immersed in clouds of tobacco-smoke, her father and Herr Meerbach were talking, while Felix, with a touch of masterly power and sweetness, was playing the "Walpurgis Night." The dreamy strains floated by Amy almost unheard. Her heart—the foolish heart of sixteen—was throbbing with pain and doubt.

Could it be true that Marchmont was a suitor of Miss Waldron's? Hugh had said so; but Hugh was not likely to be well informed with regard to such matters, and, besides, he was jealous.

"I *cannot* believe it!" she thought,

passionately; then, with a spasmodic effort, common-sense asserted itself, as she added, mentally, "What is it to me? Mr. Marchmont has never done anything except admire my singing and say I am pretty. I am a fool to think anything about him, or care if he marries Miss Waldron to-morrow! She is rich and handsome, and has been everywhere and seen everything. Oh!"—the long-drawn sigh ending in spoken words—"I *wish* I was rich!"

"Perhaps you may be, some day," said a quiet, unexpected voice very near at hand.

CHAPTER IX.

MR. TRAFFORD OFFERS ADVICE.

AMY started, and turned her head; but it was no Mephistopheles who stood at her elbow, ready to gratify her longings by driving a bargain for the ultimate possession of her soul. As far removed as possible from that sulphuric personage was the pleasant, good-humored face that met her glance—the face of a gentleman who had paused by the window and looked with amusement at the pretty, wistful countenance on which the moonlight fell broadly.

"O Mr. Trafford!" she said; "I didn't know I spoke so loud that any one could hear my foolish wish!"

"Not *any one*," replied Mr. Trafford, "but I was close at hand, and so I heard it. I am not sure about its foolishness," he added, smiling. "Wishing for riches is sometimes a first step toward obtaining them."

"I shall be rich some day," said Amy, confidently. "I am certain of that. But I want to be so *now*."

"You want the prize before you have won it? I am surprised at you!"

He spoke in a tone of half-laughing banter, as to a child; but Amy looked up gravely in his face.

"I was reading, the other day," she said, "that after we have worked a long time for a prize, when at last we gain it, it has lost its value. If we could only have things *at the start*, and not wait to be tired out, how much better it would be!"

"Well," said Mr. Trafford, with a long puff at the meerschaum which, as usual, he was smoking, "I am not sure about that. Without being much of a moralist, I have generally found that there's a good reason for most things. If we gained what we desire 'at the start,' as you say, we should not only miss the discipline of labor, but often get a great many worthless prizes. Suppose you come and take a turn round the square, and I will give you an instance of that from my personal experience?"

Amy was nothing loath. She was tired of the house and everybody in it. There was something of novelty in a moonlight stroll with Mr. Trafford, and his promise to relate a "personal experience" wakened her curiosity. She slipped out of the parlor, and in a minute stood on the pavement by his side.

"Had you not better put something on your head?" he suggested, looking at her. "No? It is true, you have no neuralgia or rheumatism to dread yet a while. I hope you don't object to my pipe? I came out to smoke."

She laughed. "I've been sitting in a room with *two* pipes," she said, "so I could hardly object to one in the open air. I rather like the odor of good tobacco, if there isn't too much of it. Oh, what a heavenly night!" she added, with a soft sigh.

"Very pretty," said Mr. Trafford, glancing round. "To-morrow night the moon will be full."

"I am always sorry for the moon to be full," said Amy, "because then it begins to decline. I wish matters had been arranged so that we could have a moon all the time."

"It is a pity you couldn't live on the

planet Saturn. Then you would have moons enough."

"I shouldn't care for more than one at a time," said Amy; but fearing that the extreme haziness of her ideas with regard to the moons of the planet Saturn might be exposed, she turned the conversation. "You promised to tell me your experience about worthless prizes," she said, glancing up at her companion.

"Yes," he answered, a little absently. They were walking slowly along the moonlit street, and he gazed ahead without speaking for a minute or two.

Then he smiled. "I haven't thought about it for years before," he said. "How old are you, my dear? Sixteen? Well, double your age—which, I suppose, you don't consider a pleasant thing to do, even in imagination—and you'll have the number of years which have elapsed since I was a young man, in love with a girl only a little older than yourself. It seems odd, doesn't it?"—rolling out a cloud of smoke as he met Amy's eyes, full of curiosity—"but it is true, and I can't flatter myself that I was any less a fool than young men are nowadays. I was desperately in love, and desperately poor. Having received an assurance of affection and constancy from the object of my passion, however, the labor of making a fortune seemed a trifle hardly worth considering. When I set to work I naturally discovered my mistake; but I struggled on, and by the time I was half-way up the hill which I proposed to climb, the girl to whom I was engaged grew tired of waiting, and married another man."

"She jilted you! Oh, how shameful!" cried Amy.

Mr. Trafford removed his pipe from his mouth to laugh. "I mustn't obtain your sympathy under false pretenses," he said. "She dissolved the engagement in the most reasonable manner, and married a man who had a fortune in hand without the trouble of making it. I don't remember that I suffered from the disease known as heart-break in any excessive degree;

but I *do* remember that, by the time I reached the top of the hill, I was heartily obliged to her for having bestowed herself upon somebody else, since life—which is like a crucible, to show what is base metal and what gold—had proved that she was a weak, extravagant woman, of bad temper and lax principles. Now, you see, if I had possessed my fortune at the start, I should have been burdened with that woman even to the present day, for she is not dead yet."

"I see," said Amy. "How glad you must be to have missed her! But, as far as *my* wish is concerned," she added, realizing that the moral of the story was intended for her benefit, "there would be nothing of that kind to fear. If I were rich, I should be able to help other people—to send Felix to Germany, to let papa rest, to give Mariette and the boys every advantage."

"Ah!" said Mr. Trafford. "I suppose you were thinking of these things when I overheard that wish you uttered so fervently a little while ago?"

Even in the moonlight Amy's deep blush was manifest. "No," she said, after a moment's hesitation, "I was not thinking of them. A—something made me think of Miss Waldron, and I wished I had money to go everywhere, and become accomplished and graceful, and be admired as she is."

"And fall a prey to some fortune-hunter, as she will probably do. How would you like that?"

"Why should you think she will probably do it?" said Amy, ignoring the question addressed to herself.

"Why should I think so? That is easily answered:

'Alas! alas! for the woman's fate
Who has from a mob to choose a mate!
'Tis a strange and painful mystery!
But the more the eggs, the worse the hatch;
The more the fish, the worse the catch;
The more the sparks, the worse the match—
Is a fact in woman's history!'"

Amy was quite astonished at this sudden "dropping into poetry" on the part of her elderly friend, and, having never read "Miss Killmansegg and her Precious Leg," the verse had the merit of novelty to her.

"I have heard the proverb about taking a crooked stick at last," she said. "I suppose it amounts to the same thing. But do you know of anybody Miss Waldron is likely to marry just — just now?"

"I have not the least knowledge of Miss Waldron's affairs, matrimonial or otherwise," replied Mr. Trafford. "I have heard some gossip about a young man named Marchmont. By-the-by, haven't you a slight acquaintance with him? On the whole, my dear—if you will excuse a bit of advice—I think you would do well to *keep* it a slight."

"Do — do you know any harm of him?" asked Amy.

Her voice quivered, but there was none of the defiance in it which had breathed for Hugh.

"I know no harm of him," answered Mr. Trafford; "but I suppose you have heard of the spider and the fly. No doubt the spider was very good-looking, and pleasant, but the fly was very silly, for all that. I should not like you to be such a fly."

"There isn't any danger of it," said Amy, and a chord of indignation thrilled in her tone.

"I hope not," said her companion. "Now tell me about this plan of your father's for sending your brother to Germany. Why does he not do it? The boy's talent ought to be cultivated."

"I should think you might know why he doesn't do it," answered Amy. "He has not the money."

"It would not take much," said Mr. Trafford.

"That depends on how you look at it," said Amy. "It might not seem much to *you*, but to papa it seems a great deal. You see"—a sigh—"it is awfully expensive to have a family!"

"I suppose so," said Mr. Trafford, with a laugh that made some loiterers on the other side of the street turn their heads. "When a man has none, however, it is only fair that he should help the over-burdened people who have. Do you think your father would be offended if I offered to send your brother abroad?"

"Offended!" Amy stopped short and clasped her hands. "O Mr. Trafford! are you in earnest? Would you *really* do it? I think papa would accept such an offer gratefully, because, you see, it is Felix you would benefit, not him—and I should *worship* you!"

"Would you? Well, then, it is a bargain. Here we are at the house. Run in and see if that German has gone. If he has, I'll speak to your father at once."

Luckily, "that German" was gone—if he had still been in the house, Amy would have been tempted to take him by the shoulders and put him out—and, more luckily still, Felix had accompanied him, while Mr. Reynolds remained at home. It was the hand of the older musician which was lingering over the keys in the dimly-lighted parlor when Amy entered, in a fever of excitement.

"O papa!" she cried, "Mr. Trafford is here, and he wants to speak to you on very particular business."

"Ask him to come in," said Mr. Reynolds, rising from the piano and fortifying himself by the thought that he did not owe Mr. Trafford any money, so "very particular business" could not have *that* significance.

Mr. Trafford came in, and, like a man of business, went directly to his point; yet there was a delicacy in his mode of doing this, which proved that his nature was not without a certain fineness which many estimable natures lack.

"He had a large income," he said, "no near relations, and very few personal wants, so that Mr. Reynolds would confer a favor if he would allow him to bear the expense of sending Felix to Germany, and providing for his musical education after he reached there."

Mr. Reynolds, who had been talking over the question of expenses with Herr Meerbach, and had realized with a sense of despair that his narrow means could not possibly be stretched to cover them, felt as if the heavens opened and an angel suddenly spoke to him. For a minute he could not answer; but, though usually one of the most undemonstrative of men, he seized Mr. Trafford's hand and wrung it until that gentleman very nearly groaned aloud.

By the time Felix returned, the matter had been settled, and there were tears on his father's lashes when he put his arm round the boy's neck and told him the wonderful news.

．　．　．　．　．　．　．

It was still wonderful news—news that seemed almost too good to be true—when Amy sat on the back piazza the next morning, and, while the sunbeams played in and out among the meshes of her curly hair, virtuously proceeded to darn Felix's socks. "If he is going away so soon, I must put his clothes in order," she had said to herself on waking, and it was in this manner she set about that arduous task. Amy's darning was very far from the perfection of art, but there was a great deal of good intention in the bungling stitches; and as her needle traveled back and forth, she was saying to herself, like a charm to keep weariness at bay, "Felix is going to Germany!"

On this refrain the sudden jingle of the door-bell broke sharply.

Down went needle and thread and sock; up sprang Amy, color flashing into her face, light into her eyes. "Callers" were unknown at the Reynolds house, therefore the person who rang in that imperative fashion could only be some one on business—as, for instance, the grocer's boy with the grocer's small account—or Marchmont.

Hope whispered strongly that it might be the latter; so Amy sped to the door

and opened it, as once before, with trembling fingers.

As once before, she encountered disappointment. Instead of Marchmont's handsome face appeared the black countenance of a well-dressed servant, who, almost without glancing at her, asked, rapidly:

"Is Miss Reynolds at home?"

"Yes, I am Miss Reynolds," answered Amy. "What do you—"

She stopped in her question, for, as she turned, she saw that a carriage was standing before the door—a carriage from which a lady bowed, and then, as the servant approached, descended.

"It is Miss Waldron," said Amy to herself. "What on earth can she want?"

Miss Waldron, when they met, shook hands and uttered her greetings in her usual pleasant, kindly fashion, but she was struck the while by the transformation in Amy's appearance since she had last seen her at anything like close quarters. In fact, Amy was at the age when a girl often astonishes even the members of her family by shooting, in a day, from childhood to womanhood. The pliant, rounded figure had gained slenderness and grace; the piquant face, womanly expression. Miss Waldron was so much struck, that she was almost guilty of staring after they entered the dingy parlor, and she was enthroned on the dingy horse-hair sofa.

"What a Hebe!" she was thinking, while she made a few commonplace inquiries and remarks.

These over, she said, frankly: "My dear, I am told that you have a beautiful voice, and I have come to ask if you will sing for me?"

Amy blushed vividly, not so much from the compliment as because the thought instantly occurred to her that only one person could have told Miss Waldron about her voice. "I am very willing to sing for you," she answered; and, rising, she turned to the music-stand, glad of an excuse to escape from the glance of the kind but keen dark eyes. "Would you like any particular song?" she asked, after a minute had elapsed, broken only by the flutter of the sheet-music.

"Not any," Miss Waldron answered. "Choose what you like best and can sing best."

So Amy chose the song she had learned last, and with her rendering of which both her father and Marchmont had professed themselves entirely satisfied. It was the beautiful music which Rubinstein has set to those exquisite words of Heine's, "Thou'rt like unto a flower."

At the first clear note Miss Waldron lifted her eyebrows, and as the full compass and exquisite quality of the voice displayed itself, she rose in uncontrollable amazement and walked to the piano.

"Beautiful!" she cried, when the song ended—"that is no term at all for your voice! It is marvelous! I had no idea of anything like it, though Mr. Marchmont did say that you were a future successor of Nilsson and Patti."

"Did he say that to *you?*" asked Amy, quickly. Then she blushed again; but, with a self-possession that did her credit, considering her sixteen years and limited opportunities, she added, "Mr. Marchmont has said some very kind things to me; but people often say such things just to be pleasant, without exactly meaning them."

"I think he meant them all," said Miss Waldron, looking at her; and, as she looked, it suddenly occurred to the young lady to wonder what that "all" included. Could any son of Adam gaze into that face without admiring its fairness?—and would not most sons of Adam utter this admiration freely to a girl so young and so unprotected?

Miss Waldron was a woman of the world, and she knew that it was hardly likely Marchmont had limited his appreciation to the voice of the future successor of Nilsson and Patti.

This thought flashed through her mind while she was uttering a few more words of sincere praise, after which she added:

"I am sorry I have not time to ask you to sing another song for me this morning, but I shall not be satisfied until I hear you again. My object in coming was to ask a favor of you—a favor which I am more anxious for you to grant since I have heard your voice. I am to give a kind of *fête*—half ball, half concert—on the tenth of May, and I shall be obliged if you will promise to sing on that occasion."

So gracious was the tone of this request, so entirely free from any suspicion of patronage, that Amy's first sensation was one of rapture.

The prospect of going to the Cedarwood *fête* was in itself ecstatic enough, but the thought of singing in public thrilled her heart to the core. Her eyes expanded, her lips sprang apart:

"Oh!" she cried, "I shall be very, very glad to do so—if papa will let me."

There was a great change of tone and expression in the last words—a change which made Miss Waldron smile.

"Do you think Mr. Reynolds will object?" she asked.

"I am afraid he will," answered Amy.

"Then I must try my powers of persuasion upon him, and I think I shall succeed in making him consent. It will be an excellent opportunity for your *début*, and so I shall tell him."

"My *début!* How delightful that sounds!" cried the girl, with sparkling eyes.

"Rather a tame *début* compared to what you will have some day," answered Miss Waldron. "But no doubt you will enjoy it; there is delight in the mere exercise of such a power as yours, I should think. Now I must say good-morning. I am very glad I came."

Glad she came! What was her gladness compared to that of Amy, who, after the carriage had rolled away, clapped her hands over her head, and cried:

"Life *has* begun! I knew it would!"

4

CHAPTER X.

"I WANDERED BY THE BROOKSIDE."

LIFE began in such earnest for Amy, that the next few days went by like a dream. Mr. Reynolds, moved to unwonted amiability by the fact that Felix was going to Germany, consented for her to sing at Miss Waldron's *fête;* but over and above the pleasure of practising for this, and the arrangement of a toilet for the occasion, was the strange, new delight which had come into her existence with Brian Marchmont. The girl was so young and inexperienced, that not all her native shrewdness availed to save her from the fate of those who love not wisely but too well.

It may be said, in palliation of her folly, that Marchmont was one of the men whom Nature gifts with exceptional powers of fascination, and that his success with women was proverbial among all who knew him.

"He has a knack of making them fall in love with him!" his friends would remark to one another; and Marchmont himself certainly was not ignorant of his attractive qualities.

There is no denying that, after his unfortunate encounter with Hugh Dinsmore, he exerted these qualities to the utmost with Amy, resolutely thrusting aside any suggestion which prudence or conscience made.

The last was too well trained to trouble him, while with regard to the first he said, with an impetuosity which was occasionally one of his characteristics, that there was only spice enough of risk to give zest to the affair, and that it was a risk well worth running, since he had not been so interested before for years.

"By heaven! that little witch is ten times more piquant and charming than any or all of the society-bred women with whom I am acquainted," he said to himself. "If she were in the remotest

degree eligible, I might be tempted to think that I had found my fate at last."

So it came to pass that Amy was led —she did not pause to consider where. Those hours in the dingy parlor when she sang for Marchmont, those hours in the neglected garden when they sat under the trees where white blossoms had given place to green leaves, and those golden hours when they wandered through the lovely spring woods, all did their work thoroughly. If any thought of warning ever came to her, she put it away. The cup of nectar which was held to her lips she drank eagerly, without pausing to consider the consequences. Like a flower exposed to a tropical sun, she seemed to grow lovelier and more mature every hour; but there was no mother's eye to note the change and read its meaning.

Her father was absent during the greater part of every day, and, though he knew Marchmont as a stranger who had been much struck with Amy's voice and came occasionally to hear her sing, his daughter was still in his eyes so entirely a child, that he never thought of the result which a woman would have been quick to foresee.

One thing which conduced to this state of security was the caution which Marchmont had of late displayed in the matter of his visits. He seldom came to the house, preferring to meet Amy in some place—like the woodland glen where he first saw her—remote from the eyes of gossips. It was not so much Hugh's expostulation which led to this, as a few words which Miss Waldron uttered.

"I went, this morning, to hear your soprano sing," she said to him, on the evening of the day when she paid her visit to Amy; "and you are right about her voice—it is wonderful! But you did not mention that her face is nearly as remarkable."

To this Marchmont, whose self-possession was imperturbable, replied: "Yes, she is very pretty; but I did not mention her face because I thought you knew all about her."

"I know all about her in a certain way—that is, I have seen her running about the streets ever since she was a little thing; but I was not in the least aware until to-day that she had shot into a woman, or that she was so beautiful. Why, she fairly dazzled me when I first saw her in that dark, narrow passage! Hebe herself never had more delicious coloring; and I hope you don't mean me to believe that you have not gone there as much to admire that bewitching face as to hear her voice!"

There was no jealousy in the tone of this remark—only a certain satirical amusement—and it was accompanied by a smile which defied contradiction. Marchmont, however, was not foolish enough to think of denying the charge.

"I always admire beauty wherever I find it," he said, calmly, "and this girl has genuine beauty. But there are plenty of pretty girls in the world, and it is only her voice which has attracted me, and made me spend some idle hours—for I can't possibly bore you with my presence *all* the time, and Edgerton is a desert to me—in her father's house."

"I suppose there is no harm in hearing her sing," said Miss Waldron, "but the girl is so singularly pretty, that I am afraid you may be tempted to amuse these idle hours by flirting with her. Nay, don't look so virtuous; I know the world, and I know the habits of the men of the world like *you*, sir! What I wish to request is, that you will forego this amusement—for my sake, if you please. I do not want that bright face shadowed before its time. Will you promise to let her alone?"

"I will promise never to see her again, if you like," he answered, carelessly; "but I think you overrate my power of doing mischief, and I am sure you overrate my intentions. Let me tell you that a man only flirts when his heart is empty—never when it is filled by—"

"Oh, never mind about that!" she interrupted, with impatience. "I am not interested in your heart, but in your conduct; and I desire you not to flirt with this child."

"And I answer to that, as to any other command you choose to lay upon me: To hear is to obey."

"I hope that I may trust you to obey," she said, looking at him steadily; and he felt a conviction that he must be careful, for this woman was no fond fool, who could be hoodwinked at a man's pleasure.

It chanced that among the guests dining at Cedarwood that evening was Mr. Trafford, and at this point he crossed the floor and installed himself in a large chair by the side of his young hostess.

"I suppose you are aware that you have made one person very happy to-day, Miss Waldron," he said, after a few preliminary remarks; while Marchmont mentally confounded his impudence, yet feared to go away, not knowing what report might be made behind his back; so he sat still, stroking his mustache, and looking supercilious—a look entirely wasted on Mr. Trafford.

"Have I?" said Beatrix. "I am glad to hear it; but I do not know to whom you allude."

"Are you, then, in the habit of making people happy?" he asked. "If so, you are a very wise young lady—and, I may add, an uncommon one."

"I should like to feel that I deserve such commendation," she answered, "but I really do not. It is very rarely that it is in my power to make any one happy, and to-day—"

"To-day you have invited a little girl to sing for you who will probably, before she dies, sing for royal personages—and have thereby given her more pleasure than the kings and queens will ever bestow."

"Do you mean Amy Reynolds? Is it possible that you know her?" said Miss Waldron, astonished, and beginning to think that Amy must be growing famous, since this orderly man of business was acquainted with her.

He smiled.

"I board at Mrs. Crenshaw's," he said, "and am, therefore, a next-door neighbor of Mr. Reynolds. The gardens of the two houses adjoin, and occasionally I look over the wall—as Mr. Marchmont is aware."

Mr. Marchmont managed to appear more indifferent than he felt.

"I remember you astonished me very much by looking over the wall *one* afternoon," he said.

"That occasion served as a warning to me," responded Mr. Trafford. "Finding that I was likely to disturb interesting conversations, I have, since then, refrained from entering an appearance unless I had good reasons for believing that the coast was clear. This afternoon, however, I heard such a tide of melody rising from the garden, that I felt constrained to glance over and ask what had inspired the songstress. Then I was told the story of your invitation," he said, looking at Miss Waldron.

"I am pleased to have made the child happy," she said. "I heard her voice this morning for the first time, and was amazed by it!"

"It is a wonderful voice," said Mr. Trafford. "She will make a sensation when she appears on the stage."

"I wish she could be saved from that," said Miss Waldron. "She is so young, so pretty!"

"Saved from it!" repeated Marchmont, with a laugh. "I do not think she would be obliged to any one who saved her. She pants for the triumph and excitement and splendor before her."

"Yes, it would be altogether useless to attempt to induce her, for any object whatever, to resign the career she has determined upon," said Mr. Trafford, with such a thorough air of knowing all about the matter that Miss Waldron betrayed in her face the surprise she felt.

At this moment General Waldron came up and carried the elder gentleman off to a whist-table, greatly to Marchmont's relief; but the evil star of the latter was plainly in the ascendant, for who should advance to take the vacant seat but Archer, whose first remark was:

"I have not been able to ask before, Miss Waldron, what you thought of the boy whom I sent here by your request?"

"Have I not yet thanked you for executing my commission so well?" she replied, with a smile. "I was exceedingly pleased with him. He is talented and modest and honest, I am sure."

"He certainly bears an excellent character, so far as I can learn," said Archer, "and, as I told you, deserves encouragement."

"Then," said Marchmont, speaking on an impulse of irritation which he could not restrain, "you will have the satisfaction of feeling yourself accountable if your *protégé* walks away with a valuable picture which Miss Waldron has intrusted to him."

"The miniature of my great-great-grandmother," said Beatrix, as Archer looked at her. "Mr. Marchmont thinks I have been imprudent; but it was impossible to look in that boy's clear eyes without feeling convinced of his integrity."

"Clear eyes are not always proofs of integrity," said Archer, smiling. "Perhaps Mr. Marchmont distrusts the boy because he knows something of him," he added, glancing at Marchmont with a keenness which that gentleman felt and resented.

"I know that he is an errand-boy, or something of the kind, in Mr. Lathrop's business-house," he answered, somewhat haughtily. "My knowledge of him begins and ends with that fact."

"It seems to me that I know more of him," said Miss Waldron, musingly. "I mean, that he is connected with some one —ah, I have it! His face was in a measure familiar to me, but I could not place it. Now I remember that I have often seen him with Amy Reynolds. I wonder if he is in love with her! What a charming match they would make!"

"Who, Beatrix?" asked a young lady not far off, attracted by the animated tone in which these words were pronounced.

"No one in whom you are interested, my dear," answered Beatrix.—"Don't you think my idea is a good one, Mr. Marchmont? Two artistic souls who begin in Bohemia and end—where shall we say?"

"Where, indeed?" said Marchmont, who could not repress his disgust. "The idea is sacrilege! The lout is no doubt in love with pretty Amy, but *she* is—"

He paused, conscious that Archer was regarding him with a rather peculiar gaze.

"Does she not like him?" asked Miss Waldron. "What a pity!

' But 'tis just these women's way,
   All the same this wide world over;
Fooled by what's most worthless, they
   Cheat in turn the honest lover.' "

"If a man had ventured to quote those sentiments, you would have called him a slanderer," said Archer.

"A man wrote them," she answered, "but I fear, alas! he was not a slanderer."

When Marchmont went away from Cedarwood that night, he told himself that he must be more cautious in his flirtation with the unfledged prima donna. He was in a position where he could not afford to lose the substance of what he most desired for a shadow, however sweet and fair that shadow might be.

Yet several reasons made it impossible for him to obey Miss Waldron's request and let Amy alone. For one thing, Amy had grown necessary to his—amusement. He was oddly conscious of being restless and ill at ease, "like a boy in love," he thought scornfully, when he did not see her; and he was far too much of an epicurean to deny himself any pleasure within his reach.

Then, Hugh's presumption was to be punished in the way Hugh would feel most, and—well, there were manifold reasons why matters should go on a little longer exactly as they were.

"After the *fête* I will make Beatrix give me a definite answer, and then I will go away for a while," he thought. "That will end everything best."

It was an eminently masculine decision, and, having made it, Mr. Marchmont felt relieved in mind. So the idle days went on in their accustomed fashion. April sun and rain made the earth more lovely every hour, and when May came, crowned with a thousand flowers, Nature seemed to welcome her favorite child with an ecstasy of rejoicing.

Into Amy's small chamber the sunshine streamed in a tide of golden brightness one afternoon, and found her standing before the mirror, trying on a hat which she had just trimmed. It was exquisitely fresh and pretty, though fashioned of the simplest materials, and the face beneath it was lovely as any blossom of the May—so lovely, that it smiled with pleasure at its own reflection.

"Are you going to walk, Amy?" inquired a small, eager voice at the half-open door. "May I go with you?"

"No, Mariette, you may not," answered Amy, with decision. "I am going out—on business. You must stay at home, like a good girl, until I come back. Oh, for pity's sake, don't cry!" as Mariette's face puckered up ominously. "You may have anything in the house to play with, if you'll only stay and keep quiet."

"I'd rather go!" said Mariette, not much impressed with this sweeping offer.

"But you can't go!" said Amy. Then, to cut the discussion short, she snatched her parasol and ran down-stairs.

When Mariette heard the house-door close, she lifted up her voice in bewailing; but there is little pleasure in crying unless somebody can be disturbed, and in the present instance there was nobody to be disturbed, for Clara—the only person left in the house—was too deaf to hear the tearless howls; consequently they soon ceased, and remembering Amy's permission with regard to having anything she liked to play with, Mariette looked round to see what she would choose. It did not take her long to decide, for Amy's treasures were few—a toilet-box, an album, usually kept out of her reach, together with a few old-fashioned, gorgeously bound annuals that had belonged to Mrs. Reynolds. On these she laid her hands, and, having piled them carefully in her apron and gathered up the hem to form a bag, she proceeded down-stairs.

It chanced that Amy, on going out, closed the house-door so carelessly behind her, that it had swung open again; and when Mariette came round the curve of the staircase, she was surprised to see a tall, handsome lady in glistening silk standing on the threshold. Such a visitor was so unexpected that the little maiden's eyes opened wide, and, in her haste to descend more rapidly, the articles in her apron slipped out of the corner thereof and came crashing down-stairs before her.

"I expected that," said the lady, advancing. Then, with her delicately gloved hands, she picked up one or two of the books. "You should not try to carry so many things at once," she said. "What are you going to do with these?"

"I am going to take them in the garden, and play keeping store with Hetty Crenshaw," replied Mariette, looking up with great, blue, unabashed eyes. "Amy said I might have anything I liked to play with. Do you want to see Amy? She's gone out."

"I am sorry for that," said Miss Waldron—for it was she—smiling, and thinking how very pretty the child was. Almost unconsciously she added, "Where has Amy gone?"

Mariette set her ringleted head on one side with an air of wisdom. "I don't know exactly," she answered.

"Amy said she was going out on business, but I expect she went to walk with Mr. Marchmont; she almost always does."

This was information Miss Waldron had not anticipated, and the blood rushed to her cheek as if she had been detected in something unworthy. It was evident that she could have learned anything else that Mariette knew, but, instead of asking further questions, she opened her card-case and drew out a card. "Give that to your sister," she said, "and tell her that I came to make some arrangements about the *fête*. Good-by, and don't try to carry so many books again."

She was passing out, when Mariette espied a bit of pasteboard lying at the foot of the staircase, which she immediately seized.

"Did you drop this?" she asked, running after Miss Waldron, who turned, glanced at the card, hesitated an instant, then took it.

On one side was Brian Marchmont's name; on the other a pressed fern was pinned, and written underneath, in an unformed, girlish hand, were a date and four words: "The beginning of life."

Mariette wondered what made the lady silent for a minute—a minute, during which she gazed at this which had oddly drifted into her hands. She knew at once that it had fallen from one of the books Mariette dropped, but she also knew that in a certain sense it was hers, since the date proved that this was the fern she had given Marchmont on the day when he asked her to be his wife.

Her resolution was quickly taken. The proud lips set themselves with a certain defiant firmness, as she opened her card-case and slipped the waif of sentiment within.

"Thank you, my dear," she said, and went away.

Amy, meanwhile, had left the streets behind and walked toward the woods, which at the present season were full of the freshest, sweetest beauty of spring.

About a quarter of a mile beyond the outskirts of the town she reached a creek, overhung by trees and draped with the vines that make Southern water-courses so wonderfully picturesque.

Turning from the road, which crossed a bridge here, she tripped lightly along the bank of the stream for some distance, with a look of expectation in her eyes—a look which suddenly changed to delight as, not far off, she saw a slender, shapely, masculine figure, clad in cool gray, lying on the green bank under the shade of overhanging boughs, while a fishing-rod was propped against a tree near by, and obligingly leaned forward so that its line touched the water.

The hat of the gentleman was pulled over his eyes, so that he would hardly have been the wiser for a dozen bites; but he heard Amy's step, and, springing up, met her with both hands outstretched in eager welcome—all listlessness gone out of his handsome face, his hat pushed back, showing the damp, dark curls that clustered round his forehead.

"So you have come at last!" he said, smiling. "I have been waiting and watching for an hour at least."

"You may have been waiting," said Amy, saucily, "but you certainly were not watching. I thought, when I came in sight, that you were asleep."

"I think I *was* asleep, and dreaming of you. But your step would wake me out of the deepest sleep that humanity knows. Don't you remember what the lover says in 'Maud'?—

'She is coming, my own, my sweet!
    Was there ever so airy a tread?
My heart would hear it and beat,
    Were it earth in an earthy bed!'"

"How much of that must I believe?" asked Amy, with a smile brimful of coquetry. "I don't think hearts like yours beat much when they are *out* of an earthy bed, and therefore they are not likely to be disturbed when in it."

He laughed—more gayly than he was in the habit of laughing.

"Have you an exhaustive knowledge of hearts like mine?" he asked. "You talk like a *blasée* flirt of thirty, and the tone is very piquant on such childish lips."

"Childish!" repeated Amy, and the lips in question curled. "If *I* am childish, who is grown? Children don't feel what I do, or desire what I do, or hate what I do. Childish! You don't know what you are talking about, Mr. Marchmont."

"Don't I?" said Mr. Marchmont, with a glitter of amusement in his eyes. "So much the better! If I am ignorant, I must be instructed. Sit down here; I arranged the seat for you. By Jove, how delightful this is! Hereafter I shall go in strongly for pastoral pleasures. Who would exchange such a place as this for any drawing-room on the face of the earth?"

"I am afraid it is damp," suggested Amy, "and a little snaky; but we don't mind about that."

"Not at all. Your friend, Mr. Trafford, might object to the dampness, but fortunately he is not here. As for the snakes, they might come in regiments, and I should defy them. Ah!"—a genuine sigh—"if life were always like this—made up of blue sky and golden sunshine, and flowers and rippling water, and crowned with the oldest and sweetest thing in existence!"

"What is that?" asked Amy, a little wonderingly.

"It is love, my dear," he answered— "love, that sooner or later makes fools of us all. Just now I am perfectly conscious of my folly; but I would not exchange it for the wisdom of sages."

"If you consider it folly, I wonder you indulge it," said Amy, who did not think this very complimentary.

"Do you wonder? That proves you can't see yourself. If you could—bah! what is the good of talking? Love exists because it exists; we know no more than that. Amy, this is not the first time

by many that I have told you I love you,
but you have never yet given me any assurance in return. I have not asked for
it, because of many fetters upon my life;
but now I feel that I must have it.
We are young, hope is strong, the future
can take care of itself; let us make the
most of the sunshine Fate has given us.
Sweetheart"—he drew her into his arms
and kissed her dewy lips passionately
once, twice, thrice—"tell me here, now,
that you love me!"

She looked up, with her eyes shining,
a scarlet fire burning on her cheek. Well
as he knew her beauty, at this moment it
almost electrified him.

"I love you with all my heart!" she
answered. "I never knew what love
meant before, but now I have—"

She stopped as if she had been shot,
and Marchmont drew her quickly back
into the deeper shade behind them. There
had been the sound of a crackling twig
crushed by a hasty foot on the other side
of the creek, and, looking across, they
saw a man's figure disappear in the shim-
mering obscurity of green-and-gold among
the brown tree-boles.

CHAPTER XI.

"WOULD YOU LIKE TO PAY YOUR DEBT?"

"How charmed I am to see you, Beatrix!" said Florence Lathrop, sweeping
into the handsome drawing-room where
Miss Waldron sat. "There is not a soul
at home but myself, and solitude does not
agree with me. Come up to my room,
won't you? It is so much more *sociable*.
What a lovely color you have! I suppose the heat has given it to you."

"Exercise, perhaps," answered Beatrix, as they left the drawing-room—
which certainly had an oppressive air of
state—crossed the hall, and ascended the
broad, easy staircase. "One of the
horses cast a shoe as we entered town; so

I sent the carriage to the blacksmith's,
and have walked from R— Street here."

"How disagreeable!" said Florence,
sympathizingly.

They entered her room as she spoke
—a boudoir-like nest of blue-and-white,
with a pleasant breeze fluttering through
the wide, lace-draped windows.

"Take this chair and rest—or will you
try the couch?"

"This is very comfortable, thank
you," answered Beatrix, sinking into the
depths of the chair and unfurling a
fan. "I am not very tired—only warm.
And so you are the only member of the
household at home? That is singular—
isn't it?"

"It may be singular that I should be
at home, but it is not at all singular that
the rest should be out. Mamma and
Anna are visiting, as usual; papa and Edward are never at home this time of day.
Eunice asked for the pony-phaeton to
drive one of her friends, and Brian has
gone fishing; so here I am all alone, and
delighted to see you!"

"Mr. Marchmont has gone fishing!"
said Beatrix, as carelessly as possible. "I
should not have imagined that he liked
such amusements."

"Nor I," responded her companion;
"but he declares that he is very fond of
it. Edward laughs at him, however, because he never brings back any fish."

"And how does he account for that?
I have observed that when people like to
do a thing, they always do it well; and
fishing, I am sure, is no exception to the
rule."

"Brian says that his object in going
fishing is not so much to catch fish as to
lie on a bank and look at the blue sky and
the green trees and the water, and enjoy
a kind of *dolce far niente*."

"Indeed!" said Miss Waldron. Her
lip curled as she bent forward and arranged a fold of her dress. "I should
never have suspected him of such pastoral
tastes."

. "Probably they have developed because he is in love. I don't know much about the tender passion myself, but I think I have heard that people grow pastoral when they are in love."

"I think I have heard so, too—especially under certain circumstances," said Beatrix, a little dryly. "We need not discuss Mr. Marchmont's tastes, however. If he likes fishing, by all means let him fish; a man whose profession is idleness must do something, I suppose."

"Oh, Beatrix! that is really too severe, when you know that Brian's abilities are so great that he is *certain* to be a very distinguished man one of these days."

Miss Waldron elevated her shapely shoulders slightly, but very significantly. Evidently Mr. Marchmont was not in her good graces at the present time.

"I am afraid somebody has been trying to prejudice you against Brian," said Miss Florence, who, being proud of her cousin, and in a manner attached to him, was sincerely anxious that he should win the young heiress. "Perhaps it was that disagreeable Mr. Archer, who plainly wants to marry you himself."

"Florence!" said Miss Waldron, "what do you mean by such an absurdity?"

"I mean exactly what I say," returned that young lady, "and you need not try to awe me by majestic looks. When Brian first suggested the idea to me, I said that, of course, you knew it—that women always know such things; and I'm sure that is true, for *I* can tell the minute a man falls in love; but when I saw you with Mr. Archer at Cedarwood the other day, I began to think you *didn't* know, and I felt I ought to give you a hint."

"You are very kind," said Beatrix, half amused, half vexed; "but I am not quite so obtuse as you imagine. I, too, can tell when a man is in love, and I am glad to be able to assure you that you are altogether mistaken with regard to Mr. Archer."

"*You* are altogether mistaken, but I am not!" said Miss Florence, energetically. "I would stake anything on the fact that the man is in love with you!"

"You would lose whatever you staked, then," said Beatrix, her vexation getting the better of amusement. "Let us change the subject."

The subject was changed, and when Miss Waldron's carriage was presently announced, she took her departure, having discovered without any trouble all that she wanted to know.

"So Mr. Marchmont goes fishing at the same time that Amy Reynolds goes to walk!" she said to herself. "Not difficult to tell what that means. The question is, how can I end the matter best?—or is it worth ending at all?".

She was still debating this question when her carriage rolled into the gates of Cedarwood, the beautiful grounds stretching away on each side, and looking doubly beautiful in the golden light and long shadows of the westering sun.

As the carriage drew up before the hall-door a young man emerged therefrom. For one moment her heart leaped, and she said to herself that she had done Marchmont injustice, since he was here to meet her—when she saw that, instead of Marchmont, it was Archer!

She was too thoroughly trained in the ways of the world to evince any sign of the recollection of Florence Lathrop's words, which came to her as soon as she saw his dark, quiet face.

She merely uttered an ordinary greeting, and gave him her hand as he assisted her to alight; then, when they were standing on the portico, she said, carelessly:

"I suppose you have been with papa, Mr. Archer?"

"No," Archer answered, "the general is not at home. I hope you will excuse my dusky appearance," he added, with a slight smile. "I have been five or six miles in the country to see a dying client, and, since the day was so fine, I walked to his house and back. I am on my way into Edgerton now, but feeling a little tired, I took the liberty of making a short cut through your grounds, and of resting for a few minutes in the house."

"I am glad you thought of doing so," said Miss Waldron, cordially. "You must come in and take some refreshment —oh, I insist upon it! You need not be afraid that I will offer you cake. I know masculine tastes better than that."

"I am afraid of nothing but kindness from your hands," he answered, with another smile; and for the first time Beatrix noticed how pleasantly his usually grave face lit up when he smiled: "but I will not trouble you, for I must go on to Edgerton. I have special business waiting for me there."

"I am inclined to think that you have forgotten the old fable about the strung bow," she said. "According to the account you give of yourself—and that every one else gives of you—you have always special business waiting for you. When a plea is brought forward so constantly, one is obliged to doubt it a little after a while. Now, will you think me impertinent if I ask what is your business this afternoon, and why it is so pressing that you cannot stay and take a cup of tea with me? I know you like tea, Mr. Archer."

If Beatrix had been questioned, she could hardly have told why she thus urged her point, except that Archer looked worn and tired—surest appeal to a woman's sympathy—and that she resolutely determined to ignore Miss Lathrop's suggestion, and not to let it influence her conduct in the least.

Nevertheless she was forced to see that something in her last speech affected Archer singularly; a strange, swift expression passed over his face, and his eyes suddenly drooped, as if unable to meet her own. He hesitated for an instant, then said, quietly:

"You are very kind, but I cannot wait —not even for the pleasure of drinking a cup of tea with you. I should not have stopped merely to rest, but I wanted a minute to think, and I went into your drawing-room as a good place to collect my thoughts and focus them into a resolution."

"That sounds mysterious," said Miss Waldron, surprised and a little curious; "but I will not be impertinent enough to ask any more point-blank questions."

"I would willingly answer your question, if I could," said Archer, looking at her now—very oddly she felt—"but it is impossible. I wonder," he said, with a change of subject so abrupt that it fairly startled her, "whether women ever care to know anything further of a man than that he is handsome, graceful, and well-versed in drawing-room accomplishments?"

"What on earth has come over him?" thought Beatrix. Aloud, she said: "I don't know about most women, but I can answer decidedly for myself, that I certainly desire to know something more than that. I would trust no man whose integrity failed to bear any test to which it could be subjected. I would never forgive"—and her eyes flashed with a quick remembrance of Marchmont—"anything that came under the head of treachery to myself or another!"

What was there in that glance of Archer's which made her feel as if he was pitying her? He only said, "I hope you may never have to endure it," bowed, and went away.

Beatrix stood still and watched him as he walked across the lawn to the side-gate. "How strange! how very strange!" she said, half aloud. "Surely he must know something. I wish I had asked him plainly what it was."

Archer, who at his best was a capital pedestrian, did not occupy many minutes in reaching Edgerton. Having entered the town, he went straight to his office, wrote a short note, inclosed it in an envelope, which he sealed and addressed to Hugh Dinsmore, and sent it to the boarding-house of the latter, with directions that it be left for him if he was not there.

It chanced that Hugh was there, having just come from Mr. Lathrop's counting-house, where he had been kept unusually busy all day. The boy felt tired in mind and body, but he knew where refreshment awaited him; and, having washed his hands and face in cool fresh water, he opened his paint-box and carried the miniature on which he was engaged, and the one he was copying, to the window, where the last sunset-light fell over them.

While he was intent on these—not painting, but merely gazing, for he knew the supper-bell would ring in a minute—a small person came tumbling up-stairs, vociferating "Hugh! Hugh!" at the top of his voice, and commenced thundering with two fists on the closed door.

"What is the matter, Bobby?" said Hugh, opening it.

Bobby—aged five—replied by extending a note which bore the impress of several dirty fingers. Notes were of unusual occurrence with Hugh, since he had no relations and few friends in Edgerton; so he received this with a sense of wonder. Was it from Amy? No; the firm, masculine hand which appeared on the address answered that question at once. Opening the envelope, he found within a few lines from Archer, requesting him to call at that gentleman's office. "Come at once, if possible," he wrote; "I have an engagement for the evening, and cannot see you after eight o'clock."

Hugh was all afire with eagerness as soon as he read these words. That the matter in hand was another commission, he did not for a moment doubt. While he glanced over the note, a clock down-stairs struck seven, and at the same moment a bell rang loudly. "There's supper!" cried Bobby, pitching away.

Though Hugh had a healthy appetite, supper was at the present moment a matter of no importance to him. Afraid that he should not find Archer if he delayed at all, he seized his hat, forgot for the first time to lock up the precious Waldron miniature, closed his door, and ran down-stairs.

Ten minutes later he entered Archer's office, and found the latter there.

"You are very prompt, Dinsmore," he said. "I did not expect you so soon."

"I started the minute I got your note," said Hugh, a little breathless from his haste. "I thought the matter might be important, so I did not even wait for supper."

"You must take supper with me, then," said Archer, smiling; "I did not mean to express such great urgency. The matter is important, but not of immediate haste. Sit down."

Hugh sat down, and, in the moment's silence which ensued, began to suspect that there was no commission in the case after all.

Archer was folding up some papers with which he had been occupied, and he put them away before he turned, and said:

"I hope you will excuse me if I ask a very abrupt and very personal question: Do you remember that evening I found you senseless in the road beyond Edgerton?"

Hugh's surprise at this unexpected question could not easily be expressed, and was strongly dashed with other feelings. For an instant he was so thoroughly "taken aback" that he could not speak; but when he answered, there was no mistaking the vibration of indignant pride in his voice, though the gathering twilight concealed the flush that burned on his face.

"I am not likely to forget it," he said; "but I don't know any reason why you should remind me of a thing that concerns nobody but myself."

"Indirectly, it may concern others besides yourself," said Archer; "and it is because of this that I have sent for you, in order to request you to be frank with me. I know that you had some kind of an altercation with Marchmont, and that he flung you—being much younger and slighter than himself—where I found you. I *know* this; what I want you to tell me is the subject of your quarrel."

"You have no right to ask me such a question!" said Hugh, with growing indignation. "You would not do so if I were a man, and your equal! I will not tell you anything about it!"

"Then I must tell *you*," said Archer. "The subject of your dispute—or whatever name you choose to give to the affair—was the daughter of Mr. Reynolds, the music-teacher."

"How did you know?" asked Hugh. Then he caught himself. "I mean, you do not know anything about it," he said; "and, if this is all you want with me, I might as well go."

He rose as he spoke; but Archer rose also, and laid a hand on his shoulder.

"This is nonsense!" Archer said. "You have betrayed yourself, even if I had not known exactly how the matter stood before. No doubt you are in love with the girl, but she is not worth shielding. I saw her with Marchmont to-day."

"You saw her!" said Hugh, with a gasp. "Where?"

"In the woods," the young lawyer answered. "Marchmont and herself were there together, and, when I came unexpectedly upon them, she was in his arms," as Hugh started and quivered from head to foot; "but this is probably only folly on *her* part. What it is on his, I won't pretend to say; but one thing is certain: if you want to end it, you had better be frank with me."

"But why do you want to know anything? How does it concern you?" said Hugh, writhing like one in pain.

"I want to know," said Archer, "because I don't choose that a man like this shall marry such a woman as Miss Waldron. I am thinking of her. Amy Reynolds is nothing to me. You owe Miss Waldron something for her kindness to you; you owe Marchmont something for the manner in which he left you lying on the highway. Would you not like to pay both these debts?"

Hugh looked up, and, even in the dusk, Archer was struck by those clear eyes of which he had heard Beatrix speak.

"I would like," he said, slowly, "to save Amy from suffering and from slander; that is all."

"To accomplish that," said Archer, "you must send Marchmont from Edgerton. As far as I know, but one thing keeps him here—his suit with Miss Waldron; and I am sure that when she is aware that, while addressing her, he has been carrying on a love-affair with a girl whom he can have no idea of marrying, she will dismiss him at once."

"Do you think so?" asked Hugh, doubtfully. "I—of course, I know nothing about such things, but I have heard people say that a woman hardly ever cares what a man has done to another woman."

"I don't believe it," said Archer, "of women in general, but I know it is not true of Miss Waldron. Such treachery as this would turn her to steel," he said, thinking of the flash he had seen in the dark eyes so short a time before. "But you have not told me yet when this—flirtation, shall I say?—began. Let me hear all about it."

Some men have a faculty for inspiring confidence, and Archer was one of these. Nobody ever felt a doubt of his entire trustworthiness, and Hugh found it almost a relief to tell all that he knew of Marchmont's acquaintance with Amy. Archer grasped the story without difficulty. An idle man of the world, lover of pleasure and admirer of beauty, a foolish, flattered girl hardly emerged from childhood—what an old combination was here! Were there any materials to work a new result? he wondered.

"Unless I am greatly mistaken, that girl is not a mere pretty doll," he thought, recalling Amy's face as he had seen it once or twice. "She may turn amusement into something else before the matter is ended."

This, however, was the merest thought in passing. Amy might be everything to Hugh, but she was nothing to him. The only person to be considered, from *his* point of view, was Beatrix Waldron. He had not the faintest hope of marrying her himself—in fact, such an idea did not enter his mind at all—but he was sternly determined to do all that lay in his power to save her from the fate of marrying Brian Marchmont.

After Hugh's story had been told, he reflected for a while, then said that he would consider how the substance could best be given to Miss Waldron. For obvious reasons he felt that it would be impossible for *him* to tell it.

"If all other expedients fail, do you think that you would have courage to go to her, Dinsmore?" he asked.

"I think I could—for Amy's sake," answered Hugh.

Archer shook his head.

"My poor fellow," he said, "you think entirely too much of Amy. When a man regards a woman in that way, do you know how she treats him?"

"I think I do," replied Hugh, ruefully.

"Generally speaking, she makes a football of him," said Archer. "But it is growing late, and I must not forget that you have had no supper. Come and take it with me at my hotel."

This Hugh declined doing.

"I can get something from Mrs. Sargent," he said; "she is very kind. I am much obliged, but I had rather not trouble you, Mr. Archer."

"Trouble!" said Archer. "I am not a housekeeper."

But Hugh still declined the invitation, and went away to his own lodging-house. In truth, supper was a matter of small consideration to him, compared to the pleasure of returning to his painting. Nevertheless, he was not sorry to find that Mrs. Sargent had put aside some bread and butter and coffee for him.

"What possessed you to run away just when supper was ready?" she said, while he sat down to these. "Bobby said you got a note; it surely must have been from your sweetheart."

"No, it wasn't," said Hugh, with as much of a sigh as was compatible with eating bread and butter. "It was from a gentleman—on business."

"Well," said the friendly woman, "I hope the business is of a kind to bring some money in your pocket, for I declare it goes to my heart to see how shabby your clothes are. Mr. Lathrop might pay you better for slaving day after day, I think."

"He pays me well enough," said Hugh; "and you know I told you, Mrs. Sargent, that the reason I dress so shabbily is, that I am saving all my money to go away some day and learn how to paint."

"A fine sight of money you will make at that!" said Mrs. Sargent, scornfully. "Why can't people be satisfied when they are well off, I say? There's Felix Reynolds, who I hear is going away to learn music—as if he couldn't see from his father's example what is to be made at that! If Mr. Reynolds would put the boy to some trade, he'd be doing a better part by him. He was here a while ago—Felix, I mean—and said he was sorry not to find you."

"Did he want anything in particular?"

"Not that I know of. I heard somebody go up-stairs to your room, and I thought perhaps it was you, till presently he came down again and put his head in the door to ask where you was. He looked white and excited-like. Somehow I don't think that boy's going to live long."

"Oh, he has an excitable temperament," said Hugh. "That don't kill people.—Well, Mrs. Sargent, I am very much obliged to you for the supper, which I have enjoyed greatly, and now I'll go up-stairs."

"And sit up all night at your painting," said Mrs. Sargent, shaking her head in warning reproof.

Hugh smiled and went away, bounding up-stairs three steps at a time. He was never so happy as when his colors were before him and his brush in his hand. His facility in executing the commission which Miss Waldron had given astonished himself. Inspiration seemed to come to his aid where technical knowledge was lacking, and, although he had worked under every possible disadvantage, the result justified his most sanguine belief in his own powers.

When he reached his room he found the door slightly ajar. This did not surprise him, for he knew that he had not locked it on going out, and that Felix had been to the room since then. He entered, struck a match, and lighted the argand-lamp, which, with its steady, powerful burner, he had found absolutely indispensable for his work, and which was one of the most precious and expensive of his few possessions. Having placed the lamp in position and arranged his things ready for painting, he turned to the casket of the miniature. To his surprise, it was open and empty. For a second, dismay seemed to grasp him like the hand of a strong man, when he remembered that he had taken the picture out just before Archer's note was brought to him. With an ejaculation on his carelessness, he turned to the window where he had been standing. There, on the ledge, lay the fold of white paper which contained his half-finished miniature, but that which had been intrusted to him was gone!

CHAPTER XII.

"AN ABSOLUTE STROKE OF LUCK."

HAVING slowly wandered home with Amy through the exquisite May twilight —twilight which seemed especially made for lovers and mocking-birds, and in which other classes of the world's population merely existed on sufferance, and were wholly out of place—Marchmont felt averse to taking leave when Mr. Reynolds's door was reached. Amy looked bewitchingly pretty in the soft gloaming; it was "the hour when lovers' vows sound sweet in every whispered word;" and, altogether, he was strongly inclined to defer his return from Bohemianism to respectability. If Amy had said "Come in to tea," he would have gone in; but Amy had no mind to say anything of the kind. Mr. Reynolds would not only have been reasonably astonished at such a step, and would certainly have demanded an explanation; but Amy shuddered when she thought of Marchmont being introduced to the family dining-room, where hideous serviceable delf alone crowned the family table. There are some rare people whose breeding is of such an exquisite quality, that they would make no sign of recognizing the difference between the table of a laborer and that of a millionaire; but she felt instinctively that Marchmont did not belong to this class. Cut-glass and silver, damask and Sèvres, were the necessities of life to him; and nothing revolted his fastidiousness so thoroughly as coarseness and ugliness in any degree.

Amy knew this as much through sympathy as anything else, for they revolted her to the centre of her soul, and had always done so. Parting was very unpleasant, but she clearly recognized the necessity for it, and held out her hand with an unmistakable gesture of farewell when they paused on the door-step.

"And must I go?" said Marchmont.

"That is very hard. I don't feel like going at all. I prefer sitting down here, and defying Mrs. Grundy to say and do her worst."

"What would Mrs. Grundy's worst be to you?" demanded Amy. "Not that I should care for anything she could say of me," she added, with a slight, defiant toss of her head; "but there's papa to be considered. He has told me not to stand here and talk to gentlemen, so I must go."

"You have stood and talked to gentlemen before, then?" said Marchmont, a little suspiciously. It is in the nature of man to be jealous, and certainly no more winsome face than Amy's at this moment ever served as an excuse for jealousy.

She caught the intonation, and laughed —a peal of mirth that rang out sweetly on the soft air. "Do you think you are the only gentleman I ever talked to?" she asked, saucily. "That's not likely— is it?"

"I think you have about as much *diablerie* in you as any of your sex whom I have ever known—and that is saying a great deal," replied Marchmont. "But let us hear the names of the gentlemen. Come! confession is good for the soul, you know."

"I don't know," said Amy, delighted at the attraction which was detaining him, yet anxious for him to go, since Mr. Reynolds, or Clara, might appear at any moment; "I think it is very foolish of people to give evidence against themselves. But I have nothing to confess," she added, with a sigh. "No doubt I should be a great flirt, if I had a chance; but nobody has ever given me a chance."

"I will!" said Marchmont. "You can practise on me! I offer myself heroically on the shrine of your future greatness, and some day, when you are breaking hearts by the score in the most scientific manner, you will give me a place in your memory as the first trophy of your skill."

The words of laughing jest were light enough, but the dark, daring eyes—irresistible eyes, a hundred young ladies had called them—were full of earnestness as they gazed at that rose-bud face. Under that gaze Amy's lashes sank, and the color wavered in her fair cheeks.

A place in her memory! There could be little doubt of that. Whether for good or evil, friend or foe, Brian Marchmont could not fail to command recollection at least.

"I wish—" she said, suddenly, and then paused.

"Well," said her companion, after waiting an instant and finding she did not go on, "what do you wish? That you were *prima-donna assoluta*, with all Paris at your feet?"

"No; I was not thinking of that," she answered, glancing at him with something of a child's wistfulness; "I was about to say that I wish I knew what you and I will be to each other—in life."

"Oh!" said Marchmont, slightly discomfited. He lifted his hand and pulled the end of his silky mustache before answering. Then he said, carelessly: "Such thoughts are unpleasant, my dear, and not worth troubling one's head over. We know nothing—absolutely nothing— about to-morrow; but we have to-day in our grasp, and we are fools if we do not take all that it offers us of pleasure. There's no better philosophy in life than that of gathering roses while we may; and you and I have gathered some this afternoon—have we not, my pretty Amy?"

The tone in which he uttered her name was equivalent to a caress, but Amy did not answer. Looking up at that moment, she saw one of the greatest gossips in the neighborhood—a stout woman, with the waddling gait that stout women often have—bearing along the sidewalk toward her.

"Dear me!" she said, under her breath, "yonder comes Mrs. Simpson, and she will stop and talk, and—and— oh, I must go! Good-by!"

She darted into the house so rapidly that Marchmont had not time for a word. In fact, he was so completely taken by surprise that he could only gaze blankly at the door for a minute, while Mrs. Simpson—who knew perfectly who *he* was—indulged in a prolonged stare at his profile. Rousing suddenly to a consciousness of this, he flung one haughty glance at her, then sprang up the step or two which intervened between himself and the door, and vanished in turn.

"If I ever saw the like!" said Mrs. Simpson to herself, as she waddled along. "He seems as much at home in the house as if he lived there. If that girl don't come to harm yet, *I'm* mistaken!"

Careless of any comments to which his conduct could give rise, Marchmont paused in the dusky passage and looked round, but there was no sign of Amy. No doubt she had ascended the staircase which wound upward before him. He would not call, for fear of rousing some one else to respond; so he entered the parlor, determined to wait and intercept her when she descended.

"I only want to say one word," he muttered to himself, in justification of this step. "I must tell her that I shall not be able to see her to-morrow."

The twilight, which by this time reigned over the outer world, was, of course, much deeper within a room which was generally in shadow at noon-day.

After stumbling against two or three pieces of furniture, Marchmont found a chair, in which he sat down. Just behind him, in a recess, was a sofa, but he was not aware of its proximity, else he might have essayed to make himself comfortable on that.

He had not been sitting here more than two minutes—though they seemed twenty—when hasty footsteps entered the house from the street. The next instant Oliver rushed into the dark parlor.

"Amy!" he cried, quickly—"Amy! are you here?"

"She is not here," said Marchmont, who did not fancy the prospect of interruption. "Is anybody dead, or dying, my good fellow, that you make such an uproar?"

"No, there's nobody dead, or dying," replied Oliver, in a tone of surprise. "You are Mr. Marchmont, aren't you?" he added, drawing nearer. "Are you here all by yourself? Where's Amy?"

"I can give no information on that point. She disappeared a minute ago, and I don't know where she has gone."

"I've got something to tell her, and something to show her!" said Oliver, in a tone of triumphant excitement. "It's the best joke on her, and on Hugh Dinsmore, that ever was! You know," he went on, "Hugh's been awful spooney about Amy for a long time, and Amy don't believe he ever thought of any other girl but her. Well, some of us boys are going to have theatricals round in Tom White's barn to-night, and I went to Hugh's room a little while ago to get him to paint me for an Indian, but he wasn't there. Then I thought I could paint myself, if I had the stuff, so I commenced rummaging among his things, when I found a picture of such a pretty girl, that I made up my mind in a minute I'd bring it and show it to Amy, and let *her* give it back to Hugh. Won't she be astonished?—and won't *he* be astonished? Ha! ha!"

"A very good joke indeed!" said Marchmont. "Let me see the picture."

"It's a stunner!" said Oliver. "But you can't see it here—come to the window."

Marchmont advanced to the window, where the lingering May twilight enabled him to see at once that the picture in question was, as he had suspected, the Waldron miniature.

The light was too dim to distinguish the painting, but the pearl setting and rich gold chain were sufficient to identify it.

He was silent for a moment, and in that moment his resolution was taken. If he could obtain possession of the picture, and induce the boy to hold his tongue, he might—after having retained it for a day or two in order to give Hugh as much trouble as he deserved—by returning it to Miss Waldron, vindicate his own opinion, and prove not only Hugh's untrustworthiness, but Archer's also, since Archer had recommended and indorsed the young artist.

The idea was tempting. The question was, how could he obtain possession of the picture in the first instance, and secure Oliver's silence in the second?

While he was considering whether or not to offer a bribe, Oliver spoke:

"You can't see it well," he said, regretfully. "It's awfully pretty! I'd go and bring a candle, only I'm expecting Tom White every minute. I wish Amy would come!"

"If she don't come in time, you can leave it with me, and I will give it to her," said Marchmont.

"She's up-stairs, I suspect; I'll take it up there," said Oliver, who had no mind to lose the pleasure of his joke. "You see, I'm going home with Tom White to-night, for all his people are away, and to-morrow we're going fishing, so I sha'n't see Amy again till to-morrow evening. Hullo! here's Tom now."

A bullet-head appeared framed in the open window, as he spoke, and a boy's voice said:

"Is that you, Oliver? Come along! The fellows will be round by eight, sharp, and we are not *near* ready!"

"You had better give me the picture," said Marchmont, in a low voice.

Oliver hesitated an instant; then, "Be sure and tell Amy that it's the likeness of Hugh's sweetheart," he said, and darted eagerly away.

It was not Marchmont's habit to indulge in soliloquy, but, after standing for a minute motionless where Oliver left him, he uttered a subdued laugh, and spoke aloud: "Hugh's sweetheart! Rather

better than that, my friend," he said. "By Jove! this is an absolute stroke of luck!"

At that moment a step sounded on the staircase, and he plunged the miniature hastily into one of the outside pockets of his coat.

It was not Amy who was descending, however — unless Amy knew how to swear.

"What the deuce is the reason that there is no light anywhere?" demanded an irritable voice. "Clara, is there to be no supper to-night?"

"Ready now, sir!" responded a voice from the farther extremity of the house, followed by an immediate clatter of dishes.

With a sigh, Marchmont resigned himself to the prospect of not seeing Amy again. He was so far gone in what he did not hesitate to term "idiocy," that he felt this to be a deprivation not easily borne. There was no alternative, however. Mr. Reynolds had gone into the dining-room; in another minute he might emerge with a lamp, and retreat be cut off.

Marchmont returned hastily to the place where he had been sitting when Oliver entered, felt about in the dark for his hat—by no means an easy task, for he came in contact with various objects, which caused him to utter some forcible ejaculations—placed that article on his head as soon as discovered, and took his departure.

. . . .

"You must have found fishing more than usually entertaining this afternoon, Brian," said Edward Lathrop, with a laugh, as they sat at dinner half an hour later—the Lathrops and Waldrons had introduced the fashion of late dining at Edgerton. "Pray, was your luck any better? When are we to have the pleasure of eating some fish of your catching?"

"I think I have remarked before," replied Marchmont, with unruffled calm-

5

ness, "that catching fish is the least agreeable feature of fishing."

"It is very fortunate that you think so," remarked Mr. Lathrop, senior, "since the fishes are plainly in no danger from you, my dear boy. If your fishing is conducted in the neighborhood of Cedarwood, that might, perhaps, account for the fact. Ha! ha! ha!"

"Oh, no, indeed, papa; you are very much mistaken," said Miss Florence. "At least, if Cedarwood is a distraction, it is a very unconscious one. Beatrix was here this afternoon, and she expressed a great deal of surprise at Brian's fancy; she had never imagined him addicted to pastoral amusements, she said."

"I suppose it would be useless to expect a woman to understand the pleasure of sport in any form," said Edward Lathrop.—"I don't at all object to fishing myself, and I think I'll go with you to-morrow, Brian, and see if the fish about here have forgotten how to bite."

"You can't go to-morrow," said Miss Anna Lathrop, "for we are all going to Cedarwood to a croquet-party."

"Is it to-morrow that you are due at Cedarwood?" said Mrs. Lathrop, looking up—in explanation of which it may be added that a croquet-club existed in Edgerton, which met weekly at the house of some one of the members.

"Yes, to-morrow," said Florence. "I am always glad when the turn of Cedarwood comes; everything is so pleasant there. It will be delightful to feel, some day, that one has a cousinly right in such a charming place," she added, with a laugh, and a mischievous glance at Brian.

"It is never wise to count chickens before they are hatched," said Mr. Lathrop, with a smile which seemed to imply that he thought there was little danger of the chickens in question not being satisfactorily hatched.

"It is not in good taste to make such remarks, Florence," said Mrs. Lathrop, with a very unusual sharpness of tone.

There was a little stir of surprise among the company. The girls looked at their mother, and then at their cousin; but the countenance of the latter was imperturbable.

"Cedarwood is certainly a charming place," he said. "I shall not much mind sacrificing myself to croquet — though generally I consider it the greatest bore of modern social life—if the sacrifice is to take place there."

Notwithstanding this nonchalance, he had a very decided foreboding of what was to come; and he was not in the least surprised when, after dinner, his aunt summoned him into the back drawing-room, where she sat alone, in a large chair near the open window, through which the air of the soft May night came laden with delicious sweetness.

The front drawing-room was brilliantly lighted, but this room was left in partial obscurity, and, when Marchmont entered, he could only perceive the outlines of Mrs. Lathrop's figure and the fan she was slowly waving back and forth.

"You will find a chair here just in front of me, Brian," she said. "Sit down; I have something to say to you."

"I am all attention," answered Brian, quietly, as he sat down.

He knew as well what Mrs. Lathrop meant to say as she knew herself, and he awaited the disclosure with a certain sense of amusement, in which irritation mingled but did not predominate.

Mrs. Lathrop on her part was glad of the semi-darkness, for she felt a sense of awkwardness altogether new to her. She, who managed all the social affairs of Edgerton, who never hesitated to advise the irresolute and admonish those who strayed from the path of right-doing, was oddly conscious of having on hand at the present moment a culprit beyond the pale of her authority—one who would probably neglect her advice and scorn her admonitions.

She hardly acknowledged this consciousness to herself, and she certainly did not mean to betray any sign of it in her manner, but instinctively she mounted a rather higher horse than usual, when she began:

"I regret to interfere in what you may probably consider no affair of mine, Brian," she said, in a very stately manner; "but since you are staying in my house—and I have always regarded you very much as I do my own sons—I feel it my duty to warn you, when I have learned that you are committing a very grave imprudence."

Marchmont smiled to himself at this address — a scornful, impatient smile, which the darkness fortunately concealed.

"Confound the woman! why can't she speak out plainly?" he thought; then, with the utmost coolness, he said:

"You are very kind, I am sure; but may I ask, Of what imprudence have I been guilty?"

"It is hardly possible that you do not know to what I allude," said Mrs. Lathrop, with an accession of dignity. "To-day I went to see Mrs. Ripley, an invalid who boards at Mrs. Crenshaw's, and there, to my utter amazement, I heard for the first time of your *intimate* acquaintance with that badly-reared girl, the daughter of Eunice's music-teacher."

"Poor little Amy!" said Marchmont, with a cadence of amusement which even caught Mrs. Lathrop's ear. "Is it possible, Aunt Caroline, that you regard my acquaintance with her in the light of a grave imprudence?"

Mrs. Lathrop felt that this was offensive levity, and she grew colder and stiffer in consequence.

"I certainly regard it in that light, when I consider the character of the girl, and your object here," she said. "You cannot blind me by any such tone as that, Brian. I have not reached my age without acquiring some knowledge of the world. If you came here to marry Be-

atrix Waldron, and if you want to marry her, you had better not spend hours every day in the society of a girl who, young as she is, has already acquired a reputation for being what is called 'fast.'"

"My acquaintance with her was entirely accidental," said Brian, who felt that he must enter a plea of defense. "I have gone to her father's house simply to hear her sing, for she has a most wonderful voice. She seemed to me a mere child—not older, I should think, than Eunice."

"If she is a mere child, she neither looks nor acts like one," said Mrs. Lathrop. "I don't think *that* alters the matter at all; and I warn you that people are talking of it, and that, if such reports come to Beatrix Waldron's ears, your chances with her will be ruined."

"I must differ with you on that point," said Marchmont, calmly. "Miss Waldron has not only heard me speak of my visits to Mr. Reynolds's house, but it was by my advice that she asked Amy to sing at her *fête*."

Mrs. Lathrop was so much surprised at this, that for a moment she was silent. It did not take her long, however, to rally her forces.

"That may be possible," she said, "and yet Beatrix may not know the extent of your intimacy, or the gossip that has risen with regard to it. No doubt you feel that it is altogether your own affair"—this was so true, that Marchmont did not contradict her—"but, although I have no good opinion of the girl, I shall make it *my* affair sufficiently to warn her father that he had better look more carefully after her, if he does not wish her to suffer seriously in her reputation."

"Aunt Caroline," said Marchmont, starting with an energy which contrasted very strongly with his previous indifference, "you surely will do no such thing!"

"I certainly shall do it, for the sake of Mr. Reynolds, whom I have known as an honest, hard-working man," answered

Mrs. Lathrop, majestically. Then she rose. "This has been an unpleasant duty, Brian, but I have discharged it *as a duty*," she said. "My conscience being clear, I shall not trouble you with the subject again. Though I do not think Beatrix and yourself calculated to make each other happy, I will not interfere in any manner with your suit; but if this matter is told to her, as it has been told to me, she is far too proud a woman to forgive it."

The clear tones ceased, the speaker swept away with a rustle of silk, and Marchmont found himself alone, with feelings more uncomfortable than he had at all anticipated.

It would be difficult to say whether, for a time, anger, disgust, or contempt possessed him most strongly. In these sentiments his aunt, himself, Beatrix, everybody except Amy, shared. It seemed incredible that *he* should be the subject of petty village gossip—should be lectured like a schoolboy, and hampered in the pursuit of any amusement that offered itself to him. "I have half a mind to turn my back on the whole affair!" he thought, with wrathful scorn. Naturally, however, other counsels prevailed. "It is fate!" he thought, with that convenient optimism which comes so easily to men. "I must stay until the last act is played. How lovely she is!" He was thinking of Amy's face as she lifted it that afternoon, when he wrung from her a confession of her love. "Many men in my place would play the villain; indeed, a few would fling all thoughts of the world to the winds! *I* shall simply linger a little longer, and then go, leaving only a girl's bruised fancy behind. Such things are often good for women who have a public career before them. She will be all the more invincible for being a little hardened."

It was natural, no doubt, that of the cost of this hardening Mr. Marchmont did not pause to think—epicurean philosophers in his position rarely do; but, as he leaned back in his chair, deaf to the strains of the piano, or the gay voices and laughter which issued from the next room, one hand unconsciously sought his coat-pocket, and the gesture reminded him of the miniature which had so strangely come into his possession a short time before.

It was not in his pocket, since he had hastily changed his dress on returning to the house in time for dinner, and he now remembered that he had left the coat which he took off lying across a chair, with the miniature still in its pocket. "How careless!" he thought, as he rose at once and went to his chamber—not because he feared that anything would befall the picture, or that any one could possibly chance to see it, but because he wished to examine it before putting it away.

The coat was lying exactly where he had thrown it, and, taking it up, he ran his hand into the pocket where the miniature had been placed. It encountered only a handkerchief! He hurriedly drew this out, and felt again; there was nothing! He turned the pocket inside out; still nothing! Then he plunged his hand in succession into all the pockets, examining each one carefully. The result with each was identical—the miniature was not to be found.

When he fully realized this, he stood gazing blankly at the coat, which he held by the collar; then he went over all the pockets again, and felt the lining carefully around each one; then he shook the garment violently, and, all measures failing to produce the missing picture, flung it aside and began examining the carpet under and around the chair over which it had been thrown. From this place his search extended throughout the room; but, after all probable and improbable places had been searched, he was obliged to face the same fact which had brought dismay to Hugh Dinsmore's breast a few hours before.

The miniature was gone!

CHAPTER XIII.

"WHERE IS THE MINIATURE?"

THE Reynolds family, with the exception of Oliver—whose absence was hardly observed and not at all remarked—were assembled at supper, when Hugh Dinsmore suddenly burst in upon them, his face white, his eyes startled, his lips apart.

"Mercy, Hugh! what is the matter?" cried Amy, who saw him first; but, for once, Hugh paid no attention to her presence or her words. He did not even seem to hear her; his eyes sought only one face, and, when they found that, he cried, breathlessly:

"Felix, for Heaven's sake, give me that picture! This is a poor jest!"

"Give you what?" asked Felix, amazed. "I have nothing of yours."

"You have!" cried Hugh. "You *must* have, Felix!" There was absolute agony in his tone. "This is no time for trifling. I ran every step of the way here as soon as I discovered the picture was gone, and I said to myself, at every step, 'Felix has taken it for a jest.' But it is a cruel jest! Give it to me."

"I don't know what you are talking about," said Felix, bewildered. "I have not any picture of yours! I went to your room a little while ago, but you were not there, so I did not stop a minute; I ran down-stairs and asked Mrs. Sargent about you, and, when she said she didn't know when you would be back, I came away. How could you think I would touch your things—much less carry anything off?"

Hugh's face seemed to sharpen momently in anxiety. He clutched the back of a chair, and looked at the boy with a gaze of passionate entreaty.

"Mrs. Sargent declares that you are the only person who went to my room during my absence," he said. "The picture that I left by the window is gone.

Who else could have taken it? Felix, I can never believe that you meant harm if you will only give it back—give it *now!*"

"What is the meaning of this?" asked Mr. Reynolds, whom astonishment had kept quiet. "What is he talking about, Felix?"

"It seems he suspects me of having taken some picture out of his room," answered Felix. "I don't know any more than that. I didn't enter his room; I only looked in, and I touched nothing."

Mr. Reynolds turned to Hugh, with the blood mounting in a dark tide to his face.

"You hear that!" he said, haughtily. "My son's denial is sufficient—though how you could have ventured to suspect him, I do not understand."

"How could I help it?" said Hugh, hoarsely. "The picture is gone—the picture that was trusted to me—and that means everything for me. No one went to my room during my absence but Felix—"

"And you dare to think that Felix took your picture!" cried Amy, with eyes all ablaze. "Hasn't he told you that he did not touch it? I never heard anything more infamous! You will say next that he *stole* it!"

"Hush, Amy!" said Felix. He alone understood the terrible blankness that came over Hugh's face, and, rising from his seat, he walked round the table and touched the elder boy's hand. "I did not take it," he said, gently. "On my honor, I touched nothing in your room. If you have lost anything valuable, let us go and look for it."

"Look for it! I *have* looked!" cried poor Hugh. "It is gone—utterly gone! If you have not got it, Felix, I am ruined!"

The despair of the last words touched even Amy.

"What was it, Hugh? Surely not Miss Waldron's miniature?" she said.

"Yes; Miss Waldron's miniature!" answered Hugh.

Then he told his woful story—how he had been called away from his room; how for the first time he had neglected to lock up the miniature, and how it had disappeared.

"God only knows what I am to do!" he said, twining and untwining his thin, nervous fingers. "I do not know where to turn—what to do! There was no one in my room but Felix—"

Mr. Reynolds pushed back his chair and rose from the table.

"You harp on that," he said, sternly, "as if you doubted Felix's assurance that he did not touch the picture. I am sorry for your misfortune, but you have plainly only your own carelessness to blame. The sooner you realize this, the better.—Felix, come with me; I am going to Herr Meerbach's."

He walked out of the room, but Felix paused to throw his arms around Hugh's neck.

"I am not vexed," he whispered. "I know you don't mean anything. I wish I had taken the picture; then I could give it back to you. I am so sorry—so sorry!"

"I am satisfied with your word that you did not take it," said Hugh, huskily. "I never thought you had done so—except as a jest."

"Was it your picture, Hugh?" asked Ernest, curiously, unable to understand such excessive concern with regard to the property of any one else.

"Eat you supper, and don't ask questions about what don't concern you!" said Amy, sharply.—"Come into the parlor with me, Hugh."

Hugh followed her, and they entered the room where, a short time before, the miniature, which was causing him so much wretchedness, had changed hands.

By the very window where Oliver and Marchmont had stood Amy sat down, while Hugh paced back and forth like an unquiet spirit.

"What is the good of taking the thing so desperately to heart, Hugh?" she said,

watching him. "I don't believe anybody has stolen the picture. What would anybody want with it? It is valuable to the Waldrons, no doubt; but nobody else would consider it so."

"You are mistaken," said Hugh. "It is not only valuable as a work of art, but it is set in very fine pearls.—I feel as if I were wasting time in staying here!" he cried out, suddenly; "but what can I do?—where can I go?"

Amy could give him no advice on this point. She offered vague consolation in the form of a remark that she had no doubt the miniature would "turn up;" but beyond that she was not able to venture.

"I have no hope of such a thing," said Hugh. "It is not lost—it has been taken. Who would take it and return it? My only hope was that Felix had done so. But, whoever has taken it, the responsibility and the suspicion fall on me."

"I am sorry," said Amy.

The words were so gentle, that, in the midst of all his trouble, Hugh's heart gave a throb. Despite his wretchedness, he could not feel that everything was lost when Amy was sorry.

"It seemed as if life was beginning for me—the kind of life I desire," he said, with something like a sob in his voice. "Now it is all over! I must go to Mr. Archer and tell him. Oh, what will he and Miss Waldron think of me?"

"Why should you go to Mr. Archer?" asked Amy. "He is a very disagreeable person—isn't he?"

"He has never been disagreeable to me," said Hugh; and then he remembered that it was Archer's summons which made him leave the miniature, and what the cause of that summons was.

So great had been his distress and anxiety that for a time he had entirely forgotten this. Now it came back to him like a dart of pain. He stopped abruptly and looked at the girl, who was sitting by the open casement in the dim light. Should he tell her?—would there be any good in telling her what he had heard?"

"Amy," he said, after a minute, "the last time that I saw you I made you angry. I shall be sorry to make you angry again, but I cannot help it. I *must* warn you once more that Marchmont is acting toward you like a scoundrel!"

"What do you know of him? What do you mean by saying such a thing to me?" asked Amy, with quick defiance. "One would think you had some right to interfere with my affairs; but you have not the least!"

"Only the right of loving you a great deal better than *he* does," said Hugh. "I would sooner die than harm you; but he is harming you more than you know. You are quite young, but have you no pride of a woman," he said, pausing before her, "that you let a man make love to you, and win your heart, when he has no idea of marrying you?"

Something in the grave, half-sorrowful words thrilled Amy. She was not so much a child but that she had a little of that "pride of a woman" of which Hugh spoke, and it now brought the blood to her cheeks in a tide.

"You don't know what you are talking about," she said, haughtily, "and you are meddling in what does not concern you. If Mr. Marchmont and I understand each other, that is enough."

"I doubt very much if you understand *him*," said Hugh. "He is amusing himself with you, my poor Amy; and, when he is tired, he will leave you, without one thought of your distress."

"I am not afraid of it," said Amy. "I know that you think me a fool; but a woman—even one so young as I am—can tell when a man really loves her."

"Then, if he really loves you," said Hugh, "what part is he playing with another woman? He certainly is trying to marry Miss Waldron."

"I don't believe it!" she flashed out. "I don't believe anything you tell me of

him! You have never liked him—you were jealous of him from the first."

"Yes, I have been jealous of him," the quiet tones replied—tones that she could hardly recognize as Hugh's; "but I am not jealous any longer. I have heard—Amy, do you know what I have heard this evening?"

"How should I know?" asked Amy; but she shrank a little as she spoke.

Conscience makes cowards of us all. She remembered how often she had met Marchmont lately, and she doubted not that some rumor of those meetings had come to Hugh's ears.

As for Hugh, the words which he would fain have uttered seemed to choke him. He felt that he literally could not repeat Archer's account. Instead of doing so, he held out his hand, abruptly.

"Good-by," he said. "I can do no good here. You will not heed me; you do not believe me. If I serve you, it must be in another way."

"There is no way in which you can serve me," answered Amy, proudly. Then she softened a little. "Good-by; and oh, I hope you will find the picture!" she said.

"Would to God I had never seen it!" Hugh answered, in a tone of despair.

From the Reynolds house he went straight to the hotel where Archer lodged, and fortunately found the latter, who heard of the loss of the miniature with great surprise and concern.

For a moment—only for a moment—he looked suspiciously at Hugh; but it was impossible to doubt the genuine distress and anxiety which the boy was enduring; and the young lawyer was too shrewd a judge of human nature to mistake reality for a counterfeit.

"I am truly sorry that the loss was owing to my summons," he said; "but this gives me an additional reason for making every possible effort to recover the picture. Whom do you suspect of the theft? Are there any dishonest servants in your boarding-house?"

"There is only one servant," answered Hugh, "and she was occupied at the time, for the family were at supper. Mrs. Sargent is positive that nobody in the house went to my room while I was out."

"Nobody *in* the house! Did somebody out of the house go to it, then?"

"Felix Reynolds went to it," answered Hugh, who knew that Mrs. Sargent would tell this if he failed to do so. 'I have been to him, but he says that he did not touch the picture—that he did not even enter the room when he found I was not there."

"What he says is of small importance," returned Mr. Archer. "If he was the only person who went to your room during your absence, he must have taken the picture."

"I am *sure* he did not!" said Hugh, eagerly. "You don't know Felix—you don't know how little he would be likely to do such a thing! I thought, at first, that he might have taken it for a jest, but I soon saw he had not. He was amazed when I spoke of it."

"I don't think that your opinion is greatly to be relied upon with regard to any of the Reynolds family," said Archer, dryly. "Come! I'll go to your boarding-house at once, and see what sort of a detective I shall make."

To the boarding-house he accordingly went, but there was nothing to be elicited beyond what Hugh had stated.

Another search demonstrated afresh the fact that the miniature was gone; while Mrs. Sargent professed her readiness to take "her Bible oath" that no one had been in Hugh's room during his absence except Felix Reynolds.

Every member of the household proved an *alibi*, and Archer was justified by the facts of the case, when he said to Hugh:

"I have perfect faith in your honesty, but you must understand this: you cannot shield young Reynolds without incurring suspicion yourself. Unless *you* have disposed of the picture, *he* must have taken it; there is no third alternative."

With these words he went away, and left poor Hugh steeped in double wretchedness. So his unhappy fate was to involve Felix as well as himself!

Although the mystery attending the disappearance of the picture grew deeper, he could not believe that Felix had taken it.

On the many miserable thoughts which haunted him, on the fears that beset him —fears of the disgrace which seemed ready to fall on his head—it is not worth while to dwell. Mrs. Sargent's sleep was sadly broken during the long hours of the night by the steady tread overhead, that never ceased until morning broke in the east.

.   .   .   .   .   .

Long, golden sunshine streaming on green, close-shorn turf, croquet-hoops set, croquet-balls rolling, brightly-dressed groups of girls and sombrely-dressed groups of young men scattered here and there, gay voices sounding, gay laughter ringing—such was the scene which the lawn of Cedarwood presented at four o'clock on the afternoon when the croquet-club met there.

For those watching the game or resting from it, chairs and rugs were placed near; but the young hostess was neither among the players nor spectators.

When the question was asked, "Where is Miss Waldron?" some one answered, with a laugh, "Sitting under the cedars with Mr. Marchmont."

Yet this fact by no means implied a withdrawal from the scene of gayety, for, although croquet was the ostensible object of the gathering, it by no means monopolized the attention of the company.

Ladies and their cavaliers strolled back and forth across the lawn, passed through the portico and hall to the dining-room, where a collation was spread, and flitted in and out of the wide-open drawing-room windows. The appearance of the entire scene was festive in the extreme.

Miss Waldron, who was seated under

the large cedars, gazed at it with absent thoughts.

"Yes," she said, in reply to a remark from her companion, "I am thoroughly out of sorts. I have been greatly shocked and distressed to-day, and all this jars upon my mood. Do you not think"—she put up her fan just here, as if to shade her eyes—"that there is something dreadful, something that one cannot easily recover from, in finding treachery where one expected fidelity?"

"It *might* be dreadful, perhaps," said Marchmont, who knew, or thought he knew, to what she alluded, "if one did not find it to be the case so often. After all, the best rule in life is that of trusting nobody. This may sound cynical, but, unhappily, cynicism is often only another name for worldly wisdom."

"And you think it wise to trust nobody?" she said, regarding him keenly. "How about yourself? Do you not trust anybody?—do you not wish any one to trust you?"

He started.

"I was not speaking of myself," he said; "I did not imagine that you would suppose so. I thought you were alluding to some dishonesty on the part of one whom you had trusted."

"I do not think I said so," she replied, "but you are right. Do you remember the miniature of which I spoke to you once or twice, and which I gave young Dinsmore to copy? You warned me against the risk of doing so, and it is a pity that I did not act on your advice, for it is lost."

"Lost!" repeated Marchmont.

He was expecting this, and had prepared all his well-trained forces of self-control, but nevertheless he was conscious of changing color, and he could utter nothing besides that word.

"Yes, lost!" said Miss Waldron, after a moment's pause. "The boy came here this morning, in deep distress, to tell me that it was taken from his room while he was absent for a short time yesterday evening. I say *taken*, because that was his story, but how much of it to believe I do not know. He looks so honest, that I am loath to suspect him of having stolen it myself, but I cannot close my eyes to the suspicious aspect of the affair."

"I told you it would be," said Marchmont, who had by this time regained his composure. "I felt that it was a great risk to intrust anything so valuable to an utterly irresponsible person."

"And you think I am right in suspecting him? I can hardly bear to think so."

"I don't see how you can avoid doing so. It is at least certain that he has been guilty of gross carelessness, if not of dishonesty. But the presumption is strong with regard to the last."

"I cannot give you any idea of how much it worries me," she said, still keeping her fan over her eyes. "I have not told papa yet, because I dislike to annoy him. If the mystery could only be cleared up, I should be so much relieved!"

"What mystery is there?" asked Marchmont, with an uneasiness which was not outwardly manifest. "You surely don't apply that term to the simple fact that the miniature has been lost?"

"The fact does not seem to be simple," she answered. "Mr. Archer was here this morning, and, like myself, he is at a loss what to believe."

"I wonder that you attach the least importance to Archer's opinion," said Marchmont, scornfully. "It was he who recommended the boy, who has proved so unworthy of your trust."

"It was at my request that he took the trouble to find out the boy's character—not to give him one," she replied, with a certain stateliness. "If there has been a mistake in the matter, it is mine, not his. But I want your opinion on the question which puzzles us both. You must understand that Mr. Archer sent for Hugh about dusk yesterday evening, and that while the boy was gone only one person went to his room. That person was one of the young Reynoldses."

"What!" said Marchmont. Surprise and dismay overmastered him, and he could not restrain the expression of both. "Great Heaven!" he thought, "can it be possible that, after all, the little wretch has betrayed me?"

"The one named Felix," said Miss Waldron, calmly. "Hugh is positive that he did not touch the picture; but, as Mr. Archer remarks, the matter lies between the two. If no one else entered the room, one or the other must be guilty."

Was it only Marchmont's fancy, or did she slightly emphasize that "if"? It was the first intimation he had had of Felix's connection with the matter, and it startled him. Clearly there was nothing to be done but to throw the weight of his opinion against Hugh.

"I have no idea that young Reynolds *did* take the picture," he said, "and Dinsmore's bringing in his name looks suspicious. If one person went to his room, why should not another have done so— some confederate, perhaps, who was to steal the picture? The fact of his going away and leaving the picture exposed, with the door open, looks very much like this!"

"Do you think so? Then you believe that he is accountable for its loss?"

Marchmont would willingly have avoided a direct answer to this question, but there was no alternative; and after all, in a certain sense, Hugh, and Hugh alone, *was* accountable for the loss of the picture. "Yes—I believe so," he answered; "I can see nothing else to believe."

Silence followed this reply. Laughter and challenging words, together with the clink of mallets and balls, came ringing from the croquet-ground, while through the open drawing-room windows floated the music of the piano and a high, clear voice singing a popular song.

"Fanny Stewart sings very well," said Miss Waldron, presently, "but there is no voice in Edgerton that can compare with that of your soprano, Mr. Marchmont."

"You mean Amy Reynolds," said Marchmont, as indifferently as possible. "She certainly has a very fine voice." Then he added, though he scarcely knew why, "Have you seen her lately?"

"I went to see her yesterday afternoon, in order to make some arrangement about her appearance at the *fête*, but I did not find her at home," answered Miss Waldron. "The little girl whom I saw —her younger sister, I believe—said she had gone to walk. Perhaps you chanced to meet her?"

"I?"—lifting his eyebrows carelessly. "Certainly not. Why should you imagine such a thing?"

She did not answer, but rose from her seat, looking very handsome, with her rich draperies sweeping round her; while, under the straw hat which she wore, her cheeks had a crimson flush, her eyes a starry gleam.

"I must not detain you here, listening to my annoyances," she said. "Are you fond of croquet? Let us go over to the ground."

"What have I done, that you should forsake the beautiful shade of these cedars for that chattering mob yonder?" asked Marchmont, with the impatience which is often the best compliment that can be paid a woman. "Pray don't go —unless you are tired of *me*."

"One grows tired of sitting still," she said, lightly. "I am naturally restless. If you object to croquet, let us go to the fernery."

"The fernery, by all means!" he answered, sauntering along by her side over the soft green turf, on which the sunshine lay like a mantle of gold.

Everything was so gay and bright around them, and the whole scene so significant of luxury, pleasure, and that holiday side of life which makes up existence for the children of prosperity, that any disturbing thought of annoyance or pain seemed like an intrusion on the harmony of the surroundings. Marchmont felt this, and, being preëminently epicurean, he found no difficulty in banishing all such reflections from his mind. The attraction which Beatrix had for him was altogether different from Amy's *seduisante* beauty, so the two did not conflict; and no woman could have desired more devotion of look and tone than was displayed in his manner.

When they entered the fernery he felt that Fate was propitious to him. Here he had made his declaration, and here all the associations were in his favor.

He was by no means an impatient suitor, and entertained no doubt as to what Miss Waldron's final answer would be; but he was not averse to exchanging suspense for comfortable certainty as soon as possible.

"Do you remember the last time we were here together?" he asked, sinking his voice to that key of perilous softness which is so often affected by men of his stamp, as they slowly walked between the graceful, broad-leafed plants.

"I remember that I tried to interest you in the different varieties of ferns, and failed utterly—if that is what you mean," said Miss Waldron.

"That is not exactly what I meant," he answered, with a slight laugh. "I am afraid I shall repeat myself, if I say that my want of interest was easily accounted for by preoccupation; but it is true, nevertheless."

"Preoccupation in me understood, I presume?" she said, coolly, and if her lip curled, he did not observe it.

"Preoccupation in you certainly understood!" he answered. "Could it be otherwise, when I was here with you?"

"That is a question which modesty forbids me to answer," she said; "but, since you recall the occasion so well, I suppose you also remember that I gave you a fern—one of these"—she paused before a plant bearing fairy-like fronds. "I wonder if you have it yet?"

If Marchmont had answered truly, he would have said that he had never thought of the fern after it had been given to him, and had not the faintest idea of its fate; but he was the last man in the world to tell an awkward or uncomplimentary truth simply because it *was* the truth. Therefore he answered, promptly:

"Of course I have it yet. Do you think I could have failed to value and preserve it?"

"I don't know," she said. "Men do not usually value trifling souvenirs of the kind. Women—not men—preserve faded flowers and leaves as if they were priceless treasures—poor fools that they are!" she added, in a tone of half-sad contempt.

"Then we are all fools together," said Marchmont, smiling, "for men are guilty of such folly as often as women. Do you remember the reason that Owen Meredith gives for something of the kind?—

'Between two leaves of Petrarch
There's a purple rose-leaf pressed,
More sweet than common roses,
For it once lay on her breast.'

The fern of which you speak never had that happiness, but still it was your gift, and, as such, a treasure to me."

"Yonder come Florence and Mr. Glenn," said Beatrix, turning abruptly away.

CHAPTER XIV.

MRS. LATHROP FULFILLS A DUTY.

THE fate of the missing miniature remained enveloped in mystery, for Oliver Reynolds, who alone could have thrown a partial light on the matter, had been frightened into holding his tongue.

Before Oliver started with Tom White on the day's fishing, Marchmont had seen him, and told him that the picture was lost. He also informed him that he had found it to be of great value, and that, if he did not wish to be apprehended as a thief, he had better not drop the least hint of having seen or touched it.

"No one can possibly suspect you, as matters stand," Marchmont said, impressively; "but if you open your lips on the subject, you are lost. Don't mention it to anybody, and *I* shall not betray you."

After mature deliberation, Oliver decided on this course, and it resulted admirably. Being of a weak, cowardly nature, he was filled with consternation, and, having pledged himself to silence, faithfully kept his pledge.

If his conscience troubled him at all, no one observed the signs thereof; but, in truth, no one had either the time or the inclination to observe Oliver.

It was known to Amy and her father, though not mentioned to the younger children, that Felix was involved in the suspicion which had fallen upon Hugh. This alone was trouble enough; but a worse sorrow was in store, and suddenly burst on Mr. Reynolds without warning.

He was at the Lathrop house, giving a music-lesson to Eunice, when, just before the hour had expired, Mrs. Lathrop entered the room and sent her daughter away.

"If you will excuse my disturbing your lesson, Mr. Reynolds," she said, "I should like to speak to you for a few minutes."

When Eunice had departed, Mr. Reynolds, who was peculiarly intolerant of parental interference, and whose temper just now was far from sunny, buttoned his coat, took his roll of music, and, without sitting down, looked at the lady in a very aggressive fashion. Mrs. Lathrop was not to be daunted, however, so she cleared her throat, and began:

"I have a very unpleasant duty to perform, Mr. Reynolds," she said; "but it is not my habit to shirk a duty, however unpleasant it may be."

Mr. Reynolds muttered something inaudible and not complimentary. He had no doubt this majestic beginning prefaced fault-finding with Eunice's progress, and he was ready to resent anything of the kind.

"I have always entertained a very friendly feeling toward you," Mrs. Lathrop proceeded, with stately condescension, "and I am truly sorry for a widower with children—especially if those children are girls. A man is so incapable of managing—one might almost say, of *understanding*—girls."

At this point Mr. Reynolds could only stare—which he did with telling effect from under his shaggy eyebrows. It occurred to him to wonder what possible connection there was between his widowed state and Eunice's music; but he was accustomed to Mrs. Lathrop's dissertations, yet felt irritably averse to listen to one just now.

"If there is anything in your daughter's progress you don't like—" he began, abruptly, but Mrs. Lathrop interrupted him suavely.

"There is nothing," she said—"nothing whatever. I am *perfectly* satisfied with her advancement. Ah! my dear Mr. Reynolds, it is not *my* daughter of whom I wish to speak, but *your* daughter."

"My daughter!" repeated Mr. Reynolds.

No suspicion of the truth came to him. He was aware that Amy's wonderful voice began to be talked of, and he expected some advice or congratulation on that score.

"Yes, your daughter," replied Mrs. Lathrop, impressively. She folded her hands in her lap, and her cap-strings quivered with the energy of her interest. "I am very sorry to shock or pain you," she went on; "but I feel that I should neglect a duty, if I did not warn you that this imprudent girl is being talked of in a way that will do her very serious injury."

"Madam!" said Mr. Reynolds, with lightning darting from his eyes, "I do not understand you!"

"I am told," said Mrs. Lathrop, now embarked on her subject, "that my nephew, Brian Marchmont, is in the habit of seeing your daughter every day, of spending hours in her society, and of taking long walks alone with her. You can judge for yourself whether such conduct is proper in a girl of her age and position. I confess that I was shocked when I first heard the gossip which has arisen on the subject."

"Gossip—about Amy!" said Mr. Reynolds, with a gasp.

He was too honestly dismayed to be indignant. There was something pathetic in the anxious look that came to his worn face.

"God forgive me!" he said, half under his breath. "I ought to have watched over her more carefully; I ought to have remembered that she has no mother.—*What* do people say?" he went on, sharply, turning to Mrs. Lathrop. "Let me hear the worst."

"I do not think they say anything at present worse than the truth—that Brian is amusing himself with her," that lady replied. "Girls' hearts, fortunately, are not easily broken; but worse may come if the matter is not stopped. I have spoken to Brian, but, of course, without effect. It rests with you to control your daughter."

Mr. Reynolds muttered something incoherent, seized his hat, and, before Mrs. Lathrop could offer any further advice, unceremoniously left the room.

Not a single recollection of pupils or appointments occurred to him as he swiftly walked along the streets toward his own house. He could think of nothing but the news which had been told; he could do nothing but execrate his own carelessness, which had suffered Amy to become the subject of amusement for a man like Brian Marchmont. His hand involuntarily clinched itself, and his brows knit closer together.

Two of his pupils who met him shrank affrighted.

"How angry Mr. Reynolds looks!" they whispered, as he passed. "Some-

body must have been doing a lesson *very* badly."

As he approached his house he heard the pure, silvery tones of Amy's voice, together with the chords of the piano; and when he entered the parlor he found Marchmont playing the accompaniment, while she stood by him singing one of the songs selected for the Cedarwood *fête*.

At her father's unexpected entrance she stopped abruptly—not so much because he entered, as because she caught at once the expression of his face, and it made her heart sink instantly.

Though by no means a tyrant in his family, all the members of it knew that Mr. Reynolds was not to be trifled with; and when his wrath was roused, they shrank before him as his pupils did.

Amy saw the signs of storm very plainly, so her voice ceased as suddenly as if a hand had been laid on her throat; and when Marchmont turned in surprise, he also beheld the fierce countenance of *monsieur le père*.

His prophetic soul warned him of a scene at once, and he rose quickly from the piano-stool; but there was no awkward consciousness of detection and guilt in his manner.

"Good-morning, Mr. Reynolds," he said, easily. "I hope you do not object to an amateur substitute. I have been playing Miss Amy's accompaniment, and venturing to offer her a little instruction."

"I object exceedingly to your presence, sir!" replied Mr. Reynolds, sternly. "I am quite able to give my daughter all the instruction she needs, and I have come to tell her that I forbid her to receive your visits or hold any further communication with you. I have just heard of your constant presence in my house," he went on, in a voice that trembled with anger, "and of the gossip to which it has given rise. You must have known this very well, and yet you have continued to take advantage of this child's youth and ignorance. You are no gentleman, and I am glad to find you here, in order that I may tell you to leave the house and never enter it again."

"Your excitement is your excuse for this insult," said Marchmont, calmly.

Since his aunt's threat he had been prepared for something of this kind, so he was not astonished, much less discomposed.

He extended his hand for his hat, which was on the top of the piano, and walked up to Amy, who looked as if the entire fabric of existence was tumbling about her ears.

"I am sorry that my presence should have caused you this annoyance," he said; "but I must thank you for the many pleasant hours I have enjoyed in your society. Good-by."

She could not utter a single word, but looked at him with eyes full of such passionate appeal, that it was only by a strong effort he maintained his composure of manner. To do so was a necessity, however, with the gaze of Mr. Reynolds upon him; he therefore turned quickly, and, without another word, passed from the house.

As the ring of his step sounded on the sidewalk below the window, and Amy realized that he was absolutely gone, a low cry broke from her lips.

"O papa! papa! how could you?" she said, bursting into tears of grief and rage.

Mr. Reynolds walked across the room and seized her arm—not harshly, but with a pressure that compelled attention and checked summarily the angry sobs.

"Listen to me!" he said. "I am willing to overlook a good deal of folly in a girl of your age, left without a mother and with little care; but you are old enough to comprehend, when I tell you that you are standing on the brink of disgrace. If you meet that man again, either in this house or out of it, you will do so at your peril, for I forbid you to see or speak to him. Now, go to your room, and do not leave it again until I send for you."

Thoroughly awed by his tone and manner, Amy obeyed. Sobbing under her breath, she slowly wended her way up-stairs and entered her chamber, closing the door behind her. Notwithstanding its being closed, she heard her father call Clara and speak to her in an energetic manner.

"He's telling her to watch me like—like a dragon, I know!" Amy said to herself as she lay prone on the bed in utter wretchedness.

This was the last drop in her full cup of anguish. To have seen Marchmont ordered from the house; to be forbidden to meet him; to be confined to her room, and to have Clara placed as sentinel over her—Amy felt that human misery could go no farther.

In truth, the girl was miserable with that intense wretchedness of youth which never looks beyond the moment. She suffered, as she enjoyed, with her whole soul; and just now her suffering was of the keenest nature.

It was not without its ray of hope, for she had a comfortable assurance that Marchmont would find some way to set everything right; neither was she indifferent to the romantic side of the distress; but these sources of consolation were at least vague, while her grievances were real.

Their reality increased very much in the course of the next few days. Marchmont, who felt that he had carried his flirtation as far as was prudent—for himself—accepted the situation, and left Amy severely and sadly alone. It cost him something to do this, but his aunt's warning had opened his eyes to the danger of his position, and he felt that he dared not trifle further with the serious interests at stake. He gave a sigh to the piquant little beauty, who, he had not the least doubt, was weeping out her eyes for him; but, on the whole, he was obliged to Mr.

Reynolds for exiling him so summarily from his paradise of roses, and giving him so good an excuse for absenting himself altogether from the shabby little house in R—— Street.

As day followed day without any word or token from him, the world for Amy seemed to come to an end. She had no idea how completely his presence filled her life until he had vanished from it, leaving so terrible a blank behind.

She pined until she was sick; she wept and watched until she was almost blind; and her fate was like that of Mariana in the moated grange.

"He must have forgotten me!" she would sob to herself. "If he *wanted* to see me, he could find some way to do so!"

Altogether a cloud rested over the Reynolds household during these days. Felix's departure for Germany was delayed, partly on account of Mr. Trafford's temporary absence from Edgerton, and partly because of the suspicion concerning the miniature, which hung over him as well as Hugh.

This mystery remained as deep as ever, and baffled every one engaged in its elucidation. Marchmont alone was easy in mind. He did not doubt but that he had dropped the picture on the street, and whoever picked it up, recognizing the value of the setting, had quietly retained it. The fact that he was accountable for its disappearance did not trouble him at all. Whether it remained lost, or whether it were found, it could not be traced to *him*—of that he felt sure, and therefore he made himself thoroughly easy.

This ease was not emulated by the rightful owners of the picture. General Waldron, outraged at the loss of such a valuable family relic, was decidedly of opinion that Hugh should be threatened with legal prosecution if it was not produced; but to this his daughter would not agree.

"It was my fault, papa," she said,

"and I cannot consent that he should bear the penalty. I may have been wrong to put the miniature in his hands, but I do not—I cannot—believe that he has taken it."

Her unsupported opinion might not have had much weight with her father, but Archer strongly indorsed it.

"That boy has no more taken the picture than I have," he said. "One has only to look at him to see that he has wasted away to a shadow through sheer anxiety since its loss."

"Somebody must have taken it," said General Waldron, positively.

"There is no doubt of that," Archer quietly replied. "Somebody certainly must have taken it."

He did not say so to any one save Beatrix, but his own impression was that Felix Reynolds had taken it. He confessed, however, that there was very little "showing of a case" against him, and that to have him arrested on a charge of theft would be an extreme step not warranted by the evidence.

Around Hugh troubles thickened at this time. To the Lathrops the fact of his guilt seemed so clear that Mr. Lathrop dismissed him from his employ.

Worse even than this, Mr. Reynolds resented so bitterly the shadow which had partly fallen on Felix, that Hugh found himself unwelcome in the house which always before had been like home to him.

That the poor boy grew wan and hollow-eyed under the burden of these accumulated misfortunes was not remarkable, and Mrs. Sargent expressed her firm belief that he would die before long if matters did not mend.

"He doesn't eat, he doesn't sleep, he does nothing but pine and mope," she said. "There's a deal of sickness in Edgerton now, and he's just in the state to go off sudden like."

While affairs were in this unsatisfactory state, many preparations for the long-talked-of Cedarwood *fête* were in progress. General Waldron, who took more interest in the matter than his daughter, personally superintended all the arrangements. The grounds were to be illuminated; the large drawing-room, which was to serve first as a concert-room and then as a ballroom, was beautifully decorated, and it was generally understood in Edgerton that "no expense was to be spared" to make the entertainment a brilliant success.

As time went on, Amy looked forward to this occasion with almost feverish anxiety, realizing as she did that it was her only chance of seeing Marchmont.

Since the morning when her father had ordered him to leave the house she had not exchanged a word with him, and she was not so much a child but that she felt keenly that this was his fault.

There could be no doubt that she was tasting the fruit of the tree of knowledge, and finding it very bitter. She was wounded not only in her heart, but in her pride, by his utter neglect.

"A word from him would make everything right," she thought, "and he will not speak it."

The inference to be drawn from this was plain even to her, and what with tearful days and sleepless nights, signs of suffering began to appear on the fair young face, which had never marred its Hebe joyousness before.

As Mrs. Sargent shook her head over Hugh, so Clara shook *her* head over Amy.

"Things are pretty bad with Miss Amy, when she don't care nothing 'bout her dress for that big party she's goin' to!" this close observer said to Felix. "I've flnted it beautiful, but she hasn't even looked at it."

This, if Clara had known it, was significant not only of Amy's grief but of Amy's age. Older women may be heart-broken, but they do not neglect their toilets.

Sixteen—foolish in this as in everything else—throws all thought of adornment to the winds, and feels, like Thekla—

"I have lived and loved, but that was to-day; Make ready my grave-clothes to-morrow."

On the day of the *fête* Amy was seated in the garden, engaged in fringing a rose-colored sash that looked as little as possible like grave-clothes.

She was silent, for of late she never sang except when she practised, but, being plunged in thought, she heard no sound of approaching steps, nor was conscious of any presence near, until a familiar voice said:

"Good-morning, my dear. I am glad to see you again."

She glanced up with a start, and saw Mr. Trafford standing before her, with a look of unmistakable pleasure on his face as he held out his hand.

"I hope you have missed me a little," he said, with a smile, after she had uttered the usual commonplace greetings. "I have been gone—let me see—eight days, I believe. What have you been doing with yourself during all that time?"

"Nothing—in particular," she faltered, remembering with how much of sadness those eight days had been fraught.

Mr. Trafford's keen glance rested on her face, and noted every line of the change there. "I am afraid it has been something very much in particular," he said. "Have you been unwell?"

"Certainly not," she answered, impatiently. "I am always well."

"Have you been unhappy, then?"

"Why do you ask me such a question?" she demanded, flushing. "Do I look wretched? I am sorry if I do, for I suppose I have no more cause to be so than many other people."

"Eight days ago you had, so far as I knew, *no* cause to be so," said Mr. Trafford, gravely. "What has wrought such a change? Come, my dear girl—I am your sincere friend, and I do not ask from idle curiosity—tell me?"

Poor Amy hesitated, and the great tears welled up into her eyes. "I—I would not mind telling you if there were any good in it," she said; "but there isn't. You couldn't help me—not at all. We have been very much worried about Felix," she went on, eagerly, anxious to lead her companion's attention away from her own trouble. "It seems too infamous that suspicion should fall on him about that miniature."

"On Felix!" said Mr. Trafford, looking amazed. "What are you talking about?"

"I forgot that it happened after you went away," she said, "so I suppose you have not heard of it."

Then she told him the story of the disappearance of the miniature, and Felix's connection therewith.

He listened attentively, and seemed struck by the fact that, up to the present time, no clew had been discovered. "Are you quite sure they have not found out anything?" he asked, more than once.

"I am perfectly sure," Amy answered. "That odious Mr. Archer has been to see Felix, and insinuated some things, for which, if I were a man," she cried, with flashing eyes, "I would shoot him!"

"And how does Felix take it?" asked Mr. Trafford.

"Felix is dreadfully distressed," she replied, "and he will not hear of going away—much as he wishes to start for Germany—until the thing is cleared up. I am afraid he will be ill from excitement and worry."

"His mind must be relieved at once," said Mr. Trafford. "If I had suspected this, I would have come back sooner."

Amy opened her eyes.

"You talk as if you had the miniature in your pocket," she said. "I don't think anything will relieve Felix's mind except some certainty about it."

"Then we must obtain the certainty," said Mr. Trafford, with the air of a man to whom everything was possible. "How about poor Dinsmore? The affair must fall heavily on him."

"No doubt it does," responded Amy, indifferently. "I have not thought of him much, and papa does not like to hear his name mentioned. The picture was in his possession, and his carelessness was the cause of its loss. Of course, therefore, he must expect to be held accountable; but Felix—"

"Yes, it is hard," said Mr. Trafford, absently. Presently, with a change of subject so abrupt that it fairly startled her, he said: "Oliver and Ernest are at school—are they not?"

"Yes," she answered; "they are always at school this time of day. Why do you ask?"—for Oliver and Ernest were by no means favorites of this eccentric gentleman.

"I want to see one of them," he answered. "Send Oliver over to me when he comes home. Do you know where I am likely to find Hugh Dinsmore?"

"At his boarding-house, I suppose," Amy answered, more and more surprised. "He is not likely to be anywhere else, for I have heard that Mr. Lathrop has discharged him."

"Humph!" said Mr. Trafford, with a significance which she only partly understood. He drew his brows together, and muttered one or two forcible words under his mustache; then he held out his hand again. "Keep up your heart, my dear," he said, "and don't sadden your pretty face for the sake of a man who is a contemptible sneak. Good-morning!"

CHAPTER XV.

A TRIUMPHANT DÉBUT.

It was impossible for Amy not to feel as if some great delight was in store for her, when she put the last touches to her toilet on the evening of the *fête* to which she had so long and so earnestly looked forward. Her dress was of simple white muslin, and flowers were her only ornaments; but the freshness of her beauty needed no further adornment, and even the dim little glass into which she gazed

6

gave back a reflection that might have satisfied the most exacting woman.

The girl looked at it with passionate eagerness. Was she beautiful? Would *he* think her so? These were the questions she was asking herself, while excitement filled her veins like electricity. She was fairly quivering with it as her slender fingers placed the rose-red roses in her hair. Ever afterward the fragrance of these particular roses was hateful to her—ever afterward it brought back that evening when she stood hoping, longing, fearing, while crowning herself with them.

The last touch had been given, the last flower placed in position, and she was gazing at herself, wishing her father was ready to go, when she heard the sound of quick steps in the hall below, and the eager tones of an excited voice.

"Who can that be?" she said. "Mariette, run down and see!"

Mariette, who had been serving as a willing candle-holder, ran at once, and in a minute came flying back. "It's Hugh," she cried; "and he says the picture's found!"

"Found!—where?" asked Amy, in amazement.

But Mariette had not waited for any details; she only knew that Hugh was in the parlor with Felix, and that he said the picture was found.

Full of eagerness, Amy ran downstairs. She had no desire to see Hugh, but the suspense of ungratified curiosity was something which, in her present mood, she was altogether unable to endure. When she entered the dusky parlor—for it was only lighted by a single candle on the high mantel-piece—Hugh, who was talking to Felix, stared at the white-robed, festive figure as if it were a vision.

"What is this about the picture?" Amy cried, before he could speak. "Who found it?—where was it found?"

"That is a secret just now," Hugh answered; "I am bound by a promise

not to tell anything about it to-night. But I felt that I *must* come and let Felix know that it is safe in Miss Waldron's hands, and that both he and I are free from blame."

"But how did it get into Miss Waldron's hands?" asked Amy, impatiently.

"What does that matter?" said Felix, who was seated as usual on the pianostool. "It is *found*—that is enough—and I shall start for Germany to-morrow."

"And I shall go with you!" said Hugh, with his eyes shining like stars. "That is glorious news, isn't it? General Waldron has offered to send me abroad to study art."

"O Hugh!" exclaimed Amy, clasping her hands. "Are you in earnest?"

"Yes, I am in earnest," answered Hugh. "It seems like a dream, but it is a fact. Are you glad, Amy?" he asked, a little wistfully.

"I am glad for you," Amy answered. "But," she added, with a sudden remembrance of all that he had been to her as a constant companion, a loyal champion, and a devoted subject, "I am sorry for myself."

"What is the use of being sorry, when you'll go away yourself before long to learn how to sing?" demanded Felix. "When you are a great singer, and Hugh's a great painter, and I'm a great musician, how glorious it will be!"

"Tremendously glorious!" exclaimed Hugh; "but just now I had rather hear that Amy is sorry, than to anticipate that splendid time."

"But it *will* be splendid!" said Felix, on whose pale, thin cheeks a feverish flush was glowing. "Some day Amy and I will give concerts together. Amy, come here and sing your songs for Hugh."

He turned quickly to the keyboard, and struck the chords of accompaniment as he spoke, while Amy, not at all unwilling, advanced to his side.

As she poured forth, in her pure, fresh voice, the songs she was to sing at Cedarwood a few hours hence, and Felix's flexile fingers swept the keys, Hugh took in the scene with a sort of lingering intensity, feeling that it would long dwell in his memory. The piano, littered with sheet-music, the dim, shadowy room, the fragile, slender boy-musician, and the beautiful young songstress who stood by his side—the picture, in all its details, struck his artistic fancy, while, with a pang, he felt that he was standing on the threshold of a change that would make this shabby old parlor, and all that it contained, part of an irrevocable past.

"I suppose you feel that you are on the eve of your first triumph, Amy," he said, when the songs were ended, and he had expressed his admiration—very sincere admiration, though tinctured with sadness.

"I hope so," answered Amy; "but I feel a little nervous. When I am on the eve of a *real* triumph, I may remember this, and think how absurd it was to be excited by a private concert."

"Little things seem great to beginners," said Hugh. "And is Felix to play your accompaniments?"

"Yes, but that is nothing—I mean, he would not go only for that. He is to play a sonata of Mozart's, which nobody will understand."

"I will make them understand it," said Felix. "Listen, Hugh!"

Then he began to play; but it is to be feared that the great waves of harmony rolled past Hugh without obtaining due appreciation, for Amy crossed the room to his side, and laid her hand on his arm.

"Tell me, Hugh," she whispered, coaxingly, "where was the miniature found?"

"I can't tell," answered Hugh, smiling. "You must wait a little while. Perhaps"—and here his voice grew more grave—"you will not be pleased when you hear everything connected with it."

"Why should I not be pleased?" she asked. "What have I to do with it?"

"You?—nothing. But don't question me, for I do not want to tell you anything.

Amy"—a pause—"do you think you will remember me after I am gone?"

"Of course I shall remember you!" replied Amy, in a matter-of-fact tone. "How could I possibly forget you, when we have been such good comrades for so long?" she asked, with a smile brimful of beguiling coquetry.

Hugh expressed his feelings by something closely resembling a groan.

"It hasn't been much comradeship with me," he said. "You know I love you better than my life, Amy; and if you would give a little hope before I go away—if you would only say that *some day* you may think well enough of me to marry me—"

"That is nonsense, Hugh!" interrupted Amy, with asperity. "A boy like you talking of marrying! I never heard anything so absurd. I have told you before that I like you as a *friend*"—very decidedly—"but I shall never like you in any other way—never!"

"You can't be sure of that—you are too young," said Hugh, making a despairing appeal against this crushing decision.

"I am just as sure as if I were fifty," answered Amy, positively. "I am fond of you in a certain way, but it is not *that* way."

She shuddered as she spoke, for something almost like repugnance came over her as she compared the figure before her with the lover for whom her heart was sick.

Youth is very cruel, especially when it suffers; therefore she felt none of the compassion which an older woman might have entertained for the boy whose hopes she was ruthlessly treading under foot, and who, during many years, had garnered all his store of affection in her.

After her last words he was silent for a few minutes, and it chanced that just then Felix was playing an exquisite *pianissimo* passage, "Soft as the memory of buried love," and sad as its lament. Hugh hardly heard it, yet it entered into his thoughts and seemed like a requiem to him. When he spoke, it was to say, slowly:

"If you are so certain, I won't trouble you any more. I never thought you could like me very much *now*, but I thought, perhaps, you could give a sort of promise when I went away, and, in case I accomplish all I hope to do, I could claim it. I should work harder for fame if I saw *you* at the end; but there is no good in talking if it is not to be. I am only sorry, oh, very sorry, that you are throwing away what is true for what is false. Somehow I have an instinct, Amy, that when you make your choice now you will make it for good."

"I hope I shall!" said Amy, with an indignant quiver in her voice.

Just here, Mr. Reynolds was heard on the staircase saying:

"Amy, are you ready?"

"Yes, papa, as soon as I get my cloak and gloves," answered Amy, darting away.

"Felix, my boy, are you sure you feel well enough to go?" the musician asked, entering the room. Then, to his surprise, he saw Hugh, and stopped with an abrupt "Humph!"

"Good-evening, Mr. Reynolds," the latter said, a little coldly, for he felt keenly the injustice to which he had been subjected. "I have only come to tell Felix that the miniature which was so mysteriously lost has been found."

"What!—found!" exclaimed Mr. Reynolds, quickly. "Where?—by whom?"

"I am not allowed to tell that to-night. Mr. Trafford will explain the whole affair to you to-morrow."

"Mr. Trafford! What has Mr. Trafford to do with it?"

"He will answer that himself," replied Hugh, quietly.

He rose as he spoke, said good-evening, and went away.

"Papa, may I start to-morrow?" asked Felix, pleadingly. "Mr. Trafford has come, and the picture is found. There is nothing now to keep me."

"Only that you are to unwell to travel," said Mr. Reynolds, gravely. "Let me feel your pulse. My boy, you have a fever now. Is it merely from excitement, or are you ill?"

"Only excitement, I suppose," Felix answered, eagerly. "Don't make me stay at home, papa! I want to go."

When Felix said "I want to" do a thing, the matter was settled with Mr. Reynolds.

Though cold, and often severe, to his other children, he idolized this boy, and indulged him beyond the ordinary measure of parental indulgence. The fact was easily accounted for on the score of his delicate health, and gentle, rarely-gifted nature. He had never been like other boys, and his father had always felt that an organization so sensitively balanced demanded the most tender care, and might at any time slip away out of the region of material things into those purely spiritual.

.   .   .   .   .   .

The grounds and windows of Cedarwood were blazing with a multitude of lights, and the company were arriving in constant detachments, when Mr. Reynolds and his children drove up to the door—Mrs. Crenshaw having kindly lent them an old-fashioned one-horse "rockaway," in which she occasionally made short journeys at a funeral pace.

Amy, who had often laughed at this sober conveyance, might at another time have felt aggrieved at the necessity of using it; but now she was too preoccupied, too eagerly anxious to reach Cedarwood, to care by what means she was conveyed there.

When she first caught sight of the house—which looked like a fairy-palace gleaming against the steel-blue sky—she uttered a cry of delight. Surely Happiness must dwell in such scenes as those! At this moment a Chrysostom could not have persuaded her to the contrary.

As they entered the house and passed along the hall, she caught a glimpse of a crimson-carpeted stage, framed in a flowery arch at the farther end of the large drawing-room. The beauty of the decoration on all sides fairly dazzled her, utterly unaccustomed as she was to such scenes.

Many *débutantes* in her position would have been awed, but Amy was only excited. The love of the world, the passionate desire for the things of the world, which had been always inherent in her, seemed to gain fresh vigor at this first contact with the object of her dreams.

"Some day I shall be rich, too!" she whispered to Felix.

And he answered:

"You will be a great artist—that will be better."

Amy did not reply, but, if she had done so, it would not have been to agree with him. Perhaps there was not the material of the real artist in her—at least it is certain that now, as ever, she thought more of the rewards of art than of its exercise.

If she had been satisfied with her appearance when it was reflected by the dim little mirror in her own chamber, she was more than satisfied—she was delighted—when she saw herself in the great cheval-glass of the dressing-room into which she was shown.

"I *am* lovely!" she thought, with a thrill of pride. "No one here to-night will be lovelier, and surely *he* will think so."

Of the "he" who filled so large a place in her thoughts she saw nothing in the interval of time which elapsed before the entertainment began.

At the end of the drawing-room a smaller apartment served as a green-room for the performers, and here she was conducted. It was filled by the gay young ladies and gentlemen of "The Cecilia," all of whom knew her slightly, and spoke with the sort of good-humored condescension to which she was accustomed, and which she always resented. To-night, however, she felt it less than usual, her mind being occupied with other considerations.

She paid little attention to the concert until it was her turn to appear. But when Felix and herself were summoned to the crimson-covered stage lined with flowers, where a grand piano stood, she felt for the first time as if her heart rose into her throat. It was purely the effect of nervous excitement, and vanished when she found herself before the audience. A sense of power came to her then, and she stood by the instrument perfectly composed and graceful, while Felix played a short prelude. There was a stir of interest among the company below—a general lifting of eye-glasses.

"What a lovely girl! Who is she?" many asked. "Is it possible that is Amy Reynolds?" said others. "By Jove! she's a regular beauty!" the younger men remarked.

But these comments ceased when she began to sing, and her voice rose so pure, so fresh, so powerful in its untried sweetness, that even those who knew least of music were amazed and enthralled. Such singing had seldom, if ever before, been heard in Edgerton, for Amy, as she had said of herself on the day when Marchmont heard her first, was "inspired." Even her father was astonished by the silvery clearness, the liquid richness, of her notes.

"It is marvelous—marvelous!" he said to himself. "There is a fortune in her voice."

She was applauded rapturously, and as she was turning to leave the stage, flushed and trembling with the delightful certainty of triumph—for she could hear the exclamations of admiration passing from lip to lip among the audience—a bouquet suddenly fell at her feet. As Felix stooped for it, she sent one swift glance in the direction whence it came, and met Marchmont's eyes.

The gaze lasted only an instant, but in that instant she read enough to set her heart beating. What telegraph is there like the human glance? What assurances can be given of love or hate, what passionate protestations silently made in less than a heart-beat of time! So it was now, as, grasping her flowers nervously, she hurried away, thinking joyously, "He is true!—he is true! He loves me yet!"

The members of "The Cecilia" crowded round her, and overwhelmed her with congratulations.

"What a beautiful, *beautiful* voice you have!" one after another cried. "Why did you never let us hear it before? You sang divinely! You will be a great prima-donna some day!"

"I am positively ashamed to sing after you!" said the star soprano.

Compliments were very pleasant to Amy, but her bouquet was best of all. She retired to a corner and buried her face in its sweetness while the concert went on. Every flower seemed to say that before the evening was over the happiness for which she longed would be hers.

Felix's sonata was a great success, for though there were only a few persons in the audience capable of appreciating the wonderful *technique* and masterly command of the instrument which the boy-musician possessed, these led the applause in which the others willingly joined.

Amy's second song was even more warmly received than the first. It was a sparkling operatic melody, which showed not only her voice, but her dramatic ability to great advantage. She was *encored* so persistently that Mr. Reynolds consented to her returning, so Felix led her back, and she sang "Within a Mile of Edinboro' Town" with charming piquancy.

"What a trump-card you have found, Beatrix!" cried a vivacious young lady rushing across the room to where Miss Waldron sat. "Who could have imagined that little Amy Reynolds, whom we have seen grow up before our eyes, would prove such a marvel? I vow she sings as well as Nillson!"

"She *will* sing as well as Nillson some day, I have no doubt," replied Miss Waldron. "She has a wonderful voice."

"And how did you find her out? Did Mr. Reynolds tell you about her?"

"No," answered Beatrix; "I am indebted to Mr. Marchmont for a knowledge of her ability, and, therefore, you are indebted to him for the pleasure you have enjoyed—since I had great trouble in persuading Mr. Reynolds to let her appear."

"Indeed!" said the young lady, turning to Marchmont, who, looking thoroughly at ease with himself and the world in general, was sitting by the young heiress's side.—"And pray, Mr. Marchmont, if I may be allowed to ask, how did *you* find her out?"

"I have a divining-rod for discovering hidden genius," replied Marchmont, calmly. "She will do my intuition credit, I think. What is this we are to have now? —a glee? It closes the concert, I believe."

"Yes, it closes the concert," said Miss Waldron. "You can fill up your ball-book as fast as you please, Emma."

"It is very nearly filled," said Emma. "Only one or two dances are yet unclaimed."

She looked at Marchmont as she spoke, but he did not offer to claim one, and, since the glee began, she was obliged to return to her seat. Then he turned to Miss Waldron and said:

"I hope you will give me the first dance, and any other you can spare."

"I hardly think I shall dance more than once or twice," she answered, carelessly; "and it has been a matter of tradition, ever since I was eighteen, that I should open my birth-night ball with one of our old friends. I have not decided who it shall be, but you know you do not belong to that class."

"Unfortunately, no; but the oldest friends are not always the best. Will you not break through the tradition to-night—for me?"

The last words were very low, the handsome eyes very soft, but she turned her own away.

"It is impossible," she said, coldly. "People would imagine—a great deal which would have no foundation. I will put you down for a quadrille later in the evening, if I should dance again, which is rather unlikely."

"I shall be grateful for anything you choose to give me," he answered, a little coldly, in turn.

It did not need this rebuff to show him that he was out of favor to-night; he had been aware of it ever since he first approached Miss Waldron. During the past few days she had fenced off all lover-like advances, and kept him very cleverly at a distance; but he had esteemed such conduct to be merely coquetry, and had given it little thought. Now, however, he was sure that some serious influence was at work, and he felt somewhat uneasy as well as considerably offended.

Under the influence of the last feeling, he left his chair and quitted the drawing-room before the glee was ended. Passing along the hall, he approached the door of the apartment behind the stage.

As he did so, the person of whom he was in search came rushing out so eagerly that she almost ran into his arms.

"What is the matter?" he asked, as she caught herself just in time to avoid a collision. "Has anything happened?"

"O Mr. Marchmont!" she exclaimed. Then she went on quickly: "Yes, something has happened. Felix has nearly fainted, and I want water for him."

"Go back, and I will bring it to you," said Marchmont.

The water was easily procured, and wine also. Followed by a servant carrying both, Marchmont went to the room, where he found Amy and Felix alone, the members of "The Cecilia" having taken leave some time before in anticipation of dancing.

Looking very wan, Felix was reclining on the end of a sofa, while Amy fanned him. He glanced up with a smile when Marchmont approached, drank the water, but declined the wine.

"I did not faint," he said. "I was only tired, and Amy was frightened. I suppose I am not well. I am a little feverish, and my throat is sore; but I will ask papa to take me home, and I shall be all right when I get to bed."

"I am afraid you have over-exerted yourself," said Marchmont, taking one of the small, burning hands.

I suppose I have," the boy answered, languidly.

The glee ended at this moment, and the performers, together with Mr. Reynolds, entered the room.

As soon as the latter caught a glimpse of Felix's face, he hurried forward, too anxious to notice Marchmont's presence.

"I was afraid it would be too much for you," he said, after the matter had been explained. "You must go home at once.—Amy, get your wraps. I will go and see about the carriage."

Amy's countenance fell so abjectly at this, that Felix interposed.

"Please don't make Amy go, papa, because I am obliged to do so," he said. "It will be too hard! Let her stay and see the dancing."

"She can't stay by herself," said Mr. Reynolds, impatiently; "and there is nobody with whom I can leave her."

Marchmont had fallen back, since he knew that to intrude himself on Mr. Reynolds's attention would seal Amy's fate, as far as immediate departure was concerned; but some one unexpectedly entered, and heard Mr. Reynolds's last words.

"What is that?" said a genial voice. "Do you want some one to look after this brilliant young débutante? Can I fill the position? It is true I am not exactly a chaperon, but I will see that no harm befalls her, and I'll take her safely home, if that will do."

"Oh, thank you, Mr. Trafford!" said

Amy, gratefully. "I am sure papa will trust me with you."

"Of course," said papa, to whom at this moment she was of the least possible importance, "if Mr. Trafford will be kind enough to look after you, I shall be obliged to him.—Feliz, my boy, I'll see about the carriage, and then we'll go."

CHAPTER XVI.

"I HAVE LIVED AND LOVED."

"Pray don't give yourself any trouble about taking care of me, Mr. Trafford," said Amy, with an earnestness which it is to be hoped was disinterested. "I know you want to play whist or something of the sort, so if you will leave me in the ballroom, I shall amuse myself very well looking on at the dancing."

"You expect to do something more than look on, I am sure," said Mr. Trafford, smiling.

"I am afraid not," she answered, with a slight sigh.

This conversation occurred after Mr. Reynolds and Felix had taken their departure; and Mr. Trafford, with his young charge, turned toward the ballroom, where the opening quadrille was being formed.

"Oh, how delightful!" exclaimed Amy, with an ecstasy which amused her companion, when the whole bright scene burst on her—a scene so common, yet to her so novel, and so entirely the realization of many dreams.

"Delightful, eh!" said the middle-aged man. "Well, it does not strike me altogether in that light. Dancing must be rather warm work to-night, I think—nevertheless, my dear, I am sorry for your sake that my dancing days are over."

"Oh," said Amy, disparagingly, "I should not think it would suit you at all. One needs to be young and active to enjoy dancing. I hope somebody will ask me!" she went on, most sincerely. "I never

had a chance before to dance in a *real* ballroom, and what charming music!"

"Of course somebody must ask you," said Mr. Trafford, looking round as if to see whom he could collar and compel to this act of social civility.

Fate at this moment interposed kindly in Amy's behalf, and spared him the necessity of any such stringent measure. Two sets had been formed on the floor, and one more couple was needed to fill out the second.

It was imperatively necessary that this deficiency should be supplied, and an unemployed young gentleman near by was called upon to get a partner and come to the rescue.

He glanced round vaguely in search of that article, and saw the nymph-like girl by Mr. Trafford's side. Being a Cecilian, he knew who she was, and felt no hesitation in addressing her; so, saying quickly, "Miss Amy do you dance? May I have the pleasure?" Amy found herself placed in position; the next moment the music began, the bows were made, and she was absolutely dancing at a "real ball."

For a little while the exhilaration consequent upon this fact, and the attention she felt it necessary to bestow on the faces and toilets round, made her forget to wonder where Marchmont was; but this preoccupation did not last very long, and in the first interval she glanced round the room for him. So far as she could ascertain, he was not to be seen, either among the dancers or the spectators.

Miss Waldron she soon singled out. The young heiress was dancing in the next set, and looking magnificently handsome in amber silk, with diamonds flashing on her neck and arms and in her dark hair.

Amy sighed as she looked at the queenly figure—a sigh which did not proceed from envy so much as from a sad realization that this woman was her rival. She seemed to feel her own insignificance as she had never felt it before, under the shadow of the prosperity which was embodied in everything around her.

A vague sense of the wildness of her folly came to her. How could she dream that a man of the world like Marchmont would turn away from all that Beatrix Waldron offered, for *her* sake?

The quadrille over, her partner deposited her in a chair, bowed, and went away, feeling no obligation to bestow any further civility upon a person of such small importance.

So the girl sat alone, and looked with dreamy eyes at the figures revolving before her like colors in a kaleidoscope. As the hum of voices and laughter fell on her ear, a consciousness of isolation began to oppress her. Mr. Trafford had vanished, and there was still no sign of Marchmont, while no one else noticed her presence in the least.

"I had better have gone home with papa and Felix," she thought, a little ruefully.

But these melancholy sensations were scattered like mists by the sun when the musicians began to play the delicious melody of a Strauss waltz, and a well-known voice said in her ear:

Chérie, will you dance?"

"Oh, you have come at last!" she said, turning, with delight involuntarily expressed by eye, lip, and cheek. "I thought I should not see you again—and yet I don't know why I should have been surprised at *that*," she added, quickly, remembering his neglect during the past few days.

"You know perfectly well why you would have had reason to be surprised at that," Marchmont answered, with a smile. "I have a great deal to say to you, and I shall make an opportunity to say it presently; but let us have our waltz first. *Allons!*"

It was like a dream to Amy when, a minute later, they were floating over the polished floor to strains that might have made a statue dance.

The golden minutes of life are very fleet, but she grasped a few of them while the blissful dance lasted.

Marchmont's choice of a partner excited a little surprise and comment among his friends and acquaintances. That one so fastidious and supercilious should, out of a whole "rose-bud garden of girls," select Amy Reynolds, appeared remarkable to those who knew nothing of what had gone before; but to those who read his conduct by the light of past events the simple act seemed very much one of defiance.

So it appeared to Mrs. Lathrop, who lowered her eye-glass with an air that expressed distinctly, "After this, we may expect anything!"

Florence paused to whisper:

"I am afraid Brian and Beatrix have had some disagreement, mamma. Do you notice how they avoid each other?"

"It is fortunately a matter of no importance to *us*," said Mrs. Lathrop, with dignity. "Your cousin must attend to his own affairs."

The cousin thus severely abjured was attending to his own affairs with great satisfaction to himself and Amy.

He had acted on an impulse—which was something very rare with him—in asking her to dance; but he could not regret it as he clasped the lissome form close to him in the circling whirl of the waltz. Episodes of flirtation were so common in his life, that it amazed him to feel how loyal his fancy was to Amy.

"There is a piquant charm about her," he thought, "which no doubt accounts for it."

Whatever accounted for it, the fact remained that this girl, in her poverty and insignificance, possessed an attraction for him which older, fairer, richer women had failed to exert.

They waltzed, with one or two short pauses for rest, until the music ceased. Then Marchmont said, abruptly:

"Let us find some cooler place; the heat and glare here are intolerable."

If he had proposed to find a furnace,

Amy would hardly have dissented, so delightful was the mere consciousness of being with him again; but she had certainly no objection to being led from the ballroom to the delightful coolness and semi-darkness of the outer world.

As they passed through one of the open windows they saw that many others, like themselves, had sought the grounds. By the light of the lamps gleaming in every direction figures in groups and pairs were to be seen sauntering to and fro, now visible, then passing into sudden eclipse with a pretty, shifting effect.

Marchmont muttered a malediction on the illumination.

"What an absurd idea to light up trees and shrubs!" he said. "I wonder if no spot has escaped the old general's rage for decoration?"

"The cedars are not lighted," said Amy. "Can we not sit under them?"

"We can, and we will," he answered, leading her toward them.

It was by Miss Waldron's special request that the cedars had been spared the "rage for decoration," and it chanced that she was sitting under them, talking earnestly to Archer, when Marchmont and Amy approached.

There were two rustic seats—each capable of holding two persons—placed so that the triple trunk of the group of cedars separated them, while the low-drooping boughs overshadowed both.

Miss Waldron and her companion were seated on the bench farthest from the house, and a pause had occurred in their conversation, when they were both startled by hearing Amy's bell-like tones exclaim:

"How pleasant this is! We can see everything without being seen, the shade is so deep here."

"Yes, blessed be the hand that planted these patriarchs, and still more blessed the one which refrained from hanging their boughs with lamps!" Marchmont answered. "And now, Amy, my darling, I have you for a little while all to myself."

"Oh, how cruel you have been!" cried Amy, with a quiver suggestive of tears in her voice. "*How* could you stay away as you have done, and—and let me break my heart, without saying a word?"

"Have you broken your heart?" he asked, in a caressing tone. "You don't look like it, my pretty one. I thought to-night, when you appeared, that I had never known how lovely you are, and that is saying a great deal, since I knew very well. But to stay away was a matter of necessity, *ma belle*. Could I go to your house, after your father had requested me to leave it? Plainly, there was nothing to do but to bide my time—and see what I have gained by doing so!"

"And do you think it a reward?" asked Amy, wistfully. "Are you really glad to be with me again?"

"Really glad? I wish I could tell you how glad I am!—for, in truth, I think you have bewitched me, you small witch! Why else should I feel, like a lovesick boy, that my only pleasure here to-night is in your society?"

"Do you feel so?" asked Amy, still wistfully. "But is it true, as I have been told," she went on, faltering and hesitating, "that—that you are trying to marry Miss Waldron? I cannot believe it," she cried, clasping her hands. "I only ask because I hear it so often."

There was a moment's pause—a pause which seemed long not only to Amy, but to the two spellbound listeners on the other side of the tree.

Archer was in a horrible state of doubt. Should he take Beatrix away from what he felt was coming, or should he let her remain and hear with her own ears the evidence of her suitor's treachery?

Beatrix, on her part, felt as if some overwhelming force was laid upon her, compelling her to await Marchmont's reply. By a strong effort she might have spoken, perhaps, but she was utterly unable to move.

Presently Marchmont spoke—slowly and gravely: "I am not sorry you have asked that question," he said. "I think it is best to tell you the truth frankly, and I am sure you will be reasonable with regard to it. I am, comparatively speaking, a poor man, my pretty Amy—that is, I am too poor for my position and the objects I have set before myself in life. To achieve these objects—one of which is political distinction—I must have money; and not only money, but certain other worldly advantages. These advantages I can best secure by a marriage with Miss Waldron. Such a marriage will be purely of convenience, and will not alter the fact that I love you."

"Come away!" said Archer, in a low, stern voice, and involuntarily he laid his hand as he spoke on Beatrix's wrist. "This is no place for you—come away!"

"One moment!" she answered in a whisper. "Wait one moment!"

If she wished to wait for Amy's answer, it came quickly enough. That sensation which the French call a *serrement du cœur* held the girl for a moment in its strong grasp, but only for a moment. Despite her folly and credulity, she was not weak, and the strength of her nature asserted itself now.

She drew herself resolutely out of the clasp of Marchmont's arms, which had encircled her, and looked at him in the dim light, with her fair, young face set in harder lines than it had ever worn before.

"So Hugh was right!" she said; and how changed her voice sounded! "I have been a fool, and you have been only trifling with me! You sought me out, you professed to love me, you have made me the object of gossip and slander; and *now* you tell me that you are going to marry another woman, and that I have only served to amuse you! Perhaps I ought to have known that a man like you would not think of me in any other way; but I have been a fool. I am a fool no longer, however!" she cried out, with a sudden burst of passion. "Don't touch me, Mr. Marchmont; I am done with you forever!"

"I did not expect this, Amy," said Marchmont, beginning to think he had made a great mistake in his explanation. "I thought that, young as you are, you had more reason than most women, and that you loved me well enough to be unselfish and understand my position."

"I understand it perfectly," replied Amy, with quivering lips; "you need not explain it any more. I have served your convenience in one way; Miss Waldron is to serve it in another. I am poor and obscure now," she went on, with a dramatic intensity all the more effective for being the natural impulse and inspiration of the passion that possessed her; "but I feel, I *know*, that I shall not always be so! and if ever it is in my power to return this upon you, Brian Marchmont, I will do so mercilessly!"

"Amy," said Marchmont, coldly, "this folly is absurd and disgusting. I had no idea you were so weak and ignorant. If you knew anything of the world, you would know that I cannot possibly act otherwise."

"I know something of the world," said a sudden voice, the tones of which were cold as ice and keen as steel, "and I am not aware that a man of the world is necessarily debarred from being a man of honor."

Marchmont sprang to his feet, for once in his life thoroughly dismayed and discomposed. Before him stood a stately figure, on which a stream of light from the windows of the ballroom fell, showing the clear-cut, scornful face turned full upon him.

"Beatrix!" he gasped.

"Miss Waldron, if you please," Beatrix answered, in the same calm, cold tones. "I have never given you the right to call me anything else, and you may be assured that I never shall do so. When you did me the honor of offering yourself to me some weeks ago, I believe I told you that I wished to be certain respecting the man I married. That question is settled with regard to you, Mr. Marchmont; I have tested you thoroughly, and I have found you devoid of honor, devoid of truth, devoid even of that principle which men call common honesty."

Marchmont threw his shoulders and his head haughtily back. With all his faults he was no coward, and, recognizing the fact that his cause was hopelessly lost with Beatrix Waldron, he was ready to make a retreat in good order.

"It is very well known," he said, "that women have an impunity in offering insults which is not allowed to men; but I hardly fancied Miss Waldron would avail herself of it, or that she would feel no hesitation in acknowledging herself an eavesdropper."

"I have no apology to make for being here," said Miss Waldron, while Archer stepped quickly forward from the shade where he had lingered and placed himself by her side. "I am glad, indeed, that I was here when you came; what I have overheard has given me no new information with regard to *you*, but it has made me think better of this poor girl.—You have spoken in a manner that does you credit," she said, turning to Amy. "In order to make you further understand what this man is, let me tell you that one word from him would have removed all suspicion from Hugh Dinsmore with regard to the loss of the miniature, which has caused so much trouble. Not content with not speaking this word, he has deliberately tried to throw suspicion on the boy whom he knew to be innocent.—You wonder, perhaps, how I gained this knowledge?" she said, addressing Marchmont, whom amazement rendered speechless. "You thought yourself alone in Mr. Reynolds's parlor when you took the miniature from Oliver; but Mr. Trafford was there before you went in. He heard everything; and, when you dropped the picture in searching for your hat, he took it and kept it, wishing to see if you would be honorable enough to avow your share in the matter. Returning to Edgerton after an absence of eight days, he found that you had *not* spoken, and so he brought the picture to me."

As her clear, incisive tones ceased, silence fell. Never in all his life had Brian Marchmont occupied such a position before—one so hopeless of explanation, so unutterably humiliating. The blood surged in his veins like fire, while mortification and rage fairly choked him.

He would fain have spoken, but for the first and last time in his life the very power of language seemed stricken from him, and it was Miss Waldron's voice which broke the silence again.

"I could go into further details, but it is not worth while. I have said enough to show that I understand everything: how you have amused yourself with this child, while trying to marry me, 'purely for convenience,' and how false you have been even to that conventional honor which worldly men respect. Our acquaintance ends here and now.—Amy, come with me."

As she extended her hand and laid it on the girl's arm, drawing her gently but firmly away, Marchmont spoke hoarsely:

"I decline to be put on my defense, or to answer the charges you have brought against me, in the presence of others; but, if I may speak to you alone—"

She turned on him with a flash of passion.

"I will never willingly speak to you again, as long as we both live!" she said. "Understand that! I am done with you, and I thank God that I never—not for one moment—loved you.—Come, Amy."

In her preoccupation she forgot Archer, and, since she said nothing to him, he hesitated to accompany her when she turned, and, taking Amy with her, swept away—a more queenly woman than ever, in the majesty of her pride and indignation—a woman whom any man might have hated to lose.

Though she forgot him, Archer was about to follow her, when Marchmont—feeling, with a sense of relief, that here at least was some one whom he could attack—moved forward a step and confronted him.

"Miss Waldron is a woman," he said, "and, as I remarked, has therefore a certain impunity in offering insult, but you are a man, and I wish to know by what right you have ventured to spy upon my conduct, to interfere with my affairs, and to play the eavesdropper to-night?"

"You can gain nothing by quarreling with me, Mr. Marchmont," replied Archer, with contemptuous coolness. "You must be aware that I have *not* spied upon your conduct, interfered with your affairs, or intentionally played the part of an eavesdropper to-night."

"You are a liar!" said Marchmont, and lifted his hand.

The other caught it in a grasp like iron.

"That is enough," he said. "It is very natural that you should not know what you are doing now; but if—when you are sane to-morrow—you still desire to hold me accountable for the part I have taken in Miss Waldron's affairs, you know where I am to be found. Good-evening."

He loosed his grasp on Marchmont's arm as he spoke, and, turning on his heel, walked deliberately away.

The other might not have allowed this but for the fact that he could not have detained him without creating a scene—which is something that, even in mortal extremity, no well-bred man desires to do.

The grounds were still full of people, though the music of a quadrille was pealing out from the ballroom. On a warm May night, coolness, fragrance, and unlimited opportunities for flirtation, seemed to the youthful mind even more desirable than dancing.

Nevertheless, there were plenty of dancers "dancing in tune" when Archer, who had little fancy for ballrooms, approached the house.

Some rather trite reflections occurred to him, as they would have been apt to occur to any one, on the different phases of human life which often come so sharply in contact—the bright and dark, the tragedy and comedy, the earnestness and frivolity, discordant elements that elbow each other constantly.

He felt profoundly grateful that Beatrix Waldron was saved from the marriage which had threatened her happiness; but he wondered, with something of a pang, how much truth there was in those last words she had uttered—those words which declared that she had never for a moment loved Marchmont. Pride would have nerved her to say that, he thought; but was it, could it be, strictly true?

He might have believed it if he could have seen Beatrix, and realized that her composure was no mere mask, but an inherent fact. When she first discovered Marchmont's perfidy, she had been moved by it, as few women under the circumstances could have failed to be moved—but that time was past. What she had heard to-night had been but a confirmation of what she had heard before, and therefore its effect had been transitory. It was of Amy she thought now, and she led the girl straight to her own apartment.

"You can be quiet here and recover yourself," she said, not ungently; "but believe me the best means of recovery will be to remember that the man with whom you have fancied yourself in love is not worth a thought—much less a tear. Mr. Trafford will tell you hereafter the whole story of the miniature. I tell you that Brian Marchmont has acted in the most dishonorable manner, both to you and to me. He has made love to you because you amused him; he has tried to marry me because I am rich. Let us put him out of our lives to-night, and never think of him again."

Amy looked up with something in her glance which the other did not exactly understand. Her face was perfectly calm, though white as marble, but her eyes were dilated and full of an expression difficult to analyze, impossible to describe.

"That may be easy to you," she answered, quietly, "because you said, out yonder, that you never loved him. I did. And one can't forget love in a minute—can one? I hate him—oh, yes, I hate him far more than you can, for he has not made a plaything of *your* heart. I will never forgive him—never as long as I live—and, if I ever have the power, I will pay my debt to him; but, all the same, I am obliged to suffer now, for I loved him!"

"Contempt is better and safer than hatred, my dear," said Miss Waldron.

Again the strange, brilliant eyes—undimmed by a tear—looked up at her.

"Contempt will do for you," she said, "but *I* must hate—because I have loved."

The elder woman was silent—in fact, she felt suddenly and oddly startled. Amy's manner was so unlike that of an ordinary girl of her age, her words were so different from those which might naturally have been expected from her lips, that Beatrix felt like one out of her reckoning. She had looked for tears, probably—for indignation, perhaps—but this calm assertion of love and hate altogether puzzled her.

After a minute's pause, she said:

"I must go down. Do you care to come with me, or will you stay here?"

"I will stay here, thank you," Amy answered, with the same immobile quiet. "Will you please tell Mr. Trafford to send for me when he wants to go?"

Promising to do this, Miss Waldron went away, leaving the pretty, graceful figure alone in the luxuriously-fitted room.

Even after the last echo of her footstep ceased Amy sat motionless, listening to the gay strains of music floating up from below, looking through the wide-open casement out on the brilliant grounds and up at the blue, starry sky,

thinking—thinking—still thinking, of the sudden blow that had darkened all things for her.

CHAPTER XVII.

"THE LIGHT IN THE DUST LIES DEAD."

MR. TRAFFORD, who had heard from Miss Waldron an account of what had occurred, was, like the latter, struck by the change in Amy when she came at his summons to go home.

There were no signs of tears on the pale, fair young face; there was no trace of agitation in the strangely composed, almost apathetic manner.

"I am quite ready to go," she said, indifferently, when he made a remark about taking her away so early.

She did not even glance toward the ballroom, which had seemed to her a palace of delight so short a time before. She took his arm as if she had been three-score, and walked out of the festive house without a glance behind.

As they drove away, she turned and said, with the same odd quiet:

"Will you tell me all about the miniature that was lost? I should like to hear the whole story. Papa will be sorry to know that Oliver was concerned in it."

"Oliver's share in the matter was very slight," said Mr. Trafford. "Do you really want to hear the story? Well," he added, partly to himself, "perhaps this is as good a time as any other. You must know, then, that, on the evening when the miniature was lost, I received a telegram summoning me away on business, and I decided to leave Edgerton that night. I had some final arrangements to make with your father about Felix, and, being uncertain as to how long I might be detained, I walked over to his house in order to make them. Every one seemed out. The door stood open, but no one answered my summons; so I entered the parlor, thinking that I would wait until some one appeared. I had been there only a short time when I heard your voice at the door. Marchmont was with you—"

"Yes, I know," she interrupted. "Never mind that."

"But it is on that that the story hinges," said Mr. Trafford. "I did not listen to your conversation. On the contrary, I retired to a corner and lay down on a sofa, to wait until the coast was clear. Presently you ran into the house and went up-stairs. A minute later Marchmont followed, stood in the hall for an instant looking round, and then entered the parlor. I lay quite still, so that he did not perceive me; and, after wandering about a little, he sat down directly in front of the recess where I was. He had not been there more than a minute, when Oliver rushed into the parlor, calling for you. Marchmont answered that you were not there, and asked what he wanted. He replied that he had been to Dinsmore's room, and had found a picture which he had brought to show you 'as a good joke.' Marchmont went to the window, looked at it, and then told Oliver to leave it with him. The boy at first refused to do this, but, when one of his associates called him, he hurriedly gave it up, bidding the other 'show it to Amy, for Hugh's sweetheart,' and went away. Left alone, as he fancied, Marchmont laughed, and uttered a few words, of which I only remember the expression, '*An absolute stroke of luck.*' Then he slipped the miniature into his pocket, and came back to the place where he had been sitting."

Here Amy interposed.

"I do not understand," she said, "what you mean to imply. You surely cannot mean that a man like—like Mr. Marchmont meant to *keep* the picture?"

"Not for its value," answered Mr. Trafford; "but, for the purpose of annoying Hugh Dinsmore, he certainly meant to keep it."

"But why should he have wished to annoy Hugh?"

"I am surprised that *you* need to ask that question!" answered Mr. Trafford, a little dryly. "You are not aware, then, that Dinsmore charged Marchmont some time before with trifling with you, and making you the subject of injurious gossip, and by way of reward was knocked down and left senseless in the highway, where Archer found him some time later?"

Amy's small hands clasped together with painful force, but her voice was still firm and even when she answered, "No, I did not know it."

"She has wonderful self-control for a woman—and so young a woman!" Mr. Trafford thought.—"It is true, nevertheless," he said, aloud; "therefore the inference is, that Marchmont's chief motive for acting as he has done was a desire to injure Dinsmore. In fact, there is no other motive which possibly explains his conduct. When he came back to the place where he had been sitting, it was to look for his hat; in doing this the miniature dropped from his pocket unobserved, and after he left the room I picked it up. A glance showed me its value, and, wondering a little how the matter would end if the picture mysteriously disappeared, I put it in *my* pocket and walked off. Two hours later I left Edgerton. When I returned and heard of the loss of the miniature, I sent for Oliver, as you know, and asked the meaning of his silence. He confessed that he had been intimidated by Marchmont, and had held his tongue from fear of the consequences. Reassured on this point, he was willing enough to speak; so I brought him and the picture to Miss Waldron, who sent at once for Dinsmore."

Silence followed his last words. What Amy thought of the story, he did not know—she uttered not a word; and a minute later the carriage drew up at Mr. Reynolds's door.

Mr. Trafford dismissed it after he had assisted her to alight, and there was something very kindly in his manner as he led her up the steps and opened the door. In the passage a lamp was burning. He paused a moment to take the cold little hand in his, to look with pity into the white young face that in an hour had been robbed of its brightness and bloom.

"Good-night, my dear," he said, gently. "I am sorry that your triumph should have been overshadowed like this. I would have had it otherwise, if I could."

"My triumph," repeated Amy, in the tone of one who vaguely recalls something forgotten. "Oh!—that does not matter! Good-night, and thank you for taking care of me."

Neither face nor voice changed in its apathetic calm, while her hand slipped out of his like a bit of ice. He was obliged to go away, in order that she might fasten the door after him, but he did so with a sense of discomfort.

"Something out of the ordinary way, there!" he thought, as he found himself on the street, proceeding toward Mrs. Crenshaw's. "If she were not so young, I should understand it better. Despite her youth, I fear the blow has struck very deep. Poor, pretty little Amy! it is hardly fair to blame her for being a fool, since we are all fools, more or less, at times in our lives!"

Amy having, meanwhile, barred the door, took the lamp and slowly went upstairs. Her quietude was no mere mask lent by pride and courage; she felt like one who had been stunned, and in whom sensation for a time was dead. When she entered her chamber, not even the recollection of the excitement, the hope, the longing, with which she went forth from it, had power to move her. She laid aside the dress which she had put on with so much innocent vanity, and took the withered roses from her hair—all with the same apathy. In truth, she felt like one in a dream. Those vivid, terrible minutes under the cedars alone seemed real, and she did not lose the memory of them for an instant.

After she had extinguished the light and crept to bed, her mind continued to go over the same thing with that maddening persistence which makes one sometimes appreciate what the agony of mental derangement must be. Every look, every word, every accent, was recalled again and again. Even her short snatches of sleep brought no relief, for memory was then, if possible, more vivid. In these brief, troubled dreams, she lived over the whole episode once more.

At daylight she was roused from this broken, unrefreshing sleep by a knock at her door. "Who is there?" she asked, starting up. "What is the matter?"

"It is I, Amy," her father replied. "Felix is ill, and I want you to go to him as quickly as possible. I am going for the doctor."

"I will be there in a minute," she answered, springing out of bed.

Her head ached from excitement and loss of sleep, while her hands trembled so that she could scarcely dress; but she managed to slip on something in the way of attire, and went to Felix's room.

A glance at the boy's face was sufficient to tell her that he was very ill. His fever, which had been high all night, had abated somewhat and left a wan pallor behind; the thin face looked thinner than ever, the great eyes were surrounded by dark-blue circles, and the lips were pale and dry.

"I am sorry papa called you," he said. "There was no need, and you must be tired. I hope you had a pleasant time."

"I am not tired. I had rather be doing something," she answered, evading a reply to his question. Then she laid her hand on his forehead, saying, "Does your head ache?"

"Yes; but it is my throat that troubles me," he answered. "I did not tell papa, but, day before yesterday, I went to see Harry Wilson, who has diphtheria. If I have that, Amy, please don't come round me, for you may take it."

"It would not matter in the least if I

did," said Amy, who at this time would not have shrunk from the plague. "I am not afraid."

When the doctor came, the first thing he did was to feel Felix's pulse, the second to look at his throat. He had no sooner glanced into the latter, than the gravity that settled over his countenance showed his opinion of the case. He asked a few questions, then walked to the window and took out his prescription-book.

Mr. Reynolds followed, and laid a nervous grasp on his arm.

"Is it anything serious?" he asked, in a husky voice. "The boy is often unwell; he is very nervous and delicate. I have not thought much of this illness."

"It is very serious, I fear," replied the doctor, gravely. "Your son has the most malignant form of diphtheria. I will do my best, but I cannot conceal from you the fact that his situation is critical. The disease is very contagious, and I advise you to send the other children out of the house at once."

"My God!" said Mr. Reynolds, turning ghastly pale.

The last words fell on his ear unheeded. What were the other children to him? He did not even give them a thought in comparison with Felix—Felix, his idol, his hope, his pride!

"Call in other advice!" he said. "Do anything—do everything! You may take all that I am worth, if you will make Felix well!"

"I shall do my best," the doctor said, again, looking with compassion at the speaker.

And so it happened that a trouble of the most real description laid its grasp on Amy, shaking her out of the self-absorption which would otherwise have overcome her.

In the terrible hours of watching and anxiety which followed by Felix's bedside, she did not forget her own pain, nor lose the heavy, aching sense of the blow that had fallen upon her; but she had no time to dwell upon it. Even in ordinary cases

there is nothing which makes such a constant demand upon the attention as the duties of a sick-room, and here the fight between life and death was short and sharp.

Very short, certainly; for, when the second morning dawned, the doctor plainly said, "No hope," and it was evident to the almost frantic father that Felix was sinking fast.

Others came and went, but he did not stir from the bedside, and his face seemed to grow momently more and more haggard as he sat watching the dying boy, as if counting every painful, fluttering breath.

"I shall not go to Germany after all, papa," Felix whispered once.

And Mr. Reynolds answered, passionately:

"You will—you must! God will not be so cruel as to take you from me."

Alas! such protests avail little when the unalterable decree has gone forth. Not to Germany, indeed, but to a far more distant country was the young traveler bound; and, before the sun sank, his painful passage thither was over, and only the fair, cold shell of mortality was left behind.

. . . .

Those who saw Mr. Reynolds's grief were not likely ever to forget it. It is seldom that human sorrow is so intense, so passionate, so bitter. Usually the poignancy of the sharpest grief is in a measure tempered by that sense of the irrevocable to which humanity is forced to submit, and against which rebellion is so absolutely hopeless. But in this instance there was not the faintest semblance of resignation. One or two people, who ventured to speak of such a thing to Mr. Reynolds, were instantly silenced by the fierce impatience with which he turned upon them. He had always possessed the high-strung, irritable temperament which is peculiar to musicians, and now grief and despair seemed to possess him like a consuming fire. He would not quit Felix's body by day or night; and, since no one dare approach him, the question of the funeral became a serious difficulty.

The difficulty, however, was at last overcome by Mr. Trafford. He alone had courage to interfere—to say what must be done, and to make the necessary arrangements for laying away that placid figure which was, and yet was not, Felix. Mr. Reynolds submitted, and after this—especially after the funeral—a change came over him. His passionate despair gave place to a melancholy from which nothing had power to rouse him. He made no effort to resume the labor of his life; he took no interest in anything. His other children were objects of indifference to him. With Felix all the purposes of his life seemed to end.

This did not last very long. Medical science sternly refuses to recognize such a disease as "heart-break;" so the doctors found some other cause to account for the fact that Mr. Reynolds's life suddenly snapped short, like a worn string. It was Hugh Dinsmore who entered the parlor, a few days after Felix's funeral, and found the musician sitting silent and motionless at the piano, with his face bowed upon the keyboard. Hugh hesitated for a moment, and then addressed him. There was no answer. He spoke again. Still no reply. Then he advanced, and, with a strange sense of awe and foreboding, touched the still figure—recoiling instantly with an involuntary cry.

There could be no doubt of the Presence which had entered before him. Sitting alone, with the instrument which was so closely associated with his dead boy, the heart-broken father had silently passed away forever.

At the time this occurred, Amy was lying dangerously ill with diphtheria—which disease, as the doctor had anticipated, she had taken from Felix. She was stricken down with it the day after the funeral, but her father had not paid the least attention to the fact. In vain Clara tried to awaken his anxiety, thinking that any distraction of mind would be an advantage to him. If he heard, he did not heed her. What was Amy's life or death to him after Felix was gone?

Poor Amy also came very near going to join "the vast majority beyond." On the border-land of life and death she hovered for days; and only the superb vitality of youth, the rallying-power of a strong constitution, saved her from sinking as Felix had sunk.

It was at this critical period that her father's death occurred. Every effort was made by Clara and the doctor, aided by Mr. Trafford, to keep the sad event from her knowledge, and they partially succeeded. The worst was over, and she had slowly and languidly entered upon the road to health before she heard of this later bereavement. The intelligence came to her accidentally, as such intelligence often does. Mariette—of whom Mrs. Crenshaw had taken charge during all this time of trouble and grief—was the bearer of the sorrowful news. When the child was admitted for the first time to see her sister, Clara forgot to warn her not to mention her father's death, and so it happened that she made some allusion to "poor papa," which told Amy the truth—a truth, it may be added, which she partly suspected from her father's absence, and from the manner in which her questions regarding him were evaded.

Nevertheless, when she heard that her fears had not outrun reality, her heart seemed to stand still, and a sense of deadly faintness rushed over her. But she did not faint; she controlled herself by a strong effort, and beckoned the child nearer to her.

"Tell me the truth, Mariette—exactly the truth," she said. "Is papa dead?"

Mariette's great blue eyes opened wide and filled with tears. "O Amy," she cried, in an awed tone, "didn't you know that? Papa's been dead a week!"

"Dead!" repeated Amy, as if she could hardly grasp the terrible fact. Then she threw up her arms with a cry of anguish. "My God! I am indeed desolate!" she said, and burst into passionate weeping.

The immediate effect of this shock was prostration, but the remote effect was to hasten the girl's recovery. Previous to this she had not seemed to care whether she lived or died, and her listless indifference had greatly retarded her convalescence. Now she became feverishly anxious to regain her health.

"Make me well—pray, make me well at once!" she said, imploringly, to the doctor. "A little while ago I wanted to die, but now I know that I cannot afford to do so. I must get well, to work for Mariette and the boys. They have nobody to depend on but me."

"You must be patient," answered the doctor; and, despite the callousness which was the result of his profession, he looked with a sense of compassion at the childish girl, who even in the depth of her desolation did not stand alone, but was burdened by others weaker than herself. "You have been very ill; you cannot recover in a day. Don't let your mind be troubled. Leave the question of what you must do when you get well to your friends. You are too young to decide."

"I have no friends," she answered. "There is nobody to decide but myself, and I have determined what I will do."

"You have at least one very kind friend," said the doctor. "That is Mr. Trafford."

"I had forgotten him," she said, quietly. "Yes, he is kind, but it is only the kindness of a stranger. He has nothing to do with my life."

Despite her anxiety, her recovery was slow; and during those long hours she lay for the most part with idle hands, gazing out of the open window at the green boughs forming a network against the blue sky—boughs in which the unnumbered sweet-voiced birds of the South sang constantly.

"How beautiful!" she exclaimed, one day, when a mocking-bird had been pouring forth a tide of melody. "I wonder if I can sing as well as that? I think I can. The doctor says I must not strain my throat; but it is quite well now, and there is no reason why I should not sing."

"Mrs. Crenshaw says she don't expect you'll ever be able to sing any more, Amy," said Mariette, who was in the room.

Amy started as if she had been struck. The idea of any injury to her voice had not occurred to her, and the suggestion was like a dart of fire.

Her hand instinctively went to her throat. What if it should be so? Was there any limit to the cruelty of Fate? Might not this power—her last plank in the midst of shipwreck—be taken from her, as everything else had been?

This thought was so appalling that she was literally unable to utter a word. Every hope and ambition for the future centred in her voice. If *that* was lost, or injured, what weapon was left her with which to fight the world?

"O Heaven! if my voice is lost, let me die!" she exclaimed, in the agony of her fear; but, fortunately for us, such prayers as these are seldom granted.

The next day, unable to endure the torture any longer, she waited until Clara had put the room in order, placed her in a large chair before the window, where of late she had been able to sit, and had finally gone away; then she clasped her white, thin hands tightly together, like one in the act of prayer, and opened her lips to sing. At first she failed to make a sound, but saying to herself, "I am nervous; that is what is the matter!" she made another effort.

The notes which she strove to utter came then, but so harsh, so flat, so utterly unlike what they had ever been before, that she paused in dismay; and at this moment the door opened, and Clara ushered the doctor in.

He was a little startled to see his patient rise from her chair and advance toward him, looking more like a spirit

than a woman in her loose white drapery,
with her great eyes shining out of her
hollow face, and one hand grasping her
throat.

"Tell me!" she cried out passionately.
"Has it gone forever?—have I *lost* my
voice?"

The doctor changed color, and glanced
sternly at Clara.

"I thought I told you not to let her
sing!" he said.

"I didn't know—" Clara began, in
self-defense, when Amy interrupted:

"How could she prevent my singing,
if I chose to do so?—and I did choose to
test my voice. I can do nothing with
it now—but will it recover its power?
Don't trifle with me!" she cried, as she
saw hesitation on his face. "I want the
truth, and I—I am strong enough to bear
it."

"I am not sure of that," said the
doctor, gravely. "This excitement is too
much for you, I am sure. Sit down.
Let me feel your pulse."

Amy sank again into her chair, because
she was unable to stand, but she drew
her wrist impatiently away from him.

"I care for nothing but my voice,"
she said. "Nothing else matters. Tell
me the truth about that!"

"My poor child, I fear that your voice
will never again be what it has been," he
answered, with sincere compassion in his
tones. "I would have spared you the
knowledge of this until you were stronger,
but since you insist—"

He stopped, for her face was growing
whiter under his gaze, her eyes dilating
with an expression which he never forgot.

"Do you mean," she said, "that I can
never sing in public?"

"It is not likely that you will ever be
able to do so," he replied, feeling that he
had no right to withhold the truth from
one who so earnestly desired to know it.
"The organs of your throat are, I fear,
hopelessly injured."

She looked at him for one moment
with a wild appeal in her eyes against

certainty. Then her head sank back, her
lids fell. Unconsciousness followed this
last, crushing blow.

CHAPTER XVIII.

"I WILL HOLD YOUR HAND BUT AS LONG AS ALL MAY."

WHEN Brian Marchmont left the
grounds of Cedarwood on the night of
the *fête*, he was tingling in every nerve
with that sense of defeat and mortification which of all sensations is the most
intolerable to a man of his stamp. Added
to this, he was so bitterly wroth with the
folly which had placed him in such a
position, that for the first time in his life
he turned savagely upon himself.

"I deserve it all," he thought, "for
the absolute insanity of which I have
been guilty! If I were twenty, the thing
would bear a different aspect, but at my
age, with my knowledge of the world, my
clearly-defined objects in life, to peril and
lose so much for the sake of an insignificant girl, there is no excuse for me—none!
By Heaven! I could almost sentence myself to a strait-waistcoat, when I think of
the madness with which I have walked
into the net spread by that fellow Archer.
I know that he has been spying upon me
from the first. I now feel sure that Amy
was right, that evening on the creek,
when she said the man on the opposite
bank was he. Then, that infernal miniature—how can I possibly put the facts he
has distorted in their true light? It may
be impossible to do so; but, at least, he
shall pay dearly for his interference."

Nor was this any vaporing threat, any
idle menace born of anger. Sybarite and
epicurean though Marchmont was, these
qualities lay merely on the surface, while
underneath was a nature possessing strong
passions, and capable of resolute and determined action when those passions were
roused.

The next morning he amazed Edward

Lathrop by requesting him to bear a challenge to Archer. That young gentleman took the cigar he was smoking from his lips, and stared at his cousin as if he thought sudden lunacy had overtaken him.

"Archer!" he repeated. "Why, there isn't a more inoffensive fellow than Archer in existence! You are surely not in earnest, Brian?"

"Am I likely to jest on such a subject?" asked Marchmont, with stern impatience. "Inoffensive! A snake may be inoffensive till it turns and strikes one; but no wise man will spare it after that."

"At least," said the other, more gravely, "you cannot expect me to act for you unless you give me some idea of the cause of the difficulty."

"That is easily given," answered Marchmont. "The fellow has made himself a spy upon my conduct for some time past—has interfered in the most insolent manner in my affairs—and has finally been successful in producing an estrangement between Miss Waldron and myself."

"Indeed!" said Lathrop. He began to comprehend the gravity of the situation, and his own countenance reflected it. "I should not have suspected Archer of such a thing," he said. "I thought him a man of honor. Are you sure there is no mistake?"

"There is no possible room for mistake," replied Marchmont. "The object he has in view is to marry Miss Waldron; I knew *that* the first time I ever saw him, but it is an object he shall not achieve. Unfortunately, it is out of my power to fight with such weapons as he has used, but pistols are no bad substitute."

"By Jove!" said Lathrop, lifting his hand and pulling his mustache.

The tone in which Marchmont uttered the last words, and the flash like blue steel from his eyes which accompanied them, made it unmistakably plain that affairs were very serious indeed. No man entertained a more rooted aversion to unpleasant things than Lathrop, and up to this point in his career he had managed to keep clear of them; but he felt that he could not refuse to stand by his cousin, however disagreeable the consequences might be.

"I am sorry, very sorry, for this," he said, presently; "but, of course, I will go to Archer if you insist upon it. Perhaps he may be able to make some explanation, to offer some apology—"

"There is no possibility of such a thing," Marchmont interrupted. "I don't think he is likely to refuse to fight. If he does, I shall know how to deal with him. Last night he said that, if I desired to hold him to account, I knew where he was to be found."

"If he said *that*, he is not likely to refuse to fight. But it is a most unfortunate affair, and will cause an immense amount of talk," said Lathrop, who now devoutly wished that Marchmont was some other man's cousin and guest.

Notwithstanding his reluctance, he bore the challenge to Archer, who received it without surprise.

"Mr. Marchmont would be wiser if he accepted the consequences of his conduct without calling attention to it," he said, quietly; "but that is altogether his own affair. If he chooses to hold me accountable for the part I have played, I am willing to afford him satisfaction."

"I know only what my cousin has told me of the matter," said Lathrop, who began to feel more and more that he was engaged in a very unpleasant thing; "but from my personal regard for your character, Mr. Archer, I hoped that some amicable settlement might be made."

"I regret that no proposal of the kind can come from me," said Archer. "Mr. Marchmont asserts that I have interfered in his private affairs in an unjustifiable manner. I acknowledge the fact of interference, but hold that every man is justified in endeavoring to unmask a scoundrel. I have, however, no intention of shirking the consequences of my acts. If

Mr. Marchmont wishes to fight, I am ready to meet him when and wherever he likes."

"You are a very impracticable and belligerent pair!" said Lathrop, in a tone of disgusted annoyance. "I have always believed that, if the principals were reasonable, such affairs as this could be arranged without difficulty; but, when the principals are *not* reasonable, there is evidently nothing to be done but to load the pistols. Of course, you will refer me to some friend, Mr. Archer?"

"I have not thought of it," replied Archer; "but I will endeavor to find some one to fill the position, and send him to you in the course of a few hours."

In the course of a few hours Mr. Archer's friend waited upon Mr. Lathrop, and all details of the affair were settled.

The meeting was arranged to take place the next morning, at a secluded place about a mile beyond the outskirts of Edgerton, and both parties agreed to keep the matter as quiet as possible.

For once this was done. No hint or rumor that a duel was impending electrified Edgerton as the day wore on—that day which Amy spent in watching by Felix's bedside; which Miss Waldron spent in her chamber at Cedarwood, with what her maid reported to be a "splitting headache;" which Marchmont spent in the Lathrop smoking-room, with a French novel for a companion; and which Archer, with a distinct knowledge of the danger before him, spent in his usual treadmill of business.

As evening began to close he threw aside the pen with which he had been occupied all day, and, leaning back in his chair, looked out of the window at which he sat.

Although his office was in the midst of buildings, it chanced that this window commanded a glimpse of the sky—a glimpse that was often like a vesper to him at the end of a weary day.

Just now the sky was flushed with the divinest beauties of sunset. Heaven itself seemed opening where the splendor burned in masses of saffron and rose, of violet and vivid gold. Green boughs, drooping with heavy foliage, interlaced across it, but the glory shone through, and fell on the worn face of the young man, whose quiet, rather sombre eyes were turned toward it. Was he thinking whether he should ever look on it again? If so, he gave no sign of such a thought; but, hearing a clock in the neighborhood strike seven, he rose, put away his papers, locked his safe, and went out.

The evening was rarely beautiful—one of those lovely, fragrant evenings of May, when the earth is so fair that day seems loath to leave it; and, as Archer felt the delicious sweetness and softness of the air on his face, almost unconsciously he turned his steps in the direction of Cedarwood.

"I shall not go in," he thought in apology for this act of weakness. "I shall only look at the place, and if possible catch a glimpse of her—for the last time, perhaps."

So, leaving the dusty streets behind, he took his way over the dewy, sweet-smelling fields which spread out like green velvet in the twilight, facing the pomp of sunset now burning faint and fainter in the far west, while a golden planet shone in the softly-tinted sky above.

When he reached the small gate giving admittance to Cedarwood, he paused, and, resting one arm on it, stood for several minutes motionless. Roses were clustering above and around him, exhaling their sweet incense on the air; a mocking-bird was singing in an oak-tree near by, as if it would fain ravish the world with melody; but he needed neither perfume nor full-throated song. His eyes swept over the lawn to where the house stood, with lights gleaming here and there from its wide-open doors and windows.

Surely her figure would pass across one of these windows—surely his passionate desire to obtain a glimpse—only a glimpse—of her, would be gratified! This desire seemed to grow in strength from his very nearness; so that he was forced to constrain himself to resist the impulse to go forward at all cost and see her, look into her eyes, touch her hand once more—for the last time, perhaps.

He had bared his head to the soft breeze blowing out of the golden west; and as he stood framed by the roses, with his yearning gaze bent on the house, the manly figure, the strong, earnest face, made a picture worth noting—worth admiring, indeed.

Beatrix Waldron thought so, as, in the course of an idle stroll around the lawn, she suddenly came in sight of the wicket-gate and paused, surprised by the appearance of Archer. At first she thought that he was simply on his way to the house; but when she saw the immobility of his attitude, and observed the intent, unchanging gaze, surprise merged into curiosity. She lingered in the shade, watching him, for some time; but he did not move, and she was obliged at last to come forward.

"Good-evening, Mr. Archer," she said, and the unexpected sound of the full, rich voice made him start. "May I ask what there is in the appearance of Cedarwood which seems to fascinate and yet repel you? I have been watching you for several minutes, and you have not stirred an inch, or taken your eyes once from the house."

"Is it possible you have been watching me?" asked Archer, coloring. "It is a little odd that I should not have felt it; there is usually so much magnetism in the gaze."

"You were so absorbed in thought, that even magnetism was unable to affect you. I should not think you would be a good subject for mesmerism."

"I am very sure I should not," he answered, looking at her with a sense of pleasure, the expression of which he vainly strove to repress from his tone and glance. Was it because he thought that he might never see her face again, that it appeared to him so fair just now? "Blessed be God who has made beautiful women," say the Arabs, and he could have echoed the benediction, as Beatrix stood in the lovely half-light of the gloaming, her graceful figure outlined by the dusky shade from which she had emerged, her stately head bare, her face more cameo-like than ever in its paleness—that soft brunette paleness which contrasts so effectively with dark eyes and hair.

"Have you come to inquire how we have survived the affair of last night?" she asked. "I have had a severe headache all day; but after dinner I came out to see if the fresh air would not help me, and it has done so. I don't want to be ungrateful to papa, but I hardly think I shall ever consent to give another ball."

"I should not imagine that there was any pleasure in it," he said, not thinking at all of what he was saying—only thinking of her, and of the difficulty of tearing himself away, now that he had obtained even more than the glimpse he had desired.

Feeling the abstraction of his manner, she glanced at him in some surprise.

"Are you not coming in?" she asked. "Papa is always glad to see you, and I—though I am very stupid—I can at least give you a cup of coffee."

"You are very kind," he said, hesitatingly; "but I did not mean to come in. I was sure you would not feel like being annoyed by visitors to-night."

"Not by ordinary visitors," she answered, with her peculiar frankness; "but I consider you very much as *ami de la maison*. Come and be bored," she said, with a smile. "I cannot allow you to stand and look over the gate and then go away."

The invitation of her voice and manner was more than Archer could resist. "For the last time, perhaps," he said to himself again, and opened the gate.

They slowly strolled across the lawn, the incense of flowers and the sweet notes of birds making the twilight delicious, and entered the drawing-room through one of the windows.

Here they found General Waldron, walking up and down with his hands behind his back.

"Good-evening, Archer," he said, brightening visibly. "I am glad to see you. Beatrix, I have been waiting for you to come in and give me a cup of coffee."

"Mr. Archer detained me, papa," said Beatrix. "I found him leaning over the gate, and it was some time before I could prevail upon him to advance any farther. But, considering the dew unwholesome, I thought it best to bring him in for a cup of coffee."

"Let us have it at once," said the general, ringing the bell.

The coffee was brought, and, having made Archer confess that he had not been to supper, Miss Waldron ordered some for him.

The general joined in doing justice to this repast, while Beatrix sat by in a low easy-chair with her coffee-cup in her hand —an indolent, graceful figure, with one slender, arched foot uncovered by the flowing sweep of her drapery, and the light catching the whiteness of her throat, the glimmer of gold around her wrists, and a fragrant yellow rose drooping among the dark braids of her hair.

As was natural under the circumstances, they talked of the entertainment of the evening before, of the toilets and the flirtations, of the concert and its success.

"Edgerton will some day be very proud of the fact that Amy Reynolds made her *début* here," said Miss Waldron.

"She has a magnificent voice," said Archer. "I had heard a good many rumors about it, but I paid little attention to them, knowing how prone to exaggeration the popular judgment is."

"I suppose her father intends her for the stage," said the general.

"Yes," answered Beatrix. Then she added, with a sigh, "Poor little Amy!"

"Is there any need to pity her?"

asked the general, with some surprise. "A petted, popular prima-donna is one of the most enviable people in the world —as the world goes."

"I am not sure of that," said Beatrix; "but I was not thinking of her public career when I spoke. I am sorry for her for other reasons."

"She does not look as if she was an object for compassion in any way," said General Waldron, recalling the Psyche-like figure, the radiant, triumph-flushed face of the night before.

Beatrix glanced at Archer, and, as their eyes met, the expression of his brought a flush to her cheek. It was an earnest, interrogative expression, which she imagined that she understood, and which she resented a little.

"How dare he imagine that *I* have suffered by the treachery of that man?" she thought; and, rising, she moved away to where the piano stood open, with its ivory keyboard gleaming in the subdued lamplight.

"Shall I sing for you, papa?" she said; and, without waiting for an answer, she sat down and began one of the ballads that the general loved.

When it ended she found that Archer had crossed the floor and was standing by her.

"You misunderstood me," he said, in a low voice. "I saw that in your face. I was thinking something very different from what you suppose. I was wondering—since you are generous enough to be sorry for that foolish girl—whether you would be sorry for some one else under other circumstances."

"You talk in enigmas," she said, looking at her hands, which were modulating a succession of soft chords. "Whether I was sorry or not, would depend upon how much sympathy or compassion 'some one else' deserved. I *am* sorry for that poor girl, foolish as she has been. I am sure she is suffering—and one can suffer very keenly at sixteen."

"Very superficially, as a rule; but

that does not matter. An aching finger is bad, if one has never known anything worse."

"And an aching heart is never matter for a sneer," said she, glancing up at him.

"Heaven forbid that I should sneer at it!" he said, with an earnestness which impressed her. "You surely did not think that I meant to do so? I only thank God that it is not *your* heart which is aching," he went on, quickly. "I was afraid—very much afraid—that you might care for that man enough to suffer from the knowledge of his treachery."

"Fortunately, my heart is not easily touched," she said, still playing softly. "I have been provoked with my insensibility once or twice; but I suppose it is for the best:

'Some there are that shadows kiss,
Some have but a shadow's bliss,'

and are content. I could not be. I can live without gold, but I cannot—I will not—accept tinsel for it."

"Yet there is gold in the world," he said, half unconsciously, and in a voice so full of passion that Beatrix suddenly started, and, instead of a chord, struck a jarring discord from the keys on which her fingers rested.

At that instant Florence Lathrop's warning—which for a time she had forgotten—recurred to her with startling force. Was it true that this man felt toward her as a lover? Had she unconsciously made discord indeed in the fair, well-ordered purpose of his life?

"Perhaps so," she answered, so absently and constrainedly that Archer knew he had betrayed himself, and then she glided into the delicate melody of one of the "Songs without Words."

He stood motionless while she played it, and when it was finished he said, with his usual manner:

"Although this is very pleasant, I must not forget that you are, of necessity, tired. Let me thank you for a delightful evening, and say good-night."

Contrary to custom, he extended his hand—extended it so gravely and quietly, that Beatrix could not hesitate to place hers in it.

For an instant—only for an instant—he held it in a close, warm grasp, looking the while into her eyes with an expression she afterward remembered and comprehended. Then, again saying "Goodnight," he turned, crossed the room, spoke to the general, and went away.

. . . . . .

The next morning, when Miss Waldron came down to breakfast, she was surprised to find her father's place vacant and her father gone. She glanced with astonishment at his coffee-cup only half emptied, at the paper thrown aside unread, and then rang the bell sharply.

"Where is your master, Price?" she said to the servant who answered it, and who had a startled look on his face.

"Master's gone into town, Miss Beatrix," answered Price, solemnly, and then paused as if uncertain whether or not to say more.

"Gone into town!" repeated Beatrix. "Why, he has not taken his breakfast!"

"No, m'm; he was only just beginning it," assented Price, gravely.

"What called him away?" she asked.

Price's face grew more solemn, but it was a solemnity mixed with pleasure—that pleasure which all people of his class feel in being the first to tell a piece of sensational news.

"Master was just beginnin' his breakfast," he said, "when he heard of a duel that's been fought in Edgerton. Bob, what brought the mail, told him; and when he heard that Mr. Archer was dead, or dying, he went right off."

Beatrix's eyes opened wide on the speaker, but, with an effort to compose herself, she said, quietly:

"Who fought the duel—and what had Mr. Archer to do with it? There is some absurd mistake—"

"Oh, no, m'm, there isn't!" interposed Price, eagerly. "Mr. Archer fought the duel—him and Mr. Marchmont, at daylight this morning—and Bob saw them bringing in Mr. Archer in a carriage. He wasn't quite dead then, but they said he couldn't live."

Beatrix sank into the chair by which she was standing, her face growing white as the morning-dress she wore. In the terrible shock of the moment her heart almost ceased to beat. With a sudden flash of intuition she understood everything. It was for his interests in *her* affairs that Marchmont had held Archer to account, and that the latter paid so dearly! As the thought occurred to her, a great sense of passionate indignation overmastered every other consideration. "The wretch!" she said, between her clinched teeth. "How dare he take such a revenge as this?"

Then she looked up at Price, pale as marble. "Take a horse and go into Edgerton at once!" she said. "Find your master, and ask him to send me word exactly how Mr. Archer is. Don't waste a minute; go and return as quickly as possible."

When the servant was gone she turned away from the breakfast-table with that terrible sickness of the heart which unnerves the whole body and sends a sensation of deadly faintness to the very tips of the fingers. The morning was exuberantly bright and glorious—one of those mornings of mingled spring and summer when Nature seems rendering joyous thanks to her Creator in every gleam of sunshine, every matin song of her feathered choir. But to Beatrix there was something ghastly in all this brightness. With earth so fair around and heaven so pure above, the life of a brave and honorable man had been put in deadly peril—cut short, perhaps—because he had tried to save her from deception and misery.

She wandered restlessly into the drawing-room; but, when her eyes fell on the spot where he had bidden her farewell the night before, a great throb of pain seized her heart; she suddenly remembered the wistful, intent gaze with which he had been regarding the house when she found him at the gate. "This was what it meant!" she cried. "And I—how cold, how constrained, how unsympathetic I was!"

There was deep wretchedness in such thoughts, but she could not banish them. She left the drawing-room and walked restlessly up and down the portico, until at last—after what seemed an interminable length of time—Price appeared in sight galloping down the road.

How long he took to reach the gates! —how long to canter up the avenue to where she stood on the steps, shivering in the warm sunshine!

Her fingers were cold as ice, and trembling so that she could scarcely control them, when she took the note he brought and tore it open. This was what the general wrote:

"Archer is desperately wounded, and the doctors seem to entertain very little hope of his recovery. He is shot through the lung, and it is surprising that he was not killed outright. Marchmont is unhurt. Both have observed great reticence with regard to the cause of the affair."

The paper dropped from her hand, and she stood gazing at the wide, beautiful prospect before her. Desperately wounded!—and that for no fault of his own, but because another man chose to be treacherous and dishonorable!

"He was mad to meet him!" she murmured, half aloud. "But, if he dies, I think I could find strength to kill Marchmont myself!"

CHAPTER XIX.

"THE THORNS I REAP ARE OF THE TREE I PLANTED."

IN all her after-life Beatrix Waldron never forgot that day—so joyous in its beauty, so full of the soft whispering of leaves, the songs of birds, the multitudinous sweet sounds of summer—when she was alone at Cedarwood with the thought that Archer was dying.

The great empty house seemed to her strangely hushed and silent, and even the golden glory of the sunshine in her imagination was full of pathos. During the long, bright hours of the morning she wandered aimlessly to and fro, hoping constantly that her father would return; but when the time for luncheon came there was still no sign of him.

Luncheon—at least the pretense of it—being over, the afternoon waned in mellow loveliness, but still the general did not come. As hour after hour passed, Beatrix's impatience and anxiety grew almost uncontrollable. Once she ordered the carriage, but countermanded the order before the horses had been harnessed. She longed to drive into Edgerton and learn exactly how matters stood; but a fear lest her name might be more closely associated with the affair than she knew deterred her from doing so. If it should be on every one's lip—as she had known other women's names in connection with duels—she felt that she could not bear to appear and run the gantlet of observation which is leveled upon the heroine of such tragedies.

Neither did she like to send another message to her father. That shadow of propriety—that question, "What will be thought of it?"—which stands by women in all hours and at all times of their lives, made her hesitate even in this. "After all, why should I be in so much haste?" she said to herself. "If the news is bad, I shall hear it soon enough. If it is good—but, alas! I fear there is little hope of that."

As this thought formed in her mind, the sound of wheels and horses' feet advancing up the avenue made her start. She moved hastily to the window, but, instead of the barouche which had been sent for her father, it was the Lathrop carriage which drew up before the door.

Surprise was her predominant sensation on recognizing the equipage—a surprise which was not lessened by the fact that Mrs. Lathrop's portly figure descended from it. At sight of this figure a swift wave of color rose into Miss Waldron's pale cheeks. "Has *he* ventured to send her here?" she thought, as she turned from the window and walked across the room. According to the usual dilatory habits of servants, several minutes elapsed before the visitor's name was brought up, and these minutes Beatrix spent at her mirror, knowing that she could not afford to appear in any disconsolate guise before the keen eyes which awaited her below.

She was quieter, cooler, rather more stately than usual, when she entered the drawing-room; this was the only change that Mrs. Lathrop perceived. That lady, however, was herself very much shaken out of her wonted repose, and therefore not altogether possessed of her usual cool judgment. Greetings having been exchanged, she plunged at once into the subject which occupied her thoughts.

"My dear," she said, when they had seated themselves, "I have come to see you chiefly to express my deep regret for this most unfortunate affair."

"I suppose," said Beatrix, coldly, "that you allude to the duel between Mr. Marchmont and Mr. Archer. But why should you come to me to express your regret with regard to it?"

"There are several reasons why I have felt impelled to do so," replied Mrs. Lathrop, with her most imposing air. "In the first place, I must tell you that I have never in my life been so mortified and grieved by any one connected with me as by my nephew, Brian Marchmont. As far as I can learn, there is no excuse for his conduct, and I am deeply provoked with Edward for acting as his second in this duel."

"There is certainly no excuse for his conduct," said Beatrix. "You are quite right with regard to that."

"It is probable that you may imagine," proceeded Mrs. Lathrop, "that I have been anxious for the success of his suit with you. Such a conclusion would be a natural but a very mistaken one. I have never, my dear, *never* thought that such a marriage would be for your happiness; and I frankly told Brian so when I remonstrated with him, several weeks ago, on his flirtation with that girl Amy Reynolds."

"If you had spoken to me on the subject," said Beatrix, in the same cold, even voice, "I might have set your mind at rest by assuring you that I had not the least intention of marrying Mr. Marchmont. I am sorry that I ever took his suit into consideration; but I knew little of him at the time, and it seemed only just to know more before deciding finally."

"It almost appears as if madness possessed him," said Mrs. Lathrop. "To bring rejection on himself, as I said to-day, and then to resent it by taking another man's life."

"Is Mr. Archer dead?" asked Beatrix, quickly.

Despite her self-control, she could not repress the sudden quiver that ran over her frame, the sudden pallor that came to her face, and Mrs. Lathrop noted both.

"He was not dead when I left Edgerton," she replied, "but I believe the doctors give little hope of his recovery. May I ask, my dear—as your sincere friend, and with a view to contradicting authoritatively the many wild rumors that are afloat—exactly *what* the ground of quarrel was? I have heard—but I can hardly believe it—that Mr. Archer was your suitor."

"He was not," said Beatrix. "He was only my friend, and as my friend he tried to serve me. Of the exact ground of quarrel I am ignorant. Though Mr. Archer was here last night," she went on, with her voice slightly faltering, "he said nothing of the affair, and hence I know no more concerning it than you do."

"Indeed!" said Mrs. Lathrop.

This astute woman, who had come to Cedarwood resolved to learn all that was possible, did not suffer that sign of faltering to escape her, and, regarding Miss Waldron closely, she went on:

"So Mr. Archer was here last night! He must possess remarkable self-control, if he did not betray any sense of the danger he was about to incur. Neither Brian nor Edward joined our family circle yesterday evening."

"Mr. Archer was altogether as usual," answered Beatrix, briefly; but as she spoke she remembered vividly that farewell glance which she now so well understood.

"With regard to the cause of the duel," said Mrs. Lathrop, after a moment's pause, "it is the general impression that Brian challenged Mr. Archer because he had produced an estrangement between him—that is, Brian—and yourself."

"He did nothing of the kind," said Beatrix. "The idea rests on an entire misconception. There is no 'estrangement' between your nephew and myself, Mrs. Lathrop. I simply discovered—partly through Mr. Archer, partly through others, but chiefly through circumstances—that, while professing to be my suitor, Mr. Marchmont was making love to another woman. That, in itself, apart from his other dishonorable conduct, was enough to make me decline any further acquaintance with him."

"I told him how it would be," said Mrs. Lathrop, shaking her head. "I warned him of such a result as soon as I heard of that affair with Amy Reynolds."

"I would rather not speak of the matter," said Beatrix, drawing her brows together. "It all seems of small account just now—of horribly small account, to cost a gallant and honorable life."

"Nevertheless, we have to think of what will be said," answered the veteran woman of the world, laying her hand impressively on her companion's arm.

"Candidly, my dear, it would be better for you to give me exactly the version of the affair you would like circulated. We cannot keep people from talking, so the best thing to do is to give them, if possible, the truth to talk about."

But Beatrix, who felt that she had borne as much as she possibly could, made a gesture of impatience.

"Let them talk as they please," she said; "I feel absolutely indifferent to anything they can say. Pray do not trouble me any further with the subject, Mrs. Lathrop. It is at once painful and disagreeable."

Mrs. Lathrop, whose curiosity and "managing" proclivities had seldom been so baffled, would have liked to press the matter further, but there was something in Miss Waldron's face and manner which made this impossible; so, after a little constrained and desultory conversation, she rose and took leave.

As her carriage was driving out of the grounds, the general's long-expected barouche entered the gates, and Beatrix had the trial of standing at the drawing-room window for fully ten minutes, watching the two equipages standing abreast while their occupants talked.

Few things are more trying to nerves and temper than such waiting for news as this, while the bearer of it is within sight; and Beatrix could have condemned Mrs. Lathrop to silence for a year before that lady finally drove off.

When the general reached the portico, he found his daughter waiting for him, with an appealing look of anxiety in her eyes.

Her first words were a question.

"How is he, papa?" she asked.

"No better," answered her father, who was deliberately alighting; "but, I am glad to say, no worse. The doctors don't give much hope, but it is my opinion he may get well. He has a good constitution to fall back upon, and I have known men more seriously wounded to recover."

"Oh, thank you, papa; it is pleasant to hear something encouraging at last! Why didn't you come back sooner? I have been so lonely and wretched all day!"

"Well, I did not like to leave the poor fellow. He has few friends, you know, and this morning the doctors thought he might die at any time. He was a fool to meet that puppy Marchmont; but, after all," said the gentleman of the old *régime*, "it is a good thing to err on the side of courage."

"He was worse than foolish—he was wrong, to meet him!" said Beatrix.

"Eh? was he?" said her father. "From what I hear, I imagine that you know more of it than any one else; and I shall be glad if you will tell me all that you know, after a while."

After a while, therefore, Beatrix complied with this request, and for the first time the general heard of the dishonorable conduct of the man who had aspired to be his son-in-law. His wrath was deep and loud.

"The scoundrel!" he said, twisting his white mustache vehemently. "He has not the faintest claim to be esteemed a gentleman! No schoolboy of average honor would have held his tongue about the miniature and allowed that poor boy to suffer. As for his conduct to you, it is difficult to characterize that as it deserves!"

"Fortunately I cared nothing for him," said Beatrix, "so it did not matter. But it is cowardly to strike at me through my friends."

"It is more than cowardly—it is infamous!" said the general, "and if Archer dies, I shall feel inclined to try *my* hand at shooting. By Jove! I don't wonder he could not refuse the challenge. I should like a crack at the fellow myself."

"The result has not been very satisfactory, so far as Mr. Archer is concerned," said Beatrix.

The next day the news from Archer

was very much of the same character, although the doctors expressed a little more hope.

It was in the course of this day that Miss Waldron was shocked to hear of the sudden death of Felix Reynolds, and she drove at once into Edgerton to offer her sympathy and condolence.

At the house of the musician she saw only Mr. Trafford, and heard from him of Amy's illness and Mr. Reynolds's despair.

"How often a narrow step alone divides brightest pleasure from deepest pain!" she said. "Do you remember the joy and pride of Mr. Reynolds's face when Felix was playing on the night of the *fête?* And poor Amy! *her* triumph was turned to bitterness even before this came. I am so very sorry for her! If I can do anything, Mr. Trafford, pray let me know—anything, I mean, in the way of assistance."

"You are very kind, my dear young lady," said Mr. Trafford, "and I will certainly call upon you if there is any need to do so. I sincerely hope that Mr. Archer may recover," he went on, looking at her with a certain friendly keenness, "and I believe he will. I saw him this morning, and I do not think he has any appearance of a man who means to die."

"I hope not," said Beatrix. Then, with a few more expressions of kindly interest, she went away.

As she was entering the carriage, Hugh Dinsmore approached the house, and, when she beckoned him to her side, she was struck by the haggard paleness of his face.

"I know this is a grief to you," she said, gently. "Felix was to have been your traveling companion—was he not?"

Hugh's eyes filled with tears. "Felix has been my companion always," he said, "and it added to my happiness, in the thought of going abroad, that I was to be with him—that we could go together and become artists, as we had so often dreamed of doing. Now—"

"It is very sad," said Miss Waldron, as his voice faltered and ceased; "but remember that the friends whom death takes we possess in a measure still; at least, nothing can dim or mar their memory. Those whom life takes from us, on the contrary, we lose utterly. If Felix had lived, you might have lost him, some day, in a worse manner than this. Try and let that thought comfort you. Will you come out to Cedarwood as soon as possible?" she added. "Papa wishes to make some arrangements about your journey."

"There would be no good in my coming just now," said Hugh, looking at her with his limpid eyes. "I cannot go away —I cannot decide anything while Amy is ill. I must know that she is well; I must see her again before I can leave Edgerton."

"That is natural," said Miss Waldron, reading the whole story at once. "Come when you like, then; papa is in no haste. Good-morning!"

As she drove away, her meditations were by no means of a cheerful order. "What a curious tangle life is!" she thought. "Here this poor boy has set his heart on a girl who cares nothing for him—who, in turn, has given *her* heart to a man who merely regarded her as a subject for idle amusement. Is it always so, I wonder? Are women's eyes always blinded by tinsel to the value of gold? Ah, not always—not always! I take no credit to myself for not loving that man. I am simply older, wiser, colder, than the child who gave him all that she had to give of passion and fancy; but I have been as blind as she to the merit of another."

.   .   .   .   .

It has been said before, that want of courage was not one of Marchmont's faults, and therefore it was not strange that he remained in Edgerton for several days after the duel. Public sentiment indignantly condemned his course, but for that very reason he defied public sentiment by his presence. His friends and relations were exceedingly anxious for his departure, but he was in no haste to gratify them. The place had become hateful to him, but he would not give people the least ground for saying that he was afraid to remain; so, for once, he compelled himself to endure an absolutely disagreeable thing.

During these days he heard of Felix's death, but the event made no impression on him; graver matters of concern had thrust Amy from his mind, and, if he thought of her at all, it was with a sense of impatient anger.

He had thrown away solid advantages and involved himself in any amount of unpleasantness on her account, and she had ventured to turn upon him with ungrateful reproaches! His idle fancy for her had died on that night, in the grounds of Cedarwood, when, instead of the pretty, piquant toy he had believed her to be, she faced him with the indignation of an outraged woman; from that moment her influence, such as it was, sank down and died, and her quondam lover only thought of her to execrate his folly.

At last the day came when Archer was, by medical authority, pronounced out of danger, and Marchmont felt that no man could venture to cast a reproach upon him if he left Edgerton. He prepared to do so with a great sense of relief.

It was impossible for him to disguise from himself the fact that he had made a complete *fiasco* of the business which had drawn him here; and if a *fiasco* is an established fact, it is at least pleasant to leave the scene of it behind.

He left this scene on an afternoon of golden beauty, when through the drooping boughs of the trees the sun's rays shot in long lances of gold, and the air seemed dissolving in amber mist—an afternoon like many of those when he had loitered with Amy among the spring woods where summer's richer robes now hung. The Lathrops obeyed very heartily the hospitable injunction to "speed the parting guest;" and it was the same sense of duty which had influenced Edward in the matter of the duel, which induced him to accompany his cousin to the railroad-station and see him off.

On their way thither they passed the church which the Lathrops attended, and where Marchmont had once or twice, in a fit of *ennui*, accompanied them. The door stood open, a few people were lingering round it, and the bell in the tower above was tolling slowly, solemnly, on the still air. Who has not sometimes been struck with the painful incongruity of such a knell with the soft loveliness of a day which alone seems fitted for life and happiness? Even Marchmont felt it now.

"It is hard lines on some poor creature to be put under the ground to-day," he said. "Who is to be buried, Ned?"

"Haven't you heard?" answered Lathrop, regarding him with an odd look. "Mr. Reynolds is dead."

Despite himself, Marchmont felt that he started and changed color. In truth, he was for a moment deeply shocked.

"Good Heaven!" he said. "Do you mean the music-teacher—Amy's father?"

"The same," his cousin answered.

"Why, what has killed him?"

"The visitation of God—as coroners' juries say—I suppose. Some people think that he died of grief from the death of his son."

"It is a great misfortune for his family, is it not?" said Marchmont, after a pause. "Have they anything to depend upon?"

"I don't know about their affairs, but I should not imagine they had. Amy will probably make a fortune some day, if she lives."

"If she lives!" repeated Marchmont. "Is she ill?"

"What! you don't know that?" asked Lathrop, in surprise. "She is dangerously ill, I believe, with diphtheria—the same disease of which Felix died."

"I had not heard it," said Marchmont,

slowly. Then, after a moment's silence, he added, "I am very sorry."

"It certainly is a pity," said the other, a little dryly—"or will be a pity if she dies—poor girl!"

Marchmont did not answer this remark; perhaps he could not. Steeped in selfishness and worldliness as he was, a thrill of shame went through him—shame for leaving, at such a time as this, without even a word of sympathy, without even learning whether she lived or died, the girl he had professed to love.

For one minute—with the deep stroke of the bell falling measuredly on his ear, and reminding him of her desolate position—he felt an inclination to return; but this did not last long.

"What good could I possibly accomplish?" he asked himself. "It would be absurd and inconvenient in every way for me to do such a thing."

"We are barely in time to catch your train, Brian," said Lathrop, as they came in sight of the station. "Yonder it stands."

"I should not like to miss it," said Marchmont.

Nor did he. By the time he reached the platform of the station a revulsion of feeling had come, and he was more anxious than ever to leave. "Our pleasant vices are made whips with which to scourge us," and some such whip the thought of Amy Reynolds had become to him. He was glad to shake hands quickly with Lathrop, to spring into the moving train, and to feel that its motion bore him swiftly away from past follies and future annoyances.

CHAPTER XX.

EXEUNT OMNES.

AFTER the last heavy blow that struck Amy to the earth, the doctor went in grave anxiety to Mr. Trafford.

"I am very uneasy about that poor girl," he said. "She has learned that her voice is ruined, and her despair is terrible—not noisy, you understand, but worse than that. When I was obliged to tell her the truth yesterday, she fainted, and since then she has hardly uttered a word. She simply lies and stares blankly out of the window, with an expression of face that might move a stone to pity. In all my life I never felt more sorry for any one. Her relations and friends—if she has any—certainly ought to be informed of her condition."

"She has no relations, and, to my knowledge, but one friend," replied Mr. Trafford, quietly. "That friend will endeavor to do the best he can for her, doctor, you may be sure."

"That friend is yourself, of course," said the doctor. "You are an extraordinary man, Mr. Trafford."

"If you mean with regard to my conduct in this matter, I should be sorry to agree with you. It is surely not extraordinary to feel compassion for the desolate and helpless."

"You ought to know the world as well as I," said the doctor, dryly, "therefore you ought to know that it *is* extraordinary for a man to feel such compassion, and more extraordinary still for him to act upon it in any practical manner. But then, you are not bound by the ties that bind most men," he added, reflectively.

"I am glad to say that I am not," answered Mr. Trafford, "if such ties would serve me, as I have seen them serve other men, as an excuse and cloak for selfishness. I am much obliged for your information," he went on, "and I will see Miss Reynolds as soon as possible. When do you think I can do so?"

"The sooner the better, I should say, if you have any comfort to offer her."

"Very well," said Mr. Trafford, meditatively.

While this conversation was in progress, some one else had forestalled the deliberation of the elder man with the impetuosity of youth, and insisted upon seeing Amy without delay.

This was Hugh Dinsmore, who had haunted the house like a restless spirit during Amy's illness, but who could not have won permission from Clara to see her now, if the faithful guardian had not thought that his presence might rouse the girl a little from that apathy of despair which alarmed her as it alarmed the doctor.

"And she has heard that her voice is lost?" cried Hugh. "Clara, I must—I *must* see her! She will die if some one does not try to help her!"

"'Deed, it looks like it!" said Clara, in a melancholy tone. "I reckon you *might* see her; it couldn't do no harm, and it might do some good. She's dressed, but she don't seem to care about leavin' her room; so I'll take you up there."

Hugh was accordingly taken up and introduced into the small, plain, spotless chamber, which, like every other corner of the house, he had known well during his years of intimacy with the Reynolds children.

His old playmate, so altered in appearance that he would scarcely have known her, sat by the window which overlooked the garden, gazing with blank, sombre eyes at the network of boughs across the soft blue sky.

"Here's Mr. Hugh Dinsmore, Miss Amy," said Clara, opening the door. "He's been makin' such a fuss to see you, that I thought I'd bring him up."

"Come in, Hugh," said Amy, turning her face, without the least variation of expression. "It is kind of you to want to see me, and you are almost the only person whom I would not *dislike* to see. That is a poor welcome," she added, with the saddest possible smile; "but you will take it for what it is worth—will you not?"

"O Amy — my poor Amy!" cried Hugh, appalled by the change in her—by the quiet of the white, thin face, by the sombre darkness of the sunken eyes, by

the entire aspect of hopeless despair. With a passionate grasp he held the frail hands which she yielded passively to him, and gazed at her with a sorrow and sympathy too deep for words.

Amy looked at him also, but it was with a far-off, absent gaze, as if she were thinking of something far beyond the actual moment.

"How long it seems since last we met, Hugh!" she said. "Do you remember? It was the night of the concert; you and I and Felix were in the parlor, and I sang for you."

"I have seen you since then," said Hugh. "Once, in Felix's room—"

"I did not see you then," she said; "but I remember that night as if I saw a picture across a great gulf: you and I and Felix, and papa coming in, and how I sang, and how excited I was, and how pretty I looked—and now! Can you count up all that I have lost since then, Hugh?"

"Don't talk of it," said Hugh, in a choked voice. "It is—it is too much for you."

"Why should I not talk of it, when I think of it all the time!" she said, looking at him with the same unchanging face. "You need not be afraid that I shall give way and cry. I do not think I shall ever shed a tear again. So much has gone, that I hardly feel as if anything was left. Papa and Felix, and my voice and my heart, and my power to be sorry, it seems—all that, Hugh, and more besides. I wonder why I got well. I thought it was to take care of Mariette and the boys. But what can I do for them, now that my voice is gone? We are only helpless children together, with not one friend on earth."

"O Amy, have you forgotten me?" cried poor Hugh. He knelt before her, and, still holding her hands fast in his own, looked appealingly at the wan young face, now bereft of all beauty save the beauty of outline. "Ever since we were little children I have been like one of

8

your brothers," he said. "Let me be your brother now. I will help you, I will work for you, I will do everything in the world I can, if you will only let me serve you—and you will, Amy—will you not?"

"It is impossible, Hugh!" said Amy, quietly; "you know it is impossible. I have no claim upon you—none in the world—unless you consider it a claim to have treated you unkindly, to have refused to listen to your advice, and to have suffered at last for my obstinacy and heedlessness, as you told me that I would suffer."

"You have the claim of our old friendship and affection," said Hugh. "I have not forgotten that the only home-life I have ever known has been in this house. Amy, I am strong, and I can work hard for you, if you will only consider me as a brother."

"You are very kind, Hugh," said Amy, touched by his pleading, but still more by his delicacy in not mentioning his love; "but I am older than you in *feeling*, and I know that such a thing is quite impossible. Besides, you forget that you have your own life to consider—that you are going abroad to study art."

"I have decided not to go," said Hugh. "I have been offered a clerkship here, and I will take it gladly, if you say so."

"And give up the career on which your heart is set?" asked Amy, looking at him in surprise.

"I would rather be of use to you than become the greatest artist in the world," he answered, simply.

"Are you in earnest?" she said, roused to interest. "Would you give up the object of your life, now that it is within your grasp, and remain here, bound to a toil you detest—all for my sake? Hugh, do you mean it?"

"I mean it with all my heart!" he replied; "and I will work as I have never worked before in all my life, Amy, if you will let me take charge of you."

Amy was silent for a moment. Her eyes left the eager face before her, and gazed out of the open window at the far blue sky with a strange, reflective expression.

"You would do all this for me?" she said, at last, slowly; "and I—what have I done for you? What sacrifice have I ever made? Hugh, I feel this moment, as I have never before felt, how shameful my conduct has been. But you are so kind, so patient, you will forgive me—will you not? I cannot accept your sacrifice—I could not be so selfish, even if other reasons did not make it impossible. You must go away and be an artist. How we three talked and dreamed of being artists together some day—do you remember? Now, Felix is dead, and my voice is dead with him, and you are the only one left to fulfill our dreams. You must do it; and if we should never see each other again, you must think 'that poor Amy, though foolish and vain, was very young; and when sorrow and desolation came, she found that she had one faithful, unselfish friend, and she never, never forgot him!'"

"And you won't let me help you?" cried Hugh, despairingly. "O Amy, you must—you must! You don't know—you don't understand what a terrible thing the world is to a girl like you. It would have been hard enough to conquer even with all the sweetness of your voice; but *now*—"

"I know it all," she said, as he paused. "I think of it until my brain seems reeling. O Hugh, if I had my voice, I should fear nothing! Was it not cruel to take my voice from me—all that I had left?"

"Hush, dear!" said Hugh. "You forget Who took it."

"I suppose you mean that God took it," she said, "and perhaps he did; but do you know who was the human cause of its loss?"

"You contracted the disease which ruined it in nursing Felix," said Hugh, uncertain as to what she meant.

"And Felix took it from a schoolfellow whom he would never have gone to see if he had sailed for Europe when papa intended that he should. He did not sail because Brian Marchmont threw on him, as well as on you, suspicion with regard to that miniature. And so it is to Brian Marchmont that I owe—everything."

"I would not think of it if I were you," said Hugh, rendered vaguely uneasy by her manner.

"I hope I shall always think of it," she said. "I trust that I shall never forget my debt until I can pay it."

Before Hugh could answer, the door opened, and Clara looked in.

"Mr. Trafford's down-stairs, and is very anxious to see you, Miss Amy," she said. "Shall I bring him up?"

"Yes," answered Amy, with the same quiet apathy that she had shown with regard to Hugh.—"Mr. Trafford has been so kind, that I cannot refuse to see him," she added, as Clara went away. "He has done a great deal for us."

"*He* has the power," said Hugh, for the first time feeling a jealous envy of Mr. Trafford.

"I am as grateful to you for having the will," she said, looking at him with her steady, sad eyes—eyes out of which the sunny joyousness of youth had died forever.

As Mr. Trafford came up-stairs he met Hugh going down, and paused for a moment to speak to the young man.

"I suppose you will soon be turning your face toward the Old World," he said, after they had exchanged greetings.

"It is by no means certain that I shall go at all," Hugh answered, rather brusquely, and passed on.

Even to Hugh's generous nature it was hard to look at the elder man and think how much he was able to do for Amy, while he himself could do nothing.

Mr. Trafford, who had not seen Amy since her illness, was, like Hugh, shocked by her wasted appearance.

Sickness, grief, and wearing anxiety,

can in a short time work a great change; and they had done their utmost here.

As Mr. Trafford entered the room, Amy rose to meet him, and held out her hand with an air of gravity which seemed to place her far above the level of the pretty girl he had noticed and admired a short time before.

"How good you have been to us!" she said, lifting her dark, circled eyes to his. "I cannot thank you now, Mr. Trafford; but some day, perhaps—"

"Never mind about that, my dear," he interrupted. "You have nothing—nothing at all—for which to thank me. I have been heartily glad to be of service, but I have done very little. I have now come to discuss how I can best serve you further," he went on, plunging hastily into his subject. "Let us sit down. My poor child, this will never do! You are a shadow—an absolute ghost!"

"Am I?" said Amy, indifferently. "Yes, I suppose so; but it does not matter."

"Excuse me," said Mr. Trafford, "but I disagree with you there. It *does* matter very much; and I see that the doctor was right—you need change of air and scene at once."

She looked a little surprised.

"I did not think the doctor was so foolish as to say such a thing of *me*," she answered. "Did he tell you the awful news that my voice—my one possession, my last hope—is gone?"

"He told me," replied Mr. Trafford, compassionately. "I was grieved, but not surprised. The disease which you have had generally injures the voice, and therefore I feared this from the first. Since it has destroyed your cherished life-plan, have you made any other?"

"How could I?" she asked, drearily. "It was only yesterday I discovered the loss of my voice. Since then I have done nothing but wonder why I did not die—I, instead of Felix! But I am alive, and I must find some way to make bread for myself and the children who will be dependent on me. Can you tell me, Mr. Trafford—you who know the world—what I can do? I am so young, and, alas, so ignorant! I could sing—that was all. What can I do, now that my voice is gone?"

Mr. Trafford rose abruptly and walked across the room and back. His eyes were suspiciously moist, and he blew his nose with an emphasis which made Amy start.

When he returned to her side and sat down again, he took one of the small, frail hands, as Hugh had done a short time before.

"My dear," he said, kindly and gravely, "I feel for you more than words can express, and this sympathy must be my excuse for what I am about to propose. You ask if I can suggest anything for you to do—you, so young, so delicate, so unfitted to cope with the world! I answer, that I have been considering the matter ever since your father's death, and I have decided that there is but one thing for you to do—if you can; that is, to marry me."

"Mr. Trafford!" gasped Amy. She could say nothing more, but her face expressed extreme amazement.

She had felt as if nothing on earth could startle her benumbed sensations; but this gave her a shock of surprise which thrilled her like a charge from a galvanic battery. She gazed at the speaker with eyes expanded and lips apart, as if doubting the evidence of her senses.

"I thought I should startle you," he said, "but there was no way to avoid it. Now, listen to me before you answer. I am a rich man, and have not a relative in the world who has any claim upon my fortune. Under these circumstances, I feel at liberty to leave it as I please, and for some time past I have decided to leave it to you. I can hardly tell what influenced me to this determination, except that I liked you—one can't analyze liking, you know; and when I heard you wishing for wealth, I felt inclined to transform myself into a sort of fairy godfather. If I had chosen to announce that I meant to make you sole heiress of a fortune larger than General Waldron's, you might have married the man with whom you fancied yourself in love a little while ago; but I think you have sense enough to be glad that I spared you such a fate. Had your father lived, I should never have asked you to become the wife of an old fellow like me; but I now see no other means of giving you the home and the protector you need. If you consent to marry me, I will do everything in my power to make you happy; and I will care for Mariette and the boys as if they were my own children. I have turned the matter over in my mind, and I can see no other plan which is not open to grave objections. However, if *you* can think of any other, I will give it careful consideration."

He paused, as if waiting for her answer; but Amy could not answer. The world seemed spinning round with her, and the pleasant face she knew so well, with its iron-gray hair and kindly eyes, seemed gazing at her out of a mist.

"Take time," he said, seeing her agitation. "I am in no haste. If you cannot answer me now, I will wait until to-morrow. Think of the matter in all its bearings, and give me your decision then."

"Stop!" said Amy, as he rose, and she laid her hand nervously on his arm. "You have forgotten—you cannot mean such a thing as this, if you remember my wretched folly—"

"I remember all that," he interrupted; "but your folly was *only* folly—nothing worse. Answer me this: if Brian Marchmont entered that door now, how would you feel toward him?"

"I should feel that I hated him with all my strength!" she answered, with a sudden light of passion flashing into her eyes.

"He is not worth bestowing hate upon," said Mr. Trafford, gravely. "Simply put him out of your mind and your heart—that will do."

"He has left me no heart," she said. "That is the worst of it. I cannot even grieve as I should for papa and Felix—I feel so dead. Nothing moves me. I am very grateful to you, Mr. Trafford, but I do not feel your kindness as I ought. I only know you must be very sorry for me, to make such a proposal as you have."

"My dear little girl," he said, gently, "I am very sorry for you; but all the sorrow in the world would not induce me to make such an offer, if I were not sincerely attached to you. I am too old for lovers' rhapsodies, but it is my heart which I offer you as well as my hand."

She looked up at him, with unutterable astonishment on her face.

"Your heart—to me!" she said. "Why, you have only known me as an ignorant, foolish, selfish child!"

"But I think there are capabilities of other things in you," he answered. "At least, such as you are I like you, and, if you can marry me, I will endeavor to make you happy. Don't answer now, however. I will be back to-morrow."

With a warm clasp of her hand, he went away, and a minute later she heard his voice, speaking to Mariette in the passage below.

The sound brought back to her memory all his kindness during the period of sorrow through which they had passed, and, sinking back into her chair, she covered her face with her hands and tried to think.

It did not take long for her to decide that she would accept Mr. Trafford's proposal. There was every motive to induce her to do so, and no reason for refusal. If he had asked her for love, she would have turned away from him; but he had not done so, and she felt an instinctive sense that she could trust him not to demand more than she could give. She had been scorched by the fire of passion until she shrank from the mere thought of it; and there was an attraction in the very calmness of the man who offered

her position and wealth, recognizing the great gulf of years between them.

Only those who have stood, like Amy, desolate and helpless, bereft of everything, can appreciate what this offered protection was to her; and when her decision was finally taken, she drew a deep breath of relief to think that all anxiety was over—anxiety for herself, and for those even more helpless than herself.

Yet it was with a great sense of sadness and pain that she bade farewell to all the past—to the careless Bohemian life—to the glorious hopes of winning fame and fortune—to the days made golden by the light of youth's romance! All were utterly dead, and the fruit of the last had turned to bitter ashes on her lips; but she could not think of them without that pang which irrevocable parting never fails to bring.

The first person who heard of her resolution was Hugh. In the evening he came again, bearing a message from Miss Waldron, who wished to see Amy, and desired to offer any assistance in her power.

"No doubt she means to be kind," Amy answered, quietly, "but I need no assistance. Since I saw you this morning, Hugh, life has changed for me; my future is assured, and all care about it is over."

A vivid flush mounted to Hugh's face. "You have taken from Mr. Trafford, then, assistance which you would not take from me!" he said. "Amy, is that kind?"

"If I had taken the assistance you mean from Mr. Trafford, I might answer that he is able to render it, and you are not," said Amy. "But I mean more than that, when I say that my future is assured; I mean, Hugh, that I am going to marry him."

"You mean—Amy, are you mad?" asked Hugh, hoarsely. "Marry!—marry a man older than your own father!"

"It does not matter to me how old

he is," said Amy, indifferently. "He is kind, he is generous, he is rich, he is willing to take care of me, and Mariette and the boys. Consider what I am—think how few men would make such a proposal—and then say whether or not I should be mad indeed to refuse it."

"Great Heaven!" said Hugh, aghast. "And it has come to this—you will sell yourself! O Amy, for God's sake, stop! Don't do this thing! It will be worse than poverty and toil—it will kill your heart—"

"You are talking folly, Hugh," interposed Amy. "I have no heart to kill. Since you are my only friend, I will tell you why I have decided on this; but you must not think that I can be shaken in my purpose."

"I don't need that you should tell me—I know everything," said Hugh, "and I see no excuse in any of it. I have been true to you through a great deal, Amy; but this is worse—a thousand times worse—than all that has gone before. If you can make this mercenary marriage—you, so young, selling yourself so utterly for money—I shall feel that I have wasted all the love that I have given to you, and I will never again think of you willingly as long as I live!"

He stood before her, white with passion and indignation, and Amy looked up at him with a sadness which he remembered long afterward.

"Good-by, then, Hugh," she answered. "I have said good-by to all the rest; you are the last link with the past, and it seems that I must leave you, too. I hope you will forget me—I am not worth remembering—though I think you are unjust to me now. So it ends—all we hoped and dreamed. Good-by!"

"Amy," cried Hugh, with one last, wild appeal, "come to me! I am young and strong, and I will work for you? Is love nothing? I love you as nobody else ever has loved or ever will love you, I am sure!"

"If you were as rich as Mr. Trafford,

Hugh, and said that, it would be enough to make me answer No," replied Amy. "You love me so much, that you would want me to love you in return; and that I can never do. I have no love for anybody, and so I am glad to marry a man who does not ask, who will not expect it."

"And you are determined—you will marry him?"

"I am determined—I shall marry him."

"Then God help me!—it is good-by forever! If I can avoid it, Amy, I will never see your face again."

He vanished from her side like a flash, as if afraid to trust himself a moment longer, and the door closed sharply. Sitting in the dusky twilight, with summer fragrance heavy on the air, and the soft lustre of the "tender star of love" shining from the delicate sky, Amy knew that she had, indeed, said farewell to all the past.

.   .   .   .   .

A week or two later—as soon as the doctor declared that Amy was able to travel—her marriage to Mr. Trafford took place. They were married early one morning, in the shabby little parlor which she was never to enter again, and the news fell on Edgerton like a clap of thunder. There had been some talk of a charitable subscription for "that poor Mr. Reynolds's family," and the well-meaning ladies who were engaged in this—Mrs. Lathrop at the helm—felt as if the whole fabric of social order was insecure, when they heard that the musician's penniless daughter had become the wife of the wealthy Mr. Trafford.

"Gone to Europe!" people said to one another in amazement. "Taken the little girl with them, and that deaf servant—sent the boys away to school—have you ever heard anything like it?"

Public curiosity was eager to learn how such an unexpected conclusion to the story of which Amy was the heroine had been reached; but the only person who could have gratified it kept silence in the most provoking manner, and only smiled when the matter was canvassed before her.

This person was Miss Waldron, who, it may be added, came in for no little share of the gossip herself. As soon as Archer was sufficiently recovered from the effect of his wound to be moved, the general had insisted upon taking him to Cedarwood for country air and quiet; and, as people sagely remarked, it was easy to tell what that meant. It meant a season of such rare pleasure and repose in the young man's life, that he would have liked to shower down benedictions on Marchmont's head for having shot him.

As the long golden days of June passed over the earth, it was nothing less than a delight to lie on the warm, dry grass, flecked by waving shadows and flickering sunlight, with Beatrix's darkly handsome face bending over her work near by, or her stately figure moving here and there, framed by the gracious beauty of the summer landscape.

It was such a day of "blissful June" as this when Amy's marriage took place; and Miss Waldron, who was the only invited guest present at the ceremony, having returned to Cedarwood, described the event to Archer.

"Nothing could have been simpler," she said; "and Amy—poor child!—looked pretty, though pale as alabaster. I have never seen any one more composed in manner than she was."

"Was it the 'stony calm' one reads about in novels of brides who give their hands where their hearts are not?" asked Archer.

"Very far from it. There was nothing stony in her manner—nothing in the least suggestive of an effort—only this grave, quiet composure. I hope she will be happy, and I hope she will make Mr. Trafford happy, for I like him very much."

"Doubtful on both sides," said Arch-er. "I can see no foundation for happiness in such a marriage."

"I can," said Beatrix. "I am sure Mr. Trafford will be kind in the extreme, and I think Amy has gained sense enough to appreciate his kindness and generosity as it deserves."

"And you think a girl of her age will be satisfied with a mild mixture of respect and gratitude for love?—or that a man of Mr. Trafford's age will not be jealous as a tiger of a young wife?"

"Amy has changed—you don't know how much she has changed; and I hardly think Mr. Trafford is the kind of man to be jealous as a tiger under any circumstances."

"You must be aware that youth is very elastic," said Archer, who never failed to maintain his opinion to the last extremity. "Grief and disappointment have no doubt changed the girl, and made her seem subdued, but the effect will soon pass. If there is not the making of a lifelong coquette in her, I am greatly mistaken, and there is nothing enviable in the position of a middle-aged man married to a young, flirting woman."

"You are evidently determined to take a dark view of the matter," said Beatrix, smiling. "But I have great hope that the marriage will prove happy—all the happier, perhaps, for the calmness of sentiment on both sides."

"You think calmness of sentiment desirable, then?" said Archer, with a quick, searching glance at her face.

A slight increase of color came to that face, but she was too entirely mistress of herself to betray discomposure in any other way.

"Surely it is a good thing," she answered. "Surely, when we see the trouble that passion brings—the feverishness, the uncertainty—one may be pardoned for thinking calmness of sentiment very desirable."

"Yet," said Archer, "it was only yesterday that I found a book of poems on your table, with this passage marked:

'He who for love has undergone
  The worst that can befall,
Is happier, thousand-fold, than one
  Who never loved at all;
A grace within his soul has reigned
  Which nothing else can bring—
Thank God for all that I have gained
  By that high offering!'"

"I suppose I marked the passage because the idea is prettily expressed," said Beatrix, with another blush brighter than the other. "You seem to have remembered the lines very well."

"I have a good memory," he answered, quietly.

Then silence fell. They were sitting on the lawn, and the sweet sights and sounds of summer were all around them. A great pride-of-china tree dropped the perfumed petals of its purple blossoms on Beatrix's head; shadow and sunshine interlaced over her white dress; bees were drowsily humming on the scented air; light breezes came and stirred the foliage with a soft rustle.

"How delightful this is!" said Archer, presently. "But I fear it is very demoralizing. After having lived in fairyland for a while, I shall find it hard to go back to the treadmill of daily life and labor. Yet it must be done—and that soon," he added, as if to himself.

"What is the need for haste?" asked Beatrix. "You have improved very much since you have been here, but you are by no means well yet."

"I am afraid I shall not recover my health here," he answered. "There are too many temptations to remain ill. I have decided to follow my doctor's advice, and go to the sea-side for a while."

Beatrix dropped her needlework with which she was occupied into the lap, and looked at him with her steady, dark eyes.

"You have decided—since when?" she asked. "This is certainly very sudden."

He moved a little uneasily.

"I have decided, Miss Waldron; is not that enough?" he said. "I always arrive at my decisions without much deliberation. You must not think that I fail to be grateful for all your kindness, and—"

"I beg that you will not talk of gratitude, Mr. Archer," said Beatrix, stiffly. "You force me to remind you that but for my unfortunate affairs you would not have incurred the wound which incapacitates you. If you wish to go, go by all means, but pray do not feel that any excuse is necessary for doing so."

She took up her work again, and, as her needle began to fly swiftly back and forth, Archer raised himself from his recumbent position on the grass.

"I see that you misunderstand me," he said; "and yet I think you ought to know better—I think you ought to feel that, however ungracious my going may seem, it is a matter of simple necessity."

On Beatrix's cheek a flush began to burn, but she did not lift her eyes, and her needle flew swifter than before, as she said, "I cannot perceive the necessity."

"But it does exist!" said Archer, with vehemence. "It is presumption, no doubt, in me to love you, Miss Waldron," he went on, without giving himself time to think, "but since I do love you with all my heart, and since I have not the faintest hope of ever winning you, it is worse than folly in me to stay here and purchase brief pleasure by long and bitter pain. Pardon me for having made this declaration," he added, after a short pause which no sound from Beatrix broke, "but I was compelled to make you understand why I must go. Now you see it, of course, as I do; and I shall leave without delay."

He rose as he spoke, and was in the act of walking away, when Beatrix's voice arrested him—a voice tremulous, though clear and sweet:

"Stop a moment, Mr. Archer," she said. "When a man makes a declaration to a woman, such as you have made, he generally waits for an answer—does he not?"

Archer turned quickly. "I did not think there was any answer possible that I would care to hear," he replied. "I am not mad, Miss Waldron. I know my position in life; I know that I have none of the advantages which the man who hopes to marry you must possess. I am poor; I am struggling; I am not fitted by nature to win a woman's heart. I can only love you," he said, with passionate bitterness, "and what is that?"

She rose, and stood before him, proud and stately, yet with a sweetness on her lips and in her eyes which no one had ever seen there before.

"If you are not mad, you are blind," she said, in a low tone of voice. "Why can you not—see? Must I answer your question? Must I tell you what your love is to me?"

He looked at her as if he could not trust his eyes, as if he could not believe his ears. He was so shaken, so amazed, at this unexpected reply, that emotion held him literally motionless for a minute. Then he said like one who speaks with an effort:

"Yes—tell me what it is to you."

She was the more self-possessed of the two, because she understood all that he felt, and the revelation of it was no surprise to her. She held out her hand quietly, but he never forgot the tone of her voice, when she answered with the word, "Everything."

PART II.

CHAPTER I.

AFTER TEN YEARS.

THE London season was opening brilliantly, and the foggy island began to wear its loveliest attire of green, when, in a small but very charming house, overlooking one of the most fashionable streets of Mayfair, an American lady, who was something of a celebrity, took up her residence.

The name of this celebrity was Mrs. Trafford, a beautiful and wealthy young widow, who in Paris, in Nice, in Florence, in Homburg, and in half a dozen other places, was well known, and whose dresses, jewels, horses, dinners, and flirtations, were topics of gossip, and the latter, perhaps, of a little scandal, wherever she went.

But Mrs. Trafford was able to set such scandal very much at defiance. The worst of gossips could not allege anything like impropriety against her; and her attractions were so many, her wealth apparently so great, that the minor transgressions of such a fascinating person were not held of much account.

Exactly who or what she was, nobody was able to say with any degree of certainty, for she was not partial to her countrymen and countrywomen, and rarely associated with them—a fact from which unpleasant things had more than once been argued concerning her.

When a report of these things reached Mrs. Trafford's ears, she only laughed—a silvery, mocking laugh well known to all her associates—and went her way with a supreme indifference which served to secure her position better than any self-assertion could have done. Apart from her wealth, the causes which gave her admittance into many usually exclusive circles were not hard to trace. She possessed beauty so extraordinary, that painters and sculptors raved over the faultless outlines of her face and figure, the exquisite tints of her complexion and hair, while her grace, her wit, her *savoir-faire*, were hardly less remarkable. It became the fashion to know her—the fashion to praise her daring yet graceful charm of manner and speech.

Of course, no woman so endowed could lack suitors, and, equally of course, there were many people to call her a heartless coquette, and say that she lived only for homage and admiration. Numberless were the stories told of the fate of her cavaliers—of her graciousness so long as they amused her, of her fickle caprices when they ceased to do so. It was at least certain that she evinced no sign of an intention to resign her freedom for any one of them.

When she first appeared in society she had propitiated Mrs. Grundy by keeping a chaperon—an elderly widow, who filled a seat in her carriage, or sat in her drawing-room and played propriety to perfection; but after a few years this lady disappeared, and her place was filled by a very different companion, a young girl, the sister of the fair widow, who added another attraction to Mrs. Trafford's already attractive house.

It would have been difficult to find a fresher, lovelier face than this girl possessed—a face which would have made her a formidable rival to most women, but which, by the side of the elder woman's regal beauty, was like a white rosebud near a "queen-rose" glowing with color, full of fragrance.

Such a comparison would have occurred to almost any one who saw the two as they sat together in Mrs. Trafford's boudoir-like drawing-room, a few days after their arrival in London.

"I think we are fairly settled at last," said the young widow, gazing meditatively out of the window at the green tops of the trees in the opposite park. "Do you know, Mariette, I am growing to be a little—just a little—tired of wandering? We have lived in so many places, that I begin to feel as if I would like a settled home."

From the luxurious chair in which she was lounging, Mariette looked at her sister with a glance of surprise. She was purely blond, with limpid eyes of turquoise blue, and hair like woven sunshine —a mass of golden softness coifed with negligent grace above the broad, white brow, and framing it with delicate babyrings, lovely enough for a seraph. Her complexion was "milk and roses" incarnate—all creamy softness and delicate bloom; while her pretty, tremulous lips parted over small, pearly teeth.

"I hope you won't think of making London that home, Amy!" she said, with the least possible shrug of her dainty shoulders. "I like it less than any place I have ever seen. How gloomy and *triste* it is, compared with Paris!"

"Wait a little," said Mrs. Trafford, with a smile. "That is one's first impression, but it wears away after a while. I have been thinking for some time that, though Continental cities are well enough in their way, London, perhaps, might be best for our headquarters. But there is no need to settle anything, since we are fortunately free as air," she added, as the expression of Mariette's face grew slightly dismayed. "We will try one season, and then, if we don't like it, nothing is easier than to take flight."

"I am sure I shall not like it," said Mariette, with slight petulance, "and I think it very odd of you to entertain such an idea, for you have often said that you disliked all English-speaking countries—I mean, all countries where English is spoken."

"That was because I disliked the idea of any association of the past," her sister replied. "But there is really no more danger of such a thing in London than in Paris or Rome. Moreover, I have learned to consider the feeling very foolish. No shadow could rise out of the past which would have power to vex or disturb me now."

"I should think not, indeed!" said Mariette, nestling deeper into her silken chair, with a comfortable sense of perfect security. To her the past of which her companion spoke was no more than a vague dream. Luxurious ease, encompassing beauty, absolute freedom from care—these things had made her life since early childhood; and hence her nymph-like face was joyous as Psyche's, her lovely eyes undimmed by the faintest shade of that trouble which is the doom of humanity.

Mrs. Trafford's face was different. Despite its wonderful beauty, its soft yet brilliant charm, no close observer could fail to be aware that this woman had suffered as well as enjoyed. In the depths of her changeful eyes the possibility of shadow lurked, and her rich, sweet voice had accents which were never learned in sunshine.

After Mariette's last words, silence fell—a silence which Mrs. Trafford had apparently little inclination to break. She lay back in the soft depths of her chair, a picture of marvelous grace in her exquisite toilet, gently waving a fan back and forth with one snowy, delicate hand —a hand fit for princes to kiss, and which no one could fancy had ever dusted and swept and darned in those long-past days to which she had alluded.

"Amy," said Mariette suddenly, "don't be vexed if I ask you a question—but do you think you will ever marry again?"

"That depends altogether upon circumstances," replied Mrs. Trafford, without the least trace of vexation. "If I could see clearly that I should gain anything by marrying, I might do so; but I have never seen that clearly yet. In such a step I should have little to gain and much to lose. My position is now as well assured as I could desire, and I like the freedom of my present existence so well, that I do not think any life which could be offered me in exchange would gain by comparison with it. I am not injured because women who are envious call me an adventuress, nor because men whom I have rejected say that I have no heart. As far as they are concerned they are right; I have no heart—not the least. I like to be amused and admired, but such but such a thing as sentiment does not exist for me. If I ever marry it will be for solid advantages—advantages which I do not need yet," she added, with a glance at her reflection in a mirror opposite.

Mariette rose and kissed her lightly.

"I am so glad you have told me this!" she said. "I have been wondering a little if our coming to England did not mean something of the kind, and—selfishly, no doubt—I did not like it. We are so charmingly situated as we are, that I could not welcome a possible brother-in-law very cordially."

"And why should you fear such a thing—especially now?" asked Mrs. Trafford.

"Oh, I don't know; except that it is easy to see how much in love both Mr. Grantham and Colonel Danesford are—"

"Choose your terms better, *petite*," interposed her sister, with a curling lip. "Boys fall in love, not men of the world like those of whom you speak. Mr.

Grantham is a diplomatist of considerable ambition and small fortune, who thinks that my fortune—also my personal gifts of beauty, cleverness, and social power—might serve his ends very well. No doubt he is right. No doubt I should make an admirable trump-card for a man in his position; but I cannot say that my pulses stir at the idea of becoming the wife of a secretary of legation who is fiftieth cousin to half a dozen peers and peeresses."

"I certainly do not think it would be a brilliant match for *you*," said Mariette.

"It would not be a brilliant match at all. I should give much and receive little. Even without birth, I have a right to look much higher. Indeed, better men have offered themselves to me before this."

"Ah, I know that!" cried Mariette, with a gay, sweet laugh. "You do not talk much of such things, but I see—I guess—a great deal."

"More than exists, perhaps," said her sister. "Now, Colonel Danesford belongs to another class. He is wealthy, he is the heir to a baronetcy, and he is a brave soldier. I like and respect him, and I think it a pity that he has suffered himself to become seriously attached to me. But one must take things as one finds them. He is an agreeable cavalier, and— *On parle du soleil, et en voici les rayons!*" she added, with a laugh, as the drawing-room door suddenly opened and a servant announced—

"Colonel Danesford."

There entered a tall, soldierly-looking man, of six or seven and thirty, very much sunburned, decidedly handsome, with a firmness of tread and a decision of bearing very significant of his rank in life. As he advanced, there were a suppressed eagerness in his manner and a glow in his dark eyes which betrayed his feeling for the fair woman who rose to meet him graciously.

"So you have come to welcome us to

London, Colonel Danesford!" she said, holding out her hand. "I was sure you would come as soon as you knew that we were here. Mariette and I were speaking of you a moment ago."

"I have been out of town until to-day, so it chances that I have only just now heard of your presence in London," he answered. "Of course I lost no time in coming to place myself at your feet, as our friends in Italy say. This is a most unexpected pleasure—one of which I had no idea when we parted in Rome."

Then he turned to Mariette, and, the commonplaces of greeting having been exchanged, the three fell at once into the easy talk of old acquaintances.

"We have been in London exactly five days," Mrs. Trafford said, in answer to a question; "but we are so practised in the art of establishing ourselves in new quarters—or, rather, we have a major-domo who is so accomplished in the art of establishing us—that we feel as if we had been settled for months. What do you think of our situation?"

"It is excellent," he said, glancing around, "and I see that you have made everything redolent of your presence. I could fancy myself back in your *salon* in Rome."

"Only that is no Roman sky," said she, pointing through the window.

"No more than Hyde Park is the Corso," said Mariette.

"I fancy, from the tone of that remark, that you do not like Hyde Park, Miss Reynolds," said Colonel Danesford. "Have you been on the Row? Can we not have a repetition of some of our delightful Roman rides?"

"Not readily, for we were always a *partie carrée* in Rome," replied Mariette; "and where shall I find, in your great London, such charming *cavalieri* as were at my service there?"

"Five days more will answer that question, I am sure," said Colonel Danesford, good-humoredly. "We may not be able to furnish such picturesque cavaliers

as your attendants in Rome; but, though Englishmen lack grace, they do not lack appreciation."

He glanced at Mrs. Trafford as he uttered these words, and, smiling, she said:

"You must excuse Mariette. Just before we left Rome we were both captivated by a young Spaniard who was of the bluest blood, handsome as a dream, and chivalrous as a crusader. He described his old castle in the Pyrenees so eloquently, that we were half inclined to go to Spain—but, instead, we have come to London."

"And I think I may venture to say that you have not made a bad choice. Have you been out much? Do your friends know that you are in town?"

"We have not been out a great deal, but our friends have already begun to gather round us, and, after to-day, we shall scarcely have an evening disengaged. We have decided, therefore, to spend this evening in a way we both like—we are going to hear Nilsson in 'Faust,' taking the opera *en connoisseur* from the beginning. If you have no other engagement, can you not join us?"

If Colonel Danesford had any other engagement, he did not give it a thought.

"I shall be most happy to do so," he answered.

"Then you will dine with us—will you not? We dine earlier than usual, of course. In fact, I ordered dinner for six o'clock."

Never did soldier yield a more ready assent to the voice of the charmer; and when, at six o'clock, they sat down, in a small but beautifully-appointed dining-room, to the most elegant of dinners, he felt himself a man to be envied.

The air of wealth and taste which pervaded everything, the profusion of flowers, the admirable attendance, the two fair women in their rich toilets, all combined to fill him with a sense of harmony and pleasure. He began to think that this was better than Rome. His foot was not only on his native heath—which is always assuring to a man who has position and ancestry behind him, and whose name means something more than the names of Smith, Jones, and Robinson—but there were as yet fewer rivals in his path than there had been in the Eternal City; and, though he knew that they would appear later, he also knew that he possessed the advantage of priority in the field.

"Priority and some favor," he said to himself—although common report had long since told him that there were few things so absolutely uncertain as Mrs. Trafford's favor.

After dinner, while Mariette retired to put a few finishing touches to her toilet, he found himself alone with the young widow, and he at once took advantage of the opportunity.

"My sister desires very much to meet you," he said, standing before her while she drew on a pair of long, primrose-tinted gloves. "She will be in town next week. I think—I hope—you will like each other."

"'You are very kind," she replied, glancing up with easy indifference. "I shall be glad to meet your sister; I think I have heard of her as a very charming woman."

"I will not venture to say what she has heard of *you*," he answered. "But it is enough to make her very anxious to know you."

"If you have made any report, and if she has taken it *au pied de la lettre*, I fear she will be sadly disappointed," said Mrs. Trafford, coolly buttoning her gloves. "I know that you are loyal and laudatory in the extreme with regard to your friends."

"It would be impossible for laudation to exaggerate what you are," he said, in a low tone. "Surely you must know that."

"I have a very good fund of vanity," she said, laughing, "but I hardly think it tells me anything so flattering.—The car-riage at the door, Johnson?" as a servant appeared. "Let Miss Reynolds know."

The last bars of the overture were being played when the two ladies and their attendant entered Mrs. Trafford's box.

Many glances were leveled upon them at once, and Colonel Danesford was not insensible to the distinction of appearing as sole cavalier of the famous beauty, who was looking even more beautiful than usual in a toilet of rich green silk, with quantities of costly white lace and emeralds at her throat and in her ears.

Seating herself in the front of the box, she lifted her glass and swept the house in the few minutes which elapsed before the curtain rose.

"I recognize a great many familiar faces," she said, dropping it and turning to Colonel Danesford. "What a very small world this is which we inhabit, after all! Does it not strike you so? If one were to attempt to escape from the orbit of one's acquaintance, it would hardly be possible to do so."

"Not for you, certainly," he answered, smiling; "at least, not in Europe. Perhaps in Australia or America you might appear without finding some one whom you knew; but I should think it doubtful."

Her face changed a little when he mentioned America.

"I have no disposition to make the experiment," she said. "I like to live in the *heart* of civilization, not on its outskirts. In Europe the higher classes are so thoroughly cosmopolitan and so very migratory, that, after a while, one will find little difference between society in St. Petersburg and London, or Paris and Vienna."

The curtain rose as she spoke, and she turned her attention to the stage; for everybody who knew Mrs. Trafford at all knew that she was so far unfashionable that she never went to an opera but as a genuine and devoted lover of music.

This evening, however, she found it

impossible to preserve her usual attention, for before the end of the first act her box was filled.

The first person who appeared was Mr. Grantham, a blond young diplomate, who was by no means pleased to find his most formidable rival in possession of the field. Following him came a Frenchman of rank, who desired to renew his acquaintance with "*la belle madame.*" Then appeared another Englishman, and then an *attaché* of the Italian embassy. Altogether, it was very evident that Mrs. Trafford's popularity was not likely to wane in London.

In a box just opposite her own, a party, consisting of two ladies and a gentleman, were meanwhile discussing her eagerly. The younger of the ladies was a rather pretty, brown-haired girl, very elaborately dressed, who scarcely paid any attention to the great prima-donna, so absorbed was she in watching Mrs. Trafford.

"She is by far the most beautiful woman I have seen since I came abroad—I am not sure that she is not the most beautiful woman I *ever* saw!" she said, enthusiastically. "If I were a man, I should fall down and worship her."

"That is going a little too far, Nelly," said the other lady; "but I should like to know who she is."

"She is a countess, no doubt," replied Nelly. "Very likely she is a duchess, or perhaps she is a foreign princess. She is not dressed like an Englishwoman."

"Why not a royal princess?" suggested the gentleman, with a laugh. "I am afraid you will let your imagination soar so high, Nelly, that it will have a grievous fall when you discover who your beauty is."

"I wish there was some one to tell us!" said Nelly, impatiently. "How unpleasant it is to be a stranger in a strange place, when one wants to know anything!—Walter, don't you think you might step into the next box and inquire?"

"I am not ambitious of being regarded as an escaped lunatic," replied Walter, calmly. "Suppose you stop talking for a little while, and listen to the 'King of Thule.'"

"A king there was in Thule,
Kept troth unto the grave,"

the silvery voice of *Marguerite* was singing, when the box-door opened and two men walked in.

One was English, unmistakably—tall, well-developed figure, florid face, mutton-chop whiskers; the other was slender, dark-eyed, and handsome, a man on whom the stamp of *blasé* was plainly set, and who looked every day of his thirty-five years.

"O Mr. Marchmont, what a pleasant surprise!" cried Nelly Paget. "You said you could not possibly come, so I had no hope of seeing you."

"I found the attraction beyond my powers of resistance," answered the last-described gentleman, advancing, "so I have not only come myself, but I have brought Bowling with me."

"I am delighted to see Mr. Bowling," said Miss Paget, frankly. "You remarked, the other day, that you knew everybody in London—at least by sight," she added, turning to Mr. Bowling. "You are just in time, therefore, to tell me the name of the most beautiful woman I have ever seen. She is in the box opposite."

"Since I was sufficiently ill-advised to make such a boast, it is as likely as not that you have pitched upon some one I do *not* know," replied Mr. Bowling, taking from her hand the glass she offered. "Where is this beauty to be seen?"

"In the box opposite—immediately across the house. As if you could mistake!"

"Tastes differ, you know," said Mr. Bowling, calmly. "Just opposite— By Jove! you are right. That woman *is* a beauty—and a famous one! I have never seen her in London before, but she is well known on the Continent. That is Mrs. Trafford."

"*Mrs.* Trafford!" echoed Nelly, crestfallen. "Not a princess—not even a countess, then?"

"Not unless princesses and countesses are made by right divine. In that case she might be one. She's regal—isn't she? And, since you admire her so much, you may be glad to hear that you can claim her as a countrywoman."

"A countrywoman—of mine?" said Nelly, incredulously.

"So I have heard; but I don't think anybody knows much of her antecedents. She is a widow—young, rich, beautiful, clever. That is enough."

"I am sure it ought to be. What more would any one have?—Did you speak to me, Mr. Marchmont?"

"I merely asked Bowling for the glass, that I might look more closely at this wonderful beauty.—Thanks!" as Bowling handed it to him.

Then he lifted and brought it to bear on the woman opposite.

———

CHAPTER II.

A SHADOW OF THE PAST.

"You seem overwhelmed, Mr. Marchmont," said Miss Paget. "I am sure I don't wonder. Isn't she divine?"

"She certainly is beautiful," answered Marchmont, slowly lowering the glass, which for several minutes he had kept leveled on Mrs. Trafford. "Her name is familiar to me," he went on, after a pause, "and I thought at first she might be an old acquaintance of mine; but, after looking at her, I do not feel as if such a thing were at all probable."

"I should not think there was any room for doubt," said Bowling. "It would hardly be possible to mistake such a face as that for any other."

"The question is, whether some other

has not developed into this," said Marchmont, lifting the glass to his eyes again.

The more he gazed, the more bewildered and incredulous he felt. Was it within the range of possibility that "little Amy Reynolds" had been transformed into *this?* Such a change seemed to him absolutely incredible. He sent his memory back over the decade of years past, and tried to summon up a picture of the girl with whom he had idly trifled when younger and more disposed for trifling than at present. But he could not recall anything tangible, try as he would. The recollection of that youthful episode had been so persistently banished, and so entirely swept away by other impressions, that, beyond a vague idea of a sparkling, Hebe face, the personality of Amy Reynolds had wholly faded from his mind.

"It is impossible!" he finally decided. "It is a mere coincident of name."—Then he said aloud to Bowling: "There is another very pretty woman in the same box—a pure blonde. Who is she?"

"I don't know her at all," Bowling answered. "It's a new face. Very lovely—don't you think so, Miss Paget?"

"I dare say I should think so, if the other peerless creature was not in view," Miss Paget replied.

"It is seldom that one woman acknowledges another woman's beauty so frankly," said Marchmont, turning to the girl with a smile.

"I was never envious of beauties—perhaps I made up my mind early to the fact that I had no beauty myself—but even if I were inclined that way, I should consider *that* woman far beyond the pale of jealousy," she answered.

"No beauty yourself!" he repeated.

"'O wad some power the giftie gie us
    To see oursels as ithers see us!'

You might change your mind on that point, and not malign your fairy godmother so much."

"Oh, I have estimated myself very exactly," she said. "I know so well what I am—especially in the matter of looks—that not even your flattery, Mr. Marchmont, can turn my head."

"I know that you are a very remarkable young lady in more ways than one," said Marchmont, in a low tone.

It was a tone which thrilled Nelly Paget's heart, and deepened the color on her cheeks. Despite her better judgment—for she was a girl of strong common-sense—her fancy was very much taken captive by this handsome, *blasé* man of the world, and she was almost ready to resign herself and her fortune into his hands.

That she was the possessor of a fortune, followed as a matter of course, since she was honored by Mr. Marchmont's attentions; for we find that distinguished gentleman as we left him—a fortune-hunter.

It must not be supposed, however, that in this interval of time he had not achieved partial success in his quest. Within twelve months after the Waldron *fiasco*, he married an heiress of uncertain wealth and more uncertain temper, whose friends settled her fortune upon her so tightly that during her life it was more of an exasperation than an assistance to her husband, and at her death—she lived six years and died childless—it returned to her family.

Thus, as he felt, providentially relieved, Mr. Marchmont, who had meanwhile made some reputation in public life, decided to be more cautious in his next matrimonial venture. His ambition was as great as ever, though he had by no means sustained his early promise; and his private affairs were very much involved, so that a short cut to wealth by the road of marriage commended itself as strongly to him now as it had done ten years before.

Having gone abroad—ostensibly for his health, but really to escape the mortification of a political defeat—he met an old friend in the person of Walter Paget, who was traveling in Europe, accompanied by his wife and sister.

At first Mr. Marchmont scarcely noticed the latter, but he was presently struck by her vivacity and shrewdness, and, being aware that she was by no means an inconsiderable heiress, as heiresses go, the idea of marrying her began to occur to him.

It was an idea which received added force from certain pecuniary embarrassments which were thickening round him, and from the consideration that, though Nelly Paget was not one of the women who prove invaluable allies in such a fight as that which he was waging, she would at least assist him to the best of her ability, and certainly never hinder him as his first wife had done.

In consequence of this opinion, deliberately formed and deliberately acted upon, he attached himself to the Paget party—that is, he discovered that his route generally lay in the same direction as theirs; and when they decided to leave the Continent for England, he saw no reason why he should not accompany them. He did accompany them, and they had been in London three or four days when this rencontre at the opera occurred.

The last act was in progress before Mrs. Trafford, who was accustomed to serving as a target for stares, observed the unusual attention which the occupants of the opposite box were paying her. It was Mariette who brought the fact to her notice.

"I do not think that, in all my experience of staring, I have ever seen people stare as those over yonder are doing!" she remarked to Colonel Danesford, who was forced to content himself with leaning over her chair, while Mr. Grantham and the Italian *attaché* monopolized as much attention as Mrs. Trafford chose to give them. "Have you observed how constantly their glasses are leveled at our box?"

"Yes, I have observed it," he answered. "They are excusable in a measure, since this is one of the first appear-

9

ances in public of Mrs. Trafford and yourself; but they should not forget good-breeding."

"Perhaps they do not possess any," said the young lady, as she raised her own glass and turned it upon the box in question, taking a quick but keen survey of each face. "Yet they look as if they *ought* to possess some," she said, "and I have a vague idea that I have seen the face of one of them before—that dark, handsome man in front."

"He may be some cursory acquaintance whom you have met and forgotten."

"Perhaps so, but Amy's memory is better than mine; in fact, it is so good that she never forgets a face. I will ask her if she knows him."

She bent forward and asked the question, and Mrs. Trafford for the first time sent a swift glance across the glittering house. Her eye fell at once on the box which Mariette indicated, and saw but one face in it—the face of Brian Marchmont.

On her part recognition was instantaneous. This was not singular, since there had not only been no such change in his appearance as in hers, but the impression which he had made upon her life, and consequently upon her memory, was far deeper than any she had made upon him.

It was the first time in all these years that she had seen any face belonging to the dead life of her youth; and now, to see *that* face, above all others, brought such a rush of old recollections over her, that for a moment—only a moment—the whole brilliant scene wavered before her eyes, and she seemed to hear the orchestra and the voices on the stage as from an immense distance.

But, by a strong effort, she recalled herself, and, though unable to prevent a variation of color, she answered Mariette's question composedly enough. "No," she said, "he is not an acquaintance of mine."

Despite her admirable self-control, something in the tone of these words struck

the well-trained ear of the man by her side. "Not an acquaintance!" Mr. Grantham thought. "But that is not saying he has not been an acquaintance. Women like madame do not change color for a trifle."

Though she did not look again toward the box where Marchmont sat, there was no doubt that Mrs. Trafford was very glad when the opera ended. The mere consciousness of being in the same assembly with her old lover gave her a sense of oppression akin to pain. The memories that she had for years thrust away came back to her with such vividness, that she felt half inclined to question whether all that had passed intermediately was not a dream. Wealth, triumph, homage, luxury — all seemed just now less real than the recollections which she hated, yet could not banish.

These recollections, however, cast no shade over her beautiful face, when, after the opera, she entertained Grantham, Danesford, and a few other privileged visitors, at the most *recherché* of suppers. She was, on the contrary, even more brilliant, more audacious, more charming than usual; and Danesford, at least, fell more deeply and hopelessly in love than ever.

But when all was over, the last guest gone, Mariette bidden good-night, and silk and lace and jewels laid aside, Mrs. Trafford, in a *robe de chambre* hardly less becoming than the toilet she had taken off, sat in a deep chair before her mirror, and, while her maid combed out the abundant masses of her hair, allowed herself for the first time to consider the meeting of the evening and all that might result from it.

"It is strange," she thought, "that my strong instinct against what Mariette calls 'English-speaking countries' should be justified by my meeting, before I have been in London a week, the first person associated with the past whom I have met all these years. I am not a fatalist, but it seems to me almost more than strange! If that man enters my life again, it must be for a purpose—it must be that I may deal back to him what he dealt to *me* long ago. But I have no desire for anything of the kind. I would rather forget that he exists. To see him, to speak to him, to recall the hateful memory of that time, would be unspeakably painful to me. I am almost coward enough to think of leaving London. But that would not do, for it would look as if I shrank from meeting him; and I have no reason to do that. I scarcely think he will venture to seek me out. If he does, the consequences must be on his own head.—That will do, Celine," she said to her maid. "Put up my hair, and let me go to bed; I am tired."

* * * * *

If Marchmont had been puzzled in the opera-house to decide whether Mrs. Trafford could be Amy Reynolds, he was still more puzzled, still more uncertain, afterward. He decided again and again that such a thing was impossible, only to find his mind going back over the same ground and debating the same question.

Directly or indirectly, he had never heard of Amy after he received the news of her marriage to Mr. Trafford. Now and then he had given her a stray thought, and wondered a little what had become of her, but no rumor concerning her had reached his ears; and it seemed, therefore, too wild an idea for probability that the music-teacher's penniless daughter should have bloomed into a social celebrity in the first capitals of Europe.

Nevertheless, he could not banish from his mind the perfect face, the dazzling presence, the high-bred grace of the woman whom he had seen at the opera. Before parting with Bowling, he extracted from that gentleman all the information of which he was possessed concerning her; and this information, meagre as it was, filled him with a vague sense of aspiration. What a prize was here for a man who should be bold enough to grasp it! Following this thought came

another, "Why should not I be the man?"

Diffidence of their power to please any and every woman is not a failing of men in general, nor was it a failing of Marchmont in particular; yet he was able to appreciate the presumption involved in this idea. He remembered the appearance of the men whom he had seen surrounding Mrs. Trafford, and he knew that to rival such men successfully would be no trifling task.

Nor was it a task to which he seriously thought of setting himself. He only thought that, if circumstances should throw him in the path of the fair widow, he would feel inclined to put forth all his energy—to stake everything—on the chance of winning her.

"Unless I am mistaken," he said to himself, "she is mistress of a fascination which would soon make a man forget everything but herself. I should like to come in contact with such a woman! I have never yet met one capable of inspiring that species of worship which borders on infatuation, and it would be something to feel, if only for the sake of a new sensation."

* * * * *

"Did you dream of my beauty of the opera last night, Mr. Marchmont?" was Nelly Paget's first question when they met at breakfast the next morning. "*I* did. I dreamed that she turned out to be the princess I thought her first, and that she came and took me to drive in a green-and-gold chariot."

"I did not dream of her, but of the person who I fancied she might be," Marchmont answered. "I mean"—as Miss Paget lifted her eyebrows interrogatively—"that I dreamed of a girl I knew long ago who became Mrs. Trafford, and who, therefore, I fancied last night this Mrs. Trafford might be."

"But, as Mr. Bowling said," observed Mrs. Paget, "how could you possibly be in doubt? One sees such a face so seldom—"

"I was in doubt because the girl whom I knew married very young, and a deluge has passed over my memory of her face," he answered, carelessly. "I only know that she was very pretty, and gave promise of greater beauty."

"I suppose you were in love with her," said Walter Paget, breaking an egg with the serious air which the operation demanded.

"Hardly that," Marchmont replied. "But we amused ourselves with tolerable satisfaction to each other for a short time. I have not heard of her, however, in quite ten years. She may be dead, or widowed, for aught I know."

"What was her name?" asked Miss Paget, with interest. "Perhaps your 'early love with her primrose face'—had she a primrose face?—and Mrs. Trafford may be the same. If so, how delightful! On the score of your old flirtation you can claim acquaintance, and introduce me. By-the-by, did you flirt with her, or did she flirt with you?"

"Nelly!" ejaculated Mrs. Paget.

"There is no harm in the question," said Nelly, calmly. "In flirting, as in everything else, one party is generally active and the other passive; in other words, one is the flirter and the other the flirtee.—Which were you in this case, Mr. Marchmont?"

Marchmont was far past the age of blushing—from a sense of guilt or any other reason—but he anathematized Miss Paget in his mind, while he answered, as composedly as possible:

"Of course I was the flirtee. From my trusting nature I could never possibly be anything else."

"How odd that truthfulness of nature is one of the last traits with which I should have thought of crediting you!" said Miss Paget, amid a general laugh; "but, of course, you know yourself best. You have not yet told me, however, the name of the girl who flirted with you?"

"I did not exactly make the statement so broad as that," said Marchmont, anathematizing this very inquisitive young lady more and more. "Her name was Reynolds—Amy Reynolds."

"Amy Reynolds?" repeated Miss Paget. "The name has a gentle, guileless sound—perhaps because it resembles Amy Robsart. Notwithstanding your truthfulness of nature, Mr. Marchmont, I am afraid you were *not* the flirtee in that affair."

"To a judgment pronounced on such accurate grounds I cannot possibly demur," said Marchmont, smiling.

"Intuition is sometimes a short road to the truth," said she, looking at him with eyes full of a laughing challenge to contradict her.

But Mr. Paget interposed here with some plan for the day's amusement, and the conversation, to Marchmont's relief, took another turn.

A day or two passed without the Paget party seeing or hearing anything more of Mrs. Trafford. Their next glimpse of her was obtained in the Park, where they were sitting one afternoon, when a quiet but handsomely-appointed park-phaeton drew up near the railing immediately in front of their chairs.

"Oh, look—there she is!" Nelly exclaimed, eagerly.—"Now you can see, Mary"—this to her sister-in-law—"whether she is not as lovely by daylight as by artificial light."

"My dear Nelly, if you don't take care she will hear you?" Mrs. Paget expostulated. "You know I only said that it was difficult to tell anything about a woman's *real* beauty, when you have only seen her at night across an opera-house."

"Well, now you can tell how real her beauty is!" said Nelly, triumphantly. "She looks even more handsome than she did the other night."

This was a slight exaggeration, perhaps; but Mrs. Trafford certainly looked very handsome, in a carriage-costume of pearl-gray silk, her fair face framed by

one of the most graceful hats ever fash-
i med in Paris, from which a soft, curling
plume drooped on the rich masses of her
chestnut hair.

Mariette's costume, though less rich,
was not less elegant, and its spring-like
tints suited her delicate loveliness, which
suggested all things fresh and dainty.

It would have been difficult to find two
more beautiful faces in all that stream of
equipages, and the loungers of the Row
manifested their appreciation by stares
and comments uttered to each other.

Among these loungers were several
of Mrs. Trafford's acquaintances, who soon
gathered round her carriage; and it
chanced that one of them, in a tone loud
enough to be heard by Nelly Paget, spoke
to or of " Miss Reynolds."

The girl started and turned to Marchmont, who was standing near, but who,
in talking to a friend whom he had encountered, had not observed the drawing-
up of Mrs. Trafford's equipage.

"Mr. Marchmont," she said, quickly,
"did you hear that? One of those gentlemen called the young lady with Mrs.
Trafford 'Miss Reynolds!'"

"Are you sure?" said Marchmont,
turning eagerly. "How do you know
that he was alluding—"

Then he stopped, for he suddenly
caught sight of the carriage and its occupants—of Mariette's exquisite face under
the shade of her rose-lined parasol, and of
Mrs. Trafford, leaning back—

"With that regal, indolent air she had,
So confident of her charm."

"There was no room for mistake," said
Miss Paget; "I heard it distinctly, and
the young lady turned in response. No
doubt she is Mrs. Trafford's sister—I
think I see some resemblance between
the two—and no doubt, also, Mrs. Trafford *is* your early love. Do, Mr. Marchmont, go and claim her acquaintance, and
say that you have a friend you would
like to present."

She looked up in his face, half laugh-

ing, half in earnest—wholly persuasive;
but Marchmont felt more singularly moved
by this discovery than he could have
imagined possible. There was something
so strange in finding, thus elevated above
him, the girl he had patronized and trifled
with, that for once his ease and readiness
in any emergency failed.

"I cannot venture to claim Mrs. Trafford's acquaintance on a mere supposition," he said; "but I will go nearer to
the carriage and see if she recognizes me
at all."

He advanced to the rails as he spoke,
and finding a vacant place near Mrs. Trafford's horses, he took his position there,
and calmly fastened his eyes on the lady's
face.

We all know the magnetism of an intent gaze, and it was not long before Mrs.
Trafford glanced toward him and their
eyes met.

There was no wavering of the color in
her cheek, no drooping of the fringed
lids. Her brilliant, dauntless eyes looked
at him for an instant as they might have
looked at any other indifferent face; then
turned carelessly back to the man with
whom she was talking.

There was no room for doubt; if this
was Amy Reynolds, she did not remember, or did not choose to recognize, him.
Either idea was so mortifying to his
vanity that he turned and moved abruptly away.

CHAPTER III.

AT LAST!

AMONG the throng in the Park that
afternoon was a man who stood in the
rear of the chairs, leaning against a tree
while he regarded with an air of calm
attention the moving stream of equipages,
with their fair occupants, and the gorgeous young men walking up and down the
Row, or lounging in knots near the rails.
The sylvan distances of the Park spread

around, the emerald foliage and grass making a beautiful setting for the brilliant picture; the level sun-rays caught the Serpentine, as it gleamed under the fine old trees that fringed it; and the air of the late afternoon was delightfully sweet and balmy.

The man who observed all this with quiet, meditative eyes was not more than twenty-eight or thirty—a man with nothing strikingly unconventional in his appearance, no unmistakable outward sign of Bohemianism about him—yet who manifestly belonged to another world than this which was on dress-parade before him.

Though not a man of fashion, he was plainly a gentleman, and his face possessed an attraction apart from its good looks—though good looks were not lacking to it. Men and women, and even children, were always attracted by the frankness of his gaze and the genial sweetness of the smile which often curved his heavily-bearded lip. His features were more strongly than regularly cut, but were not altogether deficient in grace, and his brown, curling hair was pushed carelessly back from a broad open forehead.

"What, Dinsmore! is this you?" said a young man, suddenly passing before him. "I wasn't aware that you had become an *habitué* of the Row! How goes it with the 'Duchess May?'"

"Not very well," answered Dinsmore, with a laugh, while a stout, florid matron in brown silk turned and put up her eyeglass to look at him, plainly esteeming the acquaintance of a duchess worth scrutinizing. "You know, perhaps, that it was not finished in time for the exhibition. The fact is, I cannot satisfy myself with regard to the face of the duchess. I have painted in at least a dozen faces, and painted them out again."

"That's deucedly unpleasant," said the other, in a sympathizing tone. "Perhaps you will find a face here that will serve as an inspiration," he added, nodding toward the drive.

"I was thinking the same thing myself," said Dinsmore. "But, although I have seen a score or two of lovely and high-bred faces, I fear I have *not* seen the Duchess May, nor any suggestion of her."

"Yonder is a duke's daughter, and one of the beauties of the season; will not *she* serve as an inspiration?"

Dinsmore glanced at the noble lady in question, with that quick, comprehensive artist-glance which takes in at once outline, coloring, and expression, and shook his head.

"Handsome and commonplace," was his uncompromising verdict. "Had she been the Duchess May, her 'Rhyme' would never have been written, for she would have married Leigh of Leigh in the most decorous manner from the beginning."

"Well, here comes another beauty and belle, *par excellence*, whose 'little hand holds muckle gold.' Will she do?"

"For the girl of the period—yes," answered Dinsmore, looking at the blooming heiress indicated. "For the embodiment of the beautiful and the heroic, which I need—no."

"Then yonder comes the woman you need—Lady Wriottan. No woman in London more admired; and with reason. She looks like the daughter of a Norman knight."

"And would look so under any circumstances," said Dinsmore, calmly. "A finely-chiseled face, but as cold as it is haughty. Some cold faces have possibilities of passion in them; that face has none."

"By Jove, you are hard to please!" said the other, who, it may be explained, was a painter also, but with more social pretensions than his friend. "I suppose, by-the-by, you have seen Millais's portrait of Lady Wriottan? What do you think of it?" And they plunged into professional talk.

It was in the midst of this that Dinsmore chanced to glance up a minute later, and the same instant he caught his companion's arm in a vise-like grasp.

"Look yonder, Reade!" he said. "Who is that lady in the carriage which has just drawn up by the rail?"

Reade stared round in not unnatural bewilderment.

"I see a great many carriages and a great many ladies," he said. "Which do you mean?"

"Look a little to the right—there, just in front of that plane-tree," answered Dinsmore, hoarsely—"a chestnut-haired woman in a gray-silk dress and gray hat. Who is she?"

"Oh! I see whom you mean, now, and I don't wonder at your excitement—though you might remember that my arm is not made of India-rubber. That is a very famous beauty, my dear fellow, and she is known as Mrs. Trafford. Will *she* do for the Duchess May?"

Dinsmore did not seem to hear the question, and Reade was amazed to perceive that the color had faded altogether out of his face as he gazed at Mrs. Trafford like one entranced.

Finally he drew a deep breath, and said aloud, yet evidently to himself, "At last!"

"At last!" repeated the other, too full of curiosity to be able to restrain the question which rose to his lips. "Is it possible you know Mrs. Trafford?"

Dinsmore started at this, and seemed to recollect himself.

"No," he answered. "I have never in my life spoken to *Mrs. Trafford.*"

"But you've seen her before?"

"Yes, I have seen her before," he replied; and, unconsciously to himself, there was the echo of a pang in his voice.

"Hers is a face one could not easily forget," said Reade. "I saw her in Paris two years ago, and I knew her at once when I saw her just now. There's a fascination—a sort of personal magnetism—about her that even more than her beauty serves to impress her on the memory. I can credit that she is a veritable Circe."

"Is that her reputation?" Dinsmore asked, still gazing with intent, wistful eyes at the fair face so unconscious of his scrutiny.

"If you know anything of her, I'm surprised you don't know *that!*" the other replied.

'I saw pale kings and princes, too—
  Pale warriors, death-pale were they all;
  They cried, "La belle Dame sans merci
    Hath thee in thrall."'

And that is pretty much what her captives cry, I believe."

The careless, laughing tone in which these words were uttered seemed to jar on Dinsmore. He drew his brows slightly together and turned.

"Poor Amy!" he said to himself; but Reade did not catch the words. Then he added, aloud: "I believe I must go now; you've become such a man of fashion that I suppose you have cut painting for the present. But, of course, I'll be glad to see you whenever you choose to look in at the studio. Good-day!"

He nodded and walked away in the opposite direction from Mrs. Trafford's carriage, and Reade stared after him for a second. "By Jove, I believe the fellow *has* known her, and has been badly hit, too!" he muttered. "Who would have thought it?"

He strolled on leisurely, and, a minute later, was accosted by a man whom he knew tolerably well—the same Mr. Bowling who was Marchmont's acquaintance.

"Well met, Reade!" the latter said. "You are the very man I've been wishing to see. Don't you want to be presented to a pretty, piquant American girl? She is anxious to visit some artists' studios, and, since I don't know much about such matters, I want you to take her in charge."

"Thanks for your kind intention," answered Reade. "If she is *sola*, I have no strong objection to 'taking her in charge;' but if she is one of a squad, I beg to decline the honor."

"She is one of a party of three or four, all pleasant, well - bred people. Come, don't be churlish! Do you see that brown-haired, well-dressed girl sitting yonder — no, more to the right? That is Miss Paget. I'll take you and present you at once."

There was something in the appearance of the brown-haired girl in question which prevented any further demur on Reade's part, and so it chanced that Nelly Paget glanced up as the young men were approaching, and, recognizing Bowling, smiled cordially.

"You find us quite forsaken, Mr. Bowling," she said, putting out a small, gray-gloved hand as he paused. "Walter and Mr. Marchmont have both vanished, and left Mary and myself alone. I am glad you have appeared. I had ever so many questions to ask you about the notabilities and celebrities, until the appearance of Mrs. Trafford put them all out of my head! Have you seen her? Isn't she looking superbly handsome?"

"There can't be two opinions on that score," Bowling answered, smiling at the girl's enthusiasm. "I have brought the artist-friend of whom I spoke yesterday, to present to Mrs. Paget and yourself," he went on. "Will you allow me?"

Then the introduction took place in due form, and Reade was pleased with the fresh, frank young face lifted toward him. There was never any difficulty in talking to Nelly Paget, for she was clever and always self-possessed; therefore they were soon comparing notes on the brilliant scene before them.

"Yes, I have tried the Drive and the Row," she said, in answer to a question of his, "but I think it is more amusing to sit here and enjoy the show *as* a show. I find the driving tedious, and, as for the riding, I do not like the gaits of your English horses."

"Nor our English mode of riding, perhaps?"

"I did not care to say that, but I confess I thought it. To the eye of one not accustomed to it, the English manner of riding is not graceful."

"I have heard that charge made before. In fact, it has only been a few minutes since I parted with one of your countrymen who does not hesitate to declare that the English mode of riding is only remarkable for awkwardness."

"One of my countrymen! Will you excuse me if I ask who it was? One meets a great many friends unexpectedly—"

"I am afraid you will not discover a friend in Dinsmore, though he is a capital fellow. I have heard him say that he has been in Europe ten years, and he lives the life of a recluse—paints hard all the time, and is steadily advancing in ability and success."

"He is an artist, then—like yourself?"

The young man laughed.

"He is an artist, but not at all like myself. I am a trifler and idler; he is a devoted worker, and in ten years more he will be at the top of the ladder of fame. Of that I'm confident."

"You are a very good friend to speak of him so warmly," said the girl. "But will you excuse me if I say that I think it is very odd for you to talk of yourself as 'a trifler and idler?'"

"It is generally well to speak the truth, is it not?"

"But I meant that it is odd it should *be* the truth. How can a man with such a talent neglect it?—how can he have such a profession and fail to feel enthusiasm for it?"

"Why are original sin and idleness and general depravity in the world, Miss Paget?" asked he, smiling. "It *is* a shame for a man to shrink from the drudgery of his profession; but some of us do, nevertheless. I am glad, however, that the guild of artists has found favor in your eyes."

"I am very fond of artists," she said, frankly. "They are generally original, unconventional, and strikingly unlike the men one meets in ordinary society."

"May I venture to bow? I flatter myself that I am all those things."

"I don't think you need trouble yourself," she replied, coolly. "I should never have suspected that you were an artist if I had not been told so."

"I suppose, then, that I am not unconventional enough. I should wear a velvet coat and a *sombrero*, and let my hair grow long—should I?"

He did not intend to be impertinent, but in a moment he saw that he had let flippancy carry him too far. Miss Paget's face grew cold and haughty.

"I am sorry that you are unable to distinguish between genuine unconventionality and affected Bohemianism," she said. Then she turned her graceful, silken-clad shoulder deliberately upon him. —"Mary, what can have become of Mr. Marchmont?" she asked. "He went near the rails to see if Mrs. Trafford would recognize him, and since then he has unaccountably vanished."

"I am sure I have no idea of what became of him," said Mrs. Paget, looking placidly round.

"Has he discovered yet whether or not Mrs. Trafford is his old acquaintance?" asked Bowling.

"He is not certain, but he is strongly inclined to think that she is," answered Nelly. "His acquaintance was a Miss Reynolds, and I heard some one call the young lady who is with Mrs. Trafford Miss Reynolds—which is a singular coincidence, to say the least."

"The young lady certainly is Miss Reynolds, and she also certainly is Mrs. Trafford's sister," said Bowling. "I learned that not long ago. So the evidence of identity is complete."

"Mrs. Trafford seems to have an army of old as well as of new acquaintances," said Reade. "I was standing with Dinsmore—who is one of the very last men I should have suspected of knowing a woman of her stamp—when she drove up, and he was very much struck by her appearance, evidently knew her at once,

but did not know her name—at least, her present name."

"What! the artist of whom you were speaking a moment ago?" said Nelly, turning round with complete forgetfulness of her vexation. "Did he tell you anything about her?—who she was?—when or where he had known her?"

"Not a word; and it is really mere supposition on my part that he ever knew her at all. He said that he did *not* know her—that he had only seen her before; but there was something so unusual in his manner, that I was inclined to suspect that his acquaintance had been closer than he cared to acknowledge."

"But why should he hesitate to acknowledge it?" demanded Nelly. "What a very mysterious lady Mrs. Trafford appears to be!"

"It's hardly fair to bring Mrs. Trafford in guilty of mystery because Dinsmore chooses to be reticent," said Reade. "*A propos* of Dinsmore, have you seen his pictures at the Academy, Miss Paget? They've been a good deal noticed."

"I have been to the exhibition," Nelly answered, "but I am not sure that I observed the pictures you mean, unless you tell me the subjects."

"The one which has been most admired is really admirable. It is called, with an irony which even a German could hardly fail to understand, 'Die Wacht am Rhein.'"

"Oh, yes, I remember it," the girl said. "It represents a noble old French château which the Prussians are approaching, while in the distance appear the flames of a burning village. Nothing could be finer than the spirit of the whole picture, especially the hatred and scorn on the face of the lady, who stands like a very Marguerite of Anjou in the foreground, with her trembling children and terrified servants round her."

"It is a scene from life, for Dinsmore was in France during the war, and the face of the lady is a portrait. The other picture is simply called 'Wild-flowers,' and represents a woodland glen with two figures—"

"Excuse my interrupting you," Miss Paget cried, eagerly, "but I remember *that* as well as possible, because it is a Southern scene in every feature.—Mary, don't you recollect how I clapped my hands when I recognized the live-oak and the yellow jasmine?"

"Indeed I do!" replied Mrs. Paget—"and how the people around stared at you as if you were crazy."

"I have been intending, ever since, to go back and look at that picture again," the young lady went on. "I shall certainly do so now."

"Allow me the pleasure of attending you, will you not?" asked Reade. "I shall be most happy; and, since I know the exhibition thoroughly, I may be able to find out a few things that have escaped your notice."

"That will be delightful!" said the girl, with her pleasant frankness.—"Mary, have we any engagement for to-morrow?"

"Not that I know of," answered Mrs. Paget. "Walter and Mr. Marchmont may have made some arrangement for us, however. We must consult them before we settle anything—and here they are."

The two truants appeared, with no traces of guilt on their countenances; but Marchmont seemed a trifle surprised to see a good-looking young fellow, with a flower in his button-hole, talking to Nelly Paget as if he had known her an age. It roused him to a realization of the fact that even here snares might be cast for a pretty young heiress, and that he was not making as good use of his opportunities as prudence seemed to demand that he should.

"I really thought you had deserted us," she said, turning to him with a smile. "Is Mrs. Trafford a sorceress, and did she spirit you away?—or what became of you so suddenly?"

"Mrs. Trafford is not in the least a sorceress," he answered, quietly. "I did

not think the occasion suitable for claiming her acquaintance, so I took a turn with a friend whom I chanced to meet. If I had fancied that you would miss me—"

"I don't think I mentioned anything about missing you," she interposed. "Let me introduce Mr. Reade, who has just offered kindly to act as my cicerone at the Academy Exhibition, where Mary and I are thinking of going to-morrow."

"I thought we were going to Windsor to-morrow?"

"Oh, I had quite forgotten—so we are!—Mr. Reade, have you any engagement for the next day?"

"None at all, Miss Paget. I am entirely at your command."

"Then the next day, at— But, stay! I must ask Mary."

Consultation with Mrs. Paget resulted in Mr. Reade's being asked to take luncheon with them at the Langham Hotel on the day indicated, after which they would go to the exhibition.

Mr. Reade having accepted the invitation, Mr. Paget suggested departure, to which the ladies acceded, and the party separated.

It was a peculiarity of Nelly Paget's that, when she had once taken an idea into her head, she pursued it to the last extremity, thereby often desperately boring less enthusiastic people with whom she came in contact. On the present occasion Marchmont hoped that she would drop the subject of Mrs. Trafford's identity; but as soon as they found themselves walking side by side, she began:

"Mr. Reade says that the young lady whom we saw with Mrs. Trafford *is* Miss Reynolds, and that she is Mrs. Trafford's sister; so that proves conclusively that the beautiful widow is your early love—does it not?"

"I suppose so," he answered, trying to speak carelessly, and not betray the irritation which he felt; "but my early love, as you insist on calling her, did not leave such an agreeable impression upon my mind that I should be anxious to renew my acquaintance with her. In fact, I hardly think that I shall make any attempt to do so."

"Why not?" she asked, glancing up with a disappointed expression. "Oh, excuse me! I fear I am very rude," she added, with a blush; "but I do not understand how you can resist the temptation to know such a lovely woman."

"Can you not?" said he, looking down at her with an expression which long practice had taught him perfectly how to throw into his dark, handsome eyes—an expression which had done execution upon many susceptible hearts since foolish Amy Reynolds was beguiled by it; "but suppose there is only one woman in the world for whose society I care at present?"

She blushed again, but answered readily enough: "I cannot suppose such a thing at all. Boys of twenty feel that way, perhaps, but not men of the world like you, Mr. Marchmont."

"I am a man of the world in my career, but not in my feelings," said he. "I should like you to believe that."

"I'm afraid I can't make an act of very implicit faith in it; but, fortunately, my opinion does not matter."

"You know better than that," said he; "you know that your opinion matters to me above all other opinions."

"Don't talk nonsense, please!" said she, laughing. "It really is not fair. You have so much advantage over me in the matter of experience, that there is no telling how far you might turn my head!"

"You are jesting, while I am in earnest," said he, reproachfully.

"That is certainly better than if *you* were jesting while *I* was in earnest," she replied. "I have no doubt Mrs. Trafford will in the end make you feel that—

'After all, old things are best;'

and, in that case, it would be awkward, to say the least, to have given any allegiance to the new."

"The best way to make you understand how absurd such an idea is, will be to give you an exact account of my former acquaintance with Mrs. Trafford," he said; "that is, of course, if you care to hear it."

"Don't set me down as deplorably curious if I say that I do care. The fact is, that wonderful face of hers has made such an impression upon me, that I feel an interest in everything concerning her."

"Then I must understand that it is only on her account you feel interest?"

She glanced up, smiling. There is a spice of coquetry in every daughter of Eve, and she was sufficiently heart-free and light-spirited to display hers now.

"On whose else should I feel it?" she asked. "Not on yours, when you have just assured me that it is 'absurd' to attach any importance to the matter as far as you are concerned."

"It certainly is absurd when you imply that, for the sake of a by-gone slight flirtation, I could forget—"

"Like a man!" she interrupted. "Never mind, we won't argue the matter. You shall tell me your story at the first opportunity, and I promise to give sympathy where sympathy is due."

CHAPTER IV.

IN RICHMOND PARK.

"AMY," said Mariette, as they were driving out of the Park, "I saw that same man this afternoon who stared at you so hard at the opera the other night. Surely you must have observed him! He stood by the rails and gazed at you—not with an ordinary stare, but as if trying to attract your attention."

"Yes, I saw him," answered Mrs. Trafford.

"And don't you know him? His

face is oddly familiar to me. I cannot place it—I cannot think where I ever saw it; I have only a vague sense that I have seen it somewhere, at some time."

Mrs. Trafford hesitated a moment, then said, calmly: "You are right. It is a face that you once saw often and knew well. Do you remember a man named Marchmont, who was in Edgerton when you were a child?"

Mariette looked at her sister with her bright blue eyes opening wide. Allusions to Edgerton were very rare from Amy's lips, and it was doubtful whether Marchmont's name had passed those lips in all the years that had elapsed since the old life ended so utterly.

"Yes, I remember him," the girl replied.

"Well, this is the man."

"Are you sure?"

"I am perfectly sure. He has changed very little, and I knew him at once."

"*Mon Dieu!*" said Mariette, who had not been educated in Paris for nothing. "How strange that you should meet him here! And do you—will you recognize him as an acquaintance?"

Mrs. Trafford made a gesture signifying indifference. "If he chooses to claim my acquaintance, I shall not refuse to recognize him; but, if he is wise, he will not attempt anything of the kind."

Mariette's lips parted as if she would fain have said, "Why not?" but she had learned that her sister would not endure questioning on her private affairs, and, not being very much interested in this, she closed her lips again, leaving the words unspoken.

"You know we are engaged to dine with Lady Gresham this evening," said Mrs. Trafford, when they reached home, and were about to separate for their respective toilets.

Lady Gresham was the sister of Colonel Danesford, who, immediately on arriving in town, had called on the woman with whom her brother was so infatuated. This act was dictated partly by sisterly regard, partly by policy—for the beautiful, clever widow promised to achieve as much social success in London as she had done elsewhere—and partly by curiosity.

She was a woman prone to sudden fancies, and she went away from Mrs. Trafford's house in a state of rapture. From being a source of sorrow, her brother's choice suddenly became a source of pride to her. She congratulated him on Mrs. Trafford's beauty and grace and high-bred repose, as if he was already the possessor of those charms, and she assured her husband that she could not possibly have chosen better if the matter of choice had been intrusted to her hands.

"I am very glad to hear it, my dear," said Sir Charles Gresham, who was a model husband, inasmuch as he had long since learned the futility of disputing the ideas or questioning the theories of his lively, charming wife. "You have been so much distressed about the affair, that I am glad you have found the devil less black than you painted him—or, perhaps, I should say *her*, in this case."

"I am justified in being distrustful," said Lady Gresham. "The vague statement, 'an American widow,' gave me a dreadful idea; and then, somebody—Mrs. St. John, I believe—said that she was considered in Florence to be quite fast. But I don't believe anything of the kind now."

Sir Charles looked a trifle quizzical. "I am becoming curious to see her myself, since she has worked such a change in your sentiments," he remarked.

"You will have an opportunity to do so to-morrow evening," Lady Gresham replied. "I have invited her to dine—herself and her sister."

"She has a sister, then?"

"Yes, a lovely girl."

It was a very pleasant company—though somewhat exceeding the Chesterfieldian limit—which was assembled in Lady Gresham's drawing-room the next evening when Mrs. Trafford and her sister entered. The beautiful widow looked even more beautiful than usual in a gold-colored silk with a scarf of priceless black lace draped across its shining folds. Diamonds encircled her slender throat, and shone in her ears and on her arms. Mariette was like a vision of a peri, clad all in white and silver—a costume which enhanced her delicate loveliness to such a degree that one person, at least, thought her the fairer of the two.

This person was the son and heir of the house—Stamer Gresham—young, pleasant, good-looking as men go, and not altogether devoid of an idea or two.

"By Jove! *what* a beauty!" he muttered under his mustache; but a lady to whom he had been talking overheard the words.

"Which do you mean?" she asked, smiling, for she was old enough to feel no thrill of jealousy.

"I mean the golden-haired blonde," he answered. "What a charming face! what an exquisite figure! She is a perfect picture."

"She certainly is," said the lady, elevating her eye-glass. "Yet she cannot compare with the other, who is really a superb beauty—and a beauty good for thirty years to come!"

"Immensely rich, too," said a gentleman near. "A fascinating woman and a consummate coquette. I am afraid Danesford will come to grief, as other men have come before him," he added, lowering his voice as Stamer Gresham moved away.

"That will be a pity," said the lady, in a sympathetic tone.

Though a foreboding to this effect often weighed upon Colonel Danesford, he could not feel it at present. He took Mrs. Trafford in to dinner, of course, and so gracious and charming was that beguiling lady, that he began to hope more than he had ever hoped before for a favorable issue to his suit.

"I am so glad that you are beginning to like England," he said, in reply to some remark she made. "But you must not restrict your knowledge of it to London. You must see something of the English country."

"Yes; when the London season is over, I think I shall go to the lake-country," she answered. "I spent last summer in Switzerland, and I do not care to go back there."

"I wish I could hope to be your guide in Westmoreland. I know it well."

"Then be my guide—will you not?" she said, smiling—and her companion's heart leaped under the magic of the tone and glance.

"You know that, if you chose to command my services, I would be your guide to the Mountains of the Moon," he answered. "Pending the lake-country, however, we must have a day at Richmond. Have you been down there yet? No? Then let us make a party for to-morrow, if you have no other engagement."

"I have fortunately no engagement that matters, and it will be very pleasant. How about the party, though? I have rather a horror of anything like a large number of people."

"So have I. Our Roman excursions were perfect, and, as Miss Reynolds remarked, we were always a *partie carrée* there. Shall we go to Richmond in the same manner?"

"Yes; I think that will be best. Who shall we ask to be fourth? Mr. Grantham would go, no doubt, but—"

"I was about to propose my nephew, Stamer Gresham, for the honor," he said, as she paused; "he is rather an agreeable young fellow, and, from appearances, I think Miss Reynolds and himself are inclined to be sympathetic."

"Is the young man sitting by Mariette your nephew?" she asked. "I have been wondering a little who he was. He has an exceedingly pleasant face. He is, then, Mr. Gresham?"

"Captain Gresham of the Guards."

"*Tant mieux!* Like all women, I am fond of soldiers."

"There can be no doubt that the sentiment is returned by all soldiers who have come under your spell," said he, smiling.

Meanwhile, Miss Reynolds and Captain Gresham were developing a fair amount of sympathetic tendencies. Mariette, notwithstanding her youth and slight experience, was by no means a novice in the art of beguiling, and, before dinner was over, "her sweet eyes, her low replies," had worked mischief enough in the young guardsman's heart and brain.

"I have often heard that American girls are charming, Miss Reynolds," he said, at length; "but you must pardon me if I say that I had not the least idea *how* charming they are before to-night."

Mariette laughed softly. "I should be dull with a hopeless dullness if I failed to understand what you mean, Captain Gresham," she replied. "That is a very nice compliment; but I don't know that I ought to appropriate it on on the score of being an American. I left America when I was a very small child, and I have never seen the country since."

"Yet you have never been in England before?"

"No, for I was educated and have lived altogether on the Continent."

"But I hope you like England?" This was said with an accent which seemed to imply that it was a matter of the utmost importance that she should like it.

"To be quite frank with you, I do *not* like it, though very probably I shall learn to do so. It is said, you know, that the things which grow upon one slowly are the things which one likes longest and best."

"I am not at all sure of that! Sometimes one conceives the strongest liking all in a minute."

"And isn't it rather apt to go 'all in a minute,' also?"

"I don't think so; on the contrary I believe that it often lasts longer than feelings based upon reason and—and—things of that kind."

She laughed again, and the young man thought he had never heard a sweeter sound.

"We won't enter upon a sentimental discussion," she said, gayly. "We have been told that the feelings are 'dangerous guides,' and that is, or ought to be, enough."

It was at least enough just then, for Lady Gresham rose, and, with a rustle of silken trains, the ladies swept from the room.

When the gentlemen joined them, the Richmond party was definitely arranged, and, as Captain Gresham handed Mariette into the carriage in which Colonel Danesford had already placed Mrs. Trafford, his last words were:

"What a delightful day we shall have to-morrow!"

"If the sun shines," Mariette replied; "but who can count on your capricious English climate?"

. . . .

The capricious English climate was good enough to smile upon them the next day, and the beautiful glades of Richmond Park never looked lovelier than as the long, golden spears of afternoon sunlight streamed into them and reddened the deep beds of fern where the deer were couched.

Having driven to the Star and Garter and ordered dinner, Mrs. Trafford and her party were strolling through the Park, and, as was natural under the circumstances, the two couples had wandered somewhat apart.

"I am afraid I am neglecting my duties as chaperon," said Mrs. Trafford, waking suddenly to a realization that she had seen nothing of Mariette for some time. "Where have those young people gone? This will not do!"

"I think they turned off in the direction of one of the lakes," answered Colonel Danesford. "Miss Reynolds has discovered that there is some beauty in England, after all, and Stamer is only too glad to show her as much of it as possible."

"It was very thoughtless of us to separate in this way," said Mrs. Trafford, who felt a little vexed. "Had we not better follow them?"

"That would be the worst possible way to find them. The best thing to do is, to sit down here and wait. They will come back presently to the route from which they diverged."

Mrs. Trafford hesitated. For various reasons she did not desire an extended *tête-à-tête* with her agreeable cavalier; but, since there seemed little prospect of avoiding this under any circumstances, her hesitation did not last long. She stood for a moment irresolute, with her filmy, muslin draperies lifted in one delicately-gloved hand, then glanced up with her peculiarly charming smile.

"If you think it will be best to sit down and wait, let us sit down by all means. I shall like a little leisure to take in all this wonderful beauty. See how the sunset light strikes those masses of splendid foliage, and with what a charming effect the deer pass now and then across the openings!"

"The scene is lovely, look where one will. I knew you would enjoy it, because I have often observed that your appreciation of natural beauty is greater than that of most people; in fact, you regard such things almost as an artist does."

A subtile change—almost a shadow—fell over her face. They had seated themselves under a massive oak, and, as she looked at the stretches of forest-distance, a wistful, absent expression came into her eyes. It was not often that any memory of her old life troubled her, but now her fancy went swiftly back to the far-distant and far-different woodland glades in which she first learned to regard Nature "as an artist does."

"That is not singular," she said, in answer to his last remark. "I was once associated very closely with one who had the soul and the eye of an artist; and I have not quite forgotten all that he taught me."

Absurdly enough—as he was perfectly conscious—Colonel Danesford felt a thrill of jealousy. Of Mrs. Trafford's past life he knew little; of her former masculine friends, lovers, and associates, still less; and to be vaguely jealous of every man she chanced to mention would have been uncomfortable, to say the least; but, in the present instance, there was more in her tone than in her words, and more in her face than in either, to make him suspect there was ground for jealousy.

"Artists are generally pleasant associates," he said, trying to speak as indifferently as possible, "and you have been living for years in an artist's paradise, so that you have doubtless seen a great deal of the fraternity."

"On the contrary, very little," she answered. "I have never cultivated the society of artists of any kind, and the friend of whom I speak I knew long ago —when we were both little more than children."

"But you have seen him since?"

"Never. For ten years I have not heard his name, and I do not know whether he is alive or dead, famous or obscure. Sometimes I think I should like to know—for he was a good friend to me, poor Hugh! But then, again, I think that it does not matter at all, and that it is better to let him *be* dead to me —together with all the rest."

She spoke on an impulse, half absently, half carelessly; and Danesford, who had never before heard her allude to her past, gave the words rather more than their due significance. As she said, "Poor Hugh!" there was certainly an accent of tenderness in her voice which was rather depressing to her companion's feelings.

"Hugh—whoever he may be—would be complimented if he knew how kindly he was remembered," he said.

She uttered a low and rather sad laugh.

"You are mistaken," she replied; "but it does not matter. Let us talk of something else ; old memories are among the most stupid and most disagreeable things in the world."

"Let us talk of ourselves, then," said he, in a low, eager tone. "At least, allow me to talk of myself for once, and tell you—what you cannot need to be told, however—that I love you devotedly. I had no idea of saying this when I brought you here," he added, quickly, as she started and looked at him reproachfully. "But, to be alone with you, and *not* speak, is impossible. I will not press you for an answer now, but I cannot let you remain in ignorance of my love. I wish I were able to tell you how over-mastering a passion this love is!—how it has filled and colored my whole life, and made everything else naught to me since I first saw your face—"

"Ah, pray hush!" said she, in a tone of pain. "I am not worth such love. If you could know me as I am, Colonel Danesford, you would keep that honest heart of yours for a better woman. *I* am cold and fickle, vain and heartless. I deserve all the hard things that people say of my coquetry ; and yet—I would have spared *you*, if I could."

"I have no desire to be spared." said he, quietly, but his bronzed complexion turned paler at her last words. "I mean exactly what I say, when I tell you that I would rather know you and suffer than never have known you. I have loved you—I *do* love you, as in all my life I never loved any other woman; and, if you are heart-free, I shall never give up the hope of winning you at last."

She did not answer immediately, and for a few moments silence followed his last words. With her hands lightly clasped in her lap, she sat quite motionless, gazing with unobservant eyes at the alternation of light and shadow in the beautiful scene before her. She was debating in her mind how she should an-swer this man who offered her so much, and who showed more depth of feeling and passion than she had credited him with.

"After all, why should I not marry him ?" she was saying to herself. "He is possessed of all that I have any right to ask, and he is more devoted to me than any one else will probably ever be."

While these thoughts were in her mind—though very vaguely, and by no means assuming the cast of a definite or even possible resolve—and while Danesford was watching her abstracted face with passionate eagerness on his own, a rustling step among the bracken near at hand made them both look up.

A man's figure appeared, thrown into relief by a flood of streaming, golden light behind, as he emerged from one of the glades and advanced toward the place where they were sitting. Since the radiance was behind, his face was in shadow, but every line of the figure stood clearly forth, and also a large square object—apparently a sketching portfolio—which he carried under his arm.

Mrs. Trafford was glad of any interruption, or pretext of an interruption, to end the conversation which had taken a turn so little to her taste.

"I thought that might have been Mariette and Captain Gresham," she said. "Since our waiting for them has not proved a success, suppose we go in search of them ? "

She rose as she spoke ; and the artist, who had not observed her before, started as the graceful figure suddenly stood in his path—the luminous glow falling over it, over the beautiful face and waving masses of chestnut hair tinged with gold.

He paused for a second, motionless, staring as if he had seen a spirit; then, remembering himself suddenly, he lifted his hat, and, turning abruptly, walked away in another direction.

"That fellow was certainly amazed," said Colonel Danesford, with a laugh.

"He was not expecting such an apparition, and it dazzled him."

"Do you know him? Have you any idea who he is?" asked Mrs. Trafford, looking intently after the retreating figure.

"Not the least!" Danesford answered. "He is some artist on a sketching expedition, probably. Why do you ask?" he added. "Do *you* know him?"

"No," she answered, slowly. "That is—it was fancy, I suppose; but I thought he resembled the friend of whom I was talking when we first sat down."

"The association of ideas very likely made you imagine a resemblance. Have you any reason to think that your friend is in England?"

"I know nothing about him; I have no reason to think anything of him," she answered, almost impatiently. "The resemblance merely startled me; that is all."

They walked on in silence, for Danesford felt instinctively that it would not be well to resume the subject of his declaration, until presently Mrs. Trafford paused, with a laugh. "Yonder they are!" she said. "What a pretty picture!—is it not?"

"A picture that might be painted, hung on the Accdemy-walls, and called 'Flirtation,'" said Danesford.

Mariette and Captain Gresham, of whom they spoke, appeared at the end of a long green avenue, strolling slowly, with an air of preoccupation, toward them. The girl's face was bent slightly downward, the young man's was turned toward her; bars of sunlight and shadow checkered the way; the whole framework of pastoral beauty seemed to suit their youth and grace.

CHAPTER V.

"SHOULD AULD ACQUAINTANCE BE FORGOT?"

THE rooms of the Royal Academy were well filled when Mrs. and Miss Paget, attended by Reade and Marchmont, entered them, on the day after their visit to Windsor.

The young painter's love of his art, and knowledge of it, came out strongly when he found himself with a companion so intelligent and enthusiastic as Nelly Paget.

She frankly confessed that her opportunities for art-culture had not been great; yet her taste was exceedingly good, and her apprehension very quick.

"Tell me *why* it is a good picture," she would say to him; and she listened with the most genuine interest while he discoursed of distances and perspectives, shades, tints, and tones.

This was uninteresting, however, to Mrs. Paget and Marchmont, so they did not always wait to get the benefit of Mr. Reade's criticisms and disquisitions; hence a slight separation of the party occurred. When they finally reached Hugh Dinsmore's pictures, Nelly and her companion were still lingering over one of Alma-Tadema's paintings.

"This is the picture Nelly was so much struck with the other day," said Mrs. Paget, pausing before the one entitled "Wild-Flowers." "I should not have noticed—as she did at once—that the foliage is peculiar to our woods; but I see it very clearly now. It must have been painted by some— Excuse me, Mr. Marchmont! Is anything the matter?"

Marchmont did not answer; in fact, he did not hear her. He was gazing at the painting like one who is both startled and fascinated. Nor was this singular.

What he saw before him was a picture of the glen in which he first met Amy Reynolds on an April afternoon ten years before. Every detail of the scene was familiar to him; but most familiar of all was the lovely, flower-crowned girl bending to look at herself in the crystal water.

This was the exact portrait of Amy—a portrait which made vivid again all his fading recollection of her face, and sent a sharp thrill like a dart through and through him.

There was another figure—that of a boy—but only the back of his head and form were sketched, and he was thrown in such deep shadow that a casual glance hardly discovered him.

As soon as Marchmont recovered from his first shock of amazement, he looked at his catalogue, and found exactly what he expected—the name of Hugh Dinsmore.

"Of course it could be no one else!" he muttered to himself; and then he added aloud to Mrs. Paget: "Pardon me, but I am surprised to find myself unexpectedly face to face with an old acquaintance. Does that girl remind you of any one whom you have lately seen?"

Mrs. Paget began to think that her companion was distraught. She looked at the picture, then at him, then at the picture again.

"I—really—I don't think it reminds me of any one," she said, at length. "It is a very pretty face—very pretty! Do you mean that you know the original?"

"I *did* know her very well, long ago. It is a portrait of the girl who, I have reason to believe, is now Mrs. Trafford."

Mrs. Paget stared. Before she could speak, a voice behind her said, quickly:

"Oh, how singular this is! Why, it is Amy—Amy, as she looked when I was a child!"

Marchmont turned, and faced a golden-haired girl, who was gazing at the picture with an amazement equal to his own.

"I cannot understand it!" she said, and then she, too, looked at her catalogue and uttered a cry.

"It was painted by Hugh—our own Hugh!" she said. "How strange—how very strange this is!—Captain Gresham, pray go and bring Mrs. Trafford here at once!"

"And leave you alone?" asked Captain Gresham, hesitating.

"Oh, yes—yes! that does not matter. Pray go at once!"

Her tone left the young man no room for demur, so he immediately went in search of Mrs. Trafford. That lady, attended by Mr. Grantham, who professed to be a great connoisseur of pictures, was standing with a doubtful expression before one of the latest eccentricities of the extreme pre-Raphaelite school when he approached.

"Miss Reynolds has sent me to beg that you will come to her at once, Mrs. Trafford," he said. "She has found a picture which has impressed her very much."

"With admiration, or the reverse?" asked Mrs. Trafford, smiling.

"Well, not exactly with either," replied Captain Gresham, twisting his mustache. "She seems to consider that the face on it is like yours, and she recognized the name of the artist. Stay! I will find it for you."

He took Mrs. Trafford's catalogue and hastily turned over the leaves until he found "Wild Flowers," when he gave it back, pointing to Hugh Dinsmore's name.

As her eye fell on it, the brilliant color of her cheek varied a little, and for a moment she was silent. Then she said, quietly:

"Yes, that is the name of one of our oldest friends. I am surprised—but very glad to see it here."

"May I inquire who it is?" said Mr. Grantham. "Ah! Dinsmore. He is an American artist, who is coming somewhat into note. I have heard of him once or twice lately. Do I understand that he is your friend, Mrs. Trafford?"

"He was formerly my friend," answered Mrs. Trafford; "but I have not seen him for years, and he has probably forgotten me altogether. Let us go and look at his picture."

When she came in front of it, however, her composure, perfect as it was, gave way. As her glance fell on the well-remembered glen, and on her own girlish face, the bright blood ebbed from her cheeks, and a low cry broke from her lips.

"Ah, how like it is!—how like!" she said. "Our glen—our familiar glen! And my face, as if I saw it in a mirror as it was ten years ago!"

"It is the face of a wood-nymph," said Mr. Grantham; "but the face which your mirror reflects at the present time has no need to envy or regret it."

She did not answer or heed him. She stood with her gaze fastened on the picture, as if magnetized, while her mind went back to the old existence, until her present surroundings seemed strange and unreal.

That was the real life—the babbling brook, the drooping trees, the foolish, willful girl in her Bohemian freedom. At least, it seemed so for a moment. Then she roused with a start, heard the voices round her, and remembered that Mrs. Trafford lived, and Amy Reynolds was dead forever.

It was this moment which Marchmont chose to step forward. He had drawn back a little as she approached, but he felt that, if he meant to claim her acquaintance at all, this was his best opportunity to do so. He therefore advanced, and spoke in a tone so low that his words were only audible to herself:

"Will Mrs. Trafford permit an old friend to recall himself to her recollection? We met for the first time in that glen"—he glanced at the picture—"and there is a singular appropriateness in the fact that it should be the means of our second meeting."

Instead of discomposing her, the sound of his voice seemed to steady her nerves and make them like steel. She turned, and it was Mrs. Trafford—the woman who had passed completely beyond the sphere of his influence—who now looked at him with steady eyes.

"I remember you, Mr. Marchmont," she said, quietly, but made no motion to extend her hand in token of recognition.

Her failure to perform this act of simple courtesy, and the calm coldness of her words, placed Marchmont at an almost greater disadvantage than if she had declined to know him. Her manner seemed to erect a barrier between them which it was impossible for him to pass. Yet, after a moment's pause, he made another effort to do so:

"It is a very great and unexpected happiness to me to meet you again!" he said. "You are so changed—so marvelously changed!—that but for this picture I could hardly have brought myself to believe in your identity with the girl I knew long ago in Edgerton."

She smiled slightly.

"I have no point of identity with the girl whom you knew long ago in Edgerton," she said. "I remember that she existed; that is all."

"And do you disown all the associations of that old life?" he asked, quickly.

"They are nothing to me," she answered. "Ten years have passed since I saw a face or heard a voice connected with them. Yours is the first!" she added, looking at him with a glance which seemed to say "You may judge, therefore, how utterly you are without power to move me."

He plainly recognized this, and it had on him something of the effect of a challenge. "I will move her yet!" he thought; then he said:

"If you disclaim all identity with that charming songstress of the woods"—he glanced again at the picture—"you will at least for her sake allow me the honor of your acquaintance, I hope?"

She bent her head, with the same graceful but unapproachable coldness.

"I cannot refuse such a request. The honor of my acquaintance is yours, Mr. Marchmont, if you desire it. Now be good enough to tell me if you know anything of the artist who painted this picture—my old friend Hugh Dinsmore?"

"I know no more of him than that I saw his name on the catalogue when I looked at it to learn who had—by magic, as it seemed—brought back that never-forgotten scene to me. I am in London as a mere bird of passage, and know few people."

"I must find out something concerning him," she said; and probably Marchmont had never felt a keener thrill of mortification than he experienced while contrasting her tone when speaking *of* Dinsmore with her tone in speaking *to* himself.

After a few more words—measuredly cold on her part, very deferential on his—she bowed in token of adieu, and moved away to where Mariette was standing with the two gentlemen in attendance.

"So your admirer of the opera proves to be really an old acquaintance, Mrs. Trafford?" said Mr. Grantham, when he found himself again at her side.

"My admirer of the opera!" said she, lifting her eyebrows slightly. "Oh, yes; I believe Mr. Marchmont is the same person whose persistent gaze across the opera-house was observed by Mariette the other night. Probably he was not sure of my identity with the girl he knew long ago."

"As you were not sure of his! I think you said then that you did not know him."

"I do not remember faces readily," said she, a little haughtily, for she did not fancy the tone of his remark.

She had never accorded to this ambitious aspirant for her hand a sufficient degree of favor to entitle him to presume in any way, and her quick ear warned her that there was a shade of suspicion in his tone.

This suspicion was of the kind which a new lover always feels when brought in contact with an old one. Mr. Grantham was by no means in love with Mrs. Trafford in the sentimental sense of that term, but he was most sincerely anxious to secure the valuable aid of her wealth, her beauty, her cleverness, and worldly knowledge; and he regarded with distrust the appearance of a probable rival with that glamour of the past over him which is said—often erroneously—to be so powerful in its effect on women's hearts.

Nelly Paget, meanwhile, was overwhelmed with curiosity when she heard of the encounter at the picture. In the excitement of this new interest she entirely forsook Mr. Reade, and turned an inattentive ear to his art-criticisms.

When Marchmont rejoined them after leaving Mrs. Trafford, she at once pounced upon him, and, professing for the first time to be tired of standing, carried him off to one of the seats in the middle of the room.

"Now," she said, as soon as they sat down, "tell me all about it. Mary's account has been very confused, as you can imagine. Is that girl in 'Wild-Flowers' really painted for Mrs. Trafford?—Who is the artist?—How did he chance to do it?—And did she recognize you at once?"

"Which question shall I answer first?" he asked, smiling. "Yes, the face of that girl is an exact portrait of Mrs. Trafford as I saw her first—in that very glen which is painted there."

"In that very glen!" cried Nelly, with her eyes like saucers. "If you are not playing on my credulity—"

"On my honor, I am not."

"Then how romantic it all is! But who knew of it?—who painted it? You have not told me that."

He opened the catalogue in his hand and pointed to Hugh's name, and as she read it she uttered a little cry of surprise.

"Dinsmore!" she said. "Why, that is the name of the artist of whom Mr.

Reade was talking that afternoon in the Park! Don't you remember he said—No, I believe you were not there to hear him, but he *did* say that, only a little while before Mr. Bowling introduced him to us, he was talking to this Mr. Dinsmore when Mrs. Trafford's carriage drew up, and he—Mr. Dinsmore—was so greatly agitated by her appearance that Mr. Reade was much surprised."

"So the fellow is in London!" said Marchmont, in a tone of disgust. "I am heartily sorry for that. He knew Mrs. Trafford when they both were very young, and, as he exhibited some talent for art, a wealthy philanthropist sent him over here to become a painter. He was underbred and presuming in his boyhood, and is not likely to be improved now."

"But how is it that he has carried Mrs. Trafford's face in his memory so long? Was he in love with her?"

"Very much so, if I remember rightly. Now that I think of it, I believe he was in that glen with her the evening I first saw her. So it is plain how he was able to paint the scene."

"It is altogether the most romantic affair I ever heard of!" said Miss Paget. "What an enchantress Mrs. Trafford must be! I am dying to know her! Pray, Mr. Marchmont, when you go to see her—you *are* going, are you not?—ask permission to present me to her. I don't care 'tuppence' as the people here say, whether I am violating social etiquette or not. I *must* and *will* know her!"

"To hear is to obey!" said Marchmont, smiling. "However, I have no immediate intention of going to see Mrs. Trafford."

"But you *must* have!" cried Nelly, impatiently; and he had no objection to being importuned to do as a favor to her that which he had already decided to do as soon as possible on his own account.

The next morning his card was brought to Mrs. Trafford, who glanced at it carelessly, and bade the servant say she would be down presently.

"So he will not let me alone!" she said to herself, as she sealed and addressed a note she had written. "Well, one often sees moths persist in burning themselves. If *he* persists, the penalty will fall on his own head."

Marchmont, meanwhile, was standing in the drawing-room, wondering if he was not dreaming. This *bijou* of a room, with its luxurious appointments, its flower-filled balcony, its air of wealth and culture, carried his thoughts, by very force of contrast, back to the dingy, shabby parlor in Edgerton, in which he had once spent so many hours with Amy Reynolds.

The change seemed almost incredible. The girl who, ten years before, was so socially insignificant that his careless attentions were esteemed compromising to her, and whose highest ambition had been to become an opera-singer, was to-day floating on the topmost wave of life—young, beautiful, wealthy, fashionable—as far above him now as she had been beneath him long ago. The difference was so great, that it gave him a sensation almost akin to giddiness.

"It is a prize worth an effort!" he said to himself. "If I can grasp it—and why not? Old sentiment is strong with women."

Many men lay this flattering unction to their souls, forgetting altogether that a spell once broken can never be renewed, a glamour once dispelled can never be restored, a fancy once forgotten can never be rekindled.

Presently the door opened, and Mrs. Trafford entered, wearing an exquisite morning-dress of white muslin, needlework and lace, relieved by cerise ribbons, her full yet slender figure girdled by a sash of the same color.

She greeted Marchmont as she would have greeted any ordinary acquaintance, carelessly extending a white, slender hand sparkling with jewels. Her unruffled self-possession, her easy calmness, were not calculated to give him any assurance of the power of that "old sentiment" of which he had thought; but some people are fertile in self-consolation, and he decided that these things were significantly favorable tokens.

"You have changed very little, Mr. Marchmont," she said, looking at him, with her full, brilliant glance, as he drew a chair near the couch on which she had seated herself. "It is seldom that years pass so lightly as they seem to have passed over you."

"And it is still more seldom that they work such change as I find in you!" he answered. "Pardon me if I say that, much as I admired my little friend of ten years ago, I could never have anticipated for her so magnificent a womanhood!"

"The change certainly seems to savor of enchantment," said she, as her glance swept over her surroundings. "It is impossible to express what I owe to the kind and generous friend who was the magician to bring it all about."

"You allude, of course, to your husband," said Marchmont. "The news of your marriage astounded me — may I add?—pained me; but I recognized then, as I recognize now, that you acted wisely. You were left unprotected, and I was, alas! unable to assist you; therefore a *mariage de raison* was your best resource."

"I am glad, even at this late day, to have the satisfaction of knowing that you approve of my course," said she; and the irony of her tone was so fine and delicate, that Marchmont more than half doubted whether it was irony at all.

"I wish," said he, eagerly, "that I might obtain your approbation of *my* course. I wish that I might hope that, by the light of worldly experience, you would judge it more leniently than you once did!"

"I was young and foolish—shall I say sentimental?—then," said she, with a smile glittering in her eyes. "I lacked worldly experience utterly. You are quite right; I should judge very differently *now*. I flatter myself that I am able to appreciate your motives altogether at their just value."

"Ah," said he, quickly, "it has been the hope of my life to hear you say that —to know that you appreciated the strength of the chain of circumstances which bound me. If I had been able to follow the dictates of my heart, life would have been very different; for I, too, have been married since we parted."

"Indeed!" said she, with the air of well-bred interest which people feign in things which do not interest them at all. "Is your wife with you?"

"She has been dead four years," he answered. "I am entirely alone in the world."

"That is sad!—at least some men would consider it so. Others like best to run the race of life unweighted. Unless my memory errs, you were ambitious when I had the pleasure of knowing you before, and that is a passion which gains strength with years; therefore you are ambitious still, and I hope you have been successful?"

"I have no reason to complain of want of success, though I have necessarily encountered some disappointment. I am in Europe now to recruit my health, which has suffered from my exertions in public life."

"Then you will probable not be long in London?"

"The length of my stay is altogether indefinite. I am in a measure attached to a party whose movements have regulated mine for some time. A *propos*, there is one member of it who is exceedingly anxious to make your acquaintance, and hopes you will allow her to do so. She is a very enthusiastic young lady, who has been raving about you ever since she first saw you at the opera, a few nights ago."

"I am not partial to Americans," said Mrs. Trafford, with a careless shrug of her shoulders; "but I have no objection to knowing one or two, now and then. What is the young lady's name?"

"She is Miss Paget; and I think you may like her—if it can be safely predicted that one woman will like another. Her brother, with whom she is traveling, I have known a long time; he is lately married, and his wife is a very pleasant person."

"Altogether, you fancy that I would not regret breaking through my rule in favor of the Pagets?" said she, with a smile. "I suppose they are staying at the Langham Hotel, where Americans mostly resort? If I can find time, I shall not mind dropping a card and asking them to dine, as soon as I can set a day. I may count on you for the occasion, I suppose, Mr. Marchmont?"

"With the greatest pleasure! But may I not hope to see you again before then?"

"I hardly think so. Engagements multiply around me, and, although I am very well seasoned to dissipation, I begin to think that a London season eclipses all that I have hitherto known in that line."

Silence fell for a moment, and Marchmont felt that he ought to go, yet he also felt very much averse to doing so.

"I am told that the young lady whom I have twice seen with you is your sister," he said. "She must be my little friend of old, who was then Mariette, and is now transformed into Miss Reynolds?"

"Yes, it is Mariette," Mrs. Trafford answered. "She is a very charming companion for me, and I hope I may keep her for some time to come."

"I should not fancy that it would be wise to count on such a thing, unless 'some time to come' is a period of very limited duration."

"On the contrary, it is a period of unlimited duration, I hope!" she answered.

"Subject only, I presume, to the limit of those two most uncertain arbiters of human life—fate and a woman's caprice?"

"That is understood, of course! Nothing is absolutely fixed, save death and taxation, I believe; and I am far from claiming for my plans and fancies exemption from the law of possible change."

"It is seldom a woman is so free, and, I may add, so self-sustaining, as to have only her own plans and fancies for guides," said he.

She smiled serenely.

"I find the freedom very agreeable, and my self-sustaining power is fortunately fully equal to the demand imposed upon it. Since you are in London as a tourist, I suppose you have seen all the regulation-sights?" she added, with a change of subject which made him feel as if he were thrust away at arm's-length. "Have you seen Patti?—and what do you think of this new tenor, over whom all the world is raving?"

Marchmont responded suitably, and, after a few more commonplaces on both sides, Lady Gresham was announced, and he took his departure, meditating, as he went, on the wide gulf which yawned between Amy Reynolds and Mrs. Trafford.

CHAPTER VI.

A VOICE FROM THE PAST.

"By Jove! Dinsmore, your picture has made a pretty commotion? Have you heard of it?"

It was Reade who asked the question, as he entered his friend's studio a day or two after the scene in the Royal Academy and found the latter hard at work.

Dinsmore did not look up from the canvas over which his brush was moving back and forth, nor did his somewhat impassive face betray any sign of surprise.

"I suppose I know to what you are alluding," he replied. "Mrs. Trafford has recognized the face on the picture as a likeness of herself in her girlhood. But, pray, how did you come to know anything of the matter?"

"A fine question to ask, when I knew all about it before you did! I was at the Academy that day with the American party I mentioned to you. By-the-by, that Miss Paget is a delightfully jolly girl!"

"She would be gratified, no doubt, if she knew the form your commendation takes! And so you were at the Academy that day? But I don't see how it follows that you were aware of Mrs. Trafford's recognition of the picture."

"It follows in this way: that Mrs. Trafford was not the first person who recognized it. Do you know—have you ever known—a man named Marchmont?"

Dinsmore now turned, astonishment evident on his face, while his brows drew darkly together.

"I once knew a man of the name," he said. "What of him?"

"Only that he is with the Paget party —as a suitor of Miss Paget, I suspect— and it was he who first recognized the girl in 'Wild-Flowers' to be drawn for Mrs. Trafford."

Dinsmore muttered something which might or might not have been a benediction, and after a moment's pause the other went on:

"Miss Paget and myself were unluckily loitering behind when the recognition took place. From Mrs. Paget's account, it must have been rather dramatic. First, Mr. Marchmont recognized the likeness. Then, Miss Reynolds—Mrs. Trafford's sister, you know—who chanced to come up at the same time, was struck by it. Lastly, Mrs. Trafford herself was summoned to the spot by a special messenger sent by her sister, and at once identified her own face. On the strength of this, her acquaintance was at once claimed by Marchmont, who, it seems, had before been doubtful whether he had known her or not."

A deep flush mounted to Dinsmore's face.

"The insolent puppy!" he said, be-

tween his closely-set teeth. "And did she recognize him?"

"Yes, she recognized him. It seems he had been talking a good deal of her having been his first love, or something of the kind, and Miss Paget's interest was very much roused. As soon as she heard of the meeting at the picture she was full of excitement, cross-questioned me as to how you came to paint Mrs. Trafford's portrait, and finally carried off Marchmont as soon as she could to cross-question him about the whole affair."

"She must be very much given to interfering with matters which don't concern her! A woman of that kind is my detestation!"

"I don't think Miss Paget would be your detestation if you knew her. In fact, I'm sure you'd like her, she is so pleasant and unaffected, and her curiosity is natural considering her age and her vivacity. Suppose you let me present you? Being a countryman, she would be charmed to know you."

"Charmed to have an opportunity to cross-question me, I have no doubt! So you will allow me to decline, with thanks. Besides, what you have said of Marchmont is enough. I would not make the acquaintance of a houri, if to know her would involve meeting him."

Reade looked at the speaker for a moment with a rather keen scrutiny. Then he said: "It is odd that, agreeable and well-bred as Marchmont is, I should from the first have felt a sort of distrust of him. I liked the rest of them so much—they are people that you feel to be honest and genial to the core—that this instinct was the more marked with regard to him. He is very much of a courtier, smooth and supple, and all that sort of thing—is he not?"

"He is a dishonorable scoundrel!" said Dinsmore, emphatically. "That I know; and if this Miss Paget, of whom you talk, is going to marry him, I am sincerely sorry for her!"

"She certainly is a very nice little

thing to be thrown away on a dishonor-able scoundrel!" said Reade, meditatively. "If there is no other way of saving her from such a fate, I should not mind marrying her myself!"

"It is not a bad idea, only you would have no chance at all. An honest fellow never succeeds in comparison with a man like Marchmont."

The bitterness of the tone in which those words were uttered did not escape Reade's ear, and he drew his conclusions therefrom with tolerable accuracy.

"At least it would do no harm to try!" he said, lightly. "She is remarkably attractive—not a beauty, but winsome, sensible, and good-tempered."

"Then by all means marry her—if you can! A woman of that description is worth a dozen beauties."

"That is very true; but, when it comes to the serious question of matrimony, there are other matters to be considered besides a piquant face or the rivalry of the distinguished Mr. Marchmont—for I understand that he is distinguished in America."

"He is a third-rate politician, with some showy qualities, but no real ability or sagacity—if you consider that a reputation of *that* kind constitutes distinction."

"It answers very well to travel upon. But the matters to be considered, of which I spoke, are the very mundane things called pounds, shillings, and pence. If a man can barely live upon his income, he must be a lunatic if he thinks of doubling his responsibilities upon it—must he not?"

"I am not sure. To double your responsibilities might make you paint a few pictures—which it is clear you will not do without a stimulus of some kind. I fancy, however, that in this instance you would be more likely to double your income than your responsibilities. If Marchmont is in this young lady's train, it follows of necessity that she must be an heiress."

"Indeed! That would put another complexion upon the affair. I have always sternly abjured heiresses who are not nice girls; but a nice girl who is an heiress is a phenomenon before which I should bow at once."

"I think you may bow here without loss of time, then. Marchmont was a fortune-hunter ten years ago, and men are not likely to become more disinterested as they grow older."

"Very well, then. I shall cry, 'Reade, to the rescue!' and enter the lists against your distinguished compatriot without loss of time. Probably he will transfer his attentions to the fascinating Mrs. Trafford, since the spell of old association is in her favor. Did I understand you to say that there was once a love-affair between them?"

"You understood me to say nothing whatever about Mrs. Trafford," responded Dinsmore, almost sternly.

Reade's manner changed in a moment from jesting to earnest.

"I beg pardon!" he said. "I had no intention whatever of trying to force your confidence. It was from Miss Paget, of course, that I heard the report to which I alluded."

There followed a short silence; then Dinsmore threw down his brush, and turned, with something of impatience in his manner:

"If I have not mentioned anything about my past acquaintance with Mrs. Trafford," he said, "it is simply because the subject is painful to me, and not because there is any reason for mystery attached to it. When we were both very young, I knew her; but our paths in life parted ten years ago, and I have not seen her face since then until the afternoon of which you know, in the Park. It was by the merest accident that I came to paint that picture this spring. I chanced, one day, to be looking over an old sketch-book, and there I found the outlines of the scene sketched from life. Somehow the fancy seized me to elaborate it into a painting, and I did so, never dreaming that it would meet her eye, or the eye of any one else who could identify it. If I had expected such a thing, the picture should never have left my studio. But how could I imagine that, after ten years, the people best able to identify it would meet here in London?"

"It *is* singular!" said Reade. "It makes one think of those people Dickens wrote of, who are journeying over land and sea to meet one. I don't express the idea very clearly, but you know what I mean."

"I would have cut it into shreds if I had imagined, even indirectly, that it was likely to be the means of bringing Marchmont again into her life!" Dinsmore went on, as if speaking to himself.

"But will it not bring *you* again into her life?" Reade could not refrain from saying. "With such an excellent opportunity, you surely will renew your old acquaintance!"

Dinsmore shook his head decidedly. "I have told you that our paths in life parted, and they have diverged too widely now for any acquaintance between Mrs. Trafford and myself to be pleasant or profitable to either of us. I would serve her if I could, for the sake of our old friendship; but the renewal of that friendship is out of the question. We'll drop the subject now, if you please. If you were not such a man of fashion, I'd ask you to join me in a run over into Normandy next week."

"Next week! You are not thinking of leaving London before the end of the season?"

"What is the season to me? Am *I* an attendant at kettle-drums and dinnerparties, and three or four balls a night? Don't talk nonsense, but say whether or not you'll come."

"Quite impossible now, though I may join you later, if you are anywhere this side of the Baltic. But I must be off'—glancing at his watch. "I have an engagement to drive with the Pagets down to Richmond. Don't work too hard, Dinsmore; you begin to look a trifle haggard. I'll see you again before long. Good-day!"

After the young fellow left the studio, Dinsmore laid down his palette, walked the length of the room once or twice, and finally, pausing by an open window, drew from his pocket a letter.

A note, rather; for the thick creamtinted sheet, which he slowly opened, contained only a few lines written in a woman's fair, flowing hand; and this was what they said:

"Mrs. Trafford presents her compliments to Mr. Dinsmore, and would like to become the purchaser of his picture, 'Wild-Flowers,' if it has not been already sold. She will be exceedingly obliged if he will call on her at noon to-morrow."

This, together with the date and her address, was all that the note contained. Dinsmore read it over again, as he had read it at least a dozen times before, then returned the sheet to its envelope and the envelope to his pocket, preserving the while the steady impassiveness of demeanor which he would have preserved if Reade, or any one else, had been standing by.

This composure, however, was only outward inwardly his usually well-regulated thoughts were in a strange tumult. He himself was amazed at the disturbing power of this influence which had so unexpectedly entered his life.

"What possible object can she have for wishing to see me" he muttered, aloud. "The picture is a mere excuse; I have not the least doubt of that. Why should Mrs. Trafford wish to recall anything connected with Amy Reynolds? Sometimes women of her class have a spurious sentimentality about their youth; but I should not fancy this woman likely to be subject to it. Worldly to the core, she must be by this time hard of heart and cynical of mind. Poor Amy!" he added, with his voice suddenly softening, "there were possibilities of better things in her once—at least I thought so; but I was not very capable of judging then. It can't be that any shreds of that old folly are clinging to me still!" he added, almost savagely. "If so, perhaps the best thing I can do will be to go and see her; they would not survive one interview, I am sure! But"—and here he turned and began pacing the room again—"is it worth while to give myself the useless pain of seeing the foolish, tender, wayward girl I used to love transformed into a woman of the world, who lives only for pleasure and conquest? Surely such a ghost would be sadder than any that ever stepped out of a churchyard! Can I bear to face the old memories that *must* lurk in her eyes and smile, unless those eyes and that smile have changed more utterly than I can think possible? No; it is better to stay away. Her world is not my world, nor her ways mine; we have nothing in common save a past which is dead and should be forgotten. I will write and tell her that I do not wish to sell the picture; that will end the matter at once—and forever."

Those who have observed the great tendency of human nature to make resolutions and break them will not be greatly surprised to learn that, in less than twenty-four hours, Dinsmore broke the one just recorded.

"After all, there is no reason why I should avoid Mrs. Trafford more than I would avoid any other indifferent stranger," he thought. "She is nothing to me, nor am I more to her than a painter who has ventured to take what she very likely considers an undue liberty with her face. It will seem churlish not to go and at least apologize for that."

So, with the intention of apologizing for this "undue liberty," he found himself, on the day and at the time appointed, in Mrs. Trafford's drawing-room.

During the few moments in which he was left alone he looked around with something of the same wonder which Marchmont had felt in the apartment—with the same sense of the great difference between the mistress of all this luxury and the girl he had once known, the musician's penniless daughter in her poverty-stricken home.

"She has the desire of her heart!" he thought, as his glance swept over all the indications of wealth united to taste. "How she longed for these things! How she hated the narrowness and restraint of poverty! Have they brought her happiness, I wonder? It is a very shallow nature which worldly dissipation can satisfy. When I look at her face, shall I be able to tell whether it has satisfied her or not?"

As he walked to a window and looked out over the flower-filled balcony to the green park that lay beyond in all its summer beauty, a door behind him opened, a woman's dress softly rustled across the floor, and he turned to meet once more his old companion.

CHAPTER VII.

"THE LUXURY OF REGRET."

WITH Marchmont, as we are aware, Mrs. Trafford's composure had not failed any more than it was likely to fail with Danesford, Grantham, or any other of her numerous admirers; but a strain of altogether different feeling came over her when she found herself on the eve of meeting Hugh Dinsmore.

To analyze the different emotions which entered into this feeling would be impossible, but it may be said that it bore as little reference as possible to any question of sentimentalism. To the woman of the world—the woman in whose experience passions had lived and died like mushrooms—the memory of a boy's fancy was hardly more than matter for a smile.

The thoughts which really moved her in meeting Hugh were recollections of the early life with which he was associated, and especially of her father and Felix. After her note had been sent, she was half sorry for having written it.

"What a fool I am!" she thought, "to bring upon myself the pain of reviving those old memories!"

But even those old memories passed from her mind when she entered the room and saw the man who turned to meet her—not the familiar friend of her youth, but an absolute stranger.

"Hugh?" she exclaimed, involuntarily, in a tone between wonder and doubt. "*Is* it Hugh?"

Dinsmore—who had an advantage over her, inasmuch as he had seen *her* before—advanced with a quiet grace, which she observed even in her surprise.

"It is Hugh, Mrs. Trafford," he said. "Let me thank you for having given me an opportunity to meet you again."

He took her hand as he spoke, smiling the while at her expression of astonishment.

"Have I altered beyond recognition?" he asked. "Do you doubt my identity? I can very soon convince you that I am the same person you knew of old, if you care to be convinced."

"I *now* see that you are," she said, looking into his eyes—the candid, limpid eyes she had once known so well; "but you have changed exceedingly! Not more than is natural—not more than I have, probably; but, you see, I was not thinking of you like this. I thought of my old friend; and you are not he."

Her voice sank over the last words with the softness which her admirers knew well—perilous softness it often was to those who listened; but Hugh Dinsmore answered, with the same self-possessed quietness he had already displayed:

"You are mistaken in that. I am your old friend still, Mrs. Trafford, and very glad to perceive—very glad to congratulate you on—your brilliant success in life."

"Yet you have been in no haste to congratulate me," she said, now herself again.

She sat down as she spoke, and motioned him to a chair by her side. The first surprise over, it was an absolute relief to her to perceive how greatly he had changed—to find that he hardly reminded her at all of things which she did not wish to remember. An epicurean once, an epicurean always, Amy shrank as much from painful memories and disagreeable thoughts now as she had shrunk in the past from the privations and discomforts of poverty.

"But perhaps you did not know that I was in London?" she added, as he obeyed her gesture, while her sweeping glance took in every point of his personal appearance, every detail of his manner; and she decided, as a woman of her class can decide in an instant, that her old companion was thoroughly refined, thoroughly a gentleman, thoroughly "presentable."

"Yes, I knew that you were in London," he answered. "You were pointed out to me in the Park, several days ago."

"You knew it!"—she gave him the full benefit of her beautiful eyes in a gaze of reproach—"and you waited for me to send for you! That does not speak much for the friendship in which you bid me believe."

"Pardon me," said Hugh, in his straightforward fashion, "but you must comprehend why I did not think for a moment of advancing any claim to your notice on the score of our old acquaintance. Many things have changed in the years since we parted—our respective positions most of all."

"You are famous—or, at least, on the threshold of becoming famous—I am told," said she, with the graceful tact which had rounded many an awkward conversational point. "I always knew that you would be."

"I am as little famous as any other hard-working painter with a moderately good reputation," said Hugh, uncompromisingly. "But if I *were* famous in my world, I should still be as far as ever from the world you have entered."

"What do you know of the world I have entered?" she asked.

"Little or nothing," he answered— "except that it is the world of fashion, which closes its doors on all who are workers or Bohemians; and artists are strongly suspected of belonging to both classes."

"Classes to which I belong by birth, you know," she said. "Hugh, if you really have any recollection of our old friendship, let us drop this unreal tone, and be ourselves. Do you think I have forgotten or disowned anything? Do you think I fail to remember the old life in Edgerton, with papa giving music-lessons—we growing up like young Arabs—my ambition—our plans for the future, when you and Felix and I were to be artists together? If I had forgotten any of it, your picture would have brought it all back to me. And I thought— Do you care to know what I thought when I saw that scene, torn out of our old life, and placed in such a strange, new setting?"

Despite himself, his interest was caught and held by her changing face, her vivid eyes, her rich, earnest voice. "Yes," he said; "you cannot doubt that I should like to know what you thought."

"I first thought, How strange life is! —how strange that, of we three, you alone should have fulfilled your ambition! The grass has been growing for ten years over Felix, and I—"

"You have no need to regret the loss of your career," said he, looking at her with a searching keenness of glance. "It is impossible that you can mean to imply that you do?"

"I don't mean to imply it; as you say, it would be impossible for me to do so. My position in life is all that I can ask—is far, far more brilliant than I had any right to suppose that it would be. But somehow the difference of everything

from what we hoped and planned struck me with a sense of pain when I saw your picture."

Hugh bent his head—perhaps to conceal a slightly satirical smile that curled his lip.

"It is some French writer, I think— French writers generally manage to go to the core of things—who speaks of the luxury of regret, when regret is not too poignant. In your position, Mrs. Trafford, I should say that any regret over the 'difference of everything from what we hoped and planned' must be altogether a luxury."

The color deepened swiftly, almost painfully, on her face. It had been many a day since such a tone as this—a tone of irony and half-concealed mockery—had fallen on her ear, used only to softest adulation. She felt like one who is at once rebuffed and disconcerted. If she had spoken what she thought, she would have said, "You are discourteous and unkind!" But, instead of that, she answered after a minute, without the least sign of ruffled feeling:

"I do not think I spoke of regret; I only spoke of memory, and of that pang which memory always holds. I am so little given to sentiment, I am so little fond of harrowing my emotions, that it is very seldom I indulge in what your French writer would esteem the luxury of recalling the past. But your picture made me think of it; and, since you are the only person connected with that life whom I could possibly desire to see, I venture to hold out my hand to you across all the years."

A more implacable person than Hugh would have been disarmed by the graciousness of these words, especially since Mrs. Trafford could infuse into her least utterance a charm which it is impossible to define.

"You are very kind," he replied, falling back on the conventional formulas which stand us all in good stead. "I must tell you that, apart from the pleasure of seeing you once more. I have obeyed your summons in order to make an explanation with regard to that picture. It was altogether owing to an accident that I painted it. I can hardly suppose that you remember one Sunday afternoon when we were in that glen together, and I made a sketch of you—"

She interrupted him quickly.

"I remember it perfectly. It was in April, and I told you for the first time that I meant to be a singer."

"Yes, it was that evening "—he did not say by what other token she might remember it—"I made a sketch of the scene and of yourself, and that sketch I found a few months ago in one of my old portfolios. It recalled your face to me so vividly, that I felt sure I could paint it without any other aid to memory; and I think I succeeded—moderately, at least. I should not, however, have placed the picture on exhibition if I had dreamed that there was any danger of recognition; and I offer you a sincere apology for having done so."

"There is surely no need of an apology," she said. "The girl whom you painted there is dead and gone; and I, who may be esteemed her lawful representative, give you leave to make any use you like of your old sketches of her face. Poor, pretty, foolish face! I felt sorry to look at it. But you will think that I do indulge in the 'luxury of regret' if I am absurd enough to talk like this!" she broke off, with a laugh. "May I trouble you to ring the bell? There is another old friend of yours whom I should like you to see.—Ask Miss Reynolds to come here," she said to the servant who entered a moment later.

"So it is my old friend Mariette, whom I remember as insatiable with regard to stories, and avaricious with regard to sugar-plums!" said Dinsmore. "Life is a kaleidoscope of changes, certainly. And what has become of Oliver and Ernest?"

"They are both in America. You

know, perhaps, that Mr. Trafford had an extensive business connection, and many friends. Owing to the influence of these, both Oliver and Ernest have obtained excellent business positions, and are rising in the world."

"Then they are not musicians?"

"No; both are musical, but neither a musician. Mariette has a delicious voice —not so powerful as mine was, but very sweet. You must hear her sing."

Just as Dinsmore was about to reply, the door opened, and Mariette entered— a vision fitted to charm the sight of any man who was a painter, in the exquisite freshness of her blond loveliness.

She bowed slightly to the stranger, and then addressed her sister: "You sent for me, Amy?"

"Yes," Amy answered; "I sent for you to see an old friend. Have you no idea who this is?"

Mariette turned her blue eyes on the person thus presented to her, and, after an instant's puzzled scrutiny, leaped to the right conclusion.

"It must be Hugh!" she said. "We have no other old friends in London— have we, Amy? I think it must be—ah, I know it is Hugh!" she cried, holding out a tiny, lily-leaf hand, as Dinsmore drew near, with a softer light in his eyes than had shone there for Mrs. Trafford.

"Would you like to hear the story of the 'Ugly Duckling' again, Mariette?" he asked, smiling. "You will allow me to say 'Mariette' once, for the sake of old acquaintance—will you not? My dear little playfellow, what a charming woman you have become! I believe I used to call you the 'Fair One with the Golden Locks' and the title suits you better now than ever."

"And you—oh, how handsome and nice-looking you have become!" cried the fair one, with delightful frankness. "I am so glad to see you again!—and what on earth should you call me but 'Mariette?' I remember the 'Ugly Duckling' ever so well, and I would like to hear it again. You were the very best story-teller I ever knew, Hugh—may I call you Hugh?"

"Of course you may! As you remark, what else on earth should you call me?"

"I feel very much as if I were taking a great liberty with a stranger, for there is really no sign of Hugh about you—except, perhaps, your eyes.—What do you think, Amy?—should you ever have known him?"

"Hardly, I think," Amy answered. "But we are apt to forget what a length of time ten years is, and what differences it makes. No doubt you and I are changed as much as Mr. Dinsmore."

Mr. Dinsmore! Mariette opened her eyes at that name, and would no doubt have opened them a little wider if she had known that it was the first time her sister had uttered it—an utterance due to the curious mortification with which she noted how much warmer Hugh's greeting was for Mariette than it had been for herself.

"Of course I have changed immensely," said Mariette; "but, although you have improved very much, Amy, I do not think you have altered beyond recognition. There was Mr. Marchmont, for instance, who knew you."

Involuntarily Dinsmore looked at Mrs. Trafford, but, quick as was his glance, it failed to detect any sign of discomposure on her face, while her manner was coldly careless as she answered:

"That is not exactly a case in point, Mariette. Though Mr. Marchmont had heard my name, and had seen me several times, he was not sure of my identity until it was settled by Mr. Dinsmore's picture."

"When I heard that," said Hugh, bluntly, "I was very sorry for having painted the picture, I assure you, Mrs. Trafford."

She looked at him with a smile.

"You need not be sorry," she said. "I am not. Good and evil are mixed in

everything; and the good counterbalances the evil in this, I think. But who told you anything about it?"

"A young fellow named Reade—an artist, who was at the Academy that day with the party to which Marchmont was attached."

"Some people of whom he spoke to me, probably. What is their name?"

"Paget is the name Reade mentioned. He talked a great deal of a girl to whom he has taken a fancy, in whose train Marchmont is dangling."

"Indeed! She must be an heiress."

"So I said at once; and since then I have seen an American who confirms my judgment, by telling me that she is a considerable heiress."

"Ah!" said Mrs. Trafford. She was silent for a minute, and her eyes turned absently out of the window to the green trees in the park, and the smoky-blue sky above. "And this Mr. Reade has taken a fancy to the girl, you say?" she asked. "What order of person is he? Artists belong to all classes, as we know."

"Reade belongs to Mayfair more than to Bohemia," Hugh answered. "He comes of good people, has genuine talent, but no industry, and just fortune enough to ruin him for all practical purposes."

"Agreeable?"

"Exceedingly so! At this moment I can't think of any one more agreeable."

"Then I am going to begin our new acquaintance by asking a favor of you. Present this very agreeable gentleman to me—will you not?"

"I am sure he would be most happy to be presented. But—shall I be doing him a kindness, Mrs. Trafford?"

She blushed a little, for she understood all that the grave tone, the graver eyes, implied.

"I shall not harm him, if that is what you mean," she answered. "How have you learned to think me so dangerous?"

"According to the rules of gallantry, I believe I should say I have seen you, and that is enough; but as a plain matter of truth, I must add that I have also heard of you. Mrs. Trafford's reputation is not confined to one capital of Europe."

"Mrs. Trafford's old friends—nay, it is foolish to speak in the plural, when, to be honest, one must be singular—Mrs. Trafford's old *friend* might suspend judgment until he learns how far report has dealt justly with her."

Mrs. Trafford's old friend looked at the beautiful, beguiling face, and felt his heart hardening. Like most men of his class, he had an ideal of womanhood which was as far as possible removed from a coquette who lived only to ensnare men's hearts and win their homage.

"If there had been much room to doubt its justice," he said, constrained to honesty, "I should have been convinced by a scene in Richmond Park upon which I stumbled a few days ago. My presence there was an accident, pure and simple—one of those accidents against which no foresight could guard; but you will allow me to apologize for it?"

"As well as for having painted the picture?" she said, smiling a little. "What will you apologize for next? So it *was* you in Richmond Park that evening! I had an odd instinct of your presence, though I did not recognize you. The scene upon which you stumbled was very harmless, but I suppose I could not convince you of that. Pray, do not think of going!"—as he rose. "I have planned a nice luncheon—you and Mariette and I alone. Besides, we have not settled about the picture, and I have not asked you a syllable about any of the people in Edgerton."

"We can settle about the picture in half a dozen words," said he, reluctantly.

"But those half-dozen words cannot be spoken at present," said Mariette. "Here comes Thompson to announce luncheon, and you may consider yourself a prisoner, without hope of grace."

It was too late for retreat, so Hugh made the best of the situation—certainly not one of which most men would have been inclined to complain. Even he felt little inclination to do so, when he found himself in the dining-room seated at a luncheon-table pretty enough for a picture.

Conversation was less personal and more easy here than it had been in the drawing-room; it touched lightly on many different topics, and Dinsmore soon perceived that, if Mrs. Trafford lived chiefly for the world of fashion, she had at least not failed to enlarge her mind and her sympathies by a broader culture than is usual with women.

Mariette was too young for the same result to be apparent in her, but she possessed a childlike gayety, a daring, yet graceful frankness, irresistibly attractive.

"I should like to paint you," Dinsmore said to her, presently. "Do you not think you could sit to me? I need just such a head as yours for a picture on which I am engaged."

"I shall be delighted!" she responded.—"You see my turn has come at last, Amy!—You must understand," she continued, turning to Hugh, "that the artists in Italy all raved over Amy, and would have given anything to have obtained a sitting from her. But she has never even had her portrait painted—which I think a shame!"

"Do you remember the old arrangement between us, that *you* should paint my portrait?" Amy asked, looking at her guest.

"In violet velvet and point-lace—yes, I remember," he answered. "The violet velvet and point-lace are fortunately quite practicable now: but, unfortunately, I am not a portrait-painter, and therefore not qualified to do justice to such a subject."

"You are satisfied to have done more than justice to the same subject at a different period. *A propos*, may I ask if you mean to let me become the purchaser of 'Wild-Flowers?'"

"I did not paint the picture with any intention of selling it," he replied, quietly.

"I cannot allow you to become its purchaser, but if you will accept it—"

She interrupted him decidedly, almost haughtily.

"That is altogether out of the question! Excuse me for having troubled you with regard to the matter, and let me congratulate you on your brilliant success in the 'Wacht am Rhein.' I am told that it is one of the pictures most admired in the exhibition this year."

.   .   .   .   .   .

"Well, Amy," said Mariette, an hour later, "what do you think of Hugh?"

"I think," answered Mrs. Trafford, "that there is nothing in the world more foolish than to renew old associations of any kind. Characters change quite as much as circumstances; and, after the lapse of years, people who were friends once are less than strangers. If I had ever doubted that the experiment was a rash one, I should be sure of it now."

"Then you do not like Hugh? Is that what you mean?"

"I did not exactly mean that; but there is little sympathy between us; and, in short, one had better be satisfied with those who are of one's own world, and with whom one has tastes and habits in common."

"I thought we found a great many tastes in common with Hugh," said Mariette, sauntering up to a mirror in order to regard the face at which Hugh had gazed so admiringly, "and I don't know how you feel about it, but I think that the visit to his studio, which he asked us to make, will be delightful."

———

CHAPTER VIII.

"OLD SENTIMENT."

"WILL I do, Mary? Pray tell me quite honestly if you like the effect of this dress?"

"What a question, Nelly!" said Mrs. Paget. "As if one could venture not to like a dress of Worth's? It is beautiful —ravissant, as the French say—and you look better than I ever saw you!"

"One is uncertain about these new shades," said Nelly. "They are very trying."

"I think them lovely," said Mrs. Paget, who belonged to the order of women who think anything lovely that is fashionable. "The effect is simply exquisite; you may be sure of that."

Pale-pink silk and lilac crape—could any one, save Worth, venture upon such a combination? Yet, as Mrs. Paget declared, it was "simply exquisite," and very becoming to Nelly's blooming complexion, while her pretty brown hair was coifed high, and dressed with a cluster of pale-pink roses and a spray of lilac.

If she wanted a confirmation of her sister-in-law's opinion, Marchmont's face gave it when she entered the drawing-room where he and Mr. Paget were waiting, amusing themselves the while by looking at the animated scene which the London streets presented at half-past seven o'clock on a June evening, when all the world seems to be going out for purposes of pleasure. The Paget party were also going out to dine with Mrs. Trafford. Hence Miss Paget's careful toilet and her anxiety concerning it.

As she entered, Marchmont turned, and his quick gaze of admiration brought a bright glow to the girl's cheek.

"How charming you look!" he said, advancing toward her. "I thought I knew all your capabilities for looking well, but I see I was mistaken; you have developed a new one to-night."

"I am glad you like my toilet," said she. "I know that your taste is admirable, and I trust a great deal to your opinion. Of course, with Mrs. Trafford and her beautiful sister I shall be totally eclipsed; still, I was anxious to look my modest best."

"You certainly have succeeded, and I do not think you need entertain any

11

fear of an eclipse. Modesty is a good thing, no doubt; but sometimes it is a misplaced thing—and it is grievously misplaced with you, just now. I wish you would give me leave to tell you all that I think of your appearance—and of yourself."

His voice sank low, his eyes grew eloquently soft, and Nelly's heart beat fast under her pink silk and lilac crape.

People who profess to analyze emotions, and who can tell to a nicety exactly where fancy ends and love begins, might have said that it was only her fancy which was enlisted in Marchmont's favor. Yet fancy not only borders so closely on love as to be constantly mistaken for it, but it often does duty creditably for the latter even to the end—that inevitable end of disillusionment which awaits all spurious sentiments. Whatever was the cause, her heart beat fast; of that there can be no doubt.

Within the last day or two Marchmont's devotion had unmistakably advanced toward a culmination—for had he not tested his old influence with Mrs. Trafford and found it lacking?—and does any man wise in the wisdom of the world peril a certain and positive good for an uncertain and illusory one?

After he left the house of the woman who had once loved him, and began to reckon up the chances of winning that love again, not even vanity could blind him to the fact that there was an exceedingly faint possibility of doing so. A woman of the world like Mrs. Trafford would undoubtedly marry for the things of the world. With her face, with her cleverness, above all, with her fortune—reckoned by those who knew best at a hundred thousand pounds—what matrimonial height might she not hope to gain? No; the prize was glittering, but to try to grasp it was to waste time and effort in chasing a will-o'-the-wisp, while ready to his hand was Nelly Paget and Nelly Paget's fortune, to tide over the financial ruin which threatened him.

Certain it was that, with the aid of many cigars, Mr. Marchmont weighed every *pro* and *con* of the question, and acted with his usual devotion to his own interest in deciding to abandon all hope of reviving "old sentiment" with Mrs. Trafford.

"After the life she has led for ten years, she will be altogether material in her views of things," he thought. "She will ask, 'What shall I gain by such a step?' and it is very clear that she would gain nothing, in comparison with what she now possesses. If I could only have looked into the future—if I could only have imagined that she would marry old Trafford—I should not have parted with her as I did. I should have kept a hold on her which would be useful to me now."

A vain regret, however, and, being vain, one over which Mr. Marchmont did not waste reflection. He turned his attention at once to Nelly Paget, and being anxious, for certain private reasons, to make things sure, he pressed toward the point of a declaration.

It was a point from which the girl, with the coquetry of her sex, cleverly fenced him off. She liked him, but hers was too honest a nature not to distrust him also—vaguely but decidedly. He was tender, gallant, charming, but in her heart she could not feel as if he really loved her; and this instinct held her back from loving him.

Yet, as I have said, fancy often does duty for love; so there can be no doubt of the flutter of Nelly's heart—which brings us back to the point from which we diverged.

Notwithstanding this flutter, she looked up at him with a self-possessed smile:

"I should be very glad to hear your opinion of my appearance and of myself, and have no doubt I would derive a great deal of useful information from it; but the question is, Would it be sincere?"

"You must understand very little

what you are to me, if you think it could be other than sincere!" he answered. "Nelly, you are unkind—nay, more; you are unjust—when you say such things! You may not care to accept what I offer you, but at least you should believe in it."

Nelly's hand began to tremble so that she could scarcely button the glove over which her head was bent. This, if Marchmont had only known it, was his moment of opportunity. They were, to all intents and purposes, alone, standing together in the middle of the room, while Mr. Paget remained obligingly at the window and gazed out, with the din of cabs and carriages filling his ears.

"Believe what, monsieur?" the girl asked, as lightly as she could, and then went on hastily, conscious that she had involuntarily asked a *very* leading question. "I don't believe in anything very much; I haven't faith, I suppose. I have even ventured to doubt Worth since I put on this dress. But your commendation reassures me."

"If you have faith in me that far, have faith further," said he, half jestingly.

A moment before he had been on the verge of a declaration; but, aware that Walter might turn or Mrs. Paget enter at any instant, he felt inclined to defer it now.

After all, time and opportunity were in his own hand, he thought, as many a man had thought before; forgetting that tide in the affairs of men which must be taken at the flood to lead on to fortune.

"I have perfect faith in your good taste," said she, evading the direct issue, after a fashion common with women. "If you honestly think me looking well, I shall go with a lighter heart to meet the wonderful Mrs. Trafford. By-the-by, have you ever revived the tender reminiscences of the past with her? Does she still remember anything of the old romance?"

"I have seen Mrs. Trafford only once, as you are aware, and on that occasion I certainly made no effort to revive any 'tender reminiscences.' In fact, I am by no means sure that there are any to be revived. As I told you, we had a flirtation long ago, but it did not occur to either of us to attach any importance to the affair."

"It is really edifying to hear how lightly you speak of such trifles as dead-and-gone flirtations! I wonder— Ah, Mary, here you are! I was just thinking we shall be rather late!"

"The carriage has been waiting some time," said Mr. Paget, turning round. "If you are ready, my dear, we had better go."

Twenty minutes later the party were ushered into Mrs. Trafford's drawing-room; and Mrs. Trafford, rising from a chair near one of the open, flower-filled windows came forward to receive them.

Not alone, however, had she been sitting in the cool, fragrant apartment; a masculine figure rose also, and stood in the background while she received the guests.

"Charmed to meet you, Mrs. Paget! Sorry not to have found you at home the other day.—Miss Paget, I am glad to know you, and Mr. Paget also.—Ah, Mr. Marchmont, how do you do?"

This, or something like it, was all that she said; but the grace of her manner, her voice, her smile, made the commonplace words a welcome fit for royalty. The gentleman in the background was presented as Colonel Danesford, and Nelly immediately indentified him as Mrs. Trafford's principal attendant whenever she had seen that lady in public.

Conversation for a few minutes was general, and as brilliant as it usually is on such occasions, when matters are further enlivened by an utter absence of all subjects of common interest. Then a door at the farther end of the apartment opened, and with a soft rustle of silk and muslin—azure silk under white muslin and lace—Mariette entered.

Her beauty for a moment fascinated all eyes, so fresh and nymph-like was it;

and, while her greetings were being made, another guest entered, toward whom Mrs. Trafford turned cordially, and whom the Pagets recognized, with surprise, as their friend Mr. Reade.

The surprise on Marchmont's part was altogether unmixed with pleasure. Exactly jealous of this new acquaintance he was not; but he disapproved of him for several reasons—among which his attentions to Nelly Paget and his friendship with Hugh Dinsmore stood chief. To meet him *here* was something which he certainly had not reckoned upon.

Dinner was announced almost immediately, and Mrs. Trafford laid her hand on Mr. Paget's arm, Colonel Danesford offered his to Mrs. Paget, Marchmont took Mariette, and, as a consequence of these combinations, Reade and Nelly found themselves together.

"Why did you never tell me that you knew Mrs. Trafford?" she whispered, on their way to the dining-room.

"For the very good reason that I have not seen you since I knew her," he answered. "I called yesterday, but you were out."

"Yes; we were sorry to have missed you. I think life is made up of missing people that one likes to see, and meeting those for whom one does not care."

"It is too often the case; but sometimes Fate makes amends by allowing one to meet the person that one wishes most to see—of which happy chance I am an example at the present moment."

The color deepened a little on Nelly's pretty face, but she laughed lightly.

"Does that mean Mrs. Trafford?" she asked.

"I am sure that you must know very well whom it means," he answered; and if we stretch a point, and suppose that she had *not* known, his voice would have told her.

The dinner was perfect, and passed off admirably; for Mrs. Trafford was a thorough mistress of social art, and could have made harmonious any elements more jarring than those there assembled.

As the party was small, the conversation was in a great measure general, but there were some side-interviews carried on—notably one between Marchmont and Mariette.

"Of course I remember you!" the latter said. "How could you think I would not? I was just at the age when sugar-plums sink deepest into the heart—and you were very lavish with them! Do you chance to recollect an old apple-tree in our garden? I can fancy myself seated there this moment, with a paper of sweets!"

An old apple-tree! Did Marchmont not remember it? Yet he almost felt like a man in a dream, as he looked across the table at Mrs. Trafford's beautiful face, and thought of the girl he had seen perched among its gnarled boughs.

"You were so young," he said, "and your life has been so different since that time, that I am a little surprised you should remember anything connected with that old existence!"

"I believe people say there are such things as dormant memories," she replied. "My memories were rather dormant, until I met one of our oldest friends the other day. Do you remember Hugh Dinsmore, Mr. Marchmont?"

The blue eyes looked at him with childlike innocence—it may be added, more feigned than real. As a matter of fact, Mariette remembered very well how matters stood between those two unequal rivals in the past, and shrewdly suspected how much love they bore each other in the present.

"I remember a boy of that name who used to be seen occasionally in your father's house," he answered. "He has since become a painter, I believe."

"He painted 'Wild-Flowers'—the picture in front of which I saw you at the Academy. You were struck like myself—were you not?—with the portrait of Amy?"

"So much struck that I recognized the face at once, and it enabled me to identify Mrs. Trafford as the charming girl I knew long ago. I owe Mr. Dinsmore thanks for having painted the picture, therefore—"

"Mr. Dinsmore would be gratified to receive them, I am sure," said Mariette, with a gleam of mischief under her sweeping lashes. "He has an excellent memory for everything connected with our old life, and would remember you, I have no doubt."

"Very likely," said Marchmont, with a careless air which did credit to his self-command, since at that moment he recollected only too well what good cause Hugh Dinsmore had to remember him. With the vividness of a picture there rose before him the aspect of a country-road, a sunset sky, and a shabby boy who stood before him and demanded to be heard in behalf of Amy Reynolds; how contemptuously he had thrust him out of his path then, and now— Well, well, such memories were intrusive, and by no means agreeable with good *plats* and good wines before one, and a lovely girl at one's side!

After dinner, when the ladies were alone in the drawing-room, Mrs. Trafford sat down beside Miss Paget, and asked that young lady if she entertained any predilection for artists.

"Not for any artist in particular," she said, with a soft laugh—"only for artists in general. Would you like to pay a visit to a studio? Mr. Dinsmore has kindly invited my sister and myself to go to see his paintings, and if it would entertain you to accompany us, I am sure he would be glad to see you."

"It would entertain me very much!" said Nelly. "I should like it of all things, if you think Mr. Dinsmore would not object—"

"I will answer for that. Under any circumstances, Mr. Dinsmore could only be charmed to receive you; but he feels a very special interest in you—shall I tell you why?"

"Yes, pray tell me!"—and Nelly opened her brown eyes. "I should not have fancied that he had ever heard my name."

"Not even from Mr. Reade? Then you have very little idea of the serious impression you have made upon that gentleman. *A propos*, Mr. Dinsmore tells me that he belongs to good people, and is not at all dependent upon his pictures for bread; in consequence of which, indeed, he paints very few."

"That is a pity, if he has genius!"

"Not genius, perhaps, but a great deal of talent, no doubt. Let us hope that his wife—when he gets one—will make him do better. If she has any love of art, any pride in his success, she will!"

"Those are large *ifs*," said Nelly, smiling, yet blushing, she hardly knew why.

"I don't think so," said Mrs. Trafford. "Such women are readily found, and I cannot imagine anything pleasanter than to be able to exert an influence of the kind. If I were not altogether past the age of sentiment, I should be tempted to make him fall in love with me for the sake of exerting it," she added, with another soft laugh.

"*You* past the age of sentiment!" said Nelly, looking at the beautiful, youthful face. "Pardon me, Mrs. Trafford, but I cannot believe that."

"It is true, nevertheless," said Mrs. Trafford, with an unruffled serenity.

At this point the gentlemen entered, and the fair hostess moved away, leaving a vacant seat on the sofa by Nelly, which Reade at once perceived, and toward which he quickly made his way.

Marchmont, who began to entertain an uneasy sense of possible danger in that direction, was about to follow and at least prevent a *tête-à-tête*, when Mrs. Trafford interposed, and nipped his intention in the bud.

"I have scarcely exchanged a word with you, Mr. Marchmont!"—how beguiling the sweet voice was! "Will you not take this chair, and let us recall some of our old associations?"

The chair which her hand indicated was immediately beside the one into which she gracefully sank—in her silken draperies, her soft laces, her shining jewels, a picture to fascinate any man's eye, to chain any man's attention!

It is quite unnecessary to say that her words had the intended effect upon Marchmont, and he yielded without an instant's demur to the invitation so graciously extended.

"I am only too happy to have an opportunity of recalling those old associations with you!" he said, taking the chair. "If I ever shrank from them, it was only because I did not know whether I should ever see you again, or how much I might find you changed."

"Outwardly, years change us a great deal," said she, indolently waving a fan to and fro, and sinking her voice; "but the inward change is not always in the same ratio. Despite one's self, one remembers—ah! one often remembers a great deal that one would like to forget!"

Her eyes drooped, her breast heaved in a sigh, and Marchmont—Marchmont, who had often boasted that the woman was never born who could befool him—felt himself quiver in every fibre.

How if, after all, the prize should be within his grasp! How if, after all, old sentiment still had power to sway this woman as it had, to his knowledge, swayed others of her sex!

If he had been wise, he would have recollected that she, who had once been a simple village-girl, was now one of the most consummate coquettes in Europe. But what is there that can befool a man like his own vanity? Deep-rooted in his consciousness was the belief, "She cannot have forgotten *me!*" And on this basis Mrs. Trafford, with a profound knowledge of masculine nature, proceeded to act.

"I, too, have often wished that I could forget—many things," said he, sinking his voice to its most effective key. "But who can read the future? Who knows what recompenses for the past it may hold? Even to sit here by you, is more than for many years I have dared to hope for, knowing how you might regard me—"

"Nay," said she, with her sweetest smile, "when we spoke of the past, I did not mean to revive any disagreeable memories. Did I not tell you, the other day, that I am able now to comprehend all that I may have misunderstood—shall I say—then? The world hardens one, perhaps, but it also teaches one wisdom. We can smile together over the absurdities of our youth, and be very good friends—can we not?"

Lustrous, beguiling eyes, and a half-mocking yet wholly charming smile—few men could have resisted these things combined with a half-million in the background; and Marchmont was not one of the few.

He began to feel that intoxication of the senses which leads, by no long path, to absolute enthrallment.

"Do not ask me to perjure myself," he murmured, in reply. "What you call 'the absurdities of our youth' are the memories most dear to me, of all that I possess—memories that have been—"

She interrupted him.

"That will not do," she said. "One thing which all my friends have to understand is, that I am no sentimentalist; and when people become sentimental, I am sometimes rude enough to laugh. It is better to laugh than to sigh, you know; and, perhaps, if one did not laugh, one might be tempted into sighing."

It is not worth while to record the conversation that followed. An adept in the art of ensnaring—of implying rather than saying things agreeable to the vanity of her listener—was Mrs. Trafford, and a wiser man than Marchmont might have yielded to her spell.

He grounded arms at once. Nor need it be supposed that his only motive for doing so was self-interest. There could be no doubt that this was his original and strongest motive; but the woman who looked at him with her brilliant eyes, and talked to him with her low voice, was a mistress of fascination, and before he left her side he was more in love with her than he had ever been with pretty Amy Reynolds—or, for the matter of that, with any one else. She was eminently fitted to inspire an absorbing passion, and it must be recorded of her that she deliberately set herself to inspire it here.

With long practice and surpassing attractions, she was not likely now to fail. Indeed, she succeeded to such good purpose, that the thought of Nelly Paget soon vanished from Marchmont's mind as completely as if it had never existed there.

Danesford, meanwhile, saw this oft-repeated game with a sore, sick heart. "What can you hope from such a coquette?" he often asked himself, but the answer of wisdom was given unheeded. Let her do what she would, he was her thrall until she bade him go; nevertheless, it was with a sense of bitter pain that he watched such a scene as this.

Her quick eye no doubt read the expression on his face; for presently, when she had accomplished all that she desired, she dismissed Marchmont in the manner which women of her class possess to perfection.

"Go and take Mariette to the piano," she said. "I want you to hear her sing; I want to know if you think her voice as fine as mine was."

Then she crossed over to Mrs. Paget, whom Danesford was doing his best to entertain, thanked him by a glance, and in five minutes, without seeming directly to address her attention to him, had soothed and charmed him. Presently, under cover of the music, she managed to say: "Beware of rash judgment, *mon ami*. Nay, don't disclaim! I saw that you were judging me a little while ago. I had a reason—I think a good one—for my conduct; and some day, perhaps, I may tell you what it is. Meanwhile, remember that, if women are enigmas, at the best of times, they are doubly so when you do not know their motives."

CHAPTER IX.

"FOR THE SAKE OF THE PAST."

BEFORE Mrs. Trafford parted with Miss Paget on the evening of the dinner-party, it was settled that the latter should accompany her to Hugh Dinsmore's studio on the next day.

"I do not feel at liberty to ask the rest of your party," Mrs. Trafford said. "I think we should scarcely find Mr. Dinsmore prepared for so large a company. At another time I have no doubt he would be glad to see Mr. and Mrs. Paget if they care for pictures."

"Honestly, I don't think they care very much," Nelly answered with a laugh. "Walter has more than once said that they bore him, and Mary has been almost as frank. Don't trouble about them, Mrs. Trafford. Considering the nature of the entertainment, they will be more than willing for me to go alone."

"I will call for you at five o'clock tomorrow, then, if you have no other engagement."

"No other at all."

At five o'clock the next afternoon, therefore, Mrs. Trafford's carriage drew up at the Langham Hotel, and, after a few minutes' delay, Nelly came down, attended by Marchmont.

"I must tell you, Mrs. Trafford," she cried, gayly, "that Mr. Marchmont is devoured by curiosity to know where we are going; and I think he would like exceedingly to be invited to accompany us."

"I am sorry that it is quite out of the question to invite him," said Mrs. Trafford, extending a delicate pearl-gloved hand to Marchmont. "Our destination is for the present a mystery; and when it ceases to be a mystery—when you return, and tell him where you have been —I do not think he will regret having been excluded from the expedition."

"Allow me to say that you are mistaken," replied Marchmont. "Companionship alone makes happiness; and with such companionship as the present, what place could fail to be delightful? I should enjoy—I speak advisedly—I should enjoy even a milliner's shop."

"We will not put your gallantry to such a crucial test!" said Mrs. Trafford, and her laughing manner did not altogether veil the decision of her tone. "We shall see you at the opera to-night, I suppose? Patti sings in the 'Barbiere.'"

She bowed smilingly, and the carriage drove off, leaving him standing on the pavement looking after it—an expression of doubt and irresolution on his face.

"If I could trust her!" he muttered, under his breath. "But one must run some risk in all ventures, and this—is worth a risk."

Meanwhile, Nelly turned to Mrs. Trafford, and, in her impulsive fashion, said:

"I am glad you did not ask him to go with us. I think he knew Mr. Dinsmore once, and—and I have heard him speak of him—Mr. Dinsmore, I mean—in a manner that would not make it pleasant for them to meet—at least, not in this way."

"I had no intention whatever of asking him," answered Mrs. Trafford. "I have too much regard for Mr. Dinsmore to do so; but as far as Mr. Marchmont himself is concerned," she added, with a sudden glow in her eyes, "it would be wise for him to let Hugh Dinsmore's name rest in silence. The only reason I can imagine for his failing to do so is, that we are never so implacable toward

any person as toward one whom we have injured—or attempted to injure."

She spoke with emphasis, and her words let in a flood of light on Nelly's intelligence. The latter remembered all that Marchmont had said of the boy who had once been in love with Mrs. Trafford, and she saw—or fancied she saw—proof of the truth of this in Mrs. Trafford's manner. The fragmentary knowledge of that lady's past life, which had been revealed to her, inflamed her curiosity to learn more.

"I should like to know exactly all that happened between these three people when they knew each other before," she thought. "There were romantic—perhaps dramatic—chapters in the story, I am sure."

"When you see Hugh Dinsmore, you will feel that nothing to his discredit *could* be true," said Mariette, quickly. And as Nelly noted the color deepen on her rose-leaf cheek, she began to think that here might be a new heroine for a new version of the old romance.

They were not long in reaching Dinsmore's studio, which, since he had been able to please himself in the matter of locality, was in a house on a terrace overlooking the Thames. From his windows he could see the river as it flowed by, laden with steamers, boats, and historic memories; and this fact made amends to him for any disadvantage in the situation.

Viewed outwardly, however, there was none, as the ladies agreed when the carriage drew up before the door.

"It reminds me of Florence, Amy, and our rooms overlooking the Arno!" cried Mariette. "I think Hugh ought to be glad to live in such a pleasant place! —And here he is!"

Yes, Hugh was ready to meet them— Hugh, and some one else, whom Nelly brightened and blushed to see.

"Ah, Mr. Reade—well met!" said Mrs. Trafford. "I see you could not suffer your friend to face such a feminine invasion alone.—Hugh, I have taken the liberty of bringing a young lady with me, who is anxious to see your paintings. Allow me to present you to Miss Paget."

"I am happy to make Miss Paget's acquaintance," said Hugh; and as Nelly glanced at his frank, genial face, she felt that Mariette was right—that no one could look at him and believe that anything to his discredit was true.

The studio into which the two young men ushered them was a very pleasant apartment, with great, wide windows, and heavy curtains to alter the light. It had none of those wonderful attempts at decoration which writers are more given to describing than artists are, as a general rule, to employing; yet it was a very pleasant and altogether habitable place. The windows were set wide open; there were some flowers on the balcony, half a dozen delightfully easy chairs in the room, and a broad chintz couch with cushions of the same. Besides these, there was, of course, the artist's "properties"—easels, canvases, brushes, paints, lay-figures, and a few odd bits of *bric-à-brac* here and there.

Mrs. Trafford took in every detail of the scene without saying a word, while Nelly and Mariette were chattering gayly and exclaiming over it. Around her were all the means and appliances of labor; and if there was also comfort, it was the comfort which this labor had purchased. Involuntarily she compared it with the luxury which surrounded herself, and which had come to her as a free gift, unwon by any exertion of her own.

"This is best—I am sure this is best!" she thought; and then she looked at Hugh, who was speaking to Mariette with his peculiarly winning smile.

Was it the charm of thoroughness, she wondered, that made him so attractive? Was it because he had never for an hour mingled in the artificial world in which her life had for years been passed, that his mere presence seemed to bring a sense of refreshment over her spirit?—a spirit more jaded and weary than she realized in the whirl and tumult of her life. Why else was she dimly conscious of feeling as one might who, from a rose-lined boudoir and atmosphere redolent of mille-fleurs, should step into fresh green fields and catch a breath of wild, sweet forest odors?

Life had taught this woman a great deal, and after many days she was to do justice to the nature and the heart she had once so lightly esteemed, so ignorantly cast away.

Hugh, who had as little idea as possible of what was passing in her mind, presently left Reade to act as cicerone to the two girls, and came up to her.

"I have a picture of Felix, Mrs. Trafford, which I should like you to look at," he said, "and if you think it a good likeness, I hope you will allow me to copy it for you—although you will not accept 'Wild-Flowers.'"

She looked up at him with something almost pathetic in her eyes—an expression altogether new to them, yet which, he had no doubt, was one of many artifices.

"You know why I will not accept 'Wild-Flowers,'" she said. "I am so well—so very well—able to buy it, and you—"

"I am quite able to give it away," he interposed, smiling; "otherwise I should not have been so extravagant as to offer it. I am happily past the period of struggle, Mrs. Trafford; and I am glad to say that I have a sufficient balance at my banker's to make me a respectable member of society."

"No one in the world could rejoice more over your success than I do, Hugh," she said, in a low voice. "But, for the sake of the past, you might allow me to contribute my insignificant quota to it."

"For the sake of the past, that is exactly what I cannot do!" he answered, with a sudden hardening sternness in his voice—a sternness so unexpected, that she absolutely shrank; "and we will not talk of it, if you please. May I show you the portrait now?"

It was hanging at one end of the room, and, having led her there, he drew back a curtain, and threw a broad flood of light over it.

As he did so, she started with an exclamation, for it was Felix himself who looked at her from the canvas—Felix, with delicate, shadowy face, and large, luminous eyes, sitting in his old, well-remembered attitude at the piano, with flexile, slender hands resting on the ivory keyboard.

"Oh, this is wonderful—wonderful!" she cried, with a choking in her voice suggestive of tears. "How could you reproduce his face so exactly, when even I had almost forgotten it? How it brings back everything, more—a hundred times more—than 'Wild-Flowers' did! I can see him so plainly—my poor boy!—and, if I needed anything to harden me in the task which lies before me, it would be this."

She was not aware that she had uttered the last words aloud, until she caught the expression of Hugh's face—an expression half interrogative, half keen, wholly surprise. She started then, and colored, but did not lose her self-possession in the least.

"I see you wonder what I meant by that," she said. "Shall I tell you? No, I do not think you are sufficiently interested in me, or in anything that concerns me, to care to hear."

"You are mistaken," he replied, reading accurately, as he thought, the strain of feeling in her tone. "I shall always be interested in you, Mrs. Trafford, if only on account of the old days that are dead."

"How strange it seems to remember them!" she said, shading her eyes with her face as she gazed at the picture. "How strange that you and I, so differently placed from what we were then, should meet once more—like this!"

"I have become inured to strange things," said he, rather dryly. "Life is very full of them. Do you think Mariette will recognize this face? I will bring her to see it."

As he moved to where Mariette was standing, Mrs. Trafford looked after him with a strangely varying expression in her eyes. Never before in her career of conquest had she, with all her fascinations, been so deliberately set at naught as by this man. How coolly he put aside the reminiscences which, with any one else, would have proved irresistible! Nothing seemed to touch him. With the instinct of subjecting all who approached her to her influence—an instinct stronger than any other with women of her kind—she had tried the most effective weapons of her armory upon him, and the result was absolute failure. For the first time she found a man strong enough to withstand her fascination, strong enough to look at her with calm eyes, strong enough, she felt sure, to despise all the objects of her life.

This novelty was in itself sufficient to make her think more of Hugh Dinsmore than she thought of the many men whose homage was so easily secured, whose devotion was so easily won.

"I am glad that he has forgotten his old fancy for me," she thought—for we deceive ourselves quite as often as we deceive others—"but he might forgive the pain I caused him long ago! It is unkind of him to remember it yet; for I should like to feel that I had *one* honest, genuine friend in the world; and such a friend he could be."

When Mariette was brought to the picture, she recognized it at once, and, like her sister, wondered at the faithfulness of Hugh's memory.

"My recollection of Felix had grown so dim," she said, "and this makes it vivid again. O Hugh, will you not give it to us—to Amy and me?"

"I have already told Mrs. Trafford that, with her permission, I will make a copy for her," he said. "Now come and

see the picture in which I want to put
you."

He went up to an easel and drew
aside a cloth which covered the canvas
resting thereon. A large and elaborate
painting was revealed—a painting which,
from its subject as well as from the masterly manner in which the subject was
treated, struck the attention and held it
fascinated.

Surely a strange subject viewed without a clew to its meaning. The high
battlement of a tower, on the verge of
which was a plunging, terror-stricken
horse, rearing back from the frightful
depth below ; a mail-clad rider, with his
visor raised, showing a face death-pale ;
a half-kneeling woman clinging to him in
an agony of entreaty ; and in the background a group of awe-stricken retainers.
The picture was entirely finished save the
woman's face ; this had been painted out,
but there was not a line of the figure
which did not express passionate, despairing entreaty, as she clung to his feet.

The gazers were silent for fully a
minute. Then it was Mariette who said :

"I have never seen anything more
marvelous ! one almost holds one's breath
while looking on it ! But what does it
mean, Hugh ?"

Dinsmore glanced at Mrs. Trafford,
who smiled slightly, as she said :

"I think I know what it means. It
is a scene from the 'Rhyme of the Duchess May'—is it not ? Unless my memory
fails, I can give you the very lines you
have chosen to make your text—" And
before he could speak, she repeated, in
her sweet, magnetic voice :

"Thrice he wrung her hands in twain,
   But they closed and clung again ;
Wild she clung, as one withstood
Clasps a Christ upon the rood
   In a spasm of deathly pain.

"She clung wild, and she clung mute,
   With her shuddering lips half-shut ;
Her head had fallen, as half in swound ;
Hair and knee swept on the ground,
   She clung wild to stirrup and feet.

"Back he reined his steed—back-thrown
   On the slippery coping stone ;
Back the iron hoofs did grind
On the battlement behind,
   Whence a hundred feet went down.

"And his heel did press and goad
   On the quivering flank bestrode,
'Friends and brothers, save my wife !
Pardon, sweet, in change for life,
   But I ride alone to God.' "

"Ah! yes," said Mariette, "I see it
all now. I am one of the class of people
who always see things—when they are
pointed out to them. But, O Hugh, you
cannot mean that you want to paint me
as the Duchess May ?"

"Why not ?" asked Hugh. "I think
you would make a very lovely duchess."

"I think so myself " (with a laughing
glance at a mirror), "to ride, as she said,
'through a castle-gate,' but not to 'ride
on castle-wall.' I should certainly have
let Sir Guy—wasn't his name Sir Guy?—
ride alone *there*."

"If you found Sir Guy, you might
feel differently," said he, looking with
kindly admiration at the fair, winsome
face.

But Mariette shook her head. "No,
no," she said ; "I have no such heroic
capabilities. But here is Amy ; Amy
could do such a thing as that, and never
flinch. Paint *her* for your Duchess May."

There was an instant's pause ; then
Mrs. Trafford said, quietly :

"Before you propose a substitute,
Mariette, you should be sure that the exchange would be agreeable on all sides.—
Don't be afraid to say that I am not your
ideal of the Duchess May, Mr. Dinsmore."
She looked at him with steady eyes.
"You think that I would have been
incapable of giving life for love, and
probably you are right. Such a sacrifice
certainly is out of my line.—Ah, Miss Paget" (as Nelly and Reade approached),
"you are just in time to admire this beautiful picture which Mr. Dinsmore is showing us."

The picture was admired for some

time longer, then other pictures were exhibited, and finally tea was taken, English fashion, at a table drawn up before one of the windows commanding a view of the river and of the green bank opposite.

There was no lack of merriment at this pleasant feast—merriment in which Mrs. Trafford bore her part as thoroughly, if not quite as gayly, as the two girls. Hugh played the part of host to perfection, and Reade was charmingly agreeable. Altogether time passed so swiftly, that when Mrs. Trafford presently glanced at her watch, she exclaimed:

"Why, it is nearly seven o'clock! And I have to drive home, make a toilet, and dine, then go to the opera and two balls afterward. Hugh, your hospitality has been delightful! And now you must say when you will allow me to return it —in other words, when can you dine with me?"

"When we meet in some Arcadian spot where dress-coats are unknown!" answered Hugh, smiling. "You are very kind, Mrs. Trafford, but I never dine out."

"Then it is time for you to begin to do so," said Mariette, with her pretty air of authority. "Not dine out! I never heard of anything so absurd! I am afraid you are eccentric, Mr. Dinsmore."

"I am afraid I am, Miss Reynolds."

"But your eccentricity does not reach the point of refusing to do your oldest friends a favor?"

"That depends entirely upon what the favor is."

"Bah!" she interrupted, gayly. "You are going to quibble—and I hate quibbling. In plain words, do you refuse to dine with Mrs. Trafford, and meet the present agreeable company—with an addition or two, perhaps—eh, Amy?"

Hugh's face changed, for he thought at once of Marchmont—Marchmont, who had dined with Mrs. Trafford only the evening before.

"It is impossible!" he said. "In anything else you might command me, but I regret to say that I cannot accept Mrs. Trafford's invitation."

Mrs. Trafford had been adjusting her veil, and she now turned with heightened color.

"Don't waste your persuasive eloquence, my dear," she said. "Mr. Dinsmore, I suppose, thinks that dinner is too conventional a ceremony for such an unconventional person as himself. We will hope to see him at some other time. And now I really must hurry Miss Paget and yourself away."

"Remember that I think it *very* unkind of you to act so!" said Mariette, holding out her hand to Dinsmore. "But you will come to see us soon—will you not? We have had a charming visit, and you are welcome to use my face for the Duchess May, if you like; but, honestly, I don't think it would suit the character. Amy, now— What is it, Amy? Yes, I am ready this instant."

"We certainly shall be very late!" said Mrs. Trafford. Then she shook hands with Hugh, last words were uttered, the last compliments paid, and they descended to the waiting carriage and were driven away.

CHAPTER X.

AFTER ALL, OLD THINGS ARE BEST.

WHATEVER pang of wounded feeling Mrs. Trafford felt at the obstinate coldness of her old companion, no trace of it was left on her face, or in her manner, when she made her appearance, rather late, at the opera that night.

Marchmont, from his seat in the stalls where he had been watching anxiously for her, thought that her beauty paled the beauty of all other women as she entered her box, magnificently dressed, and sparkling with diamonds.

At sight of her his heart rose with a

bound. If he had ever doubted that the prize was worth all risks, all efforts to gain it, he now doubted no longer.

Sometimes we are prophets without being aware of the fact; and such a prophet he had been when, on the first night that he saw her, he said to himself:

"She is mistress of a fascination which would soon make a man forget everything but herself. I should like to come in contact with such a woman. I have never yet met one capable of inspiring that species of worship which borders on infatuation, and it would be something to feel, if only for the sake of a new sensation."

Well, the new sensation had come. For the first time in his life he felt that for the woman herself, apart from her great advantages, he could do and dare all things. One syllable of love from those lips, one look of tenderness from those eyes—these were the rewards which already began to take the chief place in his imagination.

He was the first person to enter her box; and, when Mr. Grantham appeared there, he found the American stranger already installed in the place of honor.

Mrs. Trafford's manner was thoroughly courteous; nevertheless, the secretary of legation soon felt that his day of favor was over. No woman could make this more unmistakably evident; no woman could with more subtile grace turn her shoulder—figuratively—upon a captive of whom she had wearied. Impetuous men like Colonel Danesford—men who had really lost their hearts to the fair enchantress—rushed upon their fate despite the warning; but Mr. Grantham did not belong to this class. He saw, recognized, bowed to the inevitable at once, and had no idea of incurring the mortification of a definite and decided rejection.

Nevertheless, his vanity was sufficiently wounded for him to feel inclined to bestow a thrust or two upon the capricious beauty who had ventured to trifle

even with *his* exalted homage; and chance put it in his power to do this better than he knew.

Mrs. Trafford, after carelessly examining for a minute, through her glass, a new arrival in the box opposite, said: "Is not that the pretty, fair-haired girl who was so much admired at Nice last winter? Miss Balfour—was not that her name?"

"Yes, Miss Balfour—Nina Balfour," returned Mr. Grantham. "That is she, though she is Miss Balfour no longer."

"Ah! did mamma succeed in capturing the fat, forty, and *not* fair baronet round whom her nets were so perseveringly spread?"

"She succeeded admirably! He was landed in the most scientific manner, his house was set in order, jewels were bought, the bride's *trousseau* all ready, when lo! Miss Balfour walked quietly out of the house one morning, and was married to a captain in a marching regiment!"

Mrs. Trafford lifted her eyebrows. "What did it mean? Was the girl mad?"

"If you hold love and madness to be synonymous terms—yes. It seems there was an old boy-and-girl love-affair between them, half forgotten by both, until they met in London after her engagement; then the passion blazed up again with greater force than ever, and ended as I have said. The French, you know, have a proverb, '*On en revient toujours à ses premières amours.*' I have never had much faith in its truth, but several affairs of this kind lately are beginning to convert me. May I ask what you think? Are your sex so sentimental at heart that a first lover *always* has an advantage over later ones?"

His manner, as he asked the question, was a model of easy nonchalance; but something in the expression of his eyes, as they met Mrs. Trafford's, told her that, with the instinct of a discomfited rival, he had leaped to the right conclusion with regard to Marchmont's former acquaintance with herself.

She was also conscious that Marchmont was listening eagerly for her answer, and these things, acting on her like a defiance, steadied her in her self-possession.

"You ask a rather difficult question," she answered, indifferently. "General questions of that kind are always hard to answer, because so much depends upon the particular circumstances. Sometimes first love is a passion, sometimes only a fancy; sometimes life proves its folly, sometimes teaches its wisdom. As a rule, however, I am not a believer in 'early romance.' I hold it nearly akin to absurdity, or worse."

"What is worse than absurdity?" asked the man of the world, shrugging his shoulders lightly.

Not long after this he took his departure; and Mariette's attention being engrossed by Captain Gresham, who was bending over her chair, Marchmont felt that he could venture to speak to Mrs. Trafford as freely as if they were alone.

"Your answer to Mr. Grantham's question was very non-committal," he said, lowering his voice, and looking at her with expressive eyes; "but surely you believe, as I do, that first love is, after all, the only *real* love."

She laughed — that unembarrassed laugh which is by no means encouraging.

"I think that *first love*, as a general thing, is *first folly*," she said; "but there are exceptions to all rules—and it is often useful as a peg upon which to hang reminiscent sentiment."

The edge of sarcasm in her voice as she uttered the last words checked the "reminiscent sentiment" of which she spoke, more effectually than anything else she could have done.

Instinctively Marchmont felt that he had over-estimated the power which the past held for this woman and that the task of winning her heart again might be more difficult than he had reckoned upon.

Not for a moment, however, did the consideration occur to him that it might be impossible. It was not only vanity which blinded him to the obstacles in his way, but that sudden infatuation which such women as Mrs. Trafford inspire in the wisest of men.

As he sat by her side, looking at her, listening to her, drinking deeper and deeper from the cup of Circe which she held to his lips, he heard no tone of Patti's sweet voice, he saw hardly a feature of the brilliant, crowded opera-house. Everything began and ended for him in the face by his side.

Of this fact Mrs. Trafford was not likely to be in any doubt. Too often had she seen the signs of passion to fail in reading them now; and when they parted —when he had handed her into her carriage on her way to the balls where other men would sun themselves in her beauty and listen to her beguiling accents—her last words were:

"At three to-morrow, then. Goodnight."

"Considering that you do not like our old friend, Amy," said Mariette, as the carriage rolled away, "I think you are very gracious to him."

"Why should you imagine that I do not like him?" asked Mrs. Trafford. "I have never said so."

The other laughed.

"No, you have never said so, but I know very well when you like or dislike a person; and you dislike Mr. Marchmont—of that I am quite sure. I can't help thinking it odd, too," she added. "He is exceedingly handsome—I watched his line of profile to-night, while he talked to you—and very agreeable."

Mrs. Trafford did not choose to discuss the grounds of her dislike to this attractive gentleman, so she said: "I think you are making a serious conquest of Captain Gresham, Mariette. He seems to haunt us of late."

"He is not disagreeable—for an Englishman," said Mariette, in whose eyes the sons of Albion had not yet found favor. "He bores one a little, but one grows used to that; and if, some day, he should screw his courage to the sticking-point of proposal, it would be pleasant to be called 'My lady!'"

"I hoped you would not think of such things," said Mrs. Trafford, in a slightly troubled voice. "I hoped that you, at least, might marry for love, and love only."

Mariette's gay laugh floated out with a silver ring of mockery in it.

"What! a Saul among the prophets! *You* sentimental, Amy! You surely have forgotten what you said to me when I came to you from my Roman convent: 'Amuse yourself with men as long and as much as you like; but never believe a word they say, and, above all, *never* love them!' You see I have profited by your instruction and your example."

There was a moment's silence; then, in a grave tone, Mrs. Trafford said:

"I am sorry that I gave you such a text as that; it was a very poor one for a girl just beginning life. I understand some things better than I did then. I begin to realize that it is not wise to revenge. the falsity and cruelty of one man on all his sex. There are men whom one may believe, and men worth loving. I hoped that you, who have been shielded from all that made the bitterness of my early life, would find one of them."

"Have *you* found one, that your philosophy should change so much?" asked Mariette.

But, before Mrs. Trafford could answer that searching question, the carriage drew up before the door of the house to which they were bound.

·   ·   ·   ·   ·   ·

To say that Nelly Paget was not piqued by the open desertion of the man whose devotion to her had been that of a lover, and who had hovered so closely on the verge of a declaration that he might have felt himself as much bound in honor as if he had made it, would be to say that she was no woman. Fortunately for herself, she was not in love with him; but misplaced fancy can sometimes suffer very sensible pain, and Nelly might have known some acute pangs but for the timely advent of Mr. Reade. There is no balm to a woman for the loss of one admirer like the attentions of another. "Every one does not fail to value me," she thinks; "and what seemed common enough before rises immensely in her estimation.

So it was in the present instance. Though she had jested to Marchmont of his "early love," Nelly certainly had not expected that the same early love would so promptly, so easily reclaim him. She had not at first recognized how entirely his allegiance was transferred, but when the full realization came to her, there could be no doubt of her mortification. In such a case a woman feels that her power of charming must be weak indeed, when a man's heart can wander from her so lightly; and toward Marchmont Nelly's predominant feeling was one of keen resentment. "A man has been flirting—has been worse than flirting—when he says everything except *the words*, and then coolly walks off!" she thought. "No doubt he believes that I was ready, willing, waiting, to answer 'Yes' whenever he vouchsafed to propose. To think how he looked, how he spoke, how he held my hand! Oh, the wretch!—how dared he! I will never forgive him—never, as long as I live; and I hope Mrs. Trafford will trifle with him and fool him, as people say she has fooled other men!"

All this, however, transpired in the seclusion of her own breast. She was at once too wise and too proud to let Marchmont detect any sign of mortification or resentment. Her manner to him scarcely varied at all, save, perhaps, that it was a shade more careless than it had been before; but there was an intangible restraint on his part whenever chance threw them alone together.

Chance performed this kind office for them a day or two after the visit to Dinsmore's studio. Since that time Marchmont had seen very little of the party with which he had before been identified. His attention and thoughts were centred on Mrs. Trafford, and he became that lady's shadow whenever and wherever she would allow it.

Nevertheless, his nominal connection with the Paget party continued, and, on entering their sitting-room one day, he was a little disconcerted to find Nelly alone.

She was in carriage-costume even to her hat, and, while engaged in arranging some flowers, was standing exactly where she stood on the evening when he so nearly proposed to her—the evening they dined with Mrs. Trafford.

She glanced up and nodded with a smile, but did not pause in her occupation.

"Good-day, Mr. Marchmont," she said, easily. "I believe this is the first time I have seen you to-day?"

"I am sorry to say that it is," Marchmont answered. "I seem to see very little of you of late," he added, carrying the war into Africa with ready audacity. "My place is so entirely usurped by Mr. Reade, that I have more than once felt myself *de trop;* and since such a sensation is not pleasant to one's vanity, and I avoid on principle all unpleasant things, I have refrained from inflicting it on myself."

Nelly's bright, honest eyes looked at him with an expression approaching to scorn.

"Candor is your chief virtue—isn't it, Mr. Marchmont?" she said, with an inflection of contempt in her voice. "I should judge so. You certainly have seen and suffered a good deal from Mr. Reade's usurpation. *A propos,* how does the revival of your old friendship with Mrs. Trafford progress?"

It would have pleased him to think that this question had its origin in jeal-ousy; but, looking at the face, and meeting the smile of the speaker, he felt that it was impossible to lay such flattering unction to his soul. He was a man who had never suffered himself to be absolutely blinded by vanity, and he now recognized very plainly the unpalatable fact that his power with Nelly Paget was over.

"My old friendship with Mrs. Trafford has been revived very pleasantly," he replied. "She is a woman who would make friendship, old or new, agreeable."

"So I imagine," said Nelly, quietly. "She is also a woman who, if accounts are to be trusted, has made flirtation a fine art. I hope sincerely that you won't suffer again from her hands what you suffered once before. I believe you said she trifled with your affections long ago."

"We had a youthful episode *du cœur,*" he answered, with a laugh; "but I hardly think it amounted to trifling on either side; it was rather one of those delightful early romances that circumstances often nip in the bud."

"And later circumstances sometimes bring to full flower. That would be most romantic of all—quite like a novel, in fact, where the husbands and wives die off in the most obliging manner, so as to allow the hero and heroine to come together at last."

"What are you talking about, Nelly?" asked Mrs. Paget entering the room at the moment. She had caught the last words, and she felt a little scandalized. To talk to a widower of husbands and wives dying off in the most obliging manner, seemed to her a grave transgression of good feeling and propriety.

Nelly laughed, and, walking to a mirror, began fastening a knot of roses on the lace scarf which was crossed over her dress.

"I was congratulating Mr. Marchmont on being able to test in his own person that, 'after all, old things are best,'" she answered, lightly. "When the old things are as charming as Mrs.

Trafford, it may be so; but, for my part, I think I prefer new ones."

"As, for example, Mr. Reade?" asked Marchmont, with a slightly forced smile.

She looked at him coolly. "As, for example, Mr. Reade, or any one else who amuses me," she replied.

And it needed nothing further to assure him that, let his suit with Mrs. Trafford speed as it would, the door to fortune was barred to him *here.*

CHAPTER XI.

"I REMEMBER WELL."

THE next week or two was undoubtedly the most feverish and uncomfortable period of Amy Trafford's life. Old memories of the past tugging at her, and urging her to resentment; a struggling conscience vaguely protesting, and a heart dimly awakening—these influences, together with an amount of social dissipation calculated to tax the strongest *physique* beyond its strength, made up a state, inwardly and outwardly, to which she ever afterward looked back with a shudder.

Yet its outward aspect was certainly brilliant. Never had she floated more triumphantly on the topmost wave of life than she floated now. Her grace, her beauty, her wealth, all combined to win admittance for her to the most exclusive houses in London.

Dinners, balls, kettle-drums, garden-parties, followed one another in what, to a novice, would have been a bewildering succession; her card-basket overflowed with cards, and Mrs. Trafford's toilets, Mrs. Trafford's dinners, Mrs. Trafford's fascinations, were among the topics of the season.

To Mrs. Trafford much of this was weariness of the flesh and of the spirit; but to stop at will in the treadmill called pleasure is not allowed to those who have once fairly entered upon it.

Owing to a superb constitution, she had up to this time been able to resist the wear and tear of fashionable dissipation remarkably well; but she had always heretofore had a mind and heart at ease. Now, for the first time, neither mind nor heart was in that condition, and the result was apparent in her variations of lassitude and excitement, her sudden though not great loss of flesh and color.

In truth, she had overrated her strength in the part she undertook to play with Marchmont. Never before had she set herself to the dissimulation necessary for ensnaring a man in whom she felt no interest. That alone would have wearied her inexpressibly; but, when to want of interest was added absolute repugnance, the effort became greater than she had at all reckoned upon.

Nor was this her only source of disquietude. Colonel Danesford's devotion had reached a point when it ceased altogether to gratify, and only annoyed her. Nevertheless, she liked him sufficiently to feel averse to uttering the final words which would put an end to his hopes.

For a little while after that scene in Richmond Park she had asked herself whether she might not marry him, and had almost persuaded herself that it would be a good thing to do so. An old name, a stainless character, an ample fortune, a heart devoted to her—what more than this could she ask?

Colonel Danesford's fate, if he had only known it, hung in the balance for several days; and if—ah, these *ifs!* what a part they play in human life!—if he had urged his suit again, the answer might have been all that he desired. But there was no good fairy to whisper this, and so for him, as for many another man, the moment of opportunity slipped by unheeded.

It ended in the hour when Mrs. Trafford met the clear, honest eyes of her old friend and lover. Somehow, those eyes seemed to make her realize, as she had not realized before, the hollowness of her life and its object. To wear costumes devised by Worth, to win the admiration of men, to excite the envy of women, to go from capital to capital, and lead the same idle, aimless life in each—all this seemed suddenly very poor and empty, when Hugh Dinsmore looked at her across all the years which had separated them, and mutely asked how it had fared with her since they parted.

When a body has been wrapped in lethargy, the consciousness of pain is often a sign of returning health; and so it was with this woman's spirit. To suffer is to live—alas, that the converse of the proposition should be so often true!—and her soul, waking from the stupor in which it had lain so long, suffered with a pain which mastered all its faculties.

In truth, that nature must be very frivolous which a life such as she led can satisfy; and its multifarious amusements and occupations began to fall on her with a sense of satiety which can hardly be expressed.

These causes of dissatisfaction, taken in connection with others which need not be indicated, made this period, as has been already said, one of restless and fevered excitement to her; and so it chanced one day that she was incapacitated by a severe headache from attending a splendid garden *fête*, in anticipation of which "ravishing" toilets had been ordered from Paris for herself and Mariette.

To expect the latter to surrender the pleasure of wearing this toilet on such an occasion, would have been to ask too much from human nature, when human nature was only eighteen. Under Lady Gresham's chaperonage Mariette went to the *fête* blithe as a butterfly, while Mrs. Trafford, to her own relief, was left at home.

As the afternoon wore away, the great pain she had been enduring ceased almost altogether, but left her languid and exhausted. In this state she was lying back in a deep chair before the window of her dressing-room, when Celine entered with a card.

Mrs. Trafford motioned it away without looking at it.

"I am not at home to any one!" she said, impatiently. "Why do you trouble me in this manner?"

"A thousand pardons, madame!" said the French maid; "but this gentleman has brought a picture, and he desired that his card should be sent to madame, and, if she was not able to see him—"

"A picture!" repeated madame. "Give me the card."

She took it and read Dinsmore's name.

"Send word to Mr. Dinsmore that I will be down presently," she said, "and give orders that I am not at home to any one else. Return quickly, for I must make a toilet."

As the maid left the room, she rose and walked to a mirror. The reflection which it gave back was not calculated to gratify an exacting beauty. The severe pain which she suffered earlier in the day had left her complexion pale and her eyes dark-circled.

"I would not see any one else when I am looking so dreadfully," she murmured; "but he cares nothing for my looks. I do not think that he observes whether I am beautiful or frightful; hence it is not worth while to decline to see him—considering that he comes so seldom."

When Celine returned, therefore, she had the pleasure of dressing her mistress very plainly—far too plainly, the lively Frenchwoman thought—simply winding her soft, abundant chestnut tresses round her head.

"Gently, Celine—gently!" Mrs. Trafford said, when she touched the last. "Remember, my head is very sensitive just now. I cannot endure any elaborate coiffure; put up the hair as rapidly and easily as possible."

Celine obeyed, yet, in doing so, bestowed an artistic touch or two which gave the head a statuesque grace that suited the classic outline. "Madame is pale, but madame has never looked better," she assured her mistress, who only answered, indifferently:

"That will do. It does not matter how I look."

In this frame of mind she descended to the drawing-room; and when Hugh Dinsmore rose to meet her, he was more struck by her fair appearance than he had ever been before.

One reason of this was because his artistic eye at once noticed the absence of overloading adornment, and recognized the fact that *real* beauty is as surely enhanced by simplicity as spurious beauty is destroyed by it. Even her pallor and languor were more attractive to him than the brilliancy of dress and manner in which he always suspected effort.

"I fear I have been very inconsiderate," he said, advancing and taking her offered hand. "I was told that you were unwell, yet I persisted in sending up my card; and now I am afraid you have exerted yourself beyond your strength in seeing me."

"Do I look so shockingly?" she asked, smiling. "I flattered myself that you would not know whether I was well or ill. But I really am much better. This morning I suffered intensely with a severe headache, arising, no doubt, from irregular hours and crowded rooms; but it has worn off now, and I only feel a little exhausted."

"You are feeling more than 'a little exhausted,' as your face betokens," he said, looking at her with a kindliness of manner she had not seen him display before. "And you thought I would not know whether you were well or ill! Pray, do you think me so obtuse?—or what?"

"Indifferent, more likely. But we will not discuss my appearance, which just at present interests me very little indeed."

"I did not know that a woman's appearance—especially a beautiful woman's appearance—ever failed to interest her!" said he, with a smile.

She glanced at him with a strangely wistful expression in her eyes.

"If I were to tell you how little my appearance has interested me for some time past, you would not believe me," she said. "Therefore it is not worth while to try your credulity."

"My dear Mrs. Trafford—" he began, but she interrupted him, quickly.

"Nay, Hugh, do not attempt to be other than absolutely true. Deception—even the least form of social deception—would ill suit *you*. Do not deny that you think me steeped to the lips in artifice. Have I not seen in your face that you distrust me entirely? It is rather late for empty compliments between us."

"But I have a right to protest that you misjudge me," said he. "I should be guilty of gross presumption if I attempted to sit in judgment on your character."

"But you cannot deny that you think me artificial and insincere!"

He looked at her steadily. If truth was to be spoken between them, he was evidently ready to speak it.

"All women of the world are more or less artificial and insincere, Mrs. Trafford," he said. "And I am not sufficiently acquainted with their characteristics to be able to tell where artifice ends and sincerity begins. If I have done you an injustice, forgive me, and believe that it was most unintentional."

"You have done me *every* injustice!" she said, with sudden, passionate vehemence. "You have distrusted me without cause; you have judged and condemned me without knowledge; you have made me feel that I possess neither your liking nor respect—"

"Pardon me if I interrupt you," said he, gravely; "but may I beg to know why you should hold my opinion of sufficient importance to arraign it in this manner? If you will be kind enough to answer that question, I will promise, on my part, to answer any that you choose to ask."

For a minute an obstruction seemed to rise in her throat and choke her so that she could not reply. Then she said:

"It is strange that you should ask me such a question. Whose opinion should I value in the world, if not yours? You are the last link with my old life; and if you could know how much I need one true-hearted friend, I think that, for the sake of the old days we spent together, you would be that friend to me."

If ever there was honesty in human eyes, it was in hers as they looked at him —no longer beguiling and alluring, but sadly earnest. For an instant Dinsmore felt that he must believe in her. Then a sudden revulsion of feeling came over him, and he steeled his heart.

"One true-hearted friend!" he repeated. "That means one more trophy of conquest—one more proof of power— does it not, Mrs. Trafford? If I am rude, you will excuse me, perhaps, in memory of the old days of which you spoke a moment ago. I remember well what I was to you then—an amusement, a convenience, a subject on which to practise those arts of coquetry which make you famous now. Do you think I care to fill the same position again?—to lounge by your carriage—to have the distinction of leaning over your chair at the opera—to be invited to your dinners—to be known as the 'old friend' and latest caprice of the charming Mrs. Trafford? No! I am not the stuff of which such playthings 'for a fair woman's foot' are made *twice*. I told you, long ago, that our paths in life parted irrevocably; and I see nothing in our accidental meeting to make me change my opinion. In your own rank of life, among your own associates, you surely can find friends better able to serve you than I am."

There was a moment's silence after his voice ceased—a moment in which

Mrs. Trafford sat quiet and motionless. Never had she been so repulsed before; never, during all these years filled with adulation and homage, had any man looked at her so fearlessly, spoken to her so boldly. Rude? Yes, there could be no doubt that he was rude; but what silken words of flattery had ever stirred her heart like these? When she lifted her eyes to his face, even he was struck by the fact that there was no shadow of resentment in their depths—only the same wistful sadness deepened to appeal.

"You are more unkind and unjust than I ever thought you could be," she said. "But I suppose it is useless to argue against your convictions. You don't believe in me; that puts an end to the matter. Now, let us talk of something more entertaining. You have brought me Felix's portrait—have you not?"

"Unjust—unkind!" he said. "I should be sorry to be guilty of either of these toward any one, but especially toward you. If I mistrust you, have I not cause to do so? Look at the record of your life! Even at the present time, how many men do you keep dangling in your train, to amuse your idle hours and offer incense at your shrine? You have lately added one 'old friend' to their number. Have I not cause, then, to suspect that you would not object to playing at sentiment with another?"

A deep flush rose to her face as she understood to whom he alluded, but her eyes met his own steadily and clearly, a vivid light beginning to burn in their depths.

"Can it be possible," she said, "that you think me likely to find amusement or pleasure in the society of Brian Marchmont? Of course, it is not surprising that others should think so; but *you*—I did not fancy that you, who knew the story of the past, would be so deceived!"

He gazed at her with a surprised and doubtful expression, which almost made her smile.

"How can I know what to believe?"

he said. "Women are very strange beings. A man may be a scoundrel, and yet—sometimes, at least—a woman's heart seems to cling to him, when better men fail to touch it."

For an instant she hardly comprehended him. Then, as his meaning dawned on her—

" . . . the very nape of her fair neck
Was rosed with indignation."

"And you think that of me—that!" she said, with scorn. "This is worse than all! It is natural—I am willing to acknowledge that it is natural—that you should believe me a heartless coquette, an artificial woman of the world; but to think me so lost to every sense of pride, so narrow of mind, so weak of nature, as to love Brian Marchmont! great Heaven! what words can express the degradation involved in such an idea!"

There was no room to doubt the genuineness of passion here. It blazed in her eyes, shone in spots of crimson on her cheeks, and curved her lips back from the milk-white teeth. Dinsmore hardly knew what he was doing as he took one of her hands.

"Forgive me!" he said; "I see that I was wrong in thinking that he still had any hold on your heart. I scarcely knew what to believe. It seemed so unaccountable that you should enroll that man, of all men, in your train of followers!—that you should distinguish him by your favor—"

"And why?" she interrupted, impetuously. "Are you so dull that you cannot tell? I have marveled that even he has not understood my purpose in tolerating him. It is simply that, when his vanity has misled him far enough, and when he has lost the last chance of winning Miss Paget's fortune, I may pay the debt which I vowed ten years ago that I would pay; that I may return upon him, as far as lies in my power, all the indignity and pain he once inflicted upon me! That is why I have 'enrolled him among my followers and distinguished him by my favor.'"

Her trenchant tone, her smile, cold as ice and keen as steel, made him realize so clearly how fixed and resolute was the purpose she expressed, that he was silent for fully a minute, before he said:

"I am sorry to hear it."

She looked at him with an expression of astonishment.

"Why should you be sorry?" she asked. "What is Brian Marchmont to you?"

"Brian Marchmont is nothing to me but a dishonorable scoundrel," he answered, quietly. "You surely do not think that my regret is for him? It is of you that I am thinking—of you alone."

"And what of me?" she asked. Involuntarily her smile and her voice softened. To be thought of—to be considered in the least degree—was better than indifference.

"This of you," he replied, with a sudden impulse of frankness; "that, in descending to such a revenge, you are lowering yourself to a degree and in a manner far beyond the measure of any satisfaction which you will obtain from Marchmont's humiliation. No woman can play such a part without suffering in her self-respect—unless she has thrown self-respect more completely to the winds than I can force myself to believe that you have done, Mrs. Trafford."

"Thank you, for that much at least," she said, in a low tone. "And you are right—more right than you think. I have suffered, I am suffering, from the part I have played with this man. I feel degraded by the touch of his hand, by the glance of his eye. I almost think it has made me ill," she said, lifting her hand and pushing back the hair from her brow. "I overrated my strength, and I would gladly be done with it if I could."

"And why can you not?" said he, earnestly. "Believe me, one must stoop so low to revenge some injuries, that it is best to leave them unrevenged. Besides, if you make this man desperate, he may injure you more deeply than you can reckon upon."

Her lip curled superbly.

"I have no fear of that," she said. "It is out of Brian Marchmont's power ever to injure me again!"

"You can never be sure *where* or *how* an unscrupulous and desperate man may strike," said Dinsmore. "But for your own sake—I put *him* out of the question —you cannot end the matter too soon."

"I will end it at once—to-morrow if I can," she said. "I am anxious, fever-ishly anxious, to do so. And when it is ended—when you need no longer fear to meet him in this house—will you try to think less hardly of me, and let me see you more often?"

When a beautiful woman pleads with eyes and voice, it is difficult for a man to withstand her, let the object of her plead-ing be what it will; but when it is for a little more of his society, a degree more of his respect, refusal becomes not only difficult, but impossible. So Hugh Dins-more found it.

"I have never willingly thought hardly of you," he said, "and I am sorry indeed that I have been in any manner unjust. One from my world has little place in yours; but, if you care to see me, I shall be glad now and then to come. The por-trait which I have brought you is neglect-ed all this time, however. Will you look at it? I want your opinion on one or two points regarding the likeness."

CHAPTER XII.

"THE LITTLE LESS, AND WHAT WORLDS AWAY!".

"I AM glad to hear that you are bet-ter, Amy," said Mariette, entering her sister's dressing-room. "Celine says that you have been well enough to see a vis-itor."

"Only Hugh," Mrs. Trafford answered. "He came to bring Felix's portrait. I should not have thought of seeing any one else. I hope you have enjoyed yourself," she went on, putting out her hand caress-ingly. "Was the *fête* a very grand af-fair?"

"Oh, very! Quite the grandest affair of the season, as far as my experience goes. Everything was on a superb scale, and I saw no toilet more beautiful than mine. What a pity you were not able to go!"

"I don't feel so. I think I am grow-ing rather tired of dissipation. You can tell me all about it, and that will be better than having seen it myself.—How very, very pretty you look!"

Mariette certainly did look very pretty as she stood before her sister, still wear-ing the costume which had been one of the most charming at the *fête*, a delicate flush on her fair cheeks, a bright light in her lovely eyes. She glanced into a mir-ror, and laughed softly.

"I suppose I *am* very pretty," she said. "I cannot else imagine why Cap-tain Gresham should have asked me to marry him."

A change of interest, rather than of surprise, came over Mrs. Trafford's face. She had, for some time past, felt sure that Stamer Gresham's devotion would culminate in a proposal.

"So he has asked you to marry him?" she said. "What did you answer?"

"Is there much room for doubt?" asked Mariette, laughing again, as she drew nearer and bent over the back of her sister's chair. "Can you think it possible that I would refuse a future baronet?"

"There is no need for you to consider *that*," said Mrs. Trafford, quickly. "I mean, there is no need for you to accept him, if you do not feel sure that you care enough for him to accept him if there was no baronetcy in the question. Have you accepted him, Mariette? Do you care for him?"

"I like him very well," answered Mariette, "and—yes, I suppose I accepted him. I certainly meant to do so, but the matter was rather confused. Nevertheless, I think he understood. You cannot deny, Amy, that to be Lady Gresham some day, when Sir Charles is gathered to his fathers, will be a brilliant ending for Mariette Reynolds, whose father was a music-teacher, and whose face is her fortune."

"Whose face may be her fortune—but not *all* her fortune," said Mrs. Trafford. "I have never told you before, because there has never been any reason to do so; but I have always intended to settle half of my fortune on you at your marriage."

"Half of your fortune! O Amy!" The girl bent and kissed her eagerly. "How generous, how kind you are! But, surely, do you do not mean *half?*"

"I mean exactly and entirely half, and I make but one condition in doing so."

"And that condition?"

"Is, that you marry the man you love—not the man who bids highest for your hand."

Astonishment was for a moment Mariette's predominant sensation, then an expression of the most genuine amusement swept over her face.

"You must forgive me, Amy," she cried, with a gay peal of laughter; "but the idea of *you* as a sentimentalist is too novel not to be ludicrous! What has come over you, that you should place such unaccustomed importance upon the heart? Don't concern yourself about mine, I beg; it is not likely to trouble me. I like Stamer Gresham as well as I shall ever like any one, I suppose; at all events, I like him well enough to marry him. And, since you mean to endow me so magnificently, I presume his family will graciously consent to the alliance."

Mrs. Trafford turned so that she could gaze full into the flower-like face, and took the hand which rested nearest to her on the silken back of the chair.

"Are you in earnest, Mariette?" she asked, with gravity. "Do you really mean that you know no man whom you like better than Stamer Gresham?"

"I mean just that," Mariette answered, meeting her gaze steadily. "Whom *could* I like better? You surely do not suspect me of a hopeless fancy for one of your adorers?"

"That is not likely," Mrs. Trafford replied; but she did not say what she had suspected. "I am only anxious that you should know your own heart—that you should not make one of those terrible mistakes which women do sometimes make, and which wreck their lives more utterly than you can imagine."

"There is not the least danger of it," said Mariette, with cheerful confidence. "I assure you that I like Stamer very much, and I like the idea of being 'My lady' still better. We may, therefore, consider the matter settled—unless Sir Charles and Lady Gresham should decline to receive me as the wife of their son."

Sir Charles and Lady Gresham were certainly very much concerned when they heard of the rash conduct of that young gentleman. To countenance the beautiful and wealthy widow on whom Colonel Danesford had set his heart, was one thing; to receive an obscure and probably portionless girl as the wife of the heir and hope of the house of Gresham, was quite another. They argued, entreated, even commanded; but Stamer was firm as a rock. He loved Miss Reynolds passionately, and he had asked her to marry him. On these facts he took his position, from which nothing could make him recede. The parents, therefore, were at last forced to concessions, and, the day after the proposal had been made, Lady Gresham betook herself to Mrs. Trafford, in order to make such inquiries with regard to Miss Reynolds as were natural under the circumstances.

Mrs. Trafford received her with graceful courtesy, but without the least trace of increased cordiality. Her manner expressed very clearly that, though ready to meet any friendly advances, she did not choose to make them.

"Pray do not think it necessary to apologize," she said, quietly, when the elder lady hinted something of the kind. "It is surely right and proper that you should desire to know somewhat more of the woman your son wishes to marry than that she is a pretty, graceful girl. In point of family, I tell you frankly, we have nothing of which to boast—neither have we anything of which to be ashamed. We were left orphans at an early age, and I married a man considerably older than myself, who, after caring for me and all connected with me, when he died most generously left me his entire fortune, unfettered by a single restriction. It amounts to more than a hundred thousand pounds, and I have long intended to settle half of it on my sister. I shall direct my lawyer to take at once the proper legal steps in the matter. And, if the possession of fifty thousand pounds can make amends for her want of noble birth, you may rest satisfied, Lady Gresham, that she is endowed with that amount."

"My dear Mrs. Trafford, such wonderful generosity—" Lady Gresham began, but Mrs. Trafford quietly interposed:

"Excuse me, but I do not consider that there is any generosity in the matter. It is a duty which I have always meant to fulfill—which my husband would have fulfilled had he not known that he could trust me to do so. I am not making any bid for the honor of your alliance, Lady Gresham; I am simply telling you what I should do whoever my sister's suitor chanced to be."

The quiet tone, the haughty smile, made Lady Gresham recognize this fully. In fact, she was surprised almost beyond the power of speech—surprised at the woman who could so coolly give away fifty thousand pounds—still more surprised at Stamer's good luck; for it may be said that the fortunes of the Greshams were by no means so flourishing as they might

have been; and a girl with a dower of fifty thousand pounds, with enough beauty and grace for the bride of a prince, and whose objectionable relations—if she possessed any—were safe in a distant country, was a veritable Godsend.

"I am more than satisfied, my dear Mrs. Trafford," she said, after a moment's reflection. "You must, of course, appreciate the natural anxiety of parents when anything so important as the marriage of their son is concerned. With Miss Reynolds personally, both Sir Charles and myself have been charmed, and we shall be happy to welcome her as a daughter-in-law."

So the matter was arranged, and pretty Mariette, with her dower of fifty thousand pounds, was formally acknowledged as *fiancée* of the heir of Gresham.

It may readily be imagined that this event was more trying than gratifying to Colonel Danesford. To see his nephew win so readily the girl on whom he had set his heart, while *he*, whose wooing had been so much longer, still hung in a state of uncertainty on Mrs. Trafford's caprice, was not only far from agreeable, but brought home to him the consciousness of his own folly so strongly, that it gave him the resolution to end it.

"I will insist on a definite answer, and will abide by it," he said, as he found himself in Mrs. Trafford's drawing-room awaiting her appearance, a day or two after these events.

As if to make this resolution doubly hard for him to execute, she came in, looking more beautiful than usual, and held out one slender hand with her most graceful air of familiar friendship.

"I suppose you have heard that you are to be Mariette's uncle?" she said, with a laugh. "Have you come to offer protestations, or congratulations?"

"My congratulations have been offered to Stamer," he answered. "I think him the most fortunate fellow I know; and his wooing has been accomplished in such short order, that I can't help envying him, too. It must be a great thing to know that the happiness which one covets most is in one's grasp."

She understood so well what he meant, that even her conscience—heretofore very callous where matters of the heart were concerned—suffered a twinge. The bright bloom deepened on her cheek, though her eyes met his with their peculiar frankness.

"I am glad you have spoken thus, Colonel Danesford," she said. "It gives me an opportunity to make an explanation to you which should have been made long ago. I blame myself very much for not having made it sooner—but, alas! blaming one's self avails very little when the harm has been done."

He now knew what was coming, and, despite himself, his bronzed cheek turned a little paler. As he looked at her, there was a pleading wistfulness in his eyes which she remembered long afterward, and his voice was shaken with an intensity of feeling beyond control, as he said:

"For Heaven's sake, don't tell me that, after all, I am nothing to you!"

"I could not possibly tell you that," she said, very gently. "You are a great deal to me, and I wish—from my heart, Colonel Danesford, I wish—that you were more!"

It was not a conventional speech, and she was not a conventional woman—indeed, so strikingly unconventional, that a great part of her charm lay in that fact. It was not possible for him to doubt her sincerity or her meaning, but he could not command himself sufficiently to speak, and, after a moment's pause, she went on:

"You have a right to think that I have treated you shamefully, and I don't know that it is any excuse to say that I did not mean to do so. A few weeks ago I thought, for a little while, that I might marry you; but now I see that I should be inflicting on you the greatest possible harm and injury if I did such a thing.

Do you believe in love, Colonel Danesford?"

"You must have little idea what I feel for you, when you can ask me such a question!" he answered, hoarsely.

"Then what would you think of a woman who married you without loving you, as you so well deserve to be loved? Surely you are not like some men—surely you would not be satisfied to take the hand without the heart?"

"I should not be satisfied unless I possessed the whole heart of the woman who gave me her hand," he replied. "But why is it impossible that I should win yours? I will wait, Mrs. Trafford, even longer than I have waited already, if you can give me any hope of winning it at last."

"I am sorry," she said—"oh! very sorry!—but I must tell you frankly that there is no hope. If you could have won it, it would have been yours long ago. I have not meant to trifle with you," she went on. "I wish you would believe that. Since I have appreciated what you are, I have often wondered why I do not love you; but one cannot answer such questions. Perhaps I have no heart—at least, it is certain I have none worth giving you."

At this point, the sore jealousy which had been rankling in him for some time could not forbear expression.

"Perhaps," he said, a little bitterly, "you have thought it worth giving to your old friend Mr. Marchmont."

Her eyes looked at him with a singular expression in their lustrous depths—an expression not easily defined, but in which scorn played a large part.

"Is it possible," she said, "that you can think so poorly of me as to imagine that I would turn from you to give my heart to *him?* I do not deny that he has reason to believe such a thing, but *you* should know me better. No, Colonel Danesford, there is not a man on the face of the earth to whom I could not sooner give my heart than to my 'old friend Mr. Marchmont!'"

"And yet—" he said, then paused, remembering that he had no right to arraign her.

"And yet, you would say, you have seen me lead him on to certain disappointment and mortification. That is very true—so true, that, since I should like to retain your respect, I will tell you what reason I have for treating this man with what appears such heartlessness."

"You are mistaken," he said, "if you think that, under any circumstances, I could fail to give you other than respect. You have been the one woman in the world to me too long, for me ever to cease to think of you as one whom I admire only less than I love."

At these generous words her eyes softened with unshed tears. Once again she asked herself what perverse spirit kept her from loving this gallant gentleman? But—

"... the little more, and how much it is!
And the little less, and what worlds away!"

Such riddles are beyond all solving. Why should the "little less" not be a "little more?" Who is wise enough to answer?

"You are far kinder than I deserve, and I thank you with all my heart," she said, in a voice like spoken music. "But I think I will tell you my story. It can do no harm, and, after you have heard it, you will understand me better than you do now."

So she told him the story of the brief, ill-fated passion of her girlhood, with its attendant results on her life, and described how Fate had seemed, despite all her efforts, to thrust Marchmont into her path again, and put the means of revenge ready to her hand.

"I feel as if I were lowering myself in playing such a part," she said, in conclusion; "yet I am not only paying my debt to him, but I am saving a true-hearted girl from a marriage which could not be other than wretched."

"Nevertheless, you are lowering your-self," said Danesford, as Hugh had said before him. "The revenge is not worthy of you. And is it possible," he went on, with passionate reproach, "that you will let the shadow of this man lie on your heart and keep you from loving again —you, who could love so truly and so well?"

She shook her head.

"No," she said. "His shadow passed away from me long, long ago. But such a passion is like a fire that scorches all natural vegetation. No man who has entered my life since my widowhood has touched anything deeper than my vanity —until I met you. You have won everything except my heart."

"And for the last time," said he, taking her hand, "tell me is there no hope of winning *that* by patience and devotion?"

She was strong enough to meet his pleading eyes gravely and steadily with her own.

"I must make no more mistakes, give no more false encouragement, my dear Colonel Danesford," she said. "You must forgive me if you can—there is no hope!"

There was a moment's silence; then he bent his head and kissed her hand.

"God bless you!" he said, huskily. "I have nothing to forgive."

The next instant she found herself alone.

She sat quite motionless where he left her, gazing at the hand on which the sensation of his kiss still lingered.

"Is this wisdom, or folly?" she said to herself. "It seems incredible that I should have found one such heart in the artificial world where my life is cast. I am not likely ever to find another. Am I not mad to cast it away—for what? A mere sentiment, an unreality, which at my age should have lost all influence over me."

What would have been the end of this reflective regret, it is impossible to say; but her thoughts were suddenly dissipated by a voice at the door behind her announcing—

"Mr. Reade!"

She started, and turned quickly as the young artist advanced across the floor with a springing tread and a beaming face.

"My dear Mrs. Trafford, you will pardon me, I am sure, for intruding on you so unceremoniously, when you hear that I have come to claim your congratulations," he said, joyously. "But for your kindness, such good fortune would never have come to pass. Miss Paget has accepted me!"

"I am truly glad to hear it, and I congratulate you with all my heart!" answered Mrs. Trafford, cordially extending her hand. "It is very good of you to recognize my interests, and to come and give me the intelligence at once. I take it for granted that the engagement is not of long standing?"

"Three hours, exactly!" answered he, laughing. "I felt that I was in gratitude bound to communicate the happy result to you without loss of time, since but for your encouragement it would hardly be an accomplished fact."

"I think you are mistaken in that," said she, smiling, "though I am not averse to claiming a little share in bringing it about. I think you are a happy man, Mr. Reade. I am sure you look as if you were!"

"I am, indeed," said he. "In all England there is not a happier man. Such exaltation of feeling cannot last, of course; but Nelly is a girl whom any man might be proud, as well as happy, to win."

"I have not the least doubt of it," said Mrs. Trafford. "I was charmed with her when we first met; and I told you then — do you remember? — that you should be doubly anxious to win, since winning her meant saving her from the man who was your rival."

"I remember; and I am so well convinced that you were right, that it makes me doubly happy that I have won, and he—"

"Has lost more than he knows!" said Mrs. Trafford, with a swift flash in her eyes.

CHAPTER XIII.

"SCORES ARE SETTLED BETWEEN US."

MARCHMONT was soon destined to learn what he had lost. Despite his change of matrimonial intentions, the news of Nelly Paget's engagement was a shock to him. Without exactly saying to himself that he would hold her in his hand to fall back upon in case his ambition with regard to Mrs. Trafford failed, he had felt something of the kind, and now he was told that the prize which he had relinquished another man had grasped without loss of time. At that moment, according to a common impulse of human nature, it seemed to him better worth grasping than it had ever seemed before. Perhaps this was owing to the desperate state of his affairs, and the forebodings he entertained of Mrs. Trafford's caprice. At least, it is certain that a doubt of his own wisdom was the first thought which rose to his mind when Walter Paget told him the news.

"Honestly, I don't fancy the affair very much," that gentleman said. "A foreigner, a painter, a man that we know very little about, is by no means my ideal of a brother-in-law. But Nelly, like most women, is determined to have her own way, and there is really no very strong ground for objection."

"It seems to me that the matter has been arranged in a short time," said Marchmont, as soon as he could control his voice to speak. "Miss Paget has not known Mr. Reade very long."

"Cupid does not take long to draw his bow!" replied Mr. Paget, with a slight shrug. "I proposed to my wife on a week's acquaintance. Nelly and Reade have been very much thrown together of late—especially since you renewed your old friendship with Mrs. Trafford."

This last shot effectually stopped all further words on Marchmont's lips. Yes, there could be no doubt that the renewal of his "old friendship" with Mrs. Trafford was at the bottom of the whole affair. But for that, he knew that Nelly Paget would be engaged to *him*, instead of to this stranger who had so lately entered her life.

"If all goes well, I shall not regret it," he thought. "But the question is, *will* all go well? When I am with Amy, I cannot distrust her; but whenever I am away from her, all manner of doubts assail me. *If* she should be playing the same game with me which she has played with other men, I am simply ruined!"

So much was now staked on the venture, that he felt nervously afraid to consider it—nervously afraid to make the final plunge, and "win or lose it all." Yet he knew that the sooner this was done, the better. Other men—men with pretensions in every way higher than his own—were thronging round Mrs. Trafford, and the man who won her at all must win her boldly.

After parting with Walter Paget somewhere in the neighborhood of midnight, he smoked a cigar of meditation before retiring. He was not a man much given to reflections on the past, but it was impossible, at such a crisis as the present, to refrain from thinking of the wonderful turn which Fortune's wheel had made in his relations with the woman who had been Amy Reynolds. His mind went back vividly to those old days in Edgerton, when, in flirting with her, he had lost one of the most desirable of the succession of heiresses at whose golden shrines he had bowed. Recalling this, it began to seem to him a simple matter of poetic justice that she, who had twice stood between him and fortune, should bring fortune to him at last in her own hand.

This sanguine belief came to him strongly when he awoke the next day, and decided that before its sun went down his fate should be assured.

"Colors seen by candle-light
Do not look the same by day,"

and the doubt and indecision of the night before were altogether dissipated. Reason, instinct, knowledge of womankind—all combined to say that, when he went to woo, he also went to win. He could not seriously entertain the idea that, in leading him on as she had done, Mrs. Trafford had only been trifling. Coquette though she might be with some men, it was impossible that *he* had anything to fear—he who had once swayed her as the wind sways a reed!

He offered his congratulations to Miss Paget with a cordiality in which there was not the least suggestion of disappointment; and if Nelly had hoped, according to the fashion of women, for some such sign, she was not gratified.

Yet, it must not be supposed from this that pique had played any large part in causing her to accept Reade. That she was not averse to showing Marchmont how slight an impression he had made on her fancy, there can be no doubt; but this desire alone would never have urged her to such a step.

The young artist had found his opportunity when her mind and heart were enduring the sting of neglect, and he used it so well that he had entered into both, and possessed them as a kingdom.

She was heartily and happily in love with the man who had won her; nevertheless, she would have liked to read some token of regret in the face of the man who had lost her.

There was none, however, to be read. An adept for many years in the art of concealing all that he felt, it was not likely that such a desirable accomplishment should fail Marchmont now. It was, moreover, a consoling thought that he had not been defeated, but had voluntarily relinquished the opportunity which Fate placed in his hands. The time might come when he would regret this opportunity, but it had not come yet; it would not come while Mrs. Trafford's beauty and wealth still hung before him as a glittering prize.

Of late he had been admitted by that lady to a position of very pleasant intimacy; and he availed himself of it to-day, by presenting himself at rather an early hour in the drawing-room.

"I must apologize for such an unseasonable visit," he said, when she entered; "but I wanted so much to find you alone, that I ventured to intrude upon you at this hour. I hope you will pardon me."

"Very readily," she answered, quietly, though even her brave heart quailed a little as she thought that the issue of battle was before her. "But you must not be surprised if you find me stupid," she added. "The wear-and-tear of London dissipation is beginning to tell on me; and, if I do not soon go away in search of pastures new and fresh, I fear I shall fall into the ranks of the hopelessly dull."

"That is not very probable," he said, with a smile. "But you are looking a trifle pale."

"It is not remarkable. I have had a great deal on my mind, if not on my heart, lately. As if it were not trouble enough that I am to lose Mariette, I am harassed with legal business in connection with that loss."

"I have heard that you have been most generous in settling part of your fortune on her."

"Generous? I hate that word!" said she, impatiently. "Is it strange that I should divide a fortune already larger than my wants with the sister who has been more of a child than a sister to me?"

"When you speak of dividing, you do not mean to imply that you give *half* of it to her?" asked he, unable to re-

strain altogether the consternation which he felt.

She looked at him keenly as she answered: "I mean just that. My lawyer is now engaged in settling half on her as securely as it can be settled."

Marchmont barely escaped saying "Good Heavens!" aloud. He was dismayed to the point of disgust, and he wished most devoutly that he was in a position to remonstrate with Mrs. Trafford on her folly. But good sense and good taste both forbade such an idea, and forced him to conceal his disgust and dismay as best he could. There was no doubt that, even bereft of half her fortune, the beautiful widow was worth gaining; but the thought of that lost half annoyed him terribly.

"Miss Reynolds has a very brilliant life before her," he said, presently. "It is difficult to realize that the future Lady Gresham was ever the little golden-haired Mariette of Edgerton."

He had learned long since that she never shrank from any allusion to Edgerton and her old life there.

"Yes," said Mrs. Trafford, calmly, "it *is* difficult to realize what marvelous changes money can work. I am even more of an example than Mariette. It sometimes requires an absolute effort for me to fancy that I ever was Amy Reynolds, living in hap-hazard Bohemian poverty, and looking to stage-triumphs as my highest hope in life!"

"Yet what happy days they were!" said he, regarding her with the same glance which had thrilled her so often in the days of which they were talking. "I don't know how you may regard them, Mrs. Trafford, but to *me* they are the one spot of romance—of romance the most true and tender—in a worldly life. It would be impossible for me to tell you how often, during all these years, I have paused in the midst of excitement, toil, and struggle, to dream of the garden in which we spent so many happy hours, of the woodland glen where I found you first, and of the old parlor where you so often sang to me. Yet I never ventured to hope that we should meet again—that I should ever sit by you as now, and find the promise of your girlhood more than fulfilled in your beauty and your charms."

He held himself in check very well, mindful that in such a game as this he must make every move with caution, and his voice was eloquent with an expression which only sincerity could have given. In fact, if Marchmont ever was sincere, he was at this moment. His old love for Amy Reynolds was as water unto wine compared with the passion which he felt for the beautiful woman now before him. If he could win her! At that moment he was more than ready to pardon every unkind trick of Fortune, if only he might grasp this prize at last.

There was not much encouragement for his hopes in Mrs. Trafford's smile, if he had read that smile aright; but to do so required a coolness of judgment which he was not then in a condition to exercise.

"You are very kind," she said, quietly; "but I don't like compliments—perhaps because I have had a surfeit of them—and I am callous to the spell of old sentiment. Gardens, woodland glens, and the like haunts of flirtation, would probably not lose their attraction if one could be sixteen forever; but, happily, time bears us away from that very foolish age, and we leave its tastes as well as its absurdities behind us."

"Its absurdities, if you choose to call them so, were nearer wisdom than the cynicism which comes so readily to us now," said he, earnestly. "If you would believe and feel that as I do, something of the charm of that golden time might come back for us yet."

Looking full at him, she lifted her eyebrows with a slightly interrogative and half-mocking expression.

"Pardon me," she said, "but are you not taking a good deal for granted? Have I implied in the remotest manner that the 'golden time,' of which you speak so eloquently has any charm for me?"

He was more than a little taken aback for an instant, but recovered himself readily. Evidently this woman, with her ten years of worldly training behind her, was not to be wooed, like a schoolgirl, with mere sentiment; and, perceiving this, he changed his tone instantly.

"Do not misunderstand me," he said. "I recognize as clearly as you do the gulf of change—change in outward events, yet most of all in ourselves—which separates us from that time. I remember its miseries as well as its happiness. But neither of us is likely to deny that there *was* happiness in it; and, despite all the years and the changes which have divided us, that happiness may be ours again—if you choose, Amy."

It was the first time he had ventured to call her by the old name once so common to his lips; and, as he uttered it now, a flash came into her eyes, but she drooped her lids quickly over them, and after an instant she was able to control her voice sufficiently to reply:

"Pray explain yourself. How can the happiness of which you speak—and concerning the existence of which we will not argue—be ours again, if I choose?"

"Does not your own heart answer that question?" asked he, with genuine emotion in his face and voice. "What did our happiness spring from but love—love which we felt and expressed in the face of every obstacle? It was a romance then—bright, sweet, utterly hopeless—but it may, if you choose, be far better now. The future is in our own hands, Amy. Can we not grasp all of which Fate robbed us when it parted us ten years ago?"

He attempted to take her hand, but she drew it away, and, lifting her eyes, looked at him. In the cold, steady scorn of that glance he read his answer. Her hour for triumph and retaliation had come, and she was not likely to spare the man who had once sacrificed her heart for his idle pleasure.

"Do you not think it is time for this farce to end, Mr. Marchmont?" she asked, in a tone so keen and trenchant that it cut like a whip. "I have listened to you thus far, partly because you amused me, and partly because I was curious to see how far your forgetfulness of the past— or your reckoning on *my* forgetting it— would lead you. My curiosity is entirely satisfied. You have made a great many mistakes in your life, I doubt not; but you have never made—you never can make—a greater than when you dreamed that I had so utterly lost sight of all I owe you, that you could venture to speak to me like this!"

Coldness vanished from her speech with the last words, and a flood of passion shivered through them, while her dauntless eyes met his with a glow which no man could have been dull enough to misunderstand.

The transformation was so sudden and so complete that his first feeling was one of intense amazement, and he gazed at her like one who is incredulous of the evidence of his own ears.

Seeing this, she smiled—a haughty, contemptuous smile.

"Do you understand now," she said, "that scores are to be settled between us? If you had been wise, Mr. Marchmont, you would have chosen any other woman on earth than Amy Reynolds for the object of a fortune-hunter's scheme!"

These words seemed to restore him to himself—at least, they brought a dark-red flush to his face and a gleam into his eyes. Yet he did not lose control of himself, for in an instant he grasped the thought that, if she only distrusted his sincerity all might yet be well.

"It is impossible," he said, "that you, who know the world and the hearts of men so well, can believe that I am thinking of your fortune. You must know— you must feel to the centre of your soul —that I love you with a most passionate

devotion! It would be strange if I failed to do so, when you, mistress as you are of every fascination that can beguile, have exerted all those fascinations upon me."

"You are right," she answered. "I have endeavored to ensnare your fancy; and if I have succeeded—if you, indeed, feel for me anything approaching to a passion —it was only what I intended, to make my reprisal complete. In all your memories of the past, have you forgotten the scene of our parting? *I* remember it as if it had occurred yesterday. I remember that, when you coolly told me that I had served to amuse you, and, the time for amusement being over, all was ended between us, I warned you that, if ever any chance of life put it in my power to return upon you the suffering and mortification you had so ruthlessly inflicted, I would do so remorselessly. That time has come. You, misled by your own folly and vanity, have placed the opportunity in my hand. You chose to seek me out; you would not heed my warnings. Now take the consequences; now comprehend that I detest as deeply as I scorn you, and that there is not a beggar in the streets— nay, I will go further, there is not a felon in the prisons—whom I would not sooner marry! *Now* do you understand?"

It were needless to ask the question. If ever a man understood the full, bitter truth, Brian Marchmont understood it then. His face became more than pale; it was fairly livid, as, with a consciousness like a revealing flash of lightning, he saw everything—saw how blindly he had fallen into this woman's net, and how she had befooled and beguiled him, while Nelly Paget and Nelly Paget's fortune passed beyond his reach.

Seeing that he was absolutely incapable of speech, Mrs. Trafford rose. Though she did not feel the faintest sensation of pity—for all the memories of the past had rushed upon her with overwhelming force —she was anxious to end a scene which could only become more distinctly unpleasant with every succeeding moment.

"It is not likely that wo shall meet again," she said, in a tone cold as ice. "I have only tolerated your presence in order that I might pay the debt which I owed you; and now scores are settled between us forever."

"Not quite settled," he interposed, rising also, and advancing abruptly toward her. "Believe me, Mrs. Trafford, the last act of the drama, whether you choose to consider it tragedy, comedy, or farce, is not played yet. To retaliate upon me for the fancied injury inflicted by a flirtation ten years ago—a flirtation which cost *me* the surrender of my most brilliant worldly prospects—you have not only inspired a passion that you meant to scorn and hopes you intended to disappoint, but you cannot deny that it is chiefly owing to you that Miss Paget has engaged herself to an unknown Bohemian."

"I have no intention of denying it," replied she, calmly. "I intended from the first to save *her* and disappoint *you*. I have accomplished both."

"For the present," said he, with a calmness which equaled her own. "But did you ever hear that 'he laughs best who laughs last?' Again I say, Mrs. Trafford, the last act has yet to be played!"

She flung her head back proudly.

"I understand what you mean to imply," she said. "That you would gladly injure me if you could, I do not doubt; but I defy you! The last pang which it was in your power to inflict on me, you inflicted ten years ago in Edgerton. So long as we two live upon the earth, Brian Marchmont, it will never be in your power to harm me again."

He smiled in a manner which would have caused a less brave woman to shudder—a smile more significant than any frown.

"You have made me your debtor to a very great degree," he said, "and it remains to be seen whether there may not be yet another settlement of scores between us! For the present, however, I accept your dismissal; when we meet again, Mrs. Trafford, it may be *I* who will laugh last."

These were the final words uttered between them. He left the room with a bow; and she, standing quite still in the middle of the floor asked herself if she were dreaming, or if, indeed, her long and bitter reckoning with Brian Marchmont was settled at last.

CHAPTER XIV.

"I WILL FIND THE WAY."

IT would be vain to attempt to describe the storm of emotion which raged in Marchmont's breast when he went forth from Mrs. Trafford's presence. Never in his life before—not even on the unforgotten night when Beatrix Waldron poured out her scorn upon him—had he been so humiliated, so utterly baffled, as now. *That* defeat had seemed to him intolerable, but *this* was tenfold worse. To have been lured by any woman to such an end for such a purpose, would have proved bitter enough when the end came; but it was doubly bitter to consider that she who had so mercilessly fooled and beguiled him was no other than the woman whom he had once esteemed of such slight importance that he had cast her out of his path without a thought. It appeared to him an outrage of Fate which had thus thrown him in her power; and when he thought of the double blow which she had struck—of all that he had lost in losing Nelly Paget—he could only grind his teeth and utter impotent curses.

Impotent for the present; but, now as ever, there were powers of strong feeling and strong doing in this man's nature, which only needed a touch to waken them. Unscrupulous at all times, with the incentives of mortified pride and baffled ambition, he was ready to grasp any means by which revenge might be secured.

Nevertheless, he did not close his eyes to the fact that it was difficult to see how he could hope to strike Mrs. Trafford. She had defied him to inflict another pang on her, and he knew that the defiance was more than mere bravado—that it rested on very solid grounds. All the advantage of position was hers, and one so well supported by wealth and social prestige could afford to set at naught the malice of a discarded suitor. He recognized the situation at a glance; but he said to himself, with an emphasis which had the force of an oath:

"I will find the way!"

Absorbed in these thoughts, he did not observe where he was going, until, having walked mechanically for some distance, he found himself in Hyde Park, in the neighborhood of the Row, which at this hour was filled with equestrians.

It was a very gay and animated scene, but he scarcely took in a feature of it as he slowly strolled along the footpath. The blooming young Amazons on their handsome horses did not win a glance from him, and his mind was as far as possible away from them, when a blithe voice suddenly said:

"How do you do, Mr. Marchmont? Are you rehearsing the part of *Hamlet?* —or why is it that you so resolutely cut your friends?"

He turned, and found himself confronted by Hebe on horseback—in other words, by Mariette Reynolds, who had pulled up her horse to address him. She was laughing, and the sunlight was glinting down upon her, brightening the sheen of her golden hair until it seemed literally woven of sunbeams, showing the exquisite lines of her figure, and playing over her lovely face, with its complexion of roses and snow.

Altogether, so fair a picture was she —so radiant with youth and beauty and good spirits—that Marchmont was sud-

denly conscious that Stamer Gresham was a very fortunate man.

With this fortunate man and his sister —a handsome girl, of the substantial English order—Mariette was riding, but she had begun to find their society a trifle dull when she saw Marchmont; and, since he had twice allowed her to pass without noticing her, she acted on an impulse and reined up her horse, uttering the words recorded above.

They were words which startled him by their unexpectedness; but he was carefully trained in self-control, and the habit of years did not desert him. He swung round, and lifted his hat with a smile.

"Charmed to meet you, Miss Reynolds—and thanks for recalling me to a sense of what I was losing. I was passing along with a feeling of 'What is Hecuba'—otherwise the Row—'to me, or I to Hecuba?' But I did not know that the fairest face in London was to be seen on it!"

Not yet had compliments lost their savor to Mariette. The face of which he spoke brightened and blushed with pleasure under his gaze; and at this moment an idea darted into Marchmont's mind like a flash of inspiration. Here was his means of revenge—here was the channel through which he might strike Mrs. Trafford a blow that would forever settle scores between them! It was an idea of daring audacity, but he was a desperate man ready for desperate ventures. He could lose nothing, he might gain much; and, on the chance, with the instinct of a gambler, he was willing to stake everything.

It was the work of an instant to glance from Mariette to the commonplace young Briton by her side, and reckon the odds against success. That they were heavy, there could be no doubt—so heavy, that it seemed madness to dream of that which had occurred to him; but he was absolutely reckless. Even if he failed, he would only be where he was now; while

13

success would mean so much, that the mere thought of it sent a thrill of hope and resolution through him. Fortune favors the daring, and he determined to dare all things.

Taking advantage of Mariette's pause, Captain and Miss Gresham were talking to some friends, so that he had a moment's opportunity to speak unheard.

"I have just seen your sister, and learned that I must congratulate you," he said. "It is the old story—

> 'The smile that blest one lover's heart
> Has broken many more.'

But those that are broken have no right to complain, I suppose. Besides, broken hearts are out of fashion."

"Hearts of all kinds are," said Mariette, gayly; yet something in the glance of the dark eyes made her blush again. "Who considers them nowadays? Were you thinking of anything so obsolete, as you sauntered along, like a tragedy-hero?"

"Yes," he answered, looking straight into the blue depths of her eyes with his most effective gaze; "I was thinking of those obsolete things, and—it may be presumptuous of me, but finding you here at this moment is so strange—I should like to tell you of what I was thinking. I might bore you, however; so perhaps it is as well that I must say, instead, *au retoir*."

"Were you thinking of *me*?" she asked, quickly, curiosity rising in her breast. "I can't imagine that possible."

"Can you not?" with a smile. "Then have faith in the impossible. I was thinking a great deal which I should seriously like to tell you, but which we lack time and opportunity to discuss now. Do you feel interest enough in it to care to make an opportunity to hear it?"

"What need is there to *make* an opportunity?" asked she, with some surprise.

"Simply this need," answered he, with growing earnestness, as he felt the desperate nature of the game he was attempting to play, "that I desire to see *you*—alone, and without interruption. This, as you know, is impossible under any ordinary circumstances of meeting. Therefore, occupying almost the position of a grandfather to you—certainly having known you when you were no higher than this stick—I feel tempted to propose an *extraordinary* mode of meeting."

As was natural, his manner puzzled Mariette exceedingly, and stimulated her interest. She was not only curious, but the volatile elements in her nature caught at anything which promised excitement out of the ordinary way.

"I can appreciate the grandfatherly claim," she said, with mischievous gravity, "and I *should* like to hear the mysterious subject of your thoughts. Pray let me know what extraordinary mode of meeting you propose?"

"One not at all extraordinary save in the fact of being removed from your usual surroundings," he replied, eagerly—so eagerly that the girl's interest waxed greater. "Did I not hear you say, the other day, that you should like to spend some one of these beautiful afternoons loitering in Kensington Gardens? Unless Captain Gresham claims all your time, will you not give me the pleasure of meeting you there this afternoon?"

"Meeting me?" said she, interrogatively.

"Yes," he answered. "I cannot explain now, but I should prefer that no one knew of the meeting. Give me a chance—only a chance!" he pleaded. "I have something to tell you which may be of great—of the greatest importance. Will you come? I promise this, at least: you will not regret it."

Mariette hesitated, uncertain what to say or do. Marchmont's request, and, still more, Marchmont's manner, was so singular, that she felt more curious than can be readily expressed. After all, what objection was there to the plan he proposed? To meet an old friend—a friend of her childhood—in the pleasant shades of Kensington Gardens, and loiter away an hour or two, surely neither sister nor lover could find any wrong in that? Just as she reached this conclusion, Captain Gresham turned and asked if she was ready to ride on.

"Quite ready," she replied. Then she turned to Marchmont and said: "What hour shall we appoint? Five? Remember, I expect something *very* interesting to repay me for sacrificing a kettle-drum to which I am engaged to accompany Amy."

She bowed, smiled, and rode away, in her youth and grace, by the side of the man to whom she was engaged; while the man whom she had left standing by the rails looked after her and said to himself: "It is a desperate cast; but sometimes the desperate win."

Cleverly eluding all questions from her lover about the appointment she had made, Mariette finished her ride and went home. The more she thought of Marchmont, his singular manner and singular request, the more her curiosity was piqued, and, instead of regretting the appointment, she resolved to keep it.

"What can he have to tell me?" she thought. "It is very odd! Perhaps he has heard some dreadful story about Stamer; but he would be likely to go to Amy with *that*. Ah, I have it! He must want me to exert my influence with Amy in his behalf. If he only knew it, Love's labor is lost there. I think I'll tell him so, and then, perhaps, I shall draw out the history of the old affair, which Amy will never mention. I should like to hear it, for I have not forgotten how he used to come 'to hear her sing,' and how she met him in the woods. Such stolen romance must be very sweet—and he would make a charming lover! What eyes—ah, what eyes he has! And then, he looks like a man with a story. Poor Stamer has no such appearance, and I must confess that he is very commonplace and un-

interesting. I do *not* like Englishmen; there is no doubt of that. They do not know how to talk, and they are very heavy after one has known them a while."

With this decision—rather foreign, it would seem, to the subject of her meditation—Miss Reynolds went down to luncheon, where her attention was sufficiently disengaged to notice that Mrs. Trafford looked rather pale.

"Have you another headache, Amy?" she asked. "What a pity you did not go to ride with us! The Row was delightful. You were not condemned to solitude, however, for I met Mr. Marchmont, and he said he had just left you."

A change, slight but significant, came over Mrs. Trafford's face at the mention of Marchmont's name; but it did not occur to her to break through the reticence which she had hitherto observed regarding him.

"Yes, he was here," she answered; and then she changed the subject so quickly that Mariette's suspicions were roused.

"Something out of the ordinary way has occurred between them," she said to herself. "Perhaps I shall hear from *him* what it was. Since Amy does not choose to be frank with me, I shall not be frank with her." Then she said: "You'll excuse my going with you to Mrs. St. John's kettle-drum—will you not? Like yourself, I am rather tired of festivities—at least of that order of festivities."

"I will excuse you very readily," Mrs. Trafford answered, with a smile. "I don't wonder you are tired, and, after resting this afternoon, you will be fresher for the balls at which we are due to-night."

So Mariette carried her point without difficulty; and after Mrs. Trafford had departed to Mrs. St. John's kettle-drum, she put on a quiet but most becoming walking-costume, and set forth to keep her appointment.

. . . . . .

An hour later a lady and gentleman might have been seen pacing slowly along one of the velvet-turfed, leaf-canopied alleys of Kensington Gardens, talking with that air of thorough preoccupation which is very full of significance to lookers-on. They were no doubt taken for a pair of lovers by all who observed them, and, had they been so, they could have found no fitter place to linger than this "lovely lawn of Kensington."

It was looking its loveliest just now, in the soft beauty of the June afternoon —long, slanting, golden light lying on emerald sward, and deep shadows lying under splendid trees. Mariette had exclaimed enthusiastically over its beauty when she entered; but Nature always played a very subordinate part with her, and it was particularly subordinate now, because she was deeply interested in the story which Marchmont had brought her there to hear.

It was a very effective story, effectively told—the story of his own life viewed through the medium of his own imagination.

"You must pardon me if I am egotistical," he said, when beginning. "It is a necessary preface to what I shall tell you afterward, that I should tell you first the story of my life. I will endeavor not to be tedious, and I shall certainly be truthful."

"Don't trouble yourself with any fears of tediousness," Mariette had answered, lightly; "I am always fond of autobiography, and yours will be particularly interesting, because I hardly fancy I am wrong in thinking it is connected in certain passages with my childish recollections of persons and events."

"I know what you mean," he replied, "but you have probably heard all that from Mrs. Trafford, so I will not bore you by repeating—"

"I have never heard anything from Amy," she interrupted, eagerly, fearful that her curiosity might be ungratified at last, and, in her ignorance, giving him

exactly the assurance he wanted. "I remember, of course, how intimate you and Amy were, and I know you must have been in love with each other; but that is all I know."

"You shall know all that I can tell you," he said, with an apparent impulse of candor; and he plunged at once into the recital.

It has already been said that it was very effectively made. By a few graphic words he described his position when he first appeared in Edgerton, his ambitious hopes of entering public life, and his want of the fortune requisite for such a career. Under these circumstances, that arrangement which the French call *mariage de convenance* seemed to him the most desirable he could make, and therefore he went to Edgerton as Beatrix Waldron's suitor. But he had hardly set himself seriously at work to win the heiress's hand, when he met lovely, penniless Amy Reynolds, and fell hopelessly in love.

Then, what a pure, idyllic romance it was which followed! Had Mrs. Trafford heard his description of it, she might have been convinced that no truer-hearted lover was ever driven by the force of circumstances to resign the girl he loved.

Then came a brief sketch of the ten years' interval—"full to the brim as regarded worldly success, absolutely empty as regarded the heart," he said, pathetically. And finally he reached the present time.

It required all his most delicate diplomacy to deal with it, but he acquitted himself admirably. It is true that Mariette felt a little bewildered as she listened, a little uncertain how to reconcile her own observation with these frank statements; but, on the whole, his statements carried the day.

This was scarcely to be wondered at; everything seconded them so well! Some special pleaders can color all things with the hues of their own eloquence—can make black appear white and white seem black; and to this class Marchmont belonged. Few girls in Mariette's position could have been insensible to confidences uttered in such a thrilling voice, seconded by such a poetically-handsome face, and with every romantic influence of time and place in their favor. What soft leaf-shadows flickered over them as the breeze at intervals stirred the boughs overhead! How the level yellow sunbeams lighted up the foliage, and streaked the dark trunks of the trees with gold!

And with all these influences around—influences very potent on the impressionable heart of eighteen—what was it that she heard? Why, simply this: that when Marchmont saw Mrs. Trafford again, he strove to renew the broken links of old romance, and failed utterly.

"I found that the girl I loved had passed away forever," he said, "and left in her place a brilliant, heartless woman of the world. The nearer I came to her, the more I felt that my ideal had fled forever. Then, heart-sick and disappointed, I turned away, and, lo! the ideal, which I had fancied lost, stood before me—realized a hundred-fold! With all the tender grace of youth, all the wayward charm of a nature exquisitely fresh and fair, I found it—in you, Mariette!"

"In me!" repeated Mariette, with a start and a blush. "You surely are jesting!"

"Is it likely that I would jest on such a subject?" he asked, reproachfully. "Believe me, I am as earnest as a man can be—how earnest, indeed, I would not make you comprehend, if I could. And do not mistake me: though I found my ideal, it did not for a moment occur to me to think of winning it. I knew that such bright youth as yours should mate with bright youth—not with a life like mine, passing out of youth. I could love—nay, I do love—with a passion far deeper and stronger than that of any boy. But you would never have heard of the existence of this passion, if I had not felt that it gave me the right to utter a warning, when I saw you about to sacrifice

yourself on the altar of a worldly marriage. Mariette"—he took her hand as he spoke—"tell me, do you imagine yourself in love with the commonplace young Englishman whom you have pledged yourself to marry?"

"I—really, I don't know why you should doubt it," Mariette managed to answer with moderate self-possession. "He is very—nice."

"Just that," her companion replied, coolly. "Very nice, undoubtedly, and nothing more. While you— Mariette, is it possible you have no idea what you are?"

"I think I know pretty well," Mariette murmured. "Modesty is not one of my failings. And I like Captain Gresham very much. You must not think that I do not."

"Do you love him?"—and the grasp grew warmer on her hand. "Answer me that. If you can truly say that you do— Well, I shall try to believe you, and be satisfied."

But Mariette could not say it. Was it the clasp on her hand, or the earnest gaze of the dark eyes, which rendered her speechless—or was it some new, strange feeling in her own breast? Whatever it was, her head drooped a little, and, for answer, warm blushes came, mantling into her fair cheeks.

"I see!" said Marchmont, after a minute's pause, and he drew a deep breath as of one relieved from a great dread. "You do not love him, and you must forgive me if I implore you not to sacrifice your life, your heart, your soul, in the bondage of such a marriage. Surely there is no need for it; surely your sister—"

"My sister," said Mariette, with a faint, tremulous laugh, "has grown very sentimental of late, and declares that she wishes me only to marry the man I—love."

"She has learned what loveless marriage is, in her own experience, and she would save you from it. Why, then, do you not heed her? Has your heart not yet waked? But it *will* wake some day, and avenge the wrong you have done it, in a manner of which you could not now even dream."

She looked at him with a smile which he did not altogether understand. In truth, it had no meaning beyond the fact that she was enjoying this excitement—with its piquant taste of stolen fruit—far more than Stamer Gresham's rather monotonous love-making. The man by her side, with his musical voice and passionate eyes, was a lover of another stamp altogether, and certainly more attractive. She did not comprehend him; she had an instinct which held her back from wholly trusting him; yet she felt the power of his fascination more and more with every moment. If she had been wise, she would have left him at once; but, under temptation, few are wise. There was no harm in lingering a little longer in the mellow sunshine, beneath the spreading trees—no harm in drinking a little deeper of this sweet draught of passionate, romantic devotion. He had not asked for anything. Where was the harm of merely listening?

CHAPTER XV.

THE BLOW FALLS.

"A LADY wants to see you, Mr. Dinsmore—a lady in her carriage. Shall I ask her to walk up?"

So spoke a servant of rather grimy aspect, appearing at the door of Hugh Dinsmore's studio, where the latter was hard at work, painting as if his life depended on every stroke. He looked round in surprise.

"A lady!—to see me! What the deuce— Oh! you have her card!"

He took the card, and his surprise was not lessened when he found Mrs. Trafford's name thereon. He did not say anything, but he changed color. Putting his palette out of his hand, and motioning the servant aside, he himself went to the door. There was no mistake. It *was* Mrs. Trafford, who, when he approached the carriage in which she sat, held out her hand to him.

"Will you pardon me for taking you by surprise like this?" she asked. "But I really have a reason for it. May I go up to your studio?"

"Of course you may—of course, I am delighted to see you!" he answered, offering his arm to descend. "You find me in working-gear altogether," he added, with an apologetic glance at his painting-coat, "but you will, no doubt, excuse that."

"Excuse it! I should think so, indeed!" she answered, as they went up to the studio. "I only hope you will excuse *me*, when I tell you why I have intruded on your work."

"Surely you must know that you do not intrude upon me," he said with a gravity more reassuring than any gallantry could have been. "I shall be sincerely glad if it is in my power to serve you in any way. Let me give you a seat by the window," he went on, as they entered the studio. "You can see the river from there, and it is better worth looking at than my unfinished work."

"Your unfinished work interests me more than a hundred rivers could," she answered. "May I see what you are doing?"

Without waiting for his answer, she walked directly up to the large easel where the canvas rested on which he had been painting.

It was the scene already described from the "Rhyme of the Duchess May;" and, as Mrs. Trafford looked at it, she saw at once that the face of the duchess had been painted — a marvelously beautiful face, imploring, yet calm, despite the agony of the attitude; but it was fully a minute before she realized that it was neither more nor less than a likeness of her own face.

Hugh, who was watching her curiously, saw that she recognized it from the flush that suddenly covered her cheek and brow. Without giving herself time to think, she turned toward him quickly.

"I thought you intended to take Mariette for your model?" she said.

"I thought so, too," he answered; "but when I had painted her face—at least its outline—I found that, however lovely it might be, it was not the face of the Duchess May. Then *your* face began to haunt me in connection with the picture, until, at last, the only escape from the fascination was to paint it; and you see the result."

"I see that you have succeeded in drawing my features, yet elevating them to a higher beauty than they possess, by means of an expression totally foreign to them," she said. "Does the result satisfy you?"

"Perfectly!"

"And you could paint this without any sittings?"

"Do you think I need any sittings to paint your face?" he asked, with a slight smile. "Why, there is not a line of it that I do not know by heart—a fact not very remarkable, when you consider that you were once my only sitter, and that I taxed your patience constantly."

"Don't do yourself injustice," said she. "My recollection is, that you were considerate in that as in everything else. I am glad that my face has served you once again"—turning from the picture. "I will tell you why I have come to trouble you. It is not with regard to myself, but with regard to Mariette."

She looked at him keenly as she uttered the last words; but she failed to see that the expression of concern on his face deepened at all.

"Anything that I can do for you, or for Mariette, I will do most willingly," he answered. "Pray tell me, without hesitation, what you desire."

"What I desire is—well, I suppose it is advice," she said, with a slight, irreso-lute motion of her hands. "At least, it is nothing more definite. You know that Mariette is engaged to Captain Gresham? —yes, of course you know it. Tell me— pray, tell me frankly—what you think of the engagement."

He was surprised, and his face showed this surprise very plainly.

"Pardon me," he said, "but you have surely forgotten how little I can know of the matter. It is a brilliant match, I presume. I believe that Captain Gresham is the eldest son of a baronet. I know no more of him than that."

"I am not talking of him," said Mrs. Trafford, "but of Mariette. I was not, at the first, pleased with the idea of the engagement. I did not think that she cared enough for the man whom she thought of marrying; but, as time goes on, I am still less pleased or satisfied. I am a close observer, and Mariette's manner, of late, has made me vaguely uneasy—"

She broke off abruptly, and walked to the window, her silken skirts trailing softly over the studio-floor, while Hugh watched her, with the surprise deepening on his face. In such a matter as this, why should she come to *him?*

After a moment's pause, she went on without turning round—went on in a hurried voice:

"I may be right, or I may be wrong, in saying this to you—I cannot tell. But Mariette's manner gives me the impression that she is in love—and not with Captain Gresham."

"With whom, then?" asked Hugh, now completely overmastered by astonishment.

Mrs. Trafford turned, and, with her clear, brilliant eyes, looked full at him.

"Do not *you* know?" she asked, in reply. "I thought—I hoped—O Hugh, if I have blundered, pardon me!—but do not you care for her?"

"I!" For a moment Hugh could say no more than that; then, having grasped her meaning, he rallied his self-possession, and answered: "I care for her, most undoubtedly, as an old friend who knew and loved her in her babyhood; but not as a lover, Mrs. Trafford—if that is what you mean."

"Are you sure?" she said, drawing nearer to him, and involuntarily clasping her hands. "Hugh, *don't* suffer any false pride to ruin your happiness and hers! I have suspected from the first that you loved her; and if you do—"

"You are making a great mistake, Mrs. Trafford!" Hugh interposed, gravely. "Your penetration has misled in some unaccountable manner. The affection which I feel for Mariette now, is exactly the same which I felt for her when she was five years old. The idea of loving my old playmate as a woman has never entered my imagination—nor can it now do so. I acknowledge her loveliness, and I appreciate her charms; but my feeling toward her stops there. Why should you fear that I am deceiving you?" he added, as she still looked at him doubtfully. "Do you think"—and here his eyes kindled—"that, if I loved her, I would stand by and not make an effort to win her? Do you fancy that I should let a duke's son claim her, if she loved *me*?"

Her eyes drooped under the flash of his, and she turned her face away.

"How could I tell?" she murmured. "I thought that perhaps my wealth might stand between, and that, if you could know how happy I should be if I could benefit you, Hugh—"

"Stop!" he said, and something in his voice—a thrill of passion steadily controlled—made her quiver. "Don't let us enter upon an utterly useless discussion; don't tempt me to tell you how little I could ever think of benefiting by your wealth. The past has been sealed to us so far, Mrs. Trafford; let it remain sealed to the end."

"Oh, how cruel, how hard, how unforgiving, you are!" she cried. "What have I ever done to you, that you should treat me so?"

"How am I treating you?" he asked, regaining outward calmness. "I have only assured you that I am not, and never can be, your sister's lover. That assurance certainly ought to be a relief to you, since she is engaged to another man?"

"Instead of being a relief, it is a disappointment," she said, slowly. "I cannot help fearing for her future life, if she marries a man whom she does not sincerely love; and I hoped that she might be saved from such a fate by you."

Surely, if "woman's at best a contradiction still," man is not anything very different; for, at these words, Dinsmore's brow clouded, and his resolute lips set themselves a little more resolutely for an instant, before he answered:

"You mean kindly, no doubt, Mrs. Trafford; but I must repeat again, that you have made a great mistake. I wish that I could help you to unravel the mystery—if mystery it be—of Mariette's choice; but, unfortunately, I am utterly unable to do so."

"I may be mistaken altogether," she said. "I do not know; I cannot tell. Having made one great mistake, I have lost confidence in my judgment."

There was a minute's silence. The afternoon sunshine streamed into the studio, throwing a glory round Mrs. Trafford's erect, stately figure, brightening the shining masses of her hair, and making a picture on which Hugh's artist-eye dwelt with an admiration beyond his control. If he could but fix it on his canvas, to live forever! That was what he thought, but what he did not say. On the contrary, when he spoke, his words were very different—words which he felt actuated by some prophetic instinct to utter:

"It may seem an odd thing to say, but, if any emergency should arise, in which I could be of use, pray promise to call on me. Remember that I am your oldest friend, and think of me as you would think of your brother."

"You are very kind," she said; "but it is not easy to see what emergency could arise, or how you could be of use if it did arise. Pray, forget my blunder as soon as you can," she added, with a faint smile. "I shall not repeat it. And now I will not trespass on your time any longer."

He did not attempt to detain her, but when he placed her in her carrriage he said again, earnestly, "Promise me that you will call on me!" And she answered, almost despite herself:

"I promise—if there is need."

. . . .

When that promise was uttered, neither he who asked, nor she who gave, had any idea how soon the need for claiming it would arise. On the second day after this visit, Dinsmore received the following note:

"DEAR HUGH: Pray come to me at once! Something terrible has happened —something so terrible, that I cannot write of it!
"Yours,   A. TRAFFORD."

Surprise and consternation were equally balanced in Hugh's mind when he read this. Something terrible—something so terrible that she could not write of it! What on earth had occurred? All manner of doubts and fears took possession of him. He called a cab, promised the driver a double fare to take him as quickly as possible to Mrs. Trafford's house, and, when he arrived there, was ushered without delay into that lady's presence.

She came to meet him, so pale, so altered from the blooming beauty of only two days before, that he might have fancied she had just arisen from a severe attack of illness.

But the change in her manner was even greater than the change in her face. She held out her hand to him, and said, like one who speaks mechanically:

"It is good of you to come; but I thought, after sending, that it was useless to trouble you, for there is nothing to be done."

"Let me judge of that," he said, eagerly. "Tell me what has happened —what is the matter?"

"Have you not heard?" she asked. "Ah, I forgot! I did not tell you—and Heaven help me!" The words came through her lips with an absolute gasp. "How can I tell you!"

"Does it concern Mariette?" he asked; for his mind had at once recurred to their conversation of two days before.

"Yes, it concerns Mariette," she answered; and then she burst into tears.

Poor Hugh felt as helpless and distressed as a man of his order usually feels in presence of a woman's tears—especially the tears of such genuine, passionate grief as this. He was sorely perplexed. He felt that the trouble must indeed be of a very serious nature; but he was more and more puzzled to imagine what it could be. Knowing that the greatest kindness he could show Mrs. Trafford was to give her time to recover herself, he placed her gently in the chair from which she had risen at his entrance, and turned away.

In doing so, he struck a small table near by, and almost upset it. As he caught it, a letter fell to the ground, and, when he stooped for it, Mrs. Trafford commanded her voice sufficiently to say:

"Read it."

He needed no second invitation, but, walking to one of the windows, he opened and read the letter, which he saw at a glance was signed with Mariette's name.

"MY DEAR AMY: You have, of late, laid so much stress upon your desire that I should marry the man I love, that I am sure you will be glad to learn that I have decided to do so. Will you be surprised to hear that this man is your old friend Mr. Marchmont? I am afraid you will not be pleased, and, to avoid anything disagreeable—for Mr. Marchmont and myself both dislike disagreeable things extremely—we have decided to go over to the Continent to be married. I will write full particulars in a few days, and give you our address. Won't you join us when the season ends, and you have quite disposed of all your admirers? Trouville, for a while, would be pleasant; but we can discuss all this at length after the ceremony. I inclose a letter for Captain Gresham. Pray make my excuses as gracefully as you can. The fact is, that he is so heavy he tires me to death. But you need not mention this.

"Adieu, dear! It shall not be long before you hear again from your most affectionate

"MARIETTE."

That was all. Not another line, not another word. Hugh stood for a minute as if stunned; then he crushed the letter forcibly together in his hand, as he uttered one passionate word—

"Ingrate!"

"I do not think of—I do not care for *that!*" said Mrs. Trafford. "But think of the wretchedness which is before her! Do you understand that this is that villain's mode of striking *me?* When we had our final explanation—when he dared to speak to me of love, and I laughed in his face—he told me that scores were not settled between us yet; and I—blind fool that I was!—defied him to injure me again. This is his answer. O Hugh! Hugh! is there *no* way to save her, even yet?"

"Stop a moment—let me think," said Hugh. "I can hardly realize it. If you feared anything like this, why did you not tell me of it two days ago?"

"Fear anything like this! Why, I never dreamed of it! How could I? They had never met, to my knowledge, since last they met in this house. I never thought of him; I had no reason to do so. But I thought of *you*, because I could not connect the change in Mariette with any one else. After leaving you, I believed that I had been wholly mistaken until this morning. She left the house before I rose; and several hours later, when I began to feel anxious, her maid brought me this letter, which she pro-

fessed to have just found. Well!"—another long, gasping breath—"I did not faint. I believe one never does when one feels most. But the blow crushed me—as he meant that it should! My whole heart has been bound up in her. I could not tell you, if I would, all that I have hoped and planned: how I meant that her youth should be as bright and happy as mine was *not*, and that love should be the blessing—not the curse—of her life. And now she is the tool by which that man takes his revenge on me! O Hugh, can I do nothing—nothing to save her?"

As she laid her hand on his arm, and, in the intensity of her appeal, lifted her pallid face toward his, Hugh's heart, always easily touched by suffering of any kind, melted into tenderness, such as he had never thought to feel for her again. All his barriers of pride and reserve were suddenly broken down. He comprehended that, beneath the worldly exterior which he had so unsparingly condemned, the power of devoted, unselfish love remained; and, for the first time since their renewal of intercourse, he looked at her and listened to her without being haunted by the thought that what he saw was acting—not reality.

"I would do anything to save her—for your sake," he said. "Honestly, I have lost all desire to make such an effort for her own; but that does not matter. The question is, Can she be saved?"

"It is a question I cannot answer," Mrs. Trafford said. "I seem to have lost all power of thinking coolly; but—she is under age, you know."

"Ah!" he said, quickly. "That would be your best hope, if it were only possible to meet them before the marriage takes place. Have you the faintest idea where they have gone? She speaks indefinitely of the Continent."

"I have not the least idea; but I fancy, from her allusion to Trouville that they have gone to Paris."

"Yes," he said, reflectively, "to Paris,

most probably; but I may be able to discover something with regard to their destination by making inquiries at the Langham Hotel. Marchmont may have dropped some allusion—"

"Pray do not let this be known!" she pleaded, eagerly. "I shrink—oh! you cannot imagine how I shrink—from the thought of its being canvassed!"

"You may trust me to say nothing that will raise even a suspicion," he said, gently. "All that I mean to do is to learn where they have gone. There seems hardly a chance of your gaining anything by following; but if any accident should detain them—if the marriage should be delayed by any technicality such as might arise—you would be in time to interfere. There is a shadow of hope—no more. Are you willing to act on that?"

"How can you ask me?" she said, with a feverish color rising into her face. "I would act on the shadow of a shadow! If you say so, I will start for Paris in half an hour."

"I *don't* say so. I must have some certainty about their destination before you can think of starting. I will go at once to the Langham Hotel; and do you, meanwhile, prepare for a journey. Take care of your strength, for you may need it, and keep courage. All is not lost while the faintest hope remains."

"How glad I am that I sent for you!" she said. "How much good you have done me! I was despairing when you came, and now I feel a gleam of hope. O Hugh! if I can only save her!"

"And baffle him!" said Hugh, with a flash like unsheathed steel in his eyes. "God grant we may do both! Now there is no more time to talk. We must act! Prepare for your journey, while I go and make an effort to find the right track."

———

CHAPTER XVI.

"CHECKMATED—BY FATE."

IT seemed to Dinsmore a stroke of luck that, on the pavement in front of the Langham Hotel, he chanced to meet Reade, who had just left Nelly Paget, and was therefore able to give him all the information he was likely to obtain with regard to Marchmont. The news of Meriette's elopement had not, of course, reached the Pagets; but they had expressed considerable surprise at Marchmont's return to the Continent, since he had avowedly left it with the intention of accompanying them to America.

"I don't think they are grieved by his change of purpose," Reade added; "but it seems odd. Nelly has just suggested that perhaps the beautiful widow is at the bottom of it."

"At the bottom of it, in a certain sense, she undoubtedly is!" said Dinsmore, grimly. "Now, can you tell me—I have a special reason for asking—whether the fellow gave any intimation of where he was going first?"

Reade looked a little surprised, but was too well-bred to express the sentiment.

"I think he was going first to Paris," he answered. "At least, I heard Mrs. Paget say that he mentioned something of the kind, or something which implied an intention of the kind."

"You are sure of it?"

"Sure that he said so? Yes, perfectly sure."

"That is all I want. Thank you, and good-morning. At another time I'll explain."

He hailed a cab as he spoke, sprang in, and drove off, before Reade could utter a word. The latter gazed after the vanishing vehicle for a moment in mute astonishment; then he turned away, and, with a low whistle, said to himself:

"There's something mysterious here!

I am afraid that, despite all his protestations, Dinsmore has fallen into the toils of the enchanting Mrs. Trafford. But what has he to do with Marchmont? I must go and see if Nelly can throw any light on the affair."

While he promptly carried this resolution into execution, Dinsmore returned to Mrs. Trafford and told her what he had learned; adding that, in his opinion, it would be well to go over to Paris, even though she should gain nothing by doing so. "You will have made an effort which will set your mind at rest," he said.

"Oh, yes — yes!" she answered. "Anything is better than idly to stay here. Pardon me if I ask your advice on one more subject: What shall I do about the letter to Captain Gresham?"

"Keep it," he answered, promptly. "Don't let the story be known sooner than you can help. It is a forlorn hope, but, if we can reach her in time, we may save her."

"We cannot save her from a scandal: *that* must be, in any event."

"It shall not be!" said Hugh; and again the steel-like flash came into his eyes. "There are ways of making that dastard hold his tongue—and no one else knows of the elopement. Control yourself; tell the servants that you are called away on business; and do not take a maid with you."

Even in the midst of her distress, Mrs. Trafford looked a little dismayed at this.

"I have never made a journey alone," she said; "but if you think it necessary—"

"Alone!" he repeated. "Surely, you know that I am going with you?"

Tears sprang quickly into the eyes which she lifted to his.

"How kind you are!" she said, in a low voice. "I do not know how to thank you!"

"You must not think of thanking me," he said. "Be ready to start in half an hour—that is all."

It seemed to Amy Trafford like a dream, when, an hour later, she found herself in a railway-carriage rushing toward Dover, with Hugh for a companion. What a strange turn of events was this, which had brought them together again in their old friendly relations! Despite all that she was suffering—all her racking grief and anxiety—there was a sense of repose and relief in the consciousness of his companionship and protection.

Some men have a peculiar faculty of inspiring this feeling of reliance—this absolute trust in their capability of protecting all persons and interests under their care; and Dinsmore, though one of the most quiet, least self-asserting of men, possessed it in an extreme degree.

During the railway-journey they talked little, for both were oppressed by the uncertainty of what lay before them; but, when they found themselves on board the Calais boat, they had, in a measure, become accustomed to the situation, and it was a relief from tormenting thought to converse on subjects altogether apart from the one subject which harassed them.

Almost unconsciously Mrs. Trafford found herself speaking of her married life, and describing to Hugh—who listened with more interest than he would have believed possible—many of its incidents and scenes. But that on which she principally dwelt, with a simplicity full of truth and pathos, was the generous kindness of the husband who had taken far more the place of father than of husband to her.

As he listened, Hugh seemed to understand her story better than he had ever done before, and it was borne to him with the force of a revelation that she had acted wisely and well in making the marriage for which he had always in his heart reproached her.

"How often we are presumptuous fools, without knowing it!" he said, abruptly, as this thought pressed upon him. "I am ashamed to think of the manner in which I once ventured to arraign you for your intention of marrying Mr. Trafford; and still more ashamed to consider that years did not teach me more wisdom. A month ago I still classed you among women who sell their hearts to the bondage of a mercenary marriage; though I should have known—"

"You should have known that I had no heart to sell," she said, with a slightly sad and bitter smile. "Love was dead to me—at least, so I thought then; but in my desolate position, my undisciplined youth, I needed a protector above all things, and God sent one to me, in the person of the best and kindest friend that ever woman had."

There was silence after this for a time, and neither of them ever forgot the scene around them—the wide expanse of sea silvered with a flood of moonlight; the deck with its scattered groups here and there; the vessel throbbing and rocking after the manner of steamers; above all, the ever-recurring consciousness of the novelty and strangeness of their position.

On landing at Calais, they found the train for Paris just starting; and, after they had taken their places, Dinsmore left Mrs. Trafford for a moment. When he returned, his face was grave and pale with a new gravity and pallor; but the light was dim, and Mrs. Trafford was beginning to feel the exhaustion consequent on her day of excitement, so the fact escaped her attention, and, a few minutes later, the train started.

"Try to sleep," he said, piling shawls and cushions around her; and, though she felt, at first, that this was impossible, she presently dropped asleep from sheer fatigue, and lay unconscious, while the lamp-light shone on her face with its chiseled features, and the long lashes swept her marble-like cheeks.

Dinsmore sat alternately watching this face and the moonlit country with ghostly trees and houses flitting by. His mind was possessed with a variety of thoughts; but, through all their vagaries, his features never lost the look of new gravity which they had acquired at Calais.

The hours went on. At the stations, now and then, Mrs. Trafford stirred a little, but did not rouse herself until his hand touched her. Then she opened her eyes quickly.

"What is it?" she asked, for the train was slackening speed. "Paris already?"

"No, not Paris—Amiens," he answered. "I think it best to stop here for a few hours. I will tell you why, presently."

She glanced at him in surprise; but his quiet, composed manner put objection out of the question, and she only said:

"I am satisfied to do whatever you think best, provided that you do not wish to stop because you think I need rest."

"It is not on that account at all," he answered; and, as he spoke, the train rushed into the station.

The next thing which Mrs. Trafford—who was a little bewildered — clearly knew, she was in a *fiacre*, rattling through various narrow streets, on one side of which the moonlight poured, revealing the tall, foreign houses, that had to her a very familiar aspect.

"Why are we stopping here, Hugh?" she asked, in her perplexity.

But Hugh only answered: "Have patience. Wait a short time, and you shall know."

The hotel at which they presently alighted bore as cheerless an aspect as hotels usually do in the hours between midnight and dawning. Nevertheless, they were speedily shown to comfortable apartments; and, when Dinsmore parted with Mrs. Trafford, he said:

"Pray endeavor to rest. To-morrow morning you shall hear the cause of this delay."

"Why should I not hear it now?" she asked.

"Because I am not certain with regard to it," he replied. "Trust me, and believe that I shall not be idle while you sleep."

"I could not believe that you would ever be idle while your friends were to be served!" she said, giving him her hand.

The soft pressure lingered with him like a benediction after the door had closed upon her, and he went his way—but not to sleep. There were inquiries to be made without loss of time, doubts to be solved, and suspicions to be verified.

.   .   .   .   .

Having as it were, shifted her care to Dinsmore's shoulders, Mrs. Trafford slept for the remainder of the night; and, when she opened her eyes, the sunlight was lying in bars of gold on the floor of her chamber. For a moment her strange surroundings puzzled her; then the memory of all that had occurred flashed upon her, and, with a heavy sigh, she extended her hand and rang the bell.

The servant who answered it carried in her hand a tray on which was arranged a very dainty breakfast. It was brought by monsieur's orders, she said, and, after madame had breakfasted and made her toilet, monsieur awaited her in the saloon adjoining her apartment.

This information was sufficient to hasten madame's movements. She drank a cup of *café au lait*, and forced herself to eat a bit of bread; then her toilet was hurriedly made, and she opened the door leading into the *salon*.

Dinsmore, who was standing by one of the windows, turned, and came forward to meet her.

"I hope you slept well," he said, looking, with an expression of concern, at her pale, eager face.

"Yes, I slept very well," she answered. "I don't know how I could, unless it was because I felt that *you* were awake, and working. Now, tell me if you have any news."

"Sit down," he said, drawing a chair forward and placing her in it. "You shall hear why I stopped here, and what I have gained by stopping. Do you remember that, after putting you in the train at Calais, I left you for a few minutes? Well, during those few minutes I learned that there had been a terrible accident on the line earlier in the day, and twenty or thirty people had been killed and wounded."

She uttered a cry, her face blanching to the whiteness of snow.

"Great Heavens!" she said. "Mariette!"

"Be tranquil," he said, gently. "Mariette is unhurt. I know that now, but I did not know it then, and I was very uneasy. I could not obtain any list of names, but was told that the victims of the catastrophe were all at Amiens; and the only thing to be done to set anxiety at rest, therefore, was to stop here. If I had found no trace of them, we should have gone on to Paris two hours later; but—I have found a trace."

She gazed at him so eagerly, that the breath seemed hushed on her parted lips.

"Are they here?" she asked. "Is that what you mean?"

"That is what I mean," he answered, quietly. "I have seen them. Mariette, as I have said, is unhurt, but Marchmont is fatally injured."

The words were deliberately spoken, but she heard them with a sense of unreality which it is impossible to describe. Fatally injured! It seemed incredible that the visitation of God had fallen on the man in his pride and strength, just as he was about to strike the second blow which had fallen from his hand upon her! Ten minutes before, she would have cried out that any means which would remove him forever from her path of life would be welcome; but now she felt awed into silence by this unexpected fulfillment of her desire.

"Will he die?" she asked, presently.

"There is no hope whatever; he will certainly die," Dinsmore answered. "I found Mariette with him, and I have not undeceived her with regard to his sincerity. It seemed useless to do so. The knot is cut—she will never marry him."

"Mariette must have been greatly surprised to see you?"

"She was very much surprised, and, I think, was very glad. She met me with a cry of welcome and relief. The shock, the terror, and her strange position, have, I believe, altogether cured her romance. I told her that you were here, and she would have come to you, but that she shrank from leaving the dying man."

"I will go to her at once," said Mrs. Trafford, rising. "She must not be left in that position alone. O Hugh, I thank you from my heart for having been wise enough to stop here! What should I have done without you?"

A few minutes later, they were driving to an hotel near the railroad, where Marchmont, together with some of the other victims of the catastrophe, had been taken.

Dinsmore led his companion straight to a *salon* adjoining the apartment in which lay the dying man, and left her there while he entered the room beyond. He had hardly been gone a moment, when, from the door through which he had disappeared, Mariette entered and rushed toward her sister, like a child seeking shelter. Before Mrs. Trafford could utter a word, the eager arms were round her, the golden head resting on her shoulder.

"O Amy, how good of you to come!" she sobbed. "Oh, can you forgive me? Oh, what must you think of me! I began to realize what I had done when that awful accident came. Oh, if I had been killed, and had never seen you again!"

"Thank God, you are safe!" said Mrs. Trafford, sobbing in turn; and so the two clung together, and kissed each other, while further words were useless to tell their joy on being together again.

"Oh, I have felt so lost—so frightened!" said Mariette. "When Hugh came, his face seemed to me like the face of an angel! When he told me of your anxiety, I—I was so very sorry! I did not know—I did not think what I was doing, Amy. I should like you to believe that."

"I do believe it!" said Amy, and paused. She was about to add, "I thank God for your rescue." But she suddenly felt that it was impossible to thank him that a fellow-creature, however great his guilt, was dying near by in agony.

"We will talk of that another time," she said, with a slight shudder. "Tell me about the accident. How did you escape?"

"By the mercy of God!" answered Mariette. "There was no other possible reason why I should have been spared where others perished. It was horrible!" —she covered her face with her hands. "I shall never forget it! I think the scene will haunt me as long as I live. Then, there was yesterday and last night. Oh, when Hugh came to me," she said, again, "I was so grateful, that I could have knelt to him!"

Hugh entered the room as she spoke, and walked gravely up to them.

"That unhappy man has not many minutes to live," he said, "and he wishes to see—both of you."

Mrs. Trafford shrank back with a visible repugnance.

"He cannot wish to see me!" she said.

"He *does* wish to see you," Hugh answered; "and you cannot refuse to go."

She felt that he was right; she could not refuse to go, let Marchmont's reason for the request be what it might. Almost unconsciously, she laid her hand on Dinsmore's arm, and so they entered the room together.

The dying man, whose life was passing away in shuddering gasps, lifted his eyes and saw them. At that moment he did *not* see the face of his promised bride, who was beside him; his glance passed over her, to rest on the woman whom he had loved, forgotten, loved again, hated, and tried to injure. She paused at the foot of his couch and looked steadily at him—her large, brilliant eyes full of a solemn sadness.

"Believe me, Brian Marchmont," she said, slowly, "I am sorry that we should meet again like this."

He did not answer at once; the breath was drawn once or twice with a gasping sound between his white lips before the sentence dropped from them:

"Checkmated—by Fate!"

That was all. These three words embodied his death-bed commentary on the failure which his life had proved, and he spoke no others. Whether he had meant to say more in sending for Amy Trafford, or whether he simply wished to look on her face, can never be known.

A change, like no other of mortality, came over his countenance a minute later, and Hugh, turning to his companion, whispered:

"The end is at hand. Take Mariette away."

The end was indeed at hand! While Mariette, resisting her sister's touch, threw herself on her knees, the head fell back, a strong shiver shook the mangled frame, and the nurse said, "He is dead!"

CHAPTER XVII.

"AFTER LONG GRIEF AND PAIN."

THE horror of this tragical end to her brief romance was too much for Mariette. Excitement culminated in illness, and for many days she lay in feverish stupor alternated by feverish delirium. As soon as she had recovered sufficiently to be removed, Mrs. Trafford carried her to a quiet sea-side town in Normandy, and there they spent the summer.

When the girl was able to hear the truth respecting the unhappy man who had perished, it was told to her kindly and gently—far too kindly and gently for her to dream of doubting it. As Hugh had said, her fancy had already died as

quickly as it began; but she shuddered to think how near she had come to wrecking her life. Realizing this, and realizing, also, that but for her folly Marchmont would be alive, her remorse was very keen, and for a time a depression which was almost morbid weighed upon her.

As she recovered health and strength, however, this feeling disappeared, though it was evident to Mrs. Trafford that an impression had been made on her character which it would never lose. The nymph-like joyousness had vanished from her face; the knowledge of evil as well as of good, of pain as well as of pleasure, had set its signet on the fair features and given a new expression to the violet eyes.

The engagement with Captain Gresham was dissolved by her own act. No rumor of scandal had gone abroad, no knowledge of her elopement had transpired; but as soon as she could hold a pen she had written—a very different letter from that which Mrs. Trafford had suppressed—setting the young man free.

He did not appreciate the kindness, but, indignant and aggrieved, started at once and made his unexpected appearance in the quaint little sea-side town.

It was impossible to deny his right to an explanation; and Mariette, pale, but very composed, said to her sister:

"I shall tell him the whole truth."

"I do not think it is necessary," Mrs. Trafford answered. "Simply tell him that you do not and cannot love him. That will be enough."

"I do not feel as if it will be enough," the girl said. "I have treated him so shamefully, that it will be some *amende* to be perfectly frank—to let him know how little I am worth regretting."

The woman of the world shook her head.

"When you are older," she said, "you will know that nothing is more useless than to publish any fact to your own discredit. In this matter you must follow your own judgment; but I warn you that it will bo better to say no more than you are forced to say."

Perhaps it was not strange that Mariette did not follow this advice. She was young, she was impulsive, she was remorseful; so she told Stamer Gresham everything. To say that he was deeply shocked, gives only a faint idea of what he felt; but, if he was not brilliant in mind, he was a thorough gentleman in nature, and he uttered no word of reproach.

"I am sorry that I have annoyed you with this visit," he said, after a short, troubled silence. "I ought to have been content with what you wrote me; but I did not know—I did not suspect—anything like this."

"How could you?" said Mariette, with her golden head bent. "I have acted shamefully, and—and I tell you of it in order that you may be glad that our engagement is ended. I do not care if you let all the world know how and why the engagement was broken off. I deserve it."

"You need not fear that," he said. "I shall not even tell my mother anything more than that you cannot love me. That is surely enough. I do not deny that this is an awful blow to me," the poor fellow went on; "but I suppose I shall get over it in time. At all events, I thank you for your frankness, Miss Reynolds. You have my best wishes for your happiness, and—good-by!"

Mariette was sobbing by this time, so she did not lift her eyes; but she was aware that her hand was wrung very hard, and then Captain Gresham left the room, and was seen by her no more.

One must pay a price for everything in this world; and the price which Mariette paid for her brief romance and her tragically-ended elopement would have been esteemed, by most young ladies, very heavy.

Mariette herself did not regret the loss of the baronet's son, however. She was glad to be free—glad to feel that no one had any claim on her life.

"I see, now, that it would not be safe for me to marry without love," she said to her sister. "I will never, never make such an attempt again—not even if a prince were to ask the honor of my alliance."

"I suppose we must all learn wisdom by experience," said Mrs. Trafford; and, when it does not come too late, we ought to be thankful to learn it at any cost. Yours has not come too late. Some day you will know what love is, and then you will be grateful that you did not bind your life in the bondage of a loveless marriage."

"I am in no haste for that day to arrive," said Mariette, looking meditatively out over the wide expanse of waves washing toward the land as the incoming tide rippled high on the beach. "I have had enough—more than enough —of love and lovers, to last me for many days. When I am as old as you are, perhaps I may think again of such things. I begin to understand why you have become so sentimental of late," she added, with a smile. Then, with an arch look, she asked: "When is Hugh coming again?"

"I do not know," answered Mrs. Trafford, while a blush, brighter than the sunset glow, dyed her face.

. . . . . .

It was not long after this conversation that Hugh came. He was not expected, but Mariette received him warmly, and told him that Mrs. Trafford had gone down to the beach.

"You will find it a great deal pleasanter to go in search of her than to stay here with me," she added, frankly. "I am dull and stupid to the last degree; and, when Amy went out, I would not go with her. Now I am glad of it, for she will have a better companion."

"Probably she does not care for any companion," said Dinsmore, anxious to go, yet reluctant.

Mariette gave him a look of laughing impatience.

"How foolish you are!" she said.

"As if you do not know that Amy will be delighted to see you! Pray go."

"It is evident that you are determined to be rid of me," he said, smiling; and, without waiting for further persuasion, he went.

A path led from the village down the somewhat steep face of a cliff to the sands below. As Dinsmore descended this, he overlooked a magnificent expanse of sea, heaving and flashing as the waves swelled steadily inward, and the murmur of the tide filled the air.

There were a few figures here and there on the beach, but he soon identified the one of which he was in search—a lady who sat alone, watching the waves as they raced backward and forward and broke in sparkling foam on the sand.

He advanced upon her from behind, so that it was not until his shadow suddenly fell over her that she looked up.

She was surprised to see him, but not startled, and, without rising, she held out her hand with a smile.

"I am glad to see you," she said. "How good of you to come and cheer our solitude! But perhaps you did not come for that purpose. I believe you mentioned, when we parted, that you intended coming to Normandy on a painting-tour."

"I believe I did," he answered, sitting down beside her; "but one may sometimes combine pleasure and profit. Just at present I cannot say that painting is very much to my mind. I have come especially to see how you and Mariette are getting on."

"Thank you!"—and her eyes echoed the words; "we are getting on admirably! Have you not seen Mariette? She is regaining health and strength rapidly."

"And health of mind, I hope, as well as health of body?"

"Yes; her depression is vanishing, though she still has fits of self-reproach and remorse. Have you heard of the visitor whom we had not long ago?"

Hugh's face changed. A certain reserve—a kind of cloud—fell over it.

"No," he replied; "I have not heard of any visitor. It was Colonel Danesford, probably?"

She looked at him with evident astonishment.

"Colonel Danesford!" she repeated. "Why should you think of him? He has gone out of my life—almost out of my thoughts. No; it was Stamer Gresham who came to see Mariette."

"And what was the result?"

"The result was, that she told him everything—foolishly, I thought at the time; but now I am not so sure. There is sometimes a saving grace in frankness, even when it can serve no definite end. Do you not think so?"

"Yes," he answered, looking not at her, but out over the sea, with its waves washing up and down, and some white gulls flying far away. "We can never tell what definite end it may serve," he went on, after a moment. "False impressions may be removed, wrong ideas brushed away, by very simple explanations. Do you remember some things you said to me when we were alone on the steamer crossing from Dover to Calais? No doubt they seemed very simple truths to you; but to me they were revelations. I found that I had been looking at your life and your motives from altogether a wrong point of view, and consequently utterly mistaking them."

"It was very natural," she said, as he paused—"I mean with regard to my motives. With regard to my life, I am not sure that you were mistaken in your estimate of it. I have had time for serious reflections here—the first in ten years; and, in looking back, I see little to fill me with satisfaction. My triumphs have been very empty, and my pleasures have often left a bitter taste behind. When I was a girl, my ambition, as you may remember, was boundless. By the most extraordinary turn of Fortune's wheel, I was placed in a position to gratify that ambition to its utmost, and I have done so. Conquest, homage, admiration, wealth, and leisure, have been mine; and what is the end? Why, weariness of the soul and of the spirits, and a longing, which I can hardly restrain, to return to the simpler forms of life."

"In which you would not be contented for an hour!" said Hugh, calmly. "Do you know why it is that the life you have lived for several years does not satisfy you, as it satisfies other women? I can tell you in a few words: you have both a mind and a heart, and neither the one nor the other has had any play whatever. Your intellectual culture has been fitful and superficial, and your affections, except with regard to Mariette, have lain absolutely dormant. Consequently, both intellect and heart have risen in revolt."

She smiled faintly, and a little sadly.

"Your diagnosis may be correct," she said. "I do not know. But a physician does not content himself with *naming* a malady; he also prescribes the *remedy*."

Hugh shrugged his shoulders slightly.

"He should be certian of his skill before attempting to do so. I may be entirely mistaken. I have grown more diffident of my judgment. Modesty is a good thing to cultivate, even at a very late day. Besides, I think that I have played lecturer often enough, Mrs. Trafford. You have been very good to tolerate my presumption so long; but now—"

"Now you are going to cease speaking truth to me—you, the only person in the world who *does* speak it!" she said, as he broke off abruptly. "I am not sure that I care for your newly-found good opinion, if this is the result!"

"Why should you care for it in any event?" he asked, turning on her almost angrily. "It could only be for one reason; and surely it would be a poor triumph to draw such a man as I am to your feet!"

The color mounted swiftly into her cheeks, but her self-control was admirable; and, when he rose impetuously to his feet, she also rose and confronted him.

"So you do me injustice even yet, Hugh!" she said, gently. "Nothing has been further from my thoughts than the idea of drawing you to my feet. I am not blind, nor hopelessly obtuse. I have comprehended your dislike—I might almost say, your contempt; and, now that you are beginning to regard me with justice and kindlier feelings, I only hope to find in you my old friend."

"Who never was your friend, but always your lover!" said he, hoarsely. "I see it is useless, Amy; I cannot play the part I thought I could. When a man has loved one woman all his life, he cannot hope to forget her at my age. I must love you to the end, I suppose. But I cannot, I will not surrender all serenity of mind, all power of labor, on account of such an infatuation, and therefore it is necessary that my path of life should be apart from yours. Try and forgive this outburst. I believe that I have done you injustice, and that you did not deserve it. Shall I leave you now? Perhaps it will be best."

He turned quickly, and had taken half a dozen steps on the sand, when her dress rustled by his side and her hand touched his arm. Fortunately, they were almost entirely alone. The other figures had dispersed in different directions; only far down the beach a fisherman sat on an upturned boat, mending some nets.

At that touch, light and soft as it was, Dinsmore looked round, and the expression of the face which met his gaze made him stand motionless. Was he mad, or dreaming? What was this tender radiance on the fair outlines which he had known so long and loved so well?

"Amy!" he cried, incredulously.

"I have learned many lessons in my life, Hugh," said Amy, with that supreme quietness which sometimes comes when the height of emotion has been reached; "but the chief of them is this: that earth holds nothing better than the love of one brave, honest, constant heart like yours; and if you can forgive me—if, after all these years, you can care for a heart like mine—"

"*If* I care!" he repeated, clasping her hand in a vise-like grasp. "Amy, it cannot be that you mean that it is mine at last?"

"It is yours at last!" she answered.

And what could Hugh do, but take her in his arms, and thank God, who had granted him this crowning gift of his life—after many days!

THE END.

www.ingramcontent.com/pod-product-compliance
Lightning Source LLC
Chambersburg PA
CBHW030820270326
41928CB00007B/826